THE COGNITIVE NEUROSCIENCE OF MEMORY

Studies in Cognition Series
Published Titles

Series Editor
Glyn Humphreys, University of Birmingham, UK

Cognitive Models of Memory
Martin A. Conway (Ed.)
Language Processing
Simon Garrod & Martin Pickering (Eds.)
Knowledge, Concepts, and Categories
Koen Lamberts & David Shanks (Eds.)
Attention
Harold Pashler (Ed.)
Cognitive Neuroscience
Michael D. Rugg
Aspects of Language Production
Linda Wheeldon (Eds.)

The Cognitive Neuroscience of Memory

Encoding and Retrieval

Edited by

Amanda Parker
University of Nottingham

Edward L. Wilding
Cardiff University

and

Timothy J. Bussey
University of Cambridge

 **Psychology Press**
Taylor & Francis Group
HOVE AND NEW YORK

First published in 2002 by Psychology Press Ltd
27 Church Road, Hove, East Sussex, BN3 2FA

www.psypress.co.uk

Simultaneously published in the USA and Canada
by Psychology Press Inc
29 West 35th Street, New York, NY 10001

Psychology Press is part of the Taylor & Francis Group

Typeset in Times by RefineCatch Limited, Bungay, Suffolk
Printed and bound in Great Britain by Biddles Ltd, Guildford and King's Lynn
Cover design by Kate Williams
Cover painting *Still Life With Figures* by Ian Hopton

British Library Cataloguing in Publication Data
A catalogue record for this book is available from the British Library

Library of Congress Cataloging-in-Publication Data
The cognitive neuroscience of memory : encoding and retrieval / edited by Amanda
Parker, Edward L. Wilding & Timothy J. Bussey.
     p. cm.—(Studies in cognition)
  Includes bibliographical references and index.
  ISBN 1–84169–246–8
  1. Memory—Physiological aspects.   2. Cognitive neuroscience.   I. Parker,
Amanda, 1955–   II. Wilding, Edward L., 1968–   III. Bussey, Timothy J., 1961–
IV. Studies in cognition (Hove, England)

QP406.C635 2002
153.1′2—dc21   2002073862

ISBN 1–84169–246–8

5/7/10

Contents

List of contributors

John P. Aggleton, School of Psychology, Cardiff University, Cardiff CG10 3YG, UK

Kevin Allan, Department of Psychology, William Guild Building, Kings College, University of Aberdeen AB24 2UB, UK

Jorge L. Armony, Institute of Cognitive Neuroscience, University College London, Alexandra House, 17 Queen Square, London WC1N 3AR, UK

Mark G. Baxter, Department of Psychology, Harvard University, 906 William James Hall, 33 Kirkland Street, Cambridge MA 02138, USA

Malcolm W. Brown, MRC Centre for Synaptic Plasticity, Department of Anatomy, University of Bristol, Bristol BS8 1TD, UK

Randy L. Buckner, Howard Hughes Medical Institute, Departments of Psychology, Radiology, and Anatomy & Neurobiology, Washington University, St Louis, MO 63130, USA

Timothy J. Bussey, Department of Experimental Psychology, University of Cambridge, Cambridge CB2 3EB, UK

Robert C. Cannon, Department of Psychology and Program in Neuroscience, Boston University, 64 Cummington Street, Boston, MS 02215, USA

Helen J. Cassaday, School of Psychology, University of Nottingham, Nottingham NG7 2RD, UK

David I. Donaldson, Department of Psychology, University of Stirling, Stirling, FK9 4LA, UK

Alexander Easton, School of Psychology, University of Nottingham, Nottingham NG7 2RD, UK

Howard B. Eichenbaum, Department of Psychology, Boston University, 64 Cummington Street, Boston, MS 02215, USA

David Gaffan, Department of Experimental Psychology, University of Oxford, South Parks Road, Oxford OX1 3UD, UK

Michael E. Hasselmo, Department of Psychology, Boston University, 64 Cummington Street, Boston, MS 02215, USA

Richard N.A. Henson, Institute of Cognitive Neuroscience, University College London, Gower Street, London WC1 6BT, UK

Robert T. Knight, Helen Wills Neuroscience Institute, University of California, 3210 Tolman Hall, #1650, Berkeley, CA 94720-1650, USA

Jessica M. Logan, Department of Psychology Washington University, One Brookings Drive, Campus Box 1125, St Louis, MO 63130, USA

James M. McClelland, Center for the Neural Basis of Cognition and Department of Psychology, Carnegie Mellon University, Pittsburgh, PA 15208, USA

Janet Metcalfe, Department of Psychology, Columbia University, New York, NY 10027, USA

Christine Norman, School of Psychology, University of Nottingham, Nottingham NG7 2RD, UK

Amanda Parker, School of Psychology, University of Nottingham, Nottingham NG7 2RD, UK

Charan Ranganath, Center for Neuroscience, University of California, 3210 Tolman Hall #1650, Berkeley, CA 94720-1650, USA

Michael D. Rugg, Acting Director, Institute of Cognitive Neuroscience, 17 Queen Square, London WC1N 3AR, UK

Lisa M. Saksida, Department of Experimental Psychology, University of Cambridge, Cambridge CB2 3EB, UK

E. Clea Warburton, MRC Centre for Synaptic Plasticity, Department of Anatomy, University of Bristol, Bristol BS8 1TD, UK

Edward L. Wilding, School of Psychology, Cardiff University, Cardiff CG10 3YG, UK

Bradley P. Wyble, Department of Psychology and Program in Neuroscience, Boston University, 64 Cummington Street, Boston, MS 02215, USA

Series preface

Over the past 20 years enormous advances have been made in our understanding of basic cognitive processes concerning issues such as: What are the
basic modules of the cognitive system? How can these modules be modelled?
How are the modules implemented in the brain? The book series "Studies in
cognition" seeks to provide state-of-the-art summaries of this research,
bringing together work on experimental psychology with that on computational modelling and cognititive neuroscience. Each book contains chapters
written by leading figures in the field, which aim to provide comprehensive
summaries of current research. The books should be both accessible and
scholarly and be relevant to undergraduates, post-graduates, and research
workers alike.

Glyn Humphreys

Introduction

If understanding how the brain works is the greatest challenge left for science, cognitive neuroscience represents our best chance of rising to that challenge. Cognitive neuroscience is the umbrella term for a multidisciplinary endeavour, within which rapid progress is being made in areas once thought to be intractable, such as perception, attention, emotion, and memory. This has been accomplished primarily by combining the traditional methods of psychology with a range of approaches that investigate the relationship between neural and mental events. Neuropsychological studies of patients enable gross localisation of function in the human brain. More specific characterisations can be obtained by analysis of the behavioural deficits that ensue following discrete brain lesions in rodents and monkeys, and from electrophysiological recordings from specific cortical and subcortical areas. Additional complementary sources of information are provided by correlational methods such as functional imaging, with which it is possible to monitor changes in neural activity in awake behaving humans, and by the development of computer models of brain function. In combination, these multiple modes of enquiry can be deployed in pursuit of a more complete understanding of the relationship between cognitive operations and their neural substrates.

The chapters in this book show how these approaches have been deployed successfully in studies of memory encoding and retrieval. The book is divided into four parts, commencing with studies of memory in human participants, moving on to studies in non-human primates and then rats, and finishing with computational approaches to the study of memory. Ordering the sections in this way does not imply that the merits of any one approach outweigh another, rather, a common thread running through this volume is the view that substantial progress in our understanding of the neural and functional basis of memory can only be achieved by integrating converging sources of information that are obtained using different methodologies.

Together, these chapters summarise a wide range of approaches to the solution of a problem that for a long time looked intractable: how does the brain encode and retrieve information so that events in the past can influence behaviour in the present and in the future? The consensus that emerges, both within and between sections, is an encouraging sign that memory research has reached an exciting stage in its development. Clear research questions are being asked, and data gathered, that can be compared across species and tasks and related to the functions of specific memory systems with reasonably clear neuroanatomical bases. The chapters presented in this volume are a reflection of a vigorous, rapidly moving area of research.

PART ONE

Human imaging studies

CHAPTER ONE

Episodic memory retrieval: An (event-related) functional neuroimaging perspective

Michael D. Rugg and Richard N.A. Henson
University College London, UK

INTRODUCTION

In this chapter we focus on recent studies employing functional imaging methods to investigate human episodic memory retrieval. Episodic retrieval was one of the first aspects of memory to receive systematic study using neuroimaging methods, and has continued to be studied intensively. Many of these studies have been described in review articles published within the last few years (see Buckner & Koutstaal, 1998; Cabeza & Nyberg, 2000; Desgranges, Baron, & Eustache, 1998; Fletcher, Frith, & Rugg, 1997, for reviews of neuroimaging studies; and see Friedman & Johnson, 2000; Rugg, 1995; Rugg & Allan, 1999, for reviews of related electrophysiological work), as have some of the theoretical notions inspired by this research (Rugg & Wilding, 2000; Tulving, Kapur, Craik, Moscovitch, & Houle, 1994a; Wheeler, Stuss, & Tulving, 1997). It is not the goal of the present chapter to revisit the ground covered by these earlier reviews; instead, we concentrate on recent studies of retrieval that have employed "event-related" neuroimaging methods. We address three principal questions: (1) to what extent are the findings from event-related studies consistent with those obtained using older methodologies? (2) What do the findings tell us about the functional and neural bases of episodic retrieval? (3) What directions should be taken by future research employing these methods?

Episodic memory

For present purposes, episodic memory retrieval is defined as the cognitive operations necessary to support the explicit (conscious) retrieval of information about recently experienced events and the spatial and temporal contexts in which they occurred. The majority of neuroimaging studies of episodic memory retrieval have been conducted within the "verbal learning" tradition, wherein to-be-remembered items ("study" items) are lists of pre-experimentally familiar words. Most studies have employed memory tests that involve the presentation of cues that are in some way related to the studied items. One of the simplest and most popular tests is "yes/no" recognition memory, when entire items ("copy cues") are presented, and the participants' task is to judge whether each item was presented at study. Other tests employ less informative cues. For example, in word-stem cued recall the test items comprise the first three letters of a word (e.g. MOT__), and the task is to decide whether a word fitting the cue was presented at study.

Whatever the retrieval task that is employed, two important considerations arise. The first concerns the need to try to distinguish between "pre-" and "post-" retrieval processing (see Rugg & Wilding, 2000, for a detailed discussion of the different kinds of process that might be active during an episodic retrieval task; and see Burgess & Shallice, 1996, for a functional model of retrieval that embodies many of these processes). Preretrieval processing refers to those cognitive operations that support an attempt to use a cue to retrieve information from memory. Postretrieval processing, by contrast, involves cognitive operations that operate on the products of a retrieval attempt; these operations might include, for example, the maintenance in working memory of retrieved information and its evaluation with respect to current behavioural goals. Importantly, the notion of postretrieval processing is distinct from that of "retrieval success". The latter term refers to the situation wherein a retrieval attempt leads to successful recovery of information about a relevant past episode. Whereas retrieval success can often be sufficient to engage postretrieval processes, it is unlikely to be necessary. Postretrieval processing will be engaged to some extent whenever the products of a retrieval attempt must be evaluated prior to a memory judgement, even if the judgement is ultimately negative (signalling a failure to retrieve). The distinction implied here between processes involved in monitoring the outcome of a retrieval attempt and those that operate on the products of successful retrieval appears to be important for the interpretation of some of the findings reviewed in the later section "Event-related studies of episodic retrieval".

A second consideration when interpreting findings from functional imaging studies of memory retrieval arises from the argument that few, if any, retrieval tasks are "process pure" (Jacoby & Kelley, 1992). One well-known example of process "impurity" is the influence of explicit memory on indirect memory tests intended to assess implicit memory. But as pointed out by Jacoby and his associates (e.g. Jacoby & Kelley, 1992), performance on direct memory tests used to assess explicit memory might also be influenced by more than one kind of memory. For example, correct performance on word-stem cued recall can reflect both episodic retrieval and implicit memory (i.e. the same processes that support priming effects on word-stems; Jacoby, Toth, & Yonelinas, 1993). Clearly, if a retrieval task engages multiple kinds of memory, interpretation of the resulting imaging data will be far from straightforward. It is therefore unfortunate that the most common retrieval task in neuroimaging studies of episodic memory—recognition memory—is a task on which performance is almost certainly determined by the contribution of multiple processes (e.g. Yonelinas, 1994). It is possible to design recognition-like retrieval tasks that allow the contributions of episodic and non-episodic memory to be fractionated. For example, memory judgements based on episodic retrieval can be identified by requiring judgements of source rather than simple recognition, or alternatively by requiring recognition judgements to be accompanied by introspective report. Such tasks have been employed in several electrophysiological studies of retrieval (e.g. Rugg, Schloerscheidt, & Mark, 1998b), but they have only recently been used in studies employing functional neuroimaging methods.

Neuroimaging: Methods and measures

A description of currently available methods for the non-invasive measurement of human brain activity can be found in Rugg (1999). Irrespective of the method employed, an important distinction is that between transient changes in neural activity that follow a specific event such as the presentation of a stimulus (item-related activity), and more sustained modulations of activity that accompany engagement in a specific task and are unaffected by the presentation of specific items (state-related activity). This distinction is important because it is likely that the two kinds of activity reflect different kinds of cognitive operation (Rugg & Wilding, 2000), and also because it is central to the current debate about the functional significance of many neuroimaging findings regarding episodic retrieval.

Until relatively recently, studies employing functional neuroimaging methods based on the detection of blood flow and oxygenation—the so-called "haemodynamic" methods of positron emission tomography (PET) and functional magnetic resonance imaging (fMRI)—were designed in such a way that item- and state-related brain activity were always confounded. Because of the constraints imposed by PET methodology, PET images of regional cerebral blood flow are integrated over an acquisition period (and a corresponding block of experimental trials) lasting some 40–60s, making it impossible to distinguish between item- and state-related activity. The same problem is encountered in so-called "blocked" fMRI designs, when contrasts are performed on data from two or more blocks of trials, each representing an experimental condition. In both of these cases, any differences between experimental conditions in patterns of cerebral activity represent an unknown mixture of item- and state-related effects. Whereas it is possible in principle to design blocked studies to fractionate these effects, in practice it is difficult, if not impossible, to demonstrate that the fractionation was successful. For example, in an effort to investigate the item-related neural correlates of successful retrieval of episodic information, researchers have compared mean brain activity during recognition memory judgements made on a blocks of predominantly old versus predominantly new items (Kapur, Craik, Brown, Houle, & Tulving, 1995; Nyberg et al., 1995; Rugg et al., 1998a; Rugg, Fletcher, Frith, Frackowiak, & Dolan, 1996, 1997). Although attempts were made to disguise the manipulation of the ratio of old to new items, between-block differences in brain activity cannot be attributed unequivocally to item-related effects. Differences in state-related activity might still have occurred, for example, if participants adopted different task strategies following a few consecutive presentations of items belonging to the same class.

Historically, methods capable of distinguishing item- and state-related effects unequivocally have been based on electrophysiological rather than haemodynamic measures, notably, scalp-recorded electrical activity (the electroencephalogram or EEG). Electrophysiological methods can be employed in cognitive studies to measure time-locked modulations of the EEG elicited by a particular class of experimental items (e.g. "new" as opposed to "old" items in a recognition memory task). The resulting waveforms, known as event-related potentials (ERPs), provide a measure of that component of item-related neural activity that can be detected at the scalp (see also Chapter 2). Advances in fMRI methodology during the late 1990s led to the development of "event-related" methods, which permit functional images to be obtained in a manner analogous to that employed to record ERPs (Dale & Buckner, 1997; Josephs, Turner, & Friston, 1997; Zarahn, Aguirre, & D'Esposito, 1997). As is the case with ERPs, event-related fMRI allows item-related effects to be identified unequivocally. Whereas fMRI has by far the better spatial resolution, the sluggishness of the haemodynamic response means that the temporal resolution of event-related fMRI signals is of the order of hundreds of milliseconds. This compares unfavourably with the millisecond-level resolution that can be attained with electrophysiological measures. Thus, the two methods provide complementary perspectives on event-related brain activity.

Event-related methods have advantages that go beyond the capacity merely to detect item-related activity. First, the methods make it possible to employ randomised experimental designs, whereby trials belonging to different experimental conditions are intermixed in an unpredictable sequence. With such designs, effects on item-related measures resulting from the adoption of condition-specific "sets" are eliminated. Furthermore, by comparing the item-related activity elicited in randomised versus blocked designs, set effects can be identified and characterised. For example, using ERPs, Johnson et al. (1997b) compared the item-related activity elicited by "true" and "related lure" items in a "false memory" paradigm (see the later section "Retrieval success") when the two classes of item were randomly intermixed and when they were presented in separate test blocks. Differences in the ERPs elicited by the two kinds of item were found only for the blocked conditions, indicating that such differences depended on the adoption of different task sets (and, perhaps, on different patterns of state-related activity, although Johnson et al., 1997b, did not address this issue).

A second benefit of event-related methods, of particular importance for memory studies, is that they permit experimental trials to be allocated to different experimental conditions *post hoc*, on the basis of behavioural performance. Thus, it is possible to compare brain activity elicited by, say, "old" items in a recognition memory test according to whether the items were detected correctly or misclassified as new. The comparison of the patterns of brain activity elicited by items attracting different responses has been a cornerstone of ERP studies of memory retrieval for a considerable time (Rugg, 1995) and, as will become apparent, has already proven to be important in the case of event-related fMRI.

Despite the advantages of event-related designs in studies of memory retrieval, there remain circumstances when such designs are difficult to employ, and blocked procedures are preferable. This will be the case for example when the retrieval task does not involve the presentation of discrete retrieval cues, such as in free recall. More generally, the advantages of event-related over blocked designs will decline as the time-locking between external events and the cognitive operations of interest becomes weaker, and the inter-trial variance in the timing of item-related activity correspondingly greater.

Finally, it is important to note that the employment of event-related designs does not by itself resolve the issue of how to identify and characterise state-related changes in brain activity. It is possible however to design both electrophysiological (Duzel et al., 1999) and fMRI studies (Chawla, Rees, & Friston, 1999; Donaldson, Petersen, Ollinger, & Buckner, 2001) in such a way that item- and state-related activity can be assessed concurrently; as will become clear, there are good reasons why such designs are preferable to those focusing exclusively on event-related activity.

Interpretation of event-related fMRI data

An important issue in the interpretation of event-related data relates to the nature of the contrasts employed to identify brain regions that are active in different experimental conditions. In our view, the claim that a given brain region is selectively activated by items belonging to a given experimental condition is justified only when the event-related responses elicited by those items differs significantly from the responses elicited by items from another experimental condition. In other words, the finding that items from one condition elicit responses that differ reliably from the interstimulus baseline, whereas items from another condition do not, provides insufficient grounds for concluding that the responses elicited by the two conditions are significantly different (requiring, as it does, an acceptance of the null hypothesis).

More generally, it is arguable that "raw" event-related responses—item-related signal changes relative to an interstimulus baseline—are difficult, if not impossible, to interpret in the context of studies of higher cognitive processing. This is because the responses reflect a mixture of "low-level" processes common to all tasks, task-specific processes common to all item-classes, and processes specific to the item-class eliciting the response. Unlike, say, the simple case of visual cortex responses to brief visual stimulation against a static background, we cannot be certain what cognitive processes are engaged during the baseline periods between events in typical memory tasks. In the period prior to the presentation of a new item, for example, the participant might still be engaged in evaluating the episodic information retrieved in response to the previous old item. To separate these different kinds of item-related activity, it is necessary to contrast directly the responses elicited by the same types of item in different tasks, and by different item-types within the same task. Therefore it is important that event-related fMRI studies are designed so that differential item-related activity can be detected with adequate sensitivity. It turns out that for the kinds of randomised designs favoured in experimental psychology, sensitivity to differential activity is an inverse function of stimulus onset asynchrony (SOA) (Josephs & Henson, 1999). For this reason, the more recent event-related fMRI studies of episodic retrieval have employed relatively short SOAs (about 2–4s). With such short intervals it is not possible to obtain the "raw" response elicited by each type of item relative to the prestimulus baseline. None the less, the form of these responses can be important in constraining the interpretation of differential effects (e.g. whether the effects reflect differences in the amplitude or the latency of the responses elicited by different item classes; Henson, Price, Rugg, Turner, & Friston, 2002). It has therefore become common for event-related studies to include so-called "fixation" or "null" trials along with other trial types (Buckner et al., 1998a), effectively producing a stochastic distribution of SOAs (Friston, Zarahn, Josephs, Henson, & Dale, 1999), which allows item-related activity relative to baseline to be estimated.

BLOCKED STUDIES OF EPISODIC RETRIEVAL

In this section, we briefly review what we see as the more important of the findings to have emerged from PET and blocked fMRI studies of episodic retrieval. In these studies, several regions have been consistently reported to be active when participants engage in an episodic retrieval task relative to a non-episodic control task. Chief among these regions are dorsolateral and anterior prefrontal cortex, and medial and lateral parietal cortex. It is note-worthy that, on the basis of "classical" findings from human and animal neuropsychology, most of these regions would not be regarded as playing a central role in episodic memory.

Prefrontal cortex

Activation of prefrontal cortex has been reported in the majority of func-tional neuroimaging studies of episodic retrieval (see Desgranges et al., 1998; Fletcher & Henson, 2001; Nolde, Johnson, & Raye, 1998b, for detailed reviews of these findings). In light of reports from the neuropsychological literature of relatively subtle memory impairments following frontal lesions (Incisa Della Rocchetta & Milner, 1993; Janowsky, Shimamura, Kritchevsky, & Squire, 1989; Stuss et al., 1994) such findings were, perhaps, to be expected. What was not expected, however, was the finding that retrieval-related frontal activations were often right-lateralised, even when the experimental material was verbal. Thus, right-lateralised prefrontal activation (relative to appropri-ate control tasks) has been reported for free recall (e.g. Fletcher, Shallice, Frith, Frackowiak, & Dolan, 1998), word-stem cued recall (e.g. Squire et al., 1992), recall of paired associates (e.g. Shallice et al., 1994), and recognition memory (e.g. Nyberg et al., 1995).

The consistency with which right prefrontal activation has been reported in studies of episodic retrieval contrasts with the diversity of views that have been put forward as to its functional significance. One issue that arose early on, and that still remains to be settled fully, concerns whether retrieval-related activity in the right prefrontal cortex is state- or item-related (compare Kapur et al., 1995; Nyberg et al., 1995 with Rugg et al., 1996, 1998a). One reason why this debate has continued is that this is an issue which, for the reasons noted in the earlier section "Neuroimaging: Methods and measures", is not easy to resolve within the confines of blocked experimental designs. Thus, the findings from blocked studies leave it uncertain whether the right prefrontal activations reflect task-specific (state-related) effects, item-related effects, or some mixture thereof.

A second issue concerns the extent to which retrieval-related right pre-frontal activity can be neuroanatomically and functionally dissociated. It has been suggested, for example, that a distinction should be drawn between the retrieval functions supported by dorsolateral (BA46/9), ventrolateral (BA47), and anterior (BA10) regions (Fletcher & Henson, 2001; Henson, Shallice, Rugg, Fletcher, & Dolan, 2001; see also Christoff & Gabrieli, 2000). A further anatomical dissociation, in the form of differential lateralisation, has been proposed in light of the fact that activation of right prefrontal cortex is accompanied in many studies by activity in one or more left prefrontal regions. Nolde and colleagues (Nolde et al., 1998b) suggested that left prefrontal activity reflects the engagement of what they termed "reflective" retrieval processes, contrasting these with the "heuristic" processes supported by right prefrontal cortex.

Parietal cortex

Two parietal regions—medial and lateral—have consistently been reported to be active during episodic retrieval. Activation of medial parietal cortex often includes the precuneus (medial BA7), as reported during retrieval of paired associates (e.g. Shallice et al., 1994), cued recall (e.g. Fletcher et al., 1998), and auditory recognition memory (e.g. Tulving et al., 1994b). Posterior cingulate activations (BA23/31) have also sometimes been observed (Fletcher et al., 1998; Rugg et al., 1997). The functional significance of these findings is uncertain. There is some evidence from blocked experiments manipulating the relative proportions of old and new items that activation of the precuneus is associated with successful as opposed to unsuccessful retrieval (Kapur et al., 1995; Rugg et al., 1996), and it has been suggested that the region might support the use of visual imagery during retrieval (Fletcher et al., 1995; but see Buckner, Raichle, Miezin, & Petersen, 1996).

A second region consistently activated during episodic retrieval lies on the lateral surface of the parietal lobe, often more so on the left than the right. These activations include both inferior (and temporoparietal, BA39/40) and superior (BA7) regions (e.g. Buckner et al., 1996; Cabeza et al., 1997; Tulving et al., 1994b). Like the medial parietal region noted above, there is evidence that lateral parietal activation is associated with successful retrieval (Schacter, Alpert, Savage, Rauch, & Albert, 1996). Unlike medial parietal cortex, however, activation of lateral parietal regions appears to exhibit an element of task specificity, in that it appears to be more prominent during recognition memory than cued recall (Rugg et al., 1998a).

Medial temporal lobe

The importance of the hippocampus and adjacent regions for episodic memory is demonstrated by the many reports of profound memory impairment in humans and experimental animals following damage to the medial temporal lobe (Squire & Cohen, 1984; Zola-Morgan & Squire, 1990). In a review of medial temporal activations detected by PET, LePage, Habib, and Tulving (1998) proposed that posterior regions of the medial temporal lobe are associated with episodic retrieval (whereas anterior regions were associated with episodic encoding). Comparatively few fMRI studies have activated medial temporal regions during episodic retrieval tasks, although a review of such studies (Schacter & Wagner, 1998; see also Stark & Squire 2000a,b) failed to find an anterior–posterior distinction between encoding and retrieval. We return to this issue later.

Summary

The findings from blocked functional neuroimaging studies have revealed a wealth of data about brain regions active during episodic retrieval, only the most consistently observed of which were noted above. For reasons already discussed, the interpretation of many of these findings is hampered because of the constraints of blocked experimental designs. Thus, it is difficult on the basis of these findings to distinguish between regions activated by mere engagement in a retrieval task (thereby exhibiting state-related activity) from those activated more transiently in response to the presentation of test items (item-related activity), let alone to distinguish between activity associated with different categories of item or item/response combinations (e.g. hits versus correct rejections versus false alarms). The findings do, however, provide both an indication as to the regions where retrieval-related activations might be expected in event-related studies, and a source of hypotheses about the functional significance of these activations.

EVENT-RELATED STUDIES OF EPISODIC RETRIEVAL

Most of the studies discussed below employed as a retrieval task a variant of "yes/no" recognition memory, and were directed towards identification of the neural correlates of retrieval success—that is, patterns of brain activation associated with the retrieval of information from memory. Findings relevant to this issue thus form the bulk of the review. One study, however, also permits conclusions to be drawn about aspects of "preretrieval" processes—operations carried out on a retrieval cue in service of memory search.

Processing common to old and new items

According to Rugg and Wilding (2000), the neural correlates of preretrieval processes are best investigated by recording item-related activity elicited by retrieval cues corresponding to unstudied items (e.g. "new" items in a recognition memory test). These authors argued that such cues should be associated with minimal retrieval of information from the study episode, and hence the neural activity they elicit should be correlated primarily with processes subserving retrieval "attempt" rather than retrieval "success". This argument is not entirely convincing, however (as noted in the earlier section "Episodic memory"), even new items are likely to elicit postretrieval processing to some extent. It is arguable, however, that effects common to both new and old items are more likely candidates of preretrieval processing than are effects that vary according to item type.

Of the three studies (McDermott et al., 1999; Nolde, Johnson, & D'Esposito, 1998a; Ranganath, Johnson, & D'Esposito, 2000) that have contrasted responses elicited by items according to the nature of the task in which the items were presented, only one (Ranganath et al., 2000) assessed activity separately for cues corresponding to unstudied items. In McDermott et al. (1999) activity elicited by old and new words in a recognition task was contrasted with the activity elicited by words in an intentional encoding task. They reported a number of regions in which activity was greater during retrieval, including lateral and medial parietal cortex, and right anterior and dorsolateral prefrontal cortex. No reliable differences were found, however, for the direct contrast between old and new test items, calling into question the power of the study (compromised perhaps by the long SOA of 16.5s; see the earlier section "Neuroimaging: Methods and measures"), and making it difficult to dissociate the between-task findings into those associated with attempted versus successful retrieval. Similar problems afflict the study by Nolde et al. (1998a), in which retrieval-related activity was contrasted according to whether test items were subjected to a yes/no recognition or a source memory judgement. Three out of the four participants tested showed significantly enhanced activity during the source task in one or more regions of the left prefrontal cortex, leading Nolde et al. (1998a) to argue that the additional "reflective" retrieval operations required by source judgements were supported by left prefrontal regions (see also Nolde et al., 1998b). Intertask contrasts were, however, collapsed across old and new items.

Unlike the two studies just described, Ranganath et al. (2000) elicited event-related responses from test items presented at an SOA (4s) more suitable for detecting differences in responses to different item types. Employing a common study task (perceptual judgements about objects), and the same classes of test item (new objects, and old objects presented at a size either larger or smaller than the size at study), two test tasks were contrasted. In the "general" task, yes/no judgements were required, whereas in the specific task, participants were required to discriminate between the two classes of studied item (i.e. whether the items were larger or smaller than at study). The intertask contrast showed a relative increase in signal from left anterior prefrontal cortex (BA10) for the specific task, an effect that was apparent for both old and new test items. This finding replicates some of the results of a previous blocked study that contrasted source and recognition judgements (Rugg, Fletcher, Chua, & Dolan, 1999), and suggests that left anterior prefrontal cortex supports operations engaged preferentially when the retrieval task requires recovery of a high level of perceptual detail. Ranganath et al. (2000) conjectured that these operations involve some kind of monitoring or evaluative function carried out of the products of retrieval attempts. Equally likely possibilities are that the findings reflect either task-dependent differences in the manner in which the retrieval cues were processed (i.e. differences in retrieval "orientation", Rugg & Wilding, 2000), or differences due to the relative difficulty levels of the two tasks (i.e. differences in retrieval "effort", Schacter et al., 1996), consequential upon the fact that the specific task was the more difficult of the two.

Retrieval success

As noted previously, potential neural correlates of retrieval success are isolated by contrasting responses elicited by retrieval cues corresponding to correctly classified studied and unstudied items. In the studies discussed later, the cues have taken the form of old and new items in recognition memory tasks. Key findings from the studies using verbal material reviewed below are summarised in Tables 1.1, 1.2, 1.3, and 1.4. Note that unless stated otherwise, when describing these findings the designations "old" and "new" refer to items correctly classified as such (i.e. "hits" and "correct rejections").

Whereas old minus new contrasts will reveal activity related to successful retrieval, it is important to note that this activity can be confounded with other effects (Rugg & Wilding, 2000). These potential confounds include differences in response latency or confidence for old versus new decisions, and the fact that whereas some cognitive operations might be initiated when a retrieval attempt is successful, other operations—notably those related to memory search—will be terminated. Until all of the effects of these possible confounds have been investigated (for example, by comparing old–new effects as a function of reaction time (RT), obtaining confidence judgements, and examining responses to recognition misses and false alarms), it should not be taken for granted that differences in the responses elicited by old and new items are necessarily a direct reflection of cognitive operations supporting, or contingent upon, successful episodic retrieval.

The two earliest event-related fMRI studies of recognition memory (Buckner et al., 1998b; Schacter, Buckner, Koutstaal, Dale, & Rosen, 1997) to be described in any detail (see Friston et al., 1998, and Rugg, 1998, for brief descriptions of another early study) were unable to find any reliable differences between responses elicited by correctly classified old and new words. And as noted above, similarly negative findings were reported by McDermott et al. (1999). These null results were surprising given the ease with which

TABLE 1.1

Activation peaks by gross anatomical region and X, Y, Z Talairach coordinates (Talairach & Tournoux, 1999) for verbal retrieval success effects (old versus new) in prefrontal regions.

	Left anterior (BA9/10)	Left dorsal (BA9/46)	Left ventral (BA45/47)	Right anterior (BA9/10)	Right dorsal (BA9/46)	Right ventral (BA45/47)
Konishi et al. (2000)	−31 + 51 + 8		−45 + 27 + 16	+33 + 51 + 12		
Donaldson et al. (2001)	−40 + 51 + 6					
Saykin et al. (1999)					+54 + 14 + 32	
Henson et al. (1999b)	−12 + 63 + 18	−54 + 24 + 33	−48 + 39 − 12			
Henson et al. (1999a)	−21 + 63 + 21			+48 + 48 − 12		
Maratos et al. (2001)	−20 + 60 + 12		−52 + 30 − 10			+38 + 34 − 10
McDermott et al. (2000)	−37 + 53 + 10			+35 + 51 + 4	+45 + 23 + 30	
Cabeza et al. (2001)	−39 + 49 + 8				+38 + 38 + 6	

Note: Anterior, anterior to definition of inferior frontal sulcus (Y > +40); dorsal (lateral), within and above inferior frontal sulcus; ventral (lateral), below inferior frontal sulcus. BA, approximate Brodmann area.

TABLE 1.2

Activation peaks by gross anatomical region and X, Y, Z Talairach coordinates (Talairach & Tournoux, 1988) for verbal retrieval success effects (old versus new) in parietal regions.

	Left inferior (BA39/40)	Left superior (BA7)	Precuneus (BA7/19)	Post cingulate (BA23/31)	Right inferior (BA39/40)	Right superior (BA7)
Konishi et al. (2000)	−39 − 55 + 36	−29 − 69 + 44	−7 − 73 + 34	−5 − 39 + 34	+33 − 53 + 44	
Donaldson et al. (2001)	−40 − 51 + 39	−34 − 66 + 42	−1 − 63 + 27		+49 − 45 + 48	+34 − 63 + 45
Saykin et al. (1999)			−14 − 76 + 44			
Henson et al. (1999b)	−51 − 45 + 39	−33 − 60 + 45	−6 − 75 + 42	−6 − 24 + 27		
Henson et al. (1999a)		−48 − 57 + 48	0 − 69 + 33	+3 − 42 + 21		
Maratos et al. (2001)	−42 − 58 + 26	−36 − 62 + 56	−6 − 58 + 36	+4 − 54 + 18		+34 − 68 + 40
McDermott et al. (2000)	−37 − 51 + 36				+35 − 55 + 42	+41 − 57 + 48
Cabeza et al. (2001)	−47 − 50 + 38		+12 − 48 + 37		+40 − 51 + 22	

Note: Inferior, lateral inferior parietal/superior temporal; superior, superior parietal. For Henson et al. (1999b), old words confined to correct R judgements; for McDermott et al. (2000), hits and correct rejections of "combined" lures contrasted against correct rejections of new words; for Cabeza et al. (2001), hits and false alarms to lures contrasted against correct rejections. BA, approximate Brodmann area.

TABLE 1.3

Activation peaks by gross anatomical region and X, Y, Z Talairach coordinates (Talairach & Tournoux, 1988) for effects other than verbal retrieval success in prefrontal regions.

	Left anterior (BA9/10)	Left dorsal (BA9/46)	Left ventral (BA45/47)	Right anterior (BA10/11)	Right dorsal (BA9/46)	Right ventral (BA45/47)
Henson et al. (1999b) (Rem – Kno)	−21 + 54 + 39					
Henson et al. (1999b) (Kno – Rem)					+51 + 30 + 27	
Henson et al. (1999a) (Low – Hig)		−39 + 21 + 24			+54 + 30 + 24	
Eldridge (2000) (Rem – Kno)		−30 + 32 + 45				+55 + 7 + 25
Eldridge (2000) (Kno – Rem)				+23 + 52 + 25		
McDermott (2000) (Rec – Hit)		−49 + 31 + 24	−45 + 37 + 8		+45 + 23 + 30	
Cabeza (2001) (Fal – Tru)				+16 + 53 − 19		

Note: For Henson et al. (1999b), and Eldridge et al. (2000); Rem, correct Remember responses; Kno, correct Know responses. For Henson et al. (1999a): Low, low confidence responses; Hig, High confidence responses. For McDermott et al. (2000): Rec, recombined lures, correctly rejected; Hit, old words correctly recognised. For Cabeza et al. (2001): Fal, False alarms to semantic lures; Tru, old words correctly recognised.

TABLE 1.4

Activation peaks by gross anatomical region and X, Y, Z Talairach coordinates (Talairach & Tournoux, 1988) for effects other than verbal retrieval success in parietal regions.

	Left inferior (BA39/40)	Left superior (BA7)	Precuneus (BA7/19)	Post cingulate (BA23/31)	Right inferior (BA39/40)	Right superior (BA7)
Henson et al. (1999b) (Rem – Kno)	−57 – 51 + 39	−42 – 72 + 39		0 – 30 + 36		
Henson et al. (1999b) (Kno – Rem)			−12 – 60 + 57			
Eldridge (2000) (Rem – Kno)	−43 – 56 + 40			+13 – 23 + 45	+53 – 58 + 35	
McDermott (2000) (Hits – Rec)	−59 – 61 + 24				+47 – 49 + 30	
Cabeza (2001) (Tru – Fal)	−53 – 55 + 32					

Note: For Henson et al. (1999b), and Eldridge et al. (2000): Rem, correct Remember responses; Kno, correct Know responses. For McDermott et al. (2000): Rec, recombined lures, correctly rejected; Hit, old words correctly recognised. For Cabeza et al. (2001): Fal, False alarms to semantic lures; Tru, old words correctly recognised.

robust "old/new" effects can be obtained in recognition memory tasks with ERPs (Rugg, 1995), and almost certainly reflect no more than the lack of power of event-related fMRI studies to detect differential item-related activity when the SOA is long (16 or more seconds in the above cases; see Josephs & Henson, 1999).

In keeping with this conclusion, more recent studies that employed procedures better suited to the detection of interitem differences have consistently reported differences in the activity elicited by old and new items. In the study of Ranganath et al. (2000) already described, contrasts between old and new trials showed relatively greater activity for old items in a region of left dorsolateral prefrontal cortex (BA9), along with a small region demonstrating the opposite effect in the right ventral prefrontal cortex (BA47). Findings for regions outwith prefrontal cortex were not reported in that study.

In three studies employing simple yes/no recognition, reliable "old/new" differences were reported in both prefrontal and posterior regions. In Konishi, Wheeler, Donaldson, and Buckner (2000) words were studied in an "intentional" encoding task, and were subsequently presented at test intermixed with twice as many new items. Greater activity for old items was found in inferior (BA39/40) and superior (BA7) lateral parietal cortex bilaterally, in medial (BA7/31) parietal cortex, in several regions of prefrontal cortex, including bilateral anterior (BA10) and left ventral/dorsolateral (BA45/47/46) areas, and in anterior cingulate cortex. A potential difficulty in the interpretation of these findings arises from the relative frequencies of new and old items in the test lists (2:1), which potentially could give the old items something of the quality of task-relevant "oddball" stimuli. Because such stimuli elicit frontal and parietal activations even in simple tasks that place little or no demand on episodic memory (e.g. Stevens, Skudlarski, Gatenby, & Gore, 2000; Yoshiura et al., 1999), the findings of Konishi et al. (2000) might include effects that are only indirectly related to the memory demands of their task (see Rugg et al., 1996, for an example of a blocked design study of recognition memory that attempted to control for such oddball effects).

A similar problem pertains to the study of Saykin et al. (1999). Participants were required to listen passively to a series of 48 words, 10 of which had been presented both visually and auditorily prior to scanning. Relative to the novel words, enhanced responses to old items were found in left posterior parahippocampal cortex, a swathe of right premotor and prefrontal regions including dorsolateral prefrontal cortex (BA9), a large area of right temporal cortex, right anterior cingulate (BA8/32), and left medial parietal cortex (BA7). The reverse contrast revealed greater activity for novel words in left anterior hippocampus. As with Konishi et al. (2000) it is difficult to discern the extent to which these effects reflect cognitive operations linked to episodic memory, as opposed to the processing of two classes of item that differ markedly in their *a priori* probability of occurrence.

Donaldson et al. (2001) investigated both item- and state-related activity in a recognition memory task. Participants studied a series of word pairs, and later performed a yes/no recognition task on single words drawn from the pairs, and an equal number of new items. To allow state-related effects to be identified, the test trials were interrupted approximately every 2min by a 30s "fixation only" rest period. State-related effects were defined as the difference between activity during the recognition task (after removal of item-related effects) and activity during the interblock rest periods. Item-related activity was assessed relative to an interstimulus baseline, and in terms of direct contrasts between correctly classified old and new words. The analysis of state-related effects revealed signal changes in a number of regions, some of which overlapped those exhibiting item-related effects. Because Donaldson et al. (2001) did not include a control condition in which words were presented in the context of a task imposing no demands on memory, it is not possible to assess which, if any, of these regions exhibited activity tied specifically to the requirement to engage in recognition memory, rather than to more general aspects of word processing. Nor is it easy to make inferences about regions in which state-related effects were absent. For example, Donaldson et al. found no evidence of state-related activity in right anterior prefrontal cortex. Although this could be taken as damaging for the "retrieval mode" hypothesis of Tulving and colleagues (see the earlier section "Prefrontal cortex"), it is possible that the absence of cognitive demands during the rest periods meant that participants did not disengage fully from the task set engendered by the recognition test.

The same problems of interpretation do not exist for the contrast between responses elicited by old and new words. This contrast revealed enhanced activity for old items in several regions, including left anterior prefrontal cortex (BA10), and medial (BA18/31) and bilateral (BA40) parietal cortex (more extensive on the left). These regions agree well with those identified as being sensitive to retrieval success by Konishi et al. (2000).

In two studies, Henson and colleagues (Henson, Rugg, Shallice, & Dolan, 2000; Henson, Rugg, Shallice, Josephs, & Dolan, 1999b) investigated responses elicited during a recognition memory test when participants were required not only to judge whether a word was old or new, but also to provide information about the subjective experience accompanying the judgement. In the first of these studies, 60 words were studied incidentally in the context of a lexical decision task. At test, participants were presented with a list consisting of a mixture of these words and 30 unstudied items. (Note that this imbalance between old and new words raises the same potential problem of interpretation as was noted previously for Konishi et al. 2000, albeit in this case with oddball effects working against, rather than with, a finding of greater activation for old than new items. This issue does not arise in the case of the contrasts that were performed between different classes of old item.) The task requirement was to signal whether each word was new, whether it was judged old on the basis of recollection of some aspect of the study episode (a "Remember" response; Gardiner, 1988; Tulving, 1985), or judged old solely on the basis of an acontextual sense of familiarity (a "Know" response). Contrasts were performed between each class of old word and the new words, as well as between the two classes of old word.

Relative to new words, Remembered old words elicited enhanced activity in left ventral (BA47) and dorsal (BA9/46) lateral prefrontal cortex, in left lateral inferior and superior parietal cortex (BA7/40), medial parietal cortex (BA7), and the posterior cingulate (BA23/31), a network similar to that identified by Konishi et al. (2000) and Donaldson et al. (2001). (Henson et al. (1999b) also described a small region of activation in the left posterior medial temporal region, the localisation of which was indeterminate, and which therefore is not further discussed here.) Items assigned a Know judgement elicited greater activity relative to new items in similar left prefrontal regions to those activated by Remembered items, as well as in right ventral (BA47) and dorsal (BA46) prefrontal cortex, and anterior cingulate (BA9/32). Direct contrasts between the two classes of old item revealed relatively greater activity for Remembered items in left dorsal anterior prefrontal (BA8/9), inferior and superior lateral parietal cortex (BA40/19), and the posterior cingulate (BA24), whereas items assigned a Know judgement elicited relatively more activity in right dorsolateral prefrontal (BA46), anterior cingulate (BA9/32), and dorsal medial parietal (BA7) regions (see Table 1.2).

The second of Henson et al's studies (Henson et al., 2000) was motivated by the finding from their first study that right dorsolateral prefrontal cortex was more active for old items accorded a Know judgement than it was for Remembered items. Henson et al. (1999b) proposed that this finding reflected the role of this region in monitoring the products of retrieval attempts. They argued that, if Know judgements are on average based on weaker evidence than are Remember judgements (that is, on evidence nearer to the decision criterion; Donaldson, 1996), relatively more processing would be required to assess whether the evidence provided a sufficient basis for an "old" decision. Henson et al. (2000) reasoned that, if this proposal were correct, right dorsolateral activity should be greater when recognition decisions are based on evidence near to the "old/new" response criterion than when the evidence is well above or below the criterion. They tested this prediction by requiring participants to perform a recognition memory test in which decision confidence was signalled (sure new, unsure new, unsure old, sure old), predicting that non-confident decisions would be associated with greater right dorsolateral activity than would confident decisions. This prediction was borne out; the same region responsive to Know judgements in Henson et al. (1999b) was more active when correctly classified items (whether old or new) were assigned a nonconfident than a confident decision.

The study of Henson et al. (2000) also provided an opportunity to investigate effects related to retrieval success, although there were insufficient trials available to allow contrasts to be separated according to response confidence. The old minus new contrast revealed greater activity for old items in left lateral (BA40) and medial (BA7) parietal regions and the posterior cingulate (BA23), as well as in left anterior prefrontal cortex (BA10). In addition, a late-onsetting effect (old > new) was found in right anterior prefrontal cortex (BA10).

A further study using the Remember/Know procedure was reported by Eldridge, Knowlton, Furmanski, Bookheimer, and Engel (2000). Unlike Henson et al. (1999b), these authors employed a procedure whereby participants first signalled their old/new decision and then, for old judgements only, made a subsequent Remember/Know decision. Eldridge et al. (2000) argued that, in contrast to the procedure adopted by Henson et al. (1999b), in which a single, three-choice response was made to each item, the double response method produces a cleaner separation between recognition based on episodic retrieval and an acontextual sense of familiarity (Hicks & Marsh, 1999). However, the adoption of the double response procedure carries with it the disadvantage that whereas activity associated with Remember and Know judgements can be compared, contrasts between old and new items are confounded by the differential response requirements for the two classes of item. Among the areas reported by Eldridge et al. (2000) to be more active for Remember than Know judgements were left dorsolateral prefrontal cortex (BA8/9), right inferior prefrontal cortex (BA6/44), bilateral inferior parietal cortex (BA40), posterior cingulate cortex (BA23/31) and, importantly, left hippocampus. The reverse subtraction revealed greater activation in a region of right anterior prefrontal cortex (BA9/10) and the anterior cingulate (BA32). Thus, the findings were in some respects similar to those reported by Henson et al. (1999b). Among the more striking differences from the results from that study, however, were the greater hippocampal activation for Remember versus Know judgements, and, for the reverse contrast, greater activity in a more anterior portion of right prefrontal cortex.

Maratos, Dolan, Morris, Henson, and Rugg (2001) employed a recognition memory procedure to investigate the neural correlates of the incidental retrieval of emotional context. At study, participants gave valence ratings to a series of sentences that described emotionally negative, positive, or neutral situations. Immediately after the rating, a word from the sentence was presented on its own with the instruction to remember it for a subsequent test. These words were later presented, along with new items (giving an old/new ratio of 3:1) in a recognition memory test, during which event-related fMRI data were obtained. Of primary interest were the outcomes of contrasts between the responses elicited by the three classes of old item (i.e. items from the three different kinds of study sentences). However, Maratos et al. (2001) also reported those regions where each of the three possible old versus new contrasts demonstrated an enhanced response for recognised words. With the exception of the hippocampus, these regions included all of those discussed above, notably, bilateral (but predominantly left-sided) anterior and ventral prefrontal cortex (BA10 and BA47), bilateral medial and lateral parietal cortex (BA7 and BA40), and posterior cingulate (BA23).

The final two studies to be discussed also investigated retrieval success effects in recognition memory, but compared these with the effects elicited by "lure" items likely to elicit "false recollection" (see Roediger, 1996, and accompanying articles). In McDermott, Jones, Petersen, Lageman, and Roediger (2000), participants studied compound words such as "nosebleed" and "skydive". At test, yes/no recognition judgements were made on new words, studied words, and new words formed by recombining the component parts of some of the study words (e.g. "nosedive"). Recombined items attract considerably more false alarms than do new items formed from unstudied words and, it has been proposed (Jones & Jacoby, 2001), are rejected as old when they trigger recollection of one or both of the original study words, allowing the sense of familiarity engendered by the items to be successfully "opposed". On the basis of this proposal, McDermott et al. (2000) hypothesised that regions sensitive to retrieval success should be more active, relative to unrelated new items, for both recognised old items and correctly rejected recombined items.

Among the regions identified as showing greater activation for truly old items than for new items were bilateral parietal cortex (BA7/40) and bilateral anterior prefrontal cortex (BA10). The only region found to be more active for old words than correctly rejected recombined items was bilateral temporoparietal and inferior parietal cortex (BA39/40). By contrast, regions more active for the correctly rejected recombined items (relative to both old and new items) included bilateral dorsolateral prefrontal cortex (BA9/46) and medial frontal/anterior cingulate cortex (BA8/32). These latter findings must be interpreted with caution given that response times were longer for the recombined items than they were for either truly old or new words, raising the possibility that the findings reflect "time on task" effects (the same caution applies to the findings of Henson et al., 2000, and Henson et al., 1999b, with respect to their Know versus Remember, and Low versus High confidence judgements, respectively). However, this caution does not apply for those regions in which activity was enhanced equally for old and correctly rejected recombined items relative to new items, and indicates that, for these regions at least, the enhanced activity cannot be attributed to such factors as the detection of relatively rare "target" items, or differential processing associated with "yes" versus "no" responding.

In Cabeza, Rao, Wagner, Mayer, and Schacter (2001), a different method for eliciting false memories was employed (Deese, 1959; Roediger & McDermott, 1995) and the analyses focused not on the "lure" items that were successfully rejected, but on the items that were falsely accepted as old. At study, participants watched videos that depicted two speakers taking turns to read a list of semantically related words. Test items were presented visually and consisted of new and old words, along with "related lure" items—new words strongly related semantically to study items. Consistent with much previous research, participants incorrectly classified the great majority of these items as old. Relative to the activity elicited by new items, Cabeza et al. (2001) reported that a region of the anterior temporal lobe bilaterally, including the hippocampus, was more active for both old and related lure words (the activated region of left hippocampus was within a few millimetres of that reported by Eldridge et al., 2000). By contrast, a left posterior parahippocampal region showed enhanced activity for old words relative to the other two item classes, which did not differ. Other areas showing differential item-related activity included bilateral dorsolateral prefrontal cortex (BA46), where both old and related lure items elicited greater activity than did new words. A similar pattern was observed in bilateral temporoparietal and inferior parietal cortex (BA39/40) and precuneus (BA7/19/31). The left temporoparietal region (BA39/40) also showed greater activity for old words than related words, as did the anterior cingulate (BA24). Among areas showing relatively greater activity for related lures was a region of orbitofrontal cortex on the right (BA11).

Cabeza et al. (2001) interpreted their findings for the medial temporal lobe as evidence for a dissociation between regions subserving the retrieval of "semantic" versus "sensory" information. They argued that the more anterior, semantic, effects were responsible for the attribution of "oldness" to both lure and truly old items, whereas the posterior effect reflected the recovery of sensory detail specific to the truly old words, which the encoding task had ensured were associated with rich sensory information. As was the case for McDermott et al. (2000), Cabeza et al. (2001) interpreted their findings for the dorsolateral prefrontal cortex as evidence for the role of this region in the monitoring of retrieved information.

Summary

As already noted, with the exception of Ranganath et al. (2000), none of the reviewed studies specifically addressed item-related "preretrieval" processing. The foregoing review does, however, provide a reasonably consistent picture of regions sensitive to retrieval success during tests of recognition memory and, on the basis of the manipulations employed in the different studies, some useful hints emerge as to the possible functional significance of these effects. Across studies, the regions most consistently reported (i.e. identified in more than half of the studies reviewed) were in left anterior prefrontal cortex, left inferior and superior parietal cortex, and precuneus. Less consistently reported (but identified in more than one study) were differential activity in right anterior, left and right dorsolateral and left ventrolateral prefrontal cortex, right inferior and superior parietal cortex, and posterior cingulate. Differential activity in the medial temporal lobe was reported in three studies. Below, we discuss the possible functional significance of these findings.

FUNCTIONAL SIGNIFICANCE OF ACTIVATIONS

Prefrontal cortex

The prefrontal region most consistently associated with retrieval success in the foregoing event-related studies was anterior prefrontal cortex (mainly BA 10). In contrast with previous blocked designs, these anterior prefrontal effects were observed more often on the left than on the right. Dorsolateral prefrontal activations (BA9/46)—both left- and right-sided—were also sometimes detected. Interestingly, a recent meta-analysis of PET studies of recognition memory (Lepage, Ghaffar, Nyberg, & Tulving, 2000) identified both of these left prefrontal regions as being sensitive to the probability of successful retrieval.

The results reviewed here offer some clues as to the nature of the processes supported by left prefrontal cortex during episodic retrieval. In the case of left anterior cortex, the finding of Henson et al. (1999b) that this region was more active for recognised items accorded Remember rather than Know judgements is consistent with a role in the processing of retrieved information with a relatively high level of episodic content. A similar conclusion can be drawn from the finding of McDermott et al. (2000) that left anterior prefrontal cortex was activated both by recognised old items, and by correctly rejected "related lures" (items that, it is assumed, elicited recollection of the study episode). Just what the nature of this processing might be is unclear, although findings suggesting that left anterior prefrontal activity elicited by unstudied items is enhanced when the retrieval task requires a judgement of source, rather than mere recognition (Ranganath et al., 2000; see also Nolde et al., 1998a; Rugg et al., 1999) might turn out to be an important clue.

As already noted, the question of whether activation of right anterior prefrontal cortex during episodic retrieval reflects state- or item-related processing has been debated for several years (compare Kapur et al., 1995; Nyberg et al., 1995 with Rugg et al., 1996, 1998a—see also Nyberg et al., 2000). According to Tulving and colleagues, the functional role of right prefrontal cortex is to support "retrieval mode", a mental state in which environmental events are treated as retrieval cues, and retrieved episodic memories are experienced "autonoetically" (Tulving, 1983; Wheeler et al., 1997). From this viewpoint, right prefrontal activity should be state- rather than item-related and, critically, should not vary according to whether a retrieval attempt is successful or unsuccessful. An alternative viewpoint, bolstered by evidence from both neuroimaging (e.g. Rugg et al., 1996) and electrophysiological studies (e.g. Wilding & Rugg, 1996), posits that right prefrontal activity is both item-related and associated specifically with retrieval success.

The findings from the event-related recognition studies reviewed earlier do not clearly distinguish these two positions; whereas the studies do permit an assessment of whether right prefrontal cortex exhibits item-related activity, to date, no study has satisfactorily addressed the question of whether this region also demonstrates task-dependent state-related activity. Three of the studies (Henson et al., 2000; Konishi et al., 2000; McDermott et al., 2000) reported item-related right anterior prefrontal activation associated with retrieval success. The failure of other studies to observe this result could have arisen for a number of reasons. With regard to the conduct of future studies, arguably the most important of these reasons is the evidence suggesting that right anterior prefrontal cortex might exhibit atypical event-related responses, particularly with respect to onset latency. Buckner et al. (1998b) and Schacter et al. (1997), for example, reported a relatively delayed response in this region, and Henson et al. (2000) were able to detect differential right anterior responses to old and new words only when the data were modelled with a response function that was delayed by 3s relative to a standard, or "canonical", function. (Henson et al. proffered this result as an explanation for the failure to find right anterior prefrontal activation in their previous study (Henson et al., 1999b), when the data were modelled with a canonical response function only.) It is unclear why this region should exhibit an atypical response function. The function could be a reflection of the dynamics of the underlying neural activity, consistent with the relatively late onset and prolonged time course of the "right frontal" ERP old/new effect (Rugg & Allan, 1999). Alternatively, delayed right anterior frontal activity might merely reflect a peculiarity of vascular responses in this brain region, such that the interval between a change in neural activity and its reflection in the BOLD signal is delayed relative to other brain areas (Buckner et al., 1998b; Schacter et al., 1997). This latter explanation seems unlikely, however; it seems improbable that vascular properties of cortical regions would be laterally asymmetric, and the majority of the event-related studies reviewed here, regardless of the analysis method employed, were able to detect differential item-related activity in left anterior prefrontal cortex.

The other prefrontal region activated in some of the event-related studies reviewed above is dorsolateral prefrontal cortex. In most of these studies, dorsolateral prefrontal activation was detected during tasks with demands that exceeded those of simple recognition (see Table 1.2)—whether by virtue of the requirement to make an introspective judgement about the recognition decision (Eldridge et al., 2000; Henson et al., 1999b, 2000), or to discriminate between "true" and "false" recollections (Cabeza et al., 2001; McDermott et al., 2000). Thus, in keeping with the findings for the analogous right frontal ERP old/new effect (for review, see Rugg & Allan, 1999), it could be that differential activation of this region is more likely to be found when the retrieval task requires postretrieval demands additional to those imposed by simple recognition judgements. As suggested previously (Fletcher et al., 1998; Henson, Shallice, & Dolan, 1999a), these demands might include the engagement of monitoring processes that operate on the products of retrieval. This suggestion perhaps receives its most direct support from the aforementioned studies of false recollection when, as with tasks involving source memory, the mere "success" of a retrieval attempt does not in itself permit accurate responding.

In keeping with previous proposals (Fletcher & Henson, 2001; Henson et al. 2001), the findings discussed above add weight to the view that dorsolateral and anterior prefrontal regions play different roles in the processing of retrieved information. Support for this proposal comes from the findings of Henson et al. (2001) and McDermott et al. (2000). As already noted, the former authors found greater dorsolateral activation for low versus high confidence judgements, whether the word was old or new. They found a different pattern of findings for anterior prefrontal cortex, however, where activity was greater for old than new items. McDermott et al. (2000) found greater dorsolateral and anterior activation for old versus new items. In addition, however, they found that the dorsolateral, but not anterior, region was more active still for correctly rejected "recombined" items versus truly old items. Taken together, these findings suggest two different kinds of postretrieval processing. One kind of processing—supported by dorsolateral prefrontal cortex—operates on the products of a retrieval attempt regardless of the amount or the nature of the information retrieved. A second kind of processing—associated with anterior cortex—appears to be engaged only when a retrieval attempt culminates in the successful recovery of episodic information (i.e. recollection). It should be noted, however, that the data of Eldridge et al. (2000) complicate this picture somewhat. In contrast to Henson et al. (1999b), these authors reported greater activity in right anterior (rather than dorsolateral) prefrontal cortex for Know relative to Remember judgements, albeit in a region more superior than that identified by Henson et al. (2000) and McDermott et al. (2000) as sensitive to retrieval success. As the precise functional boundary between dorsolateral and anterior prefrontal cortex is uncertain, the extent to which the findings of Eldridge et al. (2000) conflict with previous results is not clear.

As already alluded to, the idea that right prefrontal cortex plays a role in postretrieval processing receives support from findings from ERP studies, in which correctly classified old items have been found to elicit a late-onsetting, sustained positive wave focused over the right frontal scalp (Rugg & Allan, 1999; see Chapter 2). The ERP "right frontal old/new effect" is often more prominent when elicited by items attracting high relative to low levels of recollection (as indexed, for example, by successful versus unsuccessful retrieval of source information; Wilding & Rugg, 1996), and has been interpreted as reflecting the maintenance and further processing of retrieved episodic information. Such a proposal would be consistent with the role envisaged above for the right anterior prefrontal cortex based upon event-related fMRI findings. Recently, however, prominent right frontal ERP effects have been reported for old items associated with little or no recollection and likely recognised with low confidence (Rugg, Allan, & Birch, 2000). This result is more in keeping with the findings reported by Henson et al. (2000) for right dorsolateral cortex. Thus it is possible that the right frontal ERP effect might reflect activity in disparate, functionally heterogeneous regions of prefrontal cortex and, therefore, act as a rather "impure" index of postretrieval processing.

Some of the left prefrontal regions identified in the foregoing review as being sensitive to retrieval success have been associated previously with encoding rather than retrieval (Tulving et al., 1994a). The ventrolateral region in particular has been linked with semantic and phonological processing (see Poldrack et al. 1998, for a review), and has received considerable attention as a region supporting effective episodic encoding of verbal material (e.g. Kapur et al., 1994; Shallice et al., 1994). One speculative possibility is that activation of left ventrolateral and adjacent prefrontal regions during retrieval reflects the consequences of successful cue processing. By this argument, only test items that receive a sufficiently full semantic analysis can act as effective retrieval cues. Thus, left frontal activation reflects a form of "pre-retrieval" processing that is "predictive" of subsequent retrieval success in a manner analogous to that reported for these regions in event-related studies of encoding (Henson et al., 1999b; Wagner et al., 1998; see Wagner, Koutstaal, & Schacter, 1999, for a review). Another possibility is that successful episodic retrieval reflects recapitulation of semantic processing performed at the time of study (Blaxton et al., 1996; Rugg et al., 1997).

The finding of increased left ventrolateral prefrontal activity for old versus new items during recognition memory stands in contrast to findings from studies employing indirect memory tasks such as semantic decision, when left ventrolateral activity is *lower* for old items (Demb et al., 1995; Wagner, Desmond, Demb, Glover, & Gabrieli, 1997; Wagner, Maril, & Schacter, 2000). This effect has been linked to "conceptual priming", and held to reflect reduced demands placed on semantic processing by repeated items. Thus, to the extent that the left prefrontal effects identified in studies using direct (recognition) and indirect (priming) memory tasks occur in the same regions, it follows that the relative activity levels for old and new words must vary according to task. One possibility is that the adoption of "retrieval mode" during direct memory tests (Tulving, 1983) alters the pattern of left prefrontal activity associated with processing old and new words, causing the former rather than the latter class of items to elicit the greater activity. Alternatively, it could be that the nature of the processing accorded words during recognition tasks differs sufficiently from that during study to eliminate any benefit (and any concomitant reduction in associated neural activity) arising from the repetition of the words (compare with Demb et al., 1995). By this account, under conditions of high intertask transfer, recognition-related increases in left ventrolateral activity might be offset by the neural correlates of the ensuing conceptual priming effects.

With regard to the foregoing issue, it is noteworthy that it has been reported that left ventrolateral prefrontal activity elicited by new words "studied" in the context of a recognition memory test is predictive of subsequent memory on a second, surprise recognition test (Buckner, Wheeler, & Sheridan, 2001). It would be of considerable interest to know whether the left ventrolateral activity elicited during the surprise test by these items, when they were successfully recognised, was higher or lower than the activity elicited by the new words in the test.

Parietal cortex

In the majority of studies reviewed, lateral and medial parietal cortex were found to exhibit greater activity for items eliciting successful relative to unsuccessful retrieval, regardless of the exact form of the retrieval task. In most of the studies, the lateral parietal activations were lateralised to, or more extensive, on the left, and more likely to be in inferior (BA40) than superior (BA7) parietal gyri. The findings are consistent with a number of previous studies in which retrieval success was investigated with blocked designs and, broadly speaking, with two meta-analyses of studies employing such designs (Habib & LePage, 1999; Lepage et al., 2000). There seems little reason, therefore, to doubt that activity in these regions is a correlate of successful recognition. The findings of Henson et al. (1999b) and Eldridge et al. (2000) that left lateral parietal activity was greater for items accorded Remember rather than Know responses suggest that activity in this region might be a function of the amount of episodic information retrieved in response to the test item.

The findings for these parietal regions are reminiscent of a memory-related ERP effect—the so-called "left parietal" old/new effect. This effect takes the form of a positive shift in ERPs elicited by correctly classified old items relative to waveforms elicited by new items. The effect onsets around 400–500ms poststimulus, is maximal over the left parietal scalp and, on the basis of its sensitivity to a wide variety of experimental variables, has been interpreted as a neural correlate of episodic retrieval or "recollection" (Rugg & Allan, 1999). Notably, as is the case for the parietal activations described in the foregoing event-related fMRI studies, the left parietal ERP effect is larger for items accorded Remember rather than Know judgements (Duzel, Yonelinas, Mangun, Heinze, & Tulving, 1997; Smith, 1993) and, in false memory paradigms, is elicited both by truly old items and semantically related "lures" (Duzel et al., 1997; Johnson, Kounios, & Nolde, 1997a). It has been proposed that the left parietal ERP effect reflects cortical activity supporting the hippocampally mediated "reactivation" or "reinstatement" of retrieved information (Rugg et al., 1998b). An alternative possibility, arguably more compatible with the role posited for parietal cortex in attention (Kastner & Ungerleider, 2000), is that the effect reflects some kind of attentional shift or orienting triggered by successful episodic retrieval. It is perhaps relevant in this context that attentional orienting in time has also been reported to be associated with predominantly left-lateralised parietal activation (Coull, Frith, Buchel, & Nobre, 2000).

On the basis of the studies reviewed here, the functional role of medial parietal cortex in memory would appear to be similar to that proposed for lateral parietal cortex. In the reviewed studies, posterior medial activations related to retrieval success were found in both the precuneus (BA7/19) and the posterior cingulate (BA23/31). There was little evidence, however, to suggest that activity in these two medial regions could be dissociated from one another, or from activity in lateral cortex, although other studies have demonstrated task-based dissociations between these regions (Rugg et al., 1998a; Shallice et al., 1994). Shallice et al. (1994), for example, found posterior cingulate activations associated with episodic encoding, whereas activation of the precuneus was observed at retrieval. The only hint of a dissociation in the crop of event-related studies reviewed here came from Henson et al. (1999b), who identified a region in the precuneus where activity was greater for Know than Remember judgements, in contrast to posterior cingulate and lateral parietal regions, where Remember judgements were associated with the greater levels of activity.

As already noted, a frequently cited role for the medial parietal cortex is in the support of visual imagery (Fletcher et al., 1995; but see Buckner et al., 1996). According to this argument, activation of this region during successful retrieval reflects the strong demands placed on visual imagery by the representation of episodic information. Although plausible, there is currently little direct evidence to support this proposal (although see Wheeler, Petersen, & Buckner, 2000). Finally, it should be noted that there is currently no reason why medial parietal cortex is any less likely to contribute to ERP old/new effects than are lateral and inferior parietal regions.

Medial temporal lobe

In contrast to the findings for frontal and parietal regions, only three of the studies reviewed here reported retrieval-related activation in the hippo-campus or adjacent medial temporal cortex. Indeed, if the findings of Saykin et al. (1999) are discounted (on the grounds that the study confounded mem-ory retrieval and oddball effects), the only studies to find hippocampal acti-vation were those of Cabeza et al. (2001) and Eldridge et al. (2000). These findings were obtained for test items likely to have elicited strong episodic recollection. Thus, they are consistent with the proposal that retrieval-related hippocampal activity is associated specifically with this form of memory (Rugg et al., 1997; Schacter et al., 1996) and, more generally, with the view that the hippocampus proper forms part of a circuit specialised for episodic memory rather than memory based on non-episodic information such as item familiarity (e.g. Aggleton & Brown, 1998). These findings lend weight to the possibility that the failure to find hippocampal activation in other studies of yes/no recognition reflects the fact that, as noted in the earlier section "Epi-sodic memory", this task is "process impure"; specifically, old/new decisions can be made on the basis of an acontextual sense of familiarity in the absence of the (putatively hippocampally mediated) retrieval of a study episode (Aggleton & Brown, 1998; Yonelinas, 1994). However, this possibil-ity seems unlikely to account fully for the inconsistent findings noted above for the medial temporal lobe. First, two other studies (Henson et al., 1999b; McDermott et al., 2000) also employed procedures that permitted responses to items eliciting episodic recollection to be contrasted with responses to new items, but in neither case was differential hippocampal activity reported. Second, it has been suggested that item familiarity, the "non-recollective" basis for recognition, depends upon perirhinal cortex, a medial temporal region that lies ventral and anterior to the hippocampus (Aggleton & Brown, 1998). Thus, to the extent that recognition judgements are based upon familiarity rather than episodic recollection (as is thought to be the case for items accorded "Know" judgements, for example), one might expect to see retrieval related activation in anterior medial temporal cortex.

The reasons why event-related medial temporal activations cannot be detected consistently during episodic retrieval remain unclear. One possi-bility is that this inconsistency reflects a limitation of the fMRI method, the sensitivity for which is compromised in regions, such as the anterior medial temporal lobe, which are prone to susceptibility artefact (although see Constable et al., 2000). Another possibility is that the null findings are a consequence of the neural dynamics of the hippocampus (such that retrieval-related neural activity does not generally give rise to changes in metabolic demand on a spatial scale large enough to be detected by current methods).

Finally, the lack of positive findings might be a sign that the contribution of the medial temporal lobe to retrieval is often overshadowed by encoding-related activity. By this argument (Rugg et al. 1997; but see Gabrieli, Brewer, Desmond, & Glover, 1997), the failure to find differential activity for contrasts between responses to old and new items reflects the fact that medial temporal structures are active both in support of retrieval of old information, and encoding of the new information carried by contextually novel items (but see Stark & Squire, 2000ab).

FUTURE RESEARCH

It is clear that event-related fMRI has made important contributions to the study of the neural correlates of memory retrieval within a remarkably short time. It is equally clear, however, that much remains to be done. Most pressing of all, perhaps, is the need to extend the event-related method to tasks other than those based around recognition memory. There are good grounds for thinking that some of the neural correlates of episodic memory retrieval are task-dependent (Allan, Dolan, Fletcher, & Rugg, 2000; Rugg & Allan, 1999; Rugg et al., 1998a), and it is important that hypotheses formulated on the basis of the existing, rather narrow, data set are challenged by findings from a much wider range of tasks. It is also likely that tasks other than recognition memory might reveal functional dissociations additional to those reported to date (a good candidate for such a dissociation being medial versus lateral/inferior parietal cortex).

A second issue that needs to be addressed concerns the relationship between item- and state-related activity. A promising start has been made in this regard (Donaldson et al., 2001), and there is no reason why it should not be possible to identify regions exhibiting one or the other form of activity in the same study. It will then be possible to address such important questions as whether the prefrontal regions held to support tonically maintained states such as retrieval mode are dissociable from regions that exhibit item-related activity, questions that cannot be addressed on the basis of present findings.

A third point concerns the relationship between "pre-" and "post-" retrieval processes. The majority of current event-related fMRI studies have been concerned with retrieval success (comparing responses elicited by correctly classified old and new words), revealing prefrontal activations most likely associated with postretrieval processing. It will be interesting to dissociate these activations from those produced by differences in task- or item-related effects associated with new items alone, for which episodic retrieval is minimal. This will allow investigation of so-called "retrieval orientation" effects (Rugg & Wilding, 2000).

A final issue concerns the need to clarify the findings relating to retrieval success, for example by controlling more carefully for potential confounds, such as those associated with oddball effects and differences in the effort or difficulty of responding to old versus new words. It will also prove informative to investigate the patterns of neural activity associated with retrieval of different types of material (e.g. words versus pictures), and different kinds of study processing (e.g. "deep" versus "shallow" study). Such studies will permit a delineation of the network of brain regions associated with episodic retrieval in general, as opposed to other regions in which retrieval-related activity is dependent on the nature of the stored information.

ACKNOWLEDGEMENTS

The authors and their research are supported by the Wellcome Trust. We are grateful to R.L. Buckner, D.I. Donaldson, and K.B. McDermott for their comments on an earlier version of this chapter.

REFERENCES

Aggleton, J.P., & Brown, M.W. (1999). Episodic memory, amnesia, and the hippocampal–anterior thalamic axis. *The Behavioral and Brain Sciences, 22*, 425–444.

Allan, K., Dolan, R.J., Fletcher, P.C., & Rugg, M.D. (2000). The role of the right anterior prefrontal cortex in episodic retrieval. *Neuroimage*, 11(3), 217–227.

Blaxton, T.A., Bookheimer, S.Y., Zeffiro, T.A., Figlozzi, C.M., Gaillard, W.D., & Theodore, W.H. (1996). Functional mapping of human memory using PET: Comparisons of conceptual and perceptual tasks. *Canadian Journal of Experimental Psychology, 50*, 42–56.

Buckner, R.L., Goodman, J., Burock, M., Rotte, M., Koustaal, W., Schacter, D., Rosen, B., & Dale, A.M. (1998a). Functional–anatomic correlates of object priming in humans revealed by rapid presentation event-related fMRI. *Neuron, 20*, 285–296.

Buckner, R.L., & Koutstaal, W. (1998). Functional neuroimaging studies of encoding, priming, and explicit memory retrieval. *Proceedings of the National Academy of Sciences USA, 95*(3), 891–898.

Buckner, R.L., Koutstaal, W., Schacter, D.L., Dale, A.M., Rotte, M., & Rosen, B.R. (1998b). Functional–anatomic study of episodic retrieval: II selective averaging of event-related fMRI trials to test the retrieval success hypothesis. *Neuroimage, 7*, 163–175.

Buckner, R.L., Raichle, M.E., Miezin, F.M., & Petersen, S.E. (1996). Functional anatomic studies of memory retrieval for auditory words and visual pictures. *Journal of Neuroscience, 16*, 6219–6235.

Buckner, R.L., Wheeler, M.E., & Sheridan, M. (2001). Encoding processes during retrieval tasks. *Journal of Cognitive Neuroscience, 13*, 406–415.

Burgess, P.W., & Shallice, T. (1996). Confabulation and the control of recollection. *Memory, 4*, 359–411.

Cabeza, R., Kapur, S., Craik, F.I.M., McIntosh, A.R., Houle, S., & Tulving, E. (1997). Functional neuroanatomy of recall and recognition: A PET study of episodic memory. *Journal of Cognitive Neuroscience, 9*, 254–265.

Cabeza, R., Rao, S.M., Wagner, A.D., Mayer, A.R., & Schacter, D.L. (2001). Can medial temporal lobe regions distinguish true from false? An event-related fMRI study of veridical and illusory recognition memory. *Proceedings of the National Academy of Sciences USA, 98*, 4805–4810.

Chawla, D., Rees, G., & Friston, K.J. (1999). The physiological basis of attentional modulation in extrastriate visual areas. *Nature Neuroscience, 2*(7), 671–676.

Christoff, K., & Gabrieli, J.D.E. (2000). The frontopolar cortex and human cognition: Evidence for a rostrocaudal hierarchical organization within the human prefrontal cortex. *Journal of Psychobiology*, *28*, 168–186.

Constable, R.T., Carpentier, A., Pugh, K., Westerveld, M., Oszunar, Y., & Spencer, D.D. (2000). Investigation of the human hippocampal formation using a randomized event-related paradigm and Z-shimmed functional MRI. *Neuroimage*, *12*, 55–62.

Coull, J.T., Frith, C.D., Buchel, C., & Nobre, A.C. (2000). Orienting attention in time: Behavioural and neuroanatomical distinction between exogenous and endogenous shifts. *Neuropsychologia*, *38*, 808–819.

Dale, A.M., & Buckner, R.L. (1997). Selective averaging of rapidly presented individual trials using fMRI. *Human Brain Mapping*, *5*, 329–340.

Deese, J. (1959). On the prediction of occurrence of particular verbal intrusions in immediate recall. *Journal of Experimental Psychology*, *58*, 17–22.

Demb, J.B., Desmond, J.E., Wagner, A.D., Vaidya, C.J., Glover, G.H., & Gabrieli, J.D. (1995). Semantic encoding and retrieval in the left inferior prefrontal cortex: A functional MRI study of task difficulty and process specificity. *Journal of Neuroscience*, *15*, 5870–5878.

Desgranges, B., Baron, J.-C., & Eustache, F. (1998). The functional neuroanatomy of episodic memory: the role of the frontal lobes, the hippocampal formation, and other areas. *Neuroimage*, *8*, 198–213.

Donaldson, D.J., Petersen, S.E., Ollinger, J.M., & Buckner, R.L. (2001). Separating state and item related processing during recognition memory using functional MRI. *Neuroimage*, *13*, 129–142.

Donaldson, W. (1996). The role of decision processes in remembering and knowing. *Memory & Cognition*, *24*, 523–533.

Duzel, E., Cabeza, R., Picton, T.W., Yonelinas, A.P., Scheich, H., Heinze, H.J., & Tulving, E. (1999). Task-related and item-related brain processes of memory retrieval. *Proceedings of the National Academy of Sciences USA*, *96*, 1794–1799.

Duzel, E., Yonelinas, A.P., Mangun, G.R., Heinze, H.J., & Tulving, E. (1997). Event-related brain potential correlates of two states of conscious awareness in memory. *Proceedings of the National Academy of Sciences USA*, *94*, 5973–5978.

Eldridge, L.L., Knowlton, B.J., Furmanski, C.S., Bookheimer, S.Y., & Engel, S.A. (2000). Remembering episodes: A selective role for the hippocampus during retrieval. *Nature Neuroscience*, *3*, 1149–1152.

Fletcher, P., Frith, C.D., Baker, S., Shallice, T., Frackowiak, R.S.J., & Dolan, R.J. (1995). The mind's eye – activation of the precuneus in memory related imagery. *Neuroimage*, *2*, 196–200.

Fletcher, P.C., Frith, C.D., & Rugg, M.D. (1997). The functional neuroanatomy of episodic memory. *Trends in Neuroscience*, *20*, 213–218.

Fletcher, P.C., & Henson, R.N.A. (2001). Frontal lobes and human memory – insights from functional neuroimaging. *Brain*, *124*, 849–881.

Fletcher, P.C., Shallice, T., Frith, C.D., Frackowiak, R.S.J., & Dolan, R.J. (1998). The functional roles of the prefrontal cortex in episodic memory: II Retrieval. *Brain*, *121*, 1249–1256.

Friedman, D., & Johnson, R. (2000). Event-related potential (ERP) studies of memory encoding and retrieval: A selective review. *Microscopy Research and Techniques*, *51*, 6–28.

Friston, K.J., Fletcher, P., Josephs, O., Holmes, A., Rugg, M.D., & Turner, R. (1998). Event-related fMRI: Characterizing differential responses. *Neuroimage*, *7*, 30–40.

Friston, K.J., Zarahn, E., Josephs, O., Henson, R.N., & Dale, A.M. (1999). Stochastic designs in event-related fMRI. *Neuroimage*, *10*, 607–619.

Gabrieli, J.D.E., Brewer, J.B., Desmond, J.E., & Glover, G.H. (1997). Separate neural bases of two fundamental memory processes in the human medial temporal lobe. *Science*, *276*, 264–266.

Gardiner, J.M. (1988). Functional aspects of recollective experience. *Memory & Cognition, 16*, 309–313.

Habib, R., & LePage, M. (1999). Novelty assessment in the brain. In E. Tulving (Ed.), *Memory, consciousness and the brain* (pp. 265–277). London: Psychology Press.

Henson, R.N.A., Price, C.J., Rugg, M.D., Turner, R., & Friston, K.J. (2002). Detecting latency differences in event-related BOLD responses: Application to words versus nonwords and initial versus repeated face presentations. *Neuroimage, 15*, 83–87.

Henson, R.N.A., Rugg, M.D., Shallice, T., & Dolan, R.J. (2000). Confidence in recognition memory for words: dissociating right prefrontal roles in episodic retrieval. *Journal of Cognitive Neuroscience, 12*, 913–923.

Henson, R.N.A., Rugg, M.D., Shallice, T., Josephs, O., & Dolan, R. (1999b). Recollection and familiarity in recognition memory: An event-related fMRI study. *Journal of Neuroscience, 19*, 3962–3972.

Henson, R.N.A, Shallice, T., & Dolan, R.J. (1999a). Right prefrontal cortex and episodic memory retrieval: A functional MRI test of the monitoring hypothesis. *Brain, 122*, 1367–1381.

Henson, R.N.A., Shallice, T., Rugg, M., Fletcher, P., & Dolan, R. (2001). Functional imaging dissociations within right prefrontal cortex during episodic memory retrieval. *Brain & Cognition, 47*, 79–81.

Hicks, J.L., & Marsh, R.L. (1999). Remember-know judgements can depend on how memory is tested. *Psychonomic Bulletin and Reviews, 6*, 117–122.

Incisa Della Rocchetta, A., & Milner, B. (1993). Strategic search and retrieval inhibition: The role of the frontal lobes. *Neuropsychologia, 31*, 503–524.

Jacoby, L.L., & Kelley, C. (1992). Unconscious influences of memory: Dissociations and automaticity. In A.D. Milner & M.D. Rugg (Eds.), *The neuropsychology of consciousness* (pp. 201–233). London: Academic Press.

Jacoby, L.L., Toth, J.P., & Yonelinas, A.P. (1993). Separating conscious and unconscious influences of memory: Measuring recollection. *Journal of Experimental Psychology: General, 122*, 139–154.

Janowsky, J.S., Shimamura, A.P., Kritchevsky, M., & Squire, L.R. (1989). Cognitive impairment following frontal lobe damage and its relevance to human amnesia. *Behavioral Neuroscience, 103*, 548–560.

Johnson, M.K., Kounios, J., & Nolde, S.F. (1997a). Electrophysiological brain activity and memory source monitoring. *Neuroreport, 8*, 1317–1320.

Johnson, M.K., Nolde, S.F., Mather, M., Kounios, J., Schacter, D.L., & Curran, T. (1997b). Test format can affect the similarity of brain activity associated with true and false recognition memory. *Psychological Science, 8*, 250–257.

Jones, T.C., & Jacoby, L.L. (2001). Feature and conjunction errors in recognition memory: Evidence for dual-process theory. *Journal of Memory and Language, 45*, 82–102.

Josephs, O., & Henson, R.N.A. (1999). Event-related fMRI: Modelling, inference and optimisation. *Philosophical Transactions of the Royal Society of London, 354*, 1215–1228.

Josephs, O., Turner, R., & Friston, K. (1997). Event-related fMRI. *Human Brain Mapping, 5*, 243–248.

Kapur, S., Craik, F., Brown, G.M., Houle, S., & Tulving, E. (1995). Functional role of the prefrontal cortex in memory retrieval: A PET study. *Neuroreport, 6*, 1880–1884.

Kapur, S., Craik, F.I.M., Tulving, E., Wilson, A.A., Houle, S., & Brown, G.M. (1994). Neuroanatomical correlates of encoding in episodic memory: levels of processing effect. *Proceedings of the National Academy of Sciences USA, 91*, 2008–2011.

Kastner, S., & Ungerleider, L.G. (2000). Mechanisms of visual attention in the human cortex. *Annual Review of Neurosciences, 23*, 315–341.

Konishi, S., Wheeler, M.E., Donaldson, D.I., & Buckner, R.L. (2000). Neural correlates of episodic retrieval success. *Neuroimage, 12*, 276–286.

Lepage, M., Ghaffar, O., Nyberg, L., & Tulving, E. (2000). Prefrontal cortex and episodic memory retrieval mode. *Proceedings of the National Academy of Sciences USA*, *97*, 506–511.

Lepage, M., Habib, R., & Tulving, E. (1998). Hippocampal PET activations of memory encoding and retrieval: The HIPER model. *Hippocampus*, *8*, 313–322.

Maratos, E.J., Dolan, R.J., Morris, J.S., Henson, R.N.A., & Rugg, M.D. (2001). Neural activity associated with episodic memory for emotional context. *Neuropsychologia*, *39*, 910–920.

McDermott, K.B., Jones, T.C., Petersen, S.E., Lageman, S.K., & Roediger, H.L. (2000). Retrieval success is accompanied by enhanced activation in anterior prefrontal cortex during recognition memory: An event-related fMRI study. *Journal of Cognitive Neuroscience*, *12*, 965–976.

McDermott, K.B., Ojemann, J.G., Petersen, S.E., Ollinger, J.M., Snyder, A.Z., Akbudak, E., Conturo, T.E., & Raichle, M.E. (1999). Direct comparison of episodic encoding and retrieval of words: an event-related fMRI study. *Memory*, *7*, 661–678.

Nolde, S.F., Johnson, M.K., & D'Esposito, M. (1998a). Left prefrontal activation during episodic memory: An event-related study. *Neuroreport*, *8*, 1317–1320.

Nolde, S.F., Johnson, M.K., & Raye, C.L. (1998b). The role of prefrontal cortex during tests of episodic memory. *Trends in Cognitive Sciences*, *2*, 399–406.

Nyberg, L., Persson, J., Habib, R., Tulving, E., McIntosh, A.R., Cabeza, R., & Houle, S. (2000). Large scale neurocognitive networks underlying episodic memory. *Journal of Cognitive Neuroscience*, *12*, 163–173.

Nyberg, L., Tulving, E., Habib, R., Nilsson, L.G., Kapur, S., Cabeza, R., & McIntosh, A.R. (1995). Functional brain maps of retrieval mode and recovery of episodic information. *Neuroreport*, *7*, 249–252.

Poldrack, R.A., Wagner, A.D., Prull, M.W., Desmond, J.E., Glover, G.H., & Gabrieli, J.D.E. (1998). Functional specialization for semantic and phonological processing in left inferior prefrontal cortex. *Neuroimage*, *10*, 15–35.

Ranganath, C., Johnson, M.K., & D'Esposito, M.D. (2000). Functional contributions of prefrontal regions during tests of episodic memory: Insights from event-related fMRI. *Journal of Neuroscience*, *20*, RC108(1–5).

Roediger, H.L. (1996). Memory illusions. *Journal of Memory and Language*, *35*, 286–299.

Roediger, H.L., & McDermott, K.B. (1995). Creating false memories: Remembering words not presented in lists. *Journal of Experimental Psychology: Learning, Memory & Cognition*, *21*, 803–814.

Rugg, M.D. (1995). ERP studies of memory. In M.D. Rugg & M.G.H. Coles (Eds.), *Electrophysiology of mind* (pp. 132–170). Oxford: Oxford University Press.

Rugg, M.D. (1998). Convergent approaches to electrophysiological and hemodynamic investigations of memory. *Human Brain Mapping*, *6*, 394–398.

Rugg, M.D. (1999). Functional neuroimaging in cognitive neuroscience. In P. Hagoort & C. Brown (Eds.), *Neurocognition of language* (pp. 15–36). Oxford: Oxford University Press.

Rugg, M.D., & Allan, K. (1999). Memory retrieval: An electrophysiological perspective. In M.S. Gazzaniga (Ed.), *The cognitive neurosciences, 2nd Edition* (pp. 805–816). Cambridge, MA: MIT Press.

Rugg, M.D., Allan, K., & Birch, C.S. (2000). Electrophysiological evidence for the modulation of retrieval orientation by depth of study processing. *Journal of Cognitive Neuroscience*, *12*, 664–678.

Rugg, M.D., Fletcher, P.C., Allan, K., Frith, C.D., Frackowiak, R.S.J., & Dolan, R.J. (1998a). Neural correlates of memory retrieval during recognition memory and cued recall. *Neuroimage*, *8*, 262–273.

Rugg, M.D., Fletcher, P.C., Chua, P.M.-L., & Dolan, R.J. (1999). The role of the prefrontal cortex in recognition memory and memory for source: An fMRI study. *Neuroimage, 10*, 520–529.

Rugg, M.D., Fletcher, P.C., Frith, C.D., Frackowiak, R.S.J., & Dolan, R.J. (1996). Differential activation of the prefrontal cortex in successful and unsuccessful memory retrieval. *Brain, 119*, 2073–2083.

Rugg, M.D., Fletcher, P.C., Frith, C.D., Frackowiak, R.S.J., & Dolan, R.J. (1997). Brain regions supporting intentional and incidental memory: A PET study. *Neuroreport, 8*, 1283–1287.

Rugg, M.D., Schloerscheidt, A.M., & Mark, R.E. (1998b). An electrophysiological comparison of two indices of recollection. *Journal of Memory and Language, 39*, 47–69.

Rugg, M.D., & Wilding, E.L. (2000). Retrieval processing and episodic memory. *Trends in Cognitive Science, 4*(3), 108–115.

Saykin, A.J., Johnson, S.C., Flashman, L.A., McAllister, T.W., Sparling, M., Darcey, T.M., Moritz, C.H., Guerin, S.J., Weaver, J., & Mamourian, A. (1999). Functional differentiation of medial temporal and frontal regions involved in processing novel and familiar words: An fMRI study. *Brain, 122*, 1963–1971.

Schacter, D.L., Alpert, N.M., Savage, C.R., Rauch, S.L., & Albert, M.S. (1996). Conscious recollection and the human hippocampal formation: Evidence from positron emission tomography. *Proceedings of the National Academy of Science USA, 93*, 321–325.

Schacter, D.L., Buckner, R.L., Koutstaal, W., Dale, A.M., & Rosen, B.R. (1997). Late onset of anterior prefrontal activity during true and false recognition: An event-related fMRI study. *Neuroimage, 6*, 259–269.

Schacter, D.L., & Wagner, A.D. (1999). Medial temporal lobe activations in fMRI and PET studies of episodic encoding and retrieval. *Hippocampus, 9*, 7–24.

Shallice, T., Fletcher, P., Frith, C.D., Grasby, P., Frackowiak, R.S.J., & Dolan, R.J. (1994). Brain regions associated with acquisition and retrieval of verbal episodic memory. *Nature, 368*, 633–635.

Smith, M.E. (1993). Neurophysiological manifestations of recollective experience during recognition memory judgements. *Journal of Cognitive Neuroscience, 5*, 1–13.

Squire, L., & Cohen, N.J. (1984). Human memory and amnesia. In J.L. McGaugh, G. Lynch, & N.M. Weinberger (Eds.), *The neurobiology of learning and memory* (pp. 3–64). New York: Guilford Press.

Squire, L.R., Ojemann, J.G., Miezin, F.M., Petersen, S.E., Videen, T.O., & Raichle, M.E. (1992). Activation of the hippocampus in normal humans: A functional anatomical study of memory. *Proceedings of the National Academy of Sciences USA, 89*, 1837–1841.

Stark, C.E. & Squire, L.R. (2000a). fMRI activity in the medial temporal lobe during recognition memory as a function of study-test interval. *Hippocampus, 10*, 329–337.

Stark, C.E. & Squire, L.R. (2000b). Functional magnetic resonance imaging (fMRI) activity in the hippocampal region during recognition memory. *Journal of Neuroscience, 20*, 7776–7781.

Stevens, A.A., Skudlarski, P., Gatenby, J.C., & Gore, J.C. (2000). Event-related fMRI of auditory and visual oddball tasks [In Process Citation]. *Magnetic Resonance Imaging, 18*, 495–502.

Stuss, D.T., Alexander, M.P., Palumbo, C.L., Buckle, L., Sayer, L., & Pogue, J. (1994). Organisational strategies of patients with unilateral or bilateral frontal lobe injury in word list learning tasks. *Neuropsychology, 8*, 355–373.

Talairach, J., & Tournoux, P. (1988). *Co-planar stereotaxic atlas of the human brain.* Stuttgart: George Thieme Verlag.

Tulving, E. (1983). *Elements of episodic memory.* Oxford: Oxford University Press.

Tulving, E. (1985). Memory and consciousness. *Canadian Psychologist, 26*, 1–12.

Tulving, E., Kapur, S., Craik, F.I.M., Moscovitch, M., & Houle, S. (1994a). Hemispheric encoding/retrieval asymmetry in episodic memory: Positron emission tomography findings. *Proceedings of the National Academy of Sciences USA, 91*, 2016–2020.

Tulving, E., Kapur, S., Markovitsch, H.J., Craik, F.I.M., Habib, R., & Houle, S. (1994b). Neuro-anatomical correlates of retrieval in episodic memory: Auditory sentence recognition. *Proceedings of the National Academy of Sciences USA, 91*, 2012–2015.

Wagner, A.D., Desmond, J.E., Demb, J.B., Glover, G.H., & Gabrieli, J.D.E. (1997). Semantic repetition priming for verbal and pictorial knowledge: A functional MRI study of left inferior prefrontal cortex. *Journal of Cognitive Neuroscience, 9*, 714–726.

Wagner, A.D., Koutstaal, W., & Schacter, D.L. (1999). When encoding yields remembering: Insights from event-related neuroimaging. *Philosophical Transactions of the Royal Society of London, Biological Sciences, 354*, 1307–1324.

Wagner, A.D., Maril, A., & Schacter, D.L. (2000). Interactions between forms of memory: When priming hinders new episodic learning. *Journal of Cognitive Neuroscience, 12*, 52–60.

Wagner, A.D., Schacter, D.L., Rotte, M., Koustaal, W., Maril, A., Dale, A.M., Rosen, B.R., & Buckner, R.L. (1998). Building memories: Remembering and forgetting of verbal experiences as predicted by brain activity. *Science, 21*, 188–191.

Wheeler, M.E., Petersen, S.E., & Buckner, R.L. (2000). Memory's echo: Vivid remembering reactivates sensory-specific cortex. *PNAS, 97*, 11125–11129.

Wheeler, M.A., Stuss, D.T., & Tulving, E. (1997). Toward a theory of episodic memory: The frontal lobes and autonoetic consciousness. *Psychol Bull, 121*, 331–354.

Wilding, E.L., & Rugg, M.D. (1996). An event-related potential study of recognition memory with and without retrieval of source. *Brain, 119*, 889–905.

Yonelinas, A.P. (1994). Receiver-operating characteristics in recognition memory: Evidence for a dual-process model. *Journal of Experimental Psychology: Learning, Memory & Cognition, 20*, 1341–1354.

Yoshiura, T., Zhong, J., Shibata, D.K., Kwok, W.E., Shrier, D.A., & Numaguchi, Y. (1999). Functional MRI study of auditory and visual oddball tasks. *Neuroreport, 10*, 1683–1688.

Zarahn, E., Aguirre, G., & D'Esposito, M. (1997). A trial-based experimental design for fMRI. *Neuroimage, 6*, 122–138.

Zola-Morgan, S.M., & Squire, L.R. (1990). The primate hippocampal formation: Evidence for a time-related role in memory storage. *Science, 250*, 288–290.

CHAPTER TWO

Fractionating episodic memory retrieval using event-related potentials

David I. Donaldson
Department of Psychology, University of Stirling, UK

Kevin Allan
Department of Psychology, Kings College, University of Aberdeen, UK

Edward L. Wilding
School of Psychology, Cardiff University, UK

INTRODUCTION

Episodic memory supports the ability to recollect events, for example, remembering what one had for breakfast or reminiscing about a friend's wedding. Traditionally, the cognitive operations that support episodic memory have been discussed with reference to one of three stages of processing; encoding, storage, or retrieval (see Tulving, 1983). The cognitive operations that might be engaged at each stage have been studied extensively, with perhaps the greatest atttention having been paid to retrieval.

According to Semon (1904, 1921), the core of episodic retrieval is an interaction between a retrieval cue and the stored record of a past experience to which the cue refers—the memory trace or engram. The interaction between cue and trace is termed *ecphory* (see Schacter, Eich, & Tulving, 1978; Tulving, 1983). In this framework, the cognitive operations that are engaged to bring about ecphory are distinguished from operations that mediate ecphory itself. Moreover, once ecphory has taken place, the recovered episodic information can receive further processing in order to differentiate fully its various contents. The nature of any such postretrieval processing will be determined by the specific retrieval demands.

This characterisation of episodic retrieval encapsulates the view that retrieval processing can be separated into those processes that are engaged in pursuit of retrieval, those that reflect retrieval itself, and those that operate on the products of retrieval (Rugg & Wilding, 2000). In this chapter, we focus on studies in which these three classes of process have been investigated by using a combination of behavioural and event-related potential (ERP) measures. For the most part, we focus on the findings from studies in which ERPs were recorded while participants completed recognition memory tasks (where participants are asked to distinguish studied from unstudied stimuli), or source retrieval tasks (where participants are asked to recover contextual (or source) information from episodes).

The main body of this review chapter has three sections. The first is concerned with ERP studies of the processes that are engaged in pursuit of memory retrieval. This class of processes has only recently been investigated using ERPs. ERP indices of processes that reflect or are contingent upon successful retrieval have received considerably more attention, and the second section contains a selective review of studies in which electrophysiological correlates of these two classes of process have been identified. The review in the second section provides the necessary background for the third and final section, in which we discuss how the findings in these ERP studies can be related to what can be termed the "consensus" view of the neuroanatomical basis of episodic memory (see Allan, Robb, & and Rugg, 2000). Before we turn to these sections, however, we provide a brief overview of the event-related potential technique, in order to orient readers who are unfamiliar with its strengths and weaknesses (for more detailed accounts, see Kutas & Dale, 1997; Picton, Lins, & Scherg, 1995; Rugg & Coles, 1995).

The event-related potential technique: An overview

ERPs provide a real-time record of neural activity with millisecond temporal resolution. They index changes in neural activity that are time-locked to an *event-of-interest*, such as the presentation of a stimulus or a behavioural response (Picton et al., 1995). In the majority of cognitive ERP studies, ERPs elicited on single trials are not analysed directly. Rather, all of the ERPs from the same experimental condition are averaged together. This averaging procedure is employed because, on any given trial, the neural activity evoked by a stimulus is small in comparison to the level of background electrical noise. To the extent that the noise is distributed randomly on each trial, then the averaging procedure will attenuate the noise while leaving unaffected that portion of the activity on each trial that has a consistent temporal relation with the stimulus event. It is worth noting that one consequence of the averaging procedure is that ERPs can be employed only in experiments that have multiple repetitions of an event-of-interest. Consequently, ERPs are perhaps not an appropriate technique to employ in experiments where critical classes of events occur relatively infrequently (Rugg, 1995).

ERPs are commonly plotted as graphs that denote changes in neural activity over time. These waveform plots are characterised by a series of positive and negative deflections (peaks and troughs) that have different time courses and are prominent at different scalp locations. ERPs are typically analysed by contrasting the time courses, amplitudes and scalp distributions of ERPs that are elicited in different experimental conditions. These contrasts can reveal *quantitative* as well as *qualitative* changes in neural activity (for a fuller exposition, see Rugg & Coles, 1995). Quantitative changes are manifest as differences in the amplitude (or magnitude) of ERP waveforms. They are taken to reflect variations in the degree to which the cognitive operations indexed by the waveform are engaged. Qualitative changes in neural activity are inferred from differences in the scalp distribution (or topography) of the ERP waveforms across conditions. Differences of this form are taken as evidence that not entirely the same brain regions, and thus not entirely the same cognitive processes, are engaged.

At this juncture it is also important to note two significant limitations that need to be borne in mind when ERPs are employed as a tool for studying neural and cognitive events. The first is that scalp-recorded ERPs have limited spatial resolution. Although information about the distribution of activity over the scalp indicates whether the same or different brain regions are engaged across experimental conditions, the intracerebral generators (or sources) of an ERP modulation cannot be determined unambiguously on the basis of the neural activity that is recorded at the scalp. This renders ERP data less than ideal if one is interested primarily in identifying the brain regions that carry-out a given cognitive operation (see Kutas & Dale, 1997). Thus, in the discussions that follow, any claims made about the generators of an ERP effect are based on converging sources of evidence (chiefly from neuropsychology and functional imaging), which provide additional constraints as to the likely intracerebral sources of the neural activity that is recorded in ERP studies of retrieval processing. Moreover, it is also important to note that the polarity of ERP modulations is not informative about whether excitatory or inhibitory neural activity is being measured.

The second important limitation of the ERP technique is that it does not sample activity from the brain uniformly. Neural activity can be recorded from electrodes on the scalp only if a number of conditions are met. Notably, the active neurons must be organised in a (non-radially) symmetric manner, and must be activated synchronously, if they are to give rise to detectable scalp ERP signatures (see Wood & Allison, 1981). Although many brain structures do not contain neurons that satisfy these conditions, clusters of neocortical pyramidal cells do. Thus, it is widely believed that the activity of such neurons is a principal source of the electrical activity that is detected at the scalp in cognitive ERP experiments (Allison, Wood, & McCarthy, 1986; Kutas & Dale, 1997). The fact that brain activity is not sampled uniformly is important because it forces a particular need for caution when interpreting the finding that equivalent ERP effects exist across two or more experimental conditions. Such a finding cannot be interpreted as reflecting identical underlying neural activity in each condition, because there might be differences in neural activity that is carried out in regions that do not produce an ERP signature that can be detected at the scalp. In light of this limitation, it is prudent to make relatively conservative functional interpretations in circumstances where common ERP effects are observed across experimental conditions. With these cautionary notes in mind, we turn now to studies that have employed ERPs to investigate the neural correlates of episodic memory.

ERP INDICES OF RETRIEVAL ATTEMPTS

In this section we focus on studies of episodic retrieval processing that have been employed to investigate the processes that are engaged during an attempt to retrieve information from memory. The approach in these studies has been to contrast the ERPs evoked in two or more conditions where participants are assumed to have interrogated their memories in different ways. ERP modulations that differ either quantitatively or qualitatively across such conditions might reflect differences between the processes that are engaged in pursuit of retrieval in each task. It is important to note, however, that when examined in relation to *old* (previously studied) test items, any differences could also reflect the fact that what is actually retrieved is likely to differ. That is, such comparisons confound processes engaged in pursuit of retrieval with those that are engaged according to what is actually retrieved (processes of the latter type are discussed later in the section "ERP indices of retrieval sucess"). This confound can be avoided, however, as long as contrasts are made between ERPs evoked by *new* (unstudied) test items that are encountered in tasks with different retrieval requirements. By definition, ERPs evoked by new items should not index veridical episodic retrieval because no corresponding memory trace is available. Because nominally identical sets of new items can be employed in each of a pair of tasks, any differences between classes of new items probably reflect processes that are engaged in pursuit of successful retrieval (Wilding, 1999; Rugg & Wilding, 2000; for a related commentary, see Chapter 1).

Studies investigating processes that are associated with the attempt to retrieve have taken one of two forms. In the first, participants complete a single encoding task that is followed by two or more episodic retrieval tasks, each having different instructions. The assumption is that the ways in which participants interrogate their memories will vary according to the task instructions (e.g. Wilding, 1999). In the second form of task, participants complete two or more distinct encoding tasks prior to completing a single retrieval task. In this case the assumption is that the memory retrieval operations that are engaged at test will vary according to the experience of the participants at study (e.g. Rugg, Allan, & Birch, 2000). A number of studies using these approaches have identified ERP correlates of processes engaged during retrieval attempts.

In the study by Johnson, Kounios, and Nolde (1996) two groups of participants completed encoding tasks that emphasised either perceptual or semantic processing of pictures and words. In a subsequent retrieval phase, an equal number of the participants completed either a recognition memory or a source memory task. The test stimuli (visually presented words) comprised an equal number of *new* words and *old* words that had been encountered either as a word at study or as a picture that corresponded to the meaning of a written word. Standard instructions were provided for the recognition memory task; discriminate between old and new test items. For the source memory task, participants were required to distinguish old from new items, and further, to note whether words judged old had been encountered previously as a word or as a picture.

Amongst other findings, Johnson et al. (1996) showed that ERPs elicited in the source memory task were more positive-going at frontal scalp sites than were those in the recognition task. This positivity was composed of two modulations, largest at scalp electrodes located over the left and the right hemisphere, respectively. One of the effects, the right frontal modulation, appears to reflect processes that operate on the products of retrieval. We discuss this effect further in the next section. More relevant here is the left-sided modulation (see in particular the description of this modulation in Nolde, Johnson & Raye, 1998), which had an earlier onset and shorter time course than its right-sided counterpart. The authors proposed that this left frontal effect reflected the greater requirement to engage in *reflective* processing in the source memory task in comparison to the recognition task. That is, the effect appears to be modulated by the way in which subjects interrogate their memories. Unfortunately, whether the effect truly reflected processes that operate independently of retrieval success was unclear in this case, because no contrast restricted to unstudied test items was reported.

ERP modulations with a similar left frontal maximum have, however, been observed in three recent studies that have included contrasts that were restricted to classes of unstudied test items (for what might be a related effect, see Tardif, Barry, Fox, & Johnstone, 2000). In the study by Ranganath and Paller (1999), each participant completed the same picture-encoding task followed by two different retrieval tasks. At test, each picture took one of three forms: old, new, or new but perceptually similar to old pictures (previously presented pictures were rescaled, resulting in small changes to their height and width). In one test condition (general retrieval), participants made old/new recognition judgements to pictures, responding *old* to previously studied pictures as well as to perceptually similar pictures. In the other test condition (specific retrieval), participants responded *old* only to previously studied pictures. These two conditions were designed to differ in the degree to which subjects were required to process perceptual details of the test items.

The differences between the ERPs that were evoked by the two classes of new items were most evident over left frontal scalp, where those from the specific retrieval condition (respond old only to studied pictures) were more positive-going from approximately 400 to 1200ms poststimulus (see also Ranganath & Paller, 2000). The authors reasoned that, in contrast to the general retrieval test condition, the specific retrieval condition required participants to attend more closely to perceptual features of the stimuli, and to engage in more evaluative operations before making an old/new judgement. Thus, they proposed that the differences over left frontal scalp reflected the greater demands that these information-processing operations imposed on attention and working memory in the pursuit of retrieval.

A recent study by Rugg et al. (2000) also revealed differences at left frontal scalp locations between the ERPs that were evoked by classes of unstudied test items. In this case, however, the differences were related to an encoding manipulation. Participants completed encoding tasks in which visually presented low-frequency words were processed with respect to either their semantic or their orthographic characteristics (hereafter the *deep* and *shallow* encoding tasks, respectively). In subsequent old/new recognition blocks, each block contained words that had been processed in only one of the two encoding tasks. For unstudied items, the ERPs at left frontal scalp locations were more positive-going for the blocks that contained shallowly encoded old words. Because memory was poorer in the shallow than in the deep retrieval task, it is reasonable to assume that greater demands were placed on attention and working memory in pursuit of recognition decisions in this task. The findings are, therefore, consistent with the interpretation offered by Ranganath and Paller (1999, 2000).

The findings of Rugg et al. for written words also indicate that the left frontal modulation is not a consequence of using picture stimuli at test, and that the differences observed by Ranganath and Paller (1999, 2000) probably do not reflect processes related to differential inspection of the surface features of test stimuli. Although noting that their results were consistent with a working memory-load interpretation, Rugg et al. (2000) also discussed an alternative account of the left frontal effect. They observed that participants adopted different response criteria (see Snodgrass & Corwin, 1988) in the deep and shallow retrieval blocks, and that a difference in response criterion across conditions was also evident in the behavioural data from the study of Ranganath and Paller (1999). In both cases, a more stringent (conservative) criterion was adopted in the more demanding task. The left frontal effect could therefore reflect processes related to criterion setting rather than to the differential demands placed upon working memory and/or attention (Rugg et al., 2000).

In addition to this left frontal modulation, Rugg et al. (2000) observed a second modulation that differentiated the ERPs to unstudied items in the deep and shallow retrieval conditions. This effect was largest at right hemisphere centroparietal scalp locations, and comprised a greater negativity in the ERPs to unstudied items from the deep retrieval condition. The authors suggested that this modulation is likely to index processes that are distinct from those indexed by the left frontal effect. The principal support for this proposal was drawn from the similarity between this modulation and the N400 ERP component. This negative-going component was identified initially in studies of language processing (Kutas & Hillyard, 1980) and is larger in tasks that require semantic, as opposed to non-semantic, processing of stimuli (see Rugg, Furda, & Lorist, 1988; Chwilla, Brown, & Hagoort, 1995). On the basis of this similarity, Rugg et al. (2000) proposed that participants employed retrieval strategies at test that varied according to their experiences at the time of encoding, with the N400-like modulation reflecting the greater emphasis on semantic retrieval processing in the easier of the two retrieval tasks. Whether the N400-like modulation indexes processes that are in fact distinct from those indexed by the left frontal modulation is not clear, however, as there was no statistical evidence to support the view that the two effects were either neurally or functionally dissociable.

The interpretations offered by Rugg et al. (2000) for these two ERP modulations are important, none the less, because they emphasise the distinction between two classes of process that can be engaged in pursuit of retrieval. The first, retrieval effort, refers to the differential engagement or allocation of processing resources during a retrieval attempt. One aspect of effort-related processing may be indexed by the left frontal modulation. The functional interpretations of the left frontal effect described above (Ranganath & Paller, 1999, 2000; Rugg et al., 2000) illustrate two ways in which retrieval effort can be cached out in information-processing terms. The second class of process, retrieval orientation, is a cognitive set that determines how memory will be interrogated (Wilding, 1999; Rugg & Wilding, 2000). That is, it determines the retrieval operations that will be engaged when a retrieval cue is encountered. Retrieval orientation, and the processing engendered by it, will vary when participants prepare to retrieve different types of episodic information, or the same kinds of information in different ways. Rugg et al. (2000) propose that the N400-like modulation arose because participants adopted different retrieval orientations as a result of the kind of encoding operations that old items had been subjected to at study.

In summary, the studies reviewed above indicate that ERPs recorded during memory retrieval tasks index processes that operate independently of successful retrieval.[1] This is demonstrated by the fact that reliable differences have been observed between the ERPs evoked by different classes of unstudied test items. Further studies will determine whether ERPs are in fact sensitive to processes reflecting retrieval effort as well as those that are

---

[1] ERPs evoked by unstudied test items in different experimental conditions were also reported by Johnson et al. 1996, and Wilding, 1999. We will not discuss their findings here.

engaged according to the retrieval orientation that participants adopt. The preceding discussion also raises the question as to how effort and orientation influence the process of retrieval itself, and, in turn, the postretrieval processing of mnemonic contents. For example, it is an open question whether orientation can determine what is in fact retrieved from memory, or whether it influences solely the way that retrieved information is processed (Rugg & Wilding, 2000). Of course, if ERPs are to be employed in pursuit of answers to questions of this form, the essential precursor is that ERPs are in fact sensitive to episodic retrieval success. In the following section we review findings that demonstrate that ERPs are indeed sensitive to this type of retrieval process.

ERP INDICES OF RETRIEVAL SUCCESS

A class of ERP modulations called *old/new effects* index processes associated with successful episodic memory retrieval, as well as processes that operate on the products of retrieval. These effects are manifest as differences between the neural activity that is evoked by *old* and *new* test items to which accurate memory judgements have been made (see Rugg & Allan, 1999, 2000; see Johnson, 1995, for reviews). There is a family of old/new effects, each effect being distinguishable on the basis of its time course, scalp distribution, and sensitivity to experimental variables. We focus here on two functionally and neurally dissociable old/new effects, maximal over left parietal and right frontal electrode sites, respectively, which are thought to be associated with retrieval and postretrieval processing.

THE LEFT-PARIETAL ERP OLD/NEW EFFECT

This effect has been observed in a range of episodic retrieval tasks, including old/new recognition, cued recall and source retrieval (e.g. Allan & Rugg, 1997; Paller & Kutas, 1992; Smith, 1993; Wilding & Rugg, 1996, 1997a) and is evoked by verbal as well as non-verbal stimuli (Schloerscheidt & Rugg, 1997). The effect comprises a positive shift in the waveforms evoked by correctly recognised old items (hits) compared to those evoked by correctly rejected new items (correct rejections). The effect typically onsets around 400–500ms poststimulus, lasts for 400–600ms (although see Donaldson & Rugg, 1998, 1999, discussed later), and is largest at left temporoparietal electrodes (Fig. 2.1). Importantly, the effect is not found in the ERPs evoked by old words that are classified incorrectly as new (misses), or new words that are identified incorrectly as old (false alarms: see Allan, Wilding, & Rugg, 1998). The absence of the effect for these classes of test item indicates that it does not simply reflect repetition of a stimulus, the fact that an old decision has been made, or the erroneous belief (however tentative) that an unstudied item was in fact encountered at study. In short, participants must make an accurate judgement to a studied item for the effect to be evoked, suggesting that the left parietal old/new effect is related specifically to processes associated with successful retrieval from episodic memory.

Discussion of the likely functional significance of the left parietal effect has been restricted primarily to those retrieval processes that are postulated in dual process theories of recognition memory (see Mandler, 1980; Jacoby & Dallas, 1981). According to dual process theories, there are two processes that can support accurate recognition memory judgements—participants might be able to *recollect* having studied an item, or the item might simply be *familiar*. In operational terms, recollection permits accurate judgements of the old/new status of test items, in addition to accurate judgments concerning contextual aspects of prior encounters. Familiarity, by contrast, provides no information other than the likely old/new status of an item, and the specific mechanisms that are thought to underlie familiarity vary for different dual-process accounts (compare Mandler, 1980 and Jacoby & Dallas, 1981).

The focus in a number of ERP studies of memory retrieval has been on the question of whether the left parietal old/new effect indexes recollection or familiarity. There is now considerable evidence that the effect in fact indexes recollection (see Rugg & Allan, 1999, 2000), and that the magnitude of the effect varies according to the amount of information that is retrieved from episodic memory (Rugg, Cox, Doyle, & Wells, 1995; Wilding, 2000; for discussion of a likely ERP correlate of familiarity, see Curran, 1999; Rugg et al., 1998). The strongest evidence in support of this view has come from studies in which recollection was defined as the ability to retrieve source information accurately. For example, in one approach participants were asked to distinguish old from new test items, and, for items judged old, to judge in which

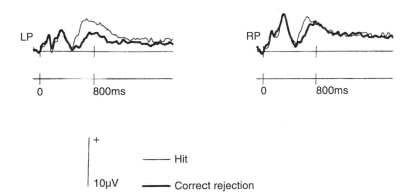

Figure 2.1.   The "left-parietal ERP old/new effect". ERPs from left and right parietal (LP, RP) electrodes elicited by correctly classified old (hit) and new (correct rejection) words in a recognition memory test (data from Allan & Rugg, 1997, figure taken from "Electrophysiological evidence for dissociable processes contributing to recollection", *Acta Psychologia*, *98*, 231–252, Copyright 1997, with permission from Elsevier Science).

of two study contexts the item had been encountered (see in particular, Wilding & Rugg, 1996). In a related approach, participants were asked to make Remember/Know judgements (Tulving, 1985) to words they believed to be old (Smith, 1993). In these studies, the largest old/new effects were observed for the classes of old items that were associated with retrieval of contextual information, providing strong evidence for a recollection interpretation of the left parietal old/new effect.

Further evidence consistent with this interpretation comes from two studies by Donaldson and Rugg (1998, 1999) in which recollection was defined operationally as the ability to retrieve associative information. In these studies participants were first presented with a list of semantically unrelated word pairs and asked to generate a sentence containing each pair (thereby encouraging subjects to encode the specific relationship between each pair of words). Donaldson and Rugg (1998, 1999) then used either *associative recognition* or *associative recall* tests to assess memory. In associative recognition, participants discriminate between test pairs that were shown in the *same* pairing at study and test and pairs that have been *rearranged* (that is, recombined into a pairing not seen at study). In associative recall, participants must report the second item from a study pair when given the first item as a cue. For each task an initial old/new recognition response was required, which was followed by either a same/rearranged judgement (associative recognition) or a verbal response (associative recall). ERPs to correctly rejected new stimuli were also collected in each case, providing a baseline equivalent to that employed in old/new recognition and source memory studies (Fig. 2.2).

The ERPs for the successful retrieval of associative information remove were associated with reliable left parietal old/new effects, although the effects were considerably longer-lasting in the case of successful associative recognition than in recognition memory or source memory. The reason for this is unclear and, to date, little research has been undertaken to investigate this issue. Regardless, in associative recall the magnitude of the left parietal old/new effect tracks the likelihood of recollection: the effect is larger when participants recall the association than when they are unable do so. Furthermore, in associative recognition the magnitude of the left parietal old/new effect is larger for the ERPs associated with correctly recognised *same* pairs than it is for correctly recognised *rearranged* pairs. This second finding is particularly difficult to reconcile with a familiarity account of the left parietal old/new effect, because presumably the words are equally familiar for same and for rearranged pairs.

THE RIGHT-FRONTAL ERP OLD/NEW EFFECT

In the study of Wilding and Rugg already mentioned (Wilding & Rugg, 1996) a second old/new effect was observed. This effect was largest over frontal electrode sites, with a tendency to be larger over the right hemisphere than

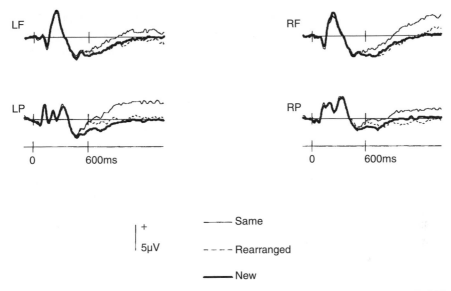

Figure 2.2.   ERP old/new effects from left- and right-frontal and parietal (LP, RP, LF, RF) electrodes elicited by correctly classified new word pairs (correct rejections) and old word pairs that were also correctly classified according to whether the words comprising the pair had been encountered in the same or different (rearranged) pairings when encountered at study (data from Donaldson & Rugg, 1998, experiment 1, "Recognition memory for new associations: Electrophysiological evidence for the role of recognition", *Neuropsychologia*, *36*, 377–395, Copyright 1998, with permission from Elsevier Science).

over the left (Fig. 2.3). The effect onset approximately 400ms poststimulus and lasted for over a second. This *right frontal old/new effect* has since been reported in a number of studies. The effect has been observed in conjunction with the retrieval of several different forms of information, and it has been demonstrated that the left parietal and right frontal effects are neurally as well as functionally dissociable (for a review see Allan, Wilding, & Rugg, 1998). In contrast with the left parietal effect, however, the functional significance of the right frontal effect is not well established. Wilding and Rugg (1996) offered an initial functional interpretation based on the distinction between *retrieval* and *postretrieval* processing. Given the time course and scalp distribution of the right frontal effect, they proposed that the effect reflected processes that operate on the products of retrieval, and were necessary for the recovery of contextual information. This interpretation has encountered a number of challenges, including findings that the effect is not always associated with accurate source judgements (Wilding & Rugg, 1997b), and the fact that it has been observed in recognition memory tasks in which there is no explicit source retrieval requirement (Allan & Rugg, 1997, 1998; see also Rugg, Allan, & Birch, 2000). In addition, there are inconsistencies across studies in respect of the way in which old/new effects at frontal sites are

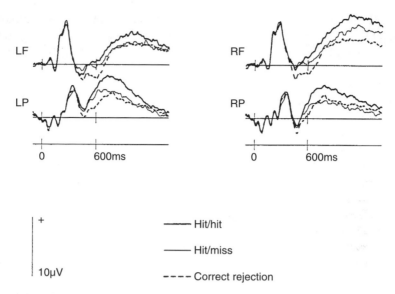

Figure 2.3. Left-parietal and right-frontal ERP old/new effects elicited by correctly classified new words (correct rejections) and old words that either were (hit/hit) or were not (hit/miss) assigned correctly to study context. Electrode sites as for Fig. 2.2 (data from Wilding & Rugg, 1996, experiment 2, with permission from Oxford University Press).

modulated according to whether accurate recognition memory judgements are also accompanied by veridical memory for study context (compare Senkfor & Van Petten, 1998; Trott, Friedman, Ritter, & Fabiani, 1997; and Wilding & Rugg, 1996). These disparate findings have led to proposals that the effect reflects the initiation and maintenance of retrieval search operations (Senkfor & Van Petten, 1998), or that it indexes retrieval monitoring operations (Rugg, Allan, & Birch, 2000). In general, the weight of evidence favours a postretrieval interpretation of the right frontal old/new effect, but the details of such an interpretation remain open to question (for relevant comments, see Chapter 1).

ERP OLD/NEW EFFECTS AND THE CONSENSUS VIEW OF EPISODIC RETRIEVAL

In the remainder of this chapter we examine how the ERP findings discussed in the previous section relate to the predominant neuroanatomical model of episodic memory; the so-called *consensus* view of how episodic memory is carried out by the brain (Damasio, 1989; McClelland, McNaughton, & O'Reilly, 1995; Rubin and Greenberg, 1998; Squire & Alvarez, 1995). According to this view, the encoding and subsequent retrieval of episodic information necessarily involves many different neocortical regions, each specialised to process some attribute of the episode. Collectively, these neocortical regions hold the entire memory trace for that episode. The loci of the neocortical regions that store each episodic trace are determined by the content of the episode—by what the subject experiences as the episode unfolds. Critically, according to this view, a record of the regions that store each episodic trace is maintained, potentially for years, within the hippocampal region, an area to which the neocortical regions project their activity via intermediate *convergence zones* lying within multimodal temporal neocortex (Damasio, 1989). Successful episodic retrieval involves gaining access, with a suitable retrieval cue, to the hippocampal *index* for the target episode.

It seems reasonable to view the overall aim of strategic preretrieval processing (discussed earlier), as a means of gaining access to the appropriate hippocampal index for a target episode. Once access to the trace is achieved, a cascade of neural events is held to ensue automatically (Moscovitch, 1992), culminating in the reinstatement of activity from a past episode in the neocortical regions that collectively hold the sought-after episodic trace. These changes in neocortical activity are driven by the hippocampus, underlie ecphory, and, furthermore, provide the information that is used by frontally based postretrieval monitoring and evaluative operations. If correct, at least in broad detail, this framework can be used to generate predictions about the patterns of neural activity that should be observed when different kinds of episode are retrieved, and consequently, the pattern of ERP correlates of these successful episodic retrieval operations.

Perhaps the most obvious prediction of the consensus view is that the loci of brain regions activated during retrieval should, at least partially, be determined by the nature of the perceptual and cognitive operations engaged during encoding (Allan, Robb, & Rugg, 2000; Fig. 2.4). Hence, the loci of brain regions activated during retrieval should change as and when different kinds of material are recollected. For example, the perceptual and cognitive operations required to process different kinds of materials, e.g. pictures versus words, would not be expected to overlap entirely. To the extent that this is the case, the recollection of verbal versus pictorial information should depend upon different brain regions.

It is particularly striking, therefore, that the nature of the encoded attribute on which source decisions are made appears to have *no* significant effect on the scalp distribution, and hence the intracerebral generators, of ERP old/new effects (see Allan & Rugg, 1998; Rugg & Allan, 2000). Source attributes employed in ERP studies have included speaker voice (Wilding & Rugg, 1996), surface form (pictures versus words: Johnson et al., 1998), presentation modality (Wilding, Doyle, & Rugg, 1995; Senkfor & van Petten, 1998), and temporal order (Allan & Rugg, 1998). Without exception, the old/new effects in source tasks have exhibited either one or both of the left parietal and the right frontal effects. Thus, even when source decisions are based upon the retrieval of different kinds of episodic attribute, qualitative differences in the ERP correlates of episodic retrieval operations have not been observed,

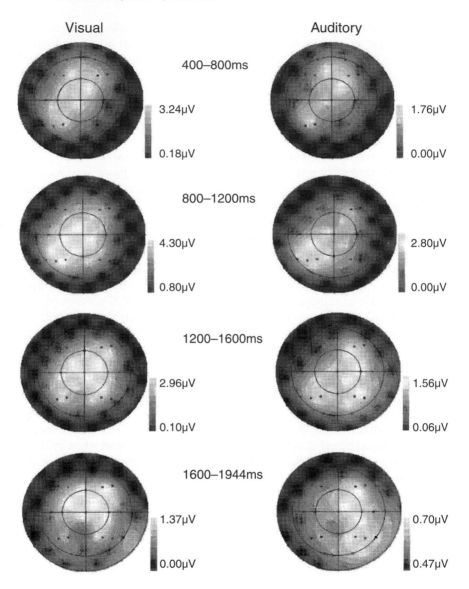

Figure 2.4. Topographic voltage maps denoting the very similar scalp distributions of the "visual" and "auditory" stem cued-recall ERP old/new effects over four poststimulus time periods. The maps were computed for each latency window by subtracting the mean amplitude measures obtained for correct rejections from those obtained for correct stem completions, separated according to study context (visual or auditory). The grey-scale bar to the right of each map indicates the mean maximum and minimum amplitudes of the effects over each time interval (data from Allan, Robb, & Rugg, 2000, experiment 2. "The effect of encoding manipulations on neural correlates of episodic retrieval", *Neuropsychologia*, *38*, 1188–1205, Copyright 2000, with permission from Elsevier Science).

counter to the predictions of the consensus view of episodic memory (although for one possible exception, see Mecklinger, 1998).

This conclusion is strengthened by the findings of two recent ERP experiments that investigated directly the consensus view described above (Allan et al., 2000). In the first experiment, Allan et al. manipulated the nature of the cognitive operations that were performed at encoding by using a depth of processing manipulation (Craik & Lockhart, 1972). This allowed two classes of study episode to be formed, termed *deep* and *shallow*. In the second experiment, different classes of study episode were formed by manipulating the sensory modality in which items were presented for study: half of the items were presented visually and half auditorally. The retrieval task in both experiments was visual word-stem cued recall. Allan et al. (2000) found that cued recall performance was substantially better for the deep than the shallowly encoded items in the first experiment. A slight but reliable cued recall advantage was also found in the second experiment for the visual compared to the auditory study items. These differences in memory performance were accompanied by a consistent pattern of modulations for the cued recall ERP old/new effects, such that in each experiment the old/new effects were largest when evoked by stems completed with items from the more memorable class of study episode. Critically, no evidence was found in either experiment for topographic differences in the old/new effects according to the class of study episode recollected. There were also no apparent differences in the time courses of the old/new effects according to the manner of their encoding.

The ERP experiments reported by Allan et al. (2000) failed to find evidence supporting the notion that the ecphory of different kinds of episodes is associated with the activation of different brain regions. Thus, Allan et al. suggested that their findings, in conjunction with the previous ERP literature on old/new effects, imply the existence of a core set of retrieval processes that are engaged (to different extents) whenever details of a prior episode are brought to mind successfully. Allan et al. (2000) did, however, propose an interpretation of their findings in keeping with the consensus view of episodic memory. They suggested that the neocortical processing reflected by the old/new effects might act in conjunction with the hippocampal region during retrieval, to bring about the reinstatement of activity within yet other modality or content specific regions of the neocortex that do not themselves generate ERP signals. Converging evidence that the medial temporal lobes, inferior frontal and inferior parietal cortices are likely locations for the generators of old/new effects associated with recognition memory comes from a study using magnetoencephalography (Tendolkar et al., 2000). This interpretation links old/new effects, and in particular the early left temporoparietally distributed effect, to a binding mechanism that plays a role in reactivating neocortical traces. In other words, the old/new effects may reflect changes in the activity of the multimodal convergence zones proposed by Damasio, 1989.

This interpretation of the ERP findings is consistent with current notions regarding the potential role of convergence zones in retrieval. It appears that these regions mediate between the hippocampal region and regions of neocortex that might hold the content or modality specific features of the episodic trace (see Mesulam, 1990). If correct, it would seem reasonable to suppose that these convergence zones are among the first neocortical regions to become activated during retrieval, and that content-specific activations of episodic information might depend upon processes that take place subsequently, involving other content-specific regions of the neocortex. Given the early onset time of the parietal old/new effect, it seems likely that it could indeed reflect an initial stage of the retrieval pathway, one that is possibly accessed prior to further modality or content specific information.

In this section we have highlighted a pattern of empirical regularities in ERP old/new effects. The intracerebral generators of these effects appear to be engaged (albeit to different extents) during episodic retrieval in a wide range of tasks, despite variations in the nature of to-be-remembered materials, and variations in the perceptual and cognitive encoding operations performed upon these materials. For example, in tests employing measures of source memory, the nature of the attribute chosen as the criterial feature evidently has little effect on the loci of the brain regions activated during retrieval, at least so far as has been established to date with scalp-recorded ERPs. When considered within the framework provided by the consensus view of episodic memory, the ERP correlates of retrieval appear likely to reflect an initial stage of processing, rather than reactivation in regions that are specific to the content of retrieval.

SUMMARY

The findings reviewed above provide an overview of ERP studies of memory retrieval, and draw important distinctions between different stages of retrieval processing. These experiments reveal ERP correlates of preretrieval processes that form what can be broadly termed a retrieval attempt, correlates of retrieval processes themselves, and correlates of postretrieval processes that may reflect the monitoring and evaluation of retrieved information. Given the high temporal resolution of ERP data it is perhaps not surprising that they reveal discrete stages of retrieval processing that are not only topographically and functionally dissociable, but temporally distinct as well.

Discussion of the ERP correlates of preretrieval processes associated with retrieval attempts highlights an important issue, that processes engaged in pursuit of retrieval of different types of information from memory may be separate from processes that reflect the cognitive effort expended during a retrieval attempt ENRfu (cf. Rugg & Wilding, 2000). In all of the studies reviewed here in which putative correlates of 'preretrieval' processes have been identified, these two classes of process have been confounded. What is required to distinguish between these two classes of process are studies which control these two variables systematically. For example, manipulations of list length and study-test interval could be used to hold retrieval orientation constant whilst varying retrieval effort. It is an open question as to whether the differences observed in relation to retrieval orientation would remain if memory performance, as well as response bias (Rugg, Allan, & Birch, 2000), were equated across conditions.

The findings in relation to ERP correlates of retrieval and postretrieval processes are clearer. Much evidence suggests that the left parietal old/new effect provides an index of recollection, but does not provide a *full* account of how different variables influence the left parietal effect. Episodic recollection is likely to involve search, retrieval and decision processes operating in an iterative manner, and differentiating how these different elements are employed flexibly may be key to specifying more completely the cognitive processes reflected by the left parietal effect. Similarly, the right frontal old/new effect appears to be linked to postretrieval monitoring processes, yet the specific nature of these processes and variables that influence them remain unclear. Further research investigating the relationship of monitoring processes to aspects of attention and working memory may prove fruitful in this regard.

We also wish to highlight another aspect related to old/new effects. Although these effects have been linked to recollection, there was no evidence for an ERP correlate of familiarity. Consequently, the data can be viewed as consistent with single process models of episodic memory. Recent evidence, however (e.g. Rugg et al., 1998; Curran, 1999), indicates that familiarity, albeit indirectly (Tsivilis, Otten, & Rugg, 2001), is indexed in the electrical record, and that this index is dissociable from the left-parietal old/new effect. These findings support the view that recognition memory depends upon at least two neurally and functionally distinct processes (Mandler, 1980).

A further, possibly more important question is why, despite the different orientation-related activity revealed by ERPs, the correlates of episodic retrieval commonly take the form of left temporo-parietal and right frontal old/new effects. Even attempts to retrieve different contents produce the same pattern of success-related old/new effects. This disparity can be seen by comparing the results from Rugg et al. (2000) and Allan, Robb and Rugg (2000), both of which employed depth of processing manipulations. Rugg et al. propose that qualitatively different processes are engaged in searching for items encoded under deep or shallow conditions, but neither study shows evidence for an analogous distinction at retrieval. Why this asymmetry exists is unclear, and the findings to date suggest that processes engaged in pursuit of retrieval have little influence on what is retrieved. The relationship between these two stages of episodic retrieval processing requires elucidation.

Finally, in relation to these outstanding questions, three points are worthy of note. First, few recent ERP studies have focused on processes that contribute to a retrieval attempt. Second, existing ERP studies of retrieval success have not exhausted the forms of episodic information that can be encoded and retrieved. Third, sophisticated data collection and analysis techniques will make it possible to determine more precisely whether the same or different generators are engaged across experimental conditions. Thus we are confident that ERPs will continue to provide insights into the memory-related processes that are engaged before, during and after retrieval from episodic memory.

ACKNOWLEDGEMENTS

We thank Indira Tendolkar, Margaret Sheridan and Mark Wheeler for helpful comments and discussion.

REFERENCES

Allan, K., Robb, W.G.K., & Rugg, M.D. (2000). The effect of encoding manipulations on neural correlates of episodic retrieval. *Neuropsychologia*, *38*, 1188–1205.

Allan, K., & Rugg, M.D. (1997). An event-related potential study of explicit memory on test of word-stem cued recall and recognition memory. *Cognitive Brain Research*, *4*, 251–262.

Allan, K., & Rugg, M.D. (1998). Neural correlates of cued-recall with and without retrieval of source memory. *Neuroreport*, *9*, 3463–3466.

Allan, K., Wilding, E.L., & Rugg, M.D. (1998). Electrophysiological evidence for dissociable processes contributing to recollection. *Acta Psychologica*, *98*, 231–252.

Allison, T., Wood, C.C., & McCarthy, G. (1986). The central nervous system. In M.G.H. Coles, E. Donchin, & S.W. Porges (Eds.) *Psychophysiology: Systems, processes and applications*. London: Guilford Press.

Chwilla, D.J., Brown, C.M., & Hagoort, P. (1995). The N400 as a function of the level of processing. *Psychophysiology*, *32*, 274–285.

Craik, F.I.M., & Lockhart, R.S. (1972). Levels of processing: A framework for memory research. *Journal of Experimental Psychology*, *86*, 77–82.

Curran, T. (1999). The electrophysiology of incidental and intentional retrieval: ERP old/new effects in lexical decision and recognition memory. *Neuropsychologia*, *37*, 771–785.

Damasio, A.R. (1989). Time-locked multiregional retroactivation: A systems-level proposal for the neural substrates of recall and recognition. *Cognition*, *33*, 25–62.

Donaldson, D.I., & Rugg, M.D. (1998). Recognition memory for new associations: Electrophysiological evidence for the role of recollection. *Neuropsychologia*, *36*, 377–395.

Donaldson, D.I., & Rugg, M.D. (1999). Event-related potential studies of associative recognition and recall: Electrophysiological evidence for context dependent retrieval processes. *Cognitive Brain Research*, *8*, 1–16.

Jacoby, L.L., & Dallas, M. (1981). On the relationship between autobiographical memory and perceptual learning. *Journal of Experimental Psychology: General*, *110*, 306–340.

Johnson, R. (1995). Event-related potential insights into the neurobiology of memory systems. In J.C. Baron & J. Grafman (Eds.) *Handbook of Neuropsychology* (vol. 9, pp. 135–164). Amsterdam: Elsevier.

Johnson, M.K., Kounios, J., & Nolde, S.F. (1996). Electrophysiological brain activity and memory source monitoring. *Neuroreport*, *8*, 1317–1320.

Kutas, M., & Dale, A. (1997). Electrical and magnetic readings of mental functions. In M.D. Rugg (Ed.) *Cognitive neuroscience* (pp. 197–242). Hove, UK: Psychology Press.

Kutas, M., & Hillyard, S.A. (1980). Reading senseless sentences: Brain potentials reflect semantic incongruity. *Science, 207*, 203–205.

Mandler, G. (1980). Recognising: The judgement of previous occurrence. *Psychological Review, 87*, 252–271.

McClelland, J.L., McNaughton, B.L. and O'Reilly, R.C. (1995). Why there are complementary learning systems in the hippocampus and neocortex: Insights from the success and failures of connectionist models of learning and memory. *Psychological Review, 102*, 419–457.

Mecklinger, A. (1998). On the modularity of recognition memory for object form and spatial location: A topographic ERP analysis. *Neuropsychologia, 36*, 441–460.

Mesulam, M.M. (1990). Large-scale neurocognitive networks and distributed processing for attention, language and memory. *Annals of Neurology, 28*, 597–613.

Moscovitch, M. (1992). Memory and working-with-memory: A component process model based on modules and central systems. *Journal of Cognitive Neuroscience, 4*, 257–267.

Nolde, S.F., Johnson, M.K., & Raye, C.L. (1998). The role of prefrontal cortex during tests of episodic memory. *Trends in Cognitive Sciences, 2*, 399–406.

Paller, K.A., & Kutas, M. (1992). Brain potentials during memory retrieval provide neurophysiological support for the distinction between conscious recollection and priming. *Journal of Cognitive Neuroscience, 4*, 375–391.

Picton, T.W., Lins, O.G., & Scherg, M. (1995). The recording and analysis of event-related potentials. In F. Boller and J. Grafman (Eds.) *Handbook of neuropsychology* (vol. 9, pp. 429–499). Amsterdam: Elsevier.

Ranganath, C., & Paller, K.A. (1999). Frontal brain potentials during recognition are modulated by requirements to retrieve perceptual details. *Neuron, 22*, 605–613.

Ranganath, C., & Paller, K.A. (2000). Neural correlates of memory retrieval and evaluation. *Cognitive Brain Research, 9*, 209–222.

Rubin, D.C., & Greenberg, D.L. (1998). Visual memory-deficit amnesia: A distinct amnesic presentation and etiology. *Proceedings of the National Academy of Science USA, 95*, 5413–5416.

Rugg, M.D. (1995). ERP studies of memory. In M.D. Rugg & M.G.H. Coles (Eds.) *Electrophysiology of mind: Event-related potentials and cognition* (pp. 132–170). Oxford: Oxford University Press.

Rugg, M.D., & Allan, K. (1999). Memory retrieval: An electrophysiological perspective. In M.S. Gazzaniga (Ed.) *The cognitive neurosciences* (2nd edn, pp. 805–816). Cambridge, MA: MIT Press.

Rugg, M.D., & Allan, K. (2000). Event-related potential studies of long-term memory. In E. Tulving & F.I.M. Craik (Eds.) *The Oxford handbook of memory* (pp. 521–538). Oxford: Oxford University Press.

Rugg, M.D., Allan, K., & Birch, C.S. (2000). Electrophysiological evidence for the modulation of retrieval orientation by depth of study processing. *Journal of Cognitive Neuroscience, 12*, 664–678.

Rugg, M.D., & Coles, M.G.H. (1995). *Electrophysiology of mind: Event-related potentials and cognition*. Oxford: Oxford University Press.

Rugg, M.D., Cox, C.J.C., Doyle, M.C., & Wells, T. (1995). Event-related potentials and the recollection of low and high frequency words. *Neuropsychologia, 33*, 471–484.

Rugg, M.D., Furda, J., & Lorist, M. (1988). The effects of task on the modulation of event-related potentials by word repetition. *Psychophysiology, 25*, 55–63.

Rugg, M.D., Mark, R.E., Walla, P., Schloerscheidt, A.M., Birch, C.S., & Allan, K. (1998). Dissociation of the neural correlates of implicit and explicit memory. *Nature, 392*, 595–598.

Rugg, M.D., & Wilding, E.L. (2000). Retrieval processing and episodic memory. *Trends in Cognitive Sciences, 4*, 108–115.

Schacter, D.L., Eich, J.E., & Tulving, E. (1978). Richard Semon's theory of memory. *Journal of Verbal Learning and Verbal Behavior, 17*, 721–743.

Schloerscheidt, A.M., & Rugg, M.D. (1997). Recognition memory for words and pictures: An event-related potential study. *Neuroreport, 8,* 3281–3285.

Semon, R.S. (1904). *The mneme.* London: Allen and Unwin.

Semon, R.S. (1921). *Die Mneme als Erhaltendes Prinzip im Wechsel des Organischen Gesechehens.* Berlin: William Engelman.

Senkfor, A.J., & Van Petten, C. (1998). Who said what? An event-related potential investigation of source and item memory. *Journal of Experimental Psychology: Learning, Memory, and Cognition, 24,* 1005–1025.

Smith, M.E. (1993). Neurophysiological manifestations of recollective experience during recognition memory judgements. *Journal of Cognitive Neuroscience, 5,* 1–13.

Snodgrass, J.G., & Corwin, J. (1988). Pragmatics of measuring recognition memory: applications to dementia and amnesia. *Journal of Experimental Psychology: General, 117,* 34–50.

Squire, L.R., & Alvarez, P. (1995). Retrograde amnesia and memory consolidation: A neurobiological perspective. *Current Opinion in Neurobiology, 5,* 169–177.

Tardif, H.P., Barry, R.J., Fox, A.M., & Johnstone, S.J. (2000) Detection of feigned recognition memory impairment using the old/new effect of the event-related potential. *International Journal of Psychophysiology, 36,* 1–9.

Tendolkar, I., Rugg, M.D., Fell, J., Vogt, H., Scholz, M., Hinrichs, H. and Heinze, H.J. (2000). A magnetoencephalographic study of brain activity related to recognition memory in healthy young human subjects. *Neuroscience Letters, 280,* 69–72.

Trott, C., Friedman, D., Ritter, W., & Fabiani, M. (1997). Item and source memory. Differential age effects revealed by event-related potentials, *Neuroreport, 8,* 3373–3378.

Tsivilis, D., Otten, J., & Rugg, M.D. (2001). Context effects on the neural correlates of recognition memory: An electrophysiological study. *Neuron, 31,* 1–20.

Tulving, E. (1983). *Elements of episodic memory.* Oxford: Oxford University Press.

Tulving, E. (1985). Memory and consciousness. *Canadian Psychologist, 26,* 1–12.

Wilding, E.L. (1999). Separating retrieval strategies from retrieval success: An event-related potential study of source memory. *Neuropsychologia, 37,* 441–454.

Wilding, E.L. (2000). In what way does the parietal old/new effect index recollection? *International Journal of Psychophysiology, 35,* 81–87.

Wilding, E.L., Doyle, M.C., & Rugg, M.D. (1995). Recognition memory with and without retrieval of context: An event-related potential study. *Neuropsychologia, 33,* 743–767.

Wilding, E.L., & Rugg, M.D. (1996). An event related potential study of recognition memory with and without retrieval of source. *Brain, 119,* 889–905.

Wilding, E.L., & Rugg, M.D. (1997a). An event-related potential study of memory for words spoken aloud or heard. *Neuropsychologia, 35,* 1185–1195.

Wilding, E.L., & Rugg, M.D. (1997b). Event-related potentials and the recognition memory exclusion task. *Neuropsychologia, 35,* 119–128.

Wood, C.C., & Allison, T. (1981). Interpretation of evoked potentials: A neurophysiological perspective. *Canadian Journal of Psychology, 35,* 113–135.

CHAPTER THREE

Frontal contributions to episodic memory encoding in the young and elderly

Randy L. Buckner
Howard Hughes Medical Institute; Departments of Radiology, and Anatomy and Neurobiology, and Department of Psychology, Washington University, USA

Jessica M. Logan
Department of Psychology, Washington University, USA

The topic of this chapter is easily illustrated by an experiment. Write down all of the events that you remember from yesterday. Be careful to write down only those events (episodes) for which you can recollect the actual experience and refrain from writing down those events that you know must have occurred but for which you have no specific memory. When you are done, examine the list carefully. It probably includes memories of episodes for which you can call up numerous details, such as the individuals with whom you shared the experience or even the thoughts you were having at the earlier time. However, it is also likely that you were not able to write down details for all the events that happened to you yesterday, and there might be little explanation for why some events are remembered and others forgotten. You probably did not attempt to memorise any of the episodes listed, yet, as illustrated by our simple experiment, when queried, many events were easily and vividly recalled. This experiment illustrates the main question explored in this chapter: why do certain events and experiences form memories?

There are many levels at which one can answer this question. On one level, theories from cognitive psychology provide an account of how certain forms of processing facilitate episodic memory formation, outlining the conditions necessary to promote these forms of processing and the many variables that can influence retrieval of episodic memories after they have formed. At another level, evidence from neuroscience provides information about the neural structures that support memory formation and characterises the operations carried out by these neural structures. The view of memory formation presented here reflects a cognitive neuroscience approach that relates these two levels of description. The aim is to understand how memory formation and its behavioural manifestations arise from the workings of underlying neural structures. Specifically, the chapter addresses neural correlates and processes that play a role in encoding events into episodic memory.

First, results from brain imaging studies will be reviewed that suggest specific regions within frontal cortex contribute to episodic memory formation. Several principles of frontal participation in encoding will be discussed including evidence for domain (code) specificity across frontal regions. Following the explication of the existing data, a cognitive neuroscience theory of how episodic memories form will be presented. The central idea of this theory is that for an episodic memory to form, an event must encourage elaboration of information within particular domain-specific frontal regions that provide critical inputs to medial temporal cortex. Medial temporal cortex then serves to facilitate binding of this information into cortical circuits. Finally, we will speculate on how the present theory relates to why memory performance is hampered in some elderly individuals. The ideas presented here overlap with those we have presented previously (Buckner, 1999; Buckner & Tulving, 1995; Buckner, Kelley, & Petersen, 1999; Buckner, Snyder, Sanders, Raichle, & Morris, 2001) as well as ideas expressed elegantly by other investigators (e.g. Moscovitch, 1992; Squire, 1987). One final preparatory note before reading this chapter is that, to limit the focus of our analysis, findings and theory directly relating to frontal contributions to episodic memory formation will be reviewed selectively. Many studies have noted important contributions of regions outside frontal cortex to memory formation. These findings, however, are outside the scope of the present explication.

FRONTAL CORTEX CONTRIBUTES TO VERBAL EPISODIC ENCODING

Human episodic memory encoding has been explored in many studies using verbal materials. Such studies have targeted correlates of brain activity associated with the active attempt to remember words or sentences (most often referred to as *intentional* encoding). In these studies, subjects are instructed to remember the materials and told that a memory test will follow. Results, obtained from both functional magnetic resonance imaging (fMRI) and positron emission tomography (PET) studies, consistently demonstrate that specific regions within left frontal cortex are active when subjects *intentionally* memorise words or sentences (Fletcher et al., 1995; Kapur et al., 1996; McDermott et al., 1999; Nyberg et al., 1996b). For example, Kapur et al. (1996) had subjects intentionally memorise word pairs. Contrasting this intentional encoding condition with a reference condition in which subjects simply read the words, the authors noted robust left frontal activation in two specific left frontal regions, one region located dorsally and a second located anterior and ventral to the first. We will return to the "specificity" of these separate regions in the next section. For now, further converging evidence that these frontal regions contribute to episodic memory encoding will be considered.

In addition to intentionally-formed memories, many instances of episodic memory formation in everyday life occur *incidentally*, without any intention to remember. As shown by studies in cognitive psychology (Postman, 1964; Hyde & Jenkins, 1973; Craik & Lockhart, 1972), episodic memories can form as a by-product of certain forms of information processing, independent of the intention to remember. For example, words that are elaborated upon in terms of their meaning and how they relate to other items in memory are better remembered than words processed in a shallow fashion in which only surface characteristics are examined—the well-known levels of processing effect (e.g. Craik & Lockhart, 1972; but see also Morris et al., 1977; Fisher & Craik, 1977, for important caveats on this principle).

Frontal regions active during *intentional* memorisation are also active during behavioural manipulations that *incidentally* alter the effectiveness of memory encoding. For example, when subjects perform tasks requiring meaning-based judgements on words, multiple regions within left frontal cortex are activated. Those words are remembered even though the subjects make no direct attempt at memorisation (Demb et al., 1995; Gabrieli et al., 1998; Kapur et al., 1994; Wagner et al., 1998b). By contrast, when subjects perform a task where words are judged to be in uppercase or lowercase letters (a surface characteristic), left frontal activity is diminished, and memory for the words is poor.

Cognitive investigations also reveal that dividing attentional resources can influence episodic memory formation. When attention is directed away from an item at the time of encoding, that item is likely to be forgotten even if a subject is attempting to remember it (Craik, Govoni, Naveh-Benjamin, & Anderson, 1996). Consistent with this behavioural observation, an influential PET study demonstrated that adding a secondary distracting task during intentional memorisation caused brain activity in frontal cortex to diminish and memory to be impaired (Fletcher et al., 1995).

A final behavioural manipulation that has related encoding processes with frontal activity stems from studies of stimulus novelty. Novel materials are better encoded than familiar materials (Jacoby & Craik, 1979). Several studies comparing novel to repeated words have noted left frontal activity (e.g. Buckner et al., 2000; Demb et al., 1995; Raichle et al., 1994). For example, Raichle et al. (1994) had subjects perform a word generation task using either novel or well-practised words as cues. Frontal activity was present during performance with the novel items but reduced significantly to the repeated items. Although not tested explicitly in that study, new episodic encoding was probably diminished or absent in the highly repeated condition. Dolan and Fletcher (1997) extended this basic observation and suggested that left frontal activity is most sensitive to the novel re-pairing of verbal materials, such as might be expected in situations where a new meaningful connection must be established for verbal items. Thus, studies across a wide range of behavioural manipulations, such as those based on levels of processing, those that divide attention between conditions, and manipulations of stimulus novelty, consistently suggest a link between activity within specific left frontal regions and processes associated with verbal encoding.

Further evidence for a link between left frontal activity and verbal encoding comes from neuroimaging studies that have examined activity on a moment-by-moment basis based on whether a particular item is remembered or forgotten. These studies perhaps most closely parallel the phenomenon observed in the experimental demonstration at the beginning of this chapter. The basic idea for these investigations came from early studies using electrical scalp recording techniques (Fabiani, Karis, & Donchin, 1986; Paller, 1990; for reviews see Rugg, 1995; Wagner, Koustaal, & Schacter, 1999). These studies recorded evoked-response potentials (ERPs) from subjects at the time of memorisation and revealed differences for words that were later remembered as compared to those that were later forgotten. Developments in fMRI methods (Buckner et al., 1996a; Dale & Buckner, 1997; Josephs, Turner, & Friston, 1997; Kim, Richter, & Ugurbil, 1997; Konishi et al., 1996; Zarahn, Aguirrr, & D'Esposito, 1997) have allowed similar phenomena to be examined with better spatial (anatomical) localisation.

Across the fMRI studies, subjects performed tasks encouraging semantic processing on words without any expectation of a later memory test. Then, during a later surprise recognition test, those words that were remembered were sorted and compared with those words that were forgotten, with neural correlates that predicted memory performance identified. Consistent with the aforementioned results, specific regions of frontal cortex were among those most strongly correlated with subsequent memory performance (Buckner, Wheeler, & Sheridan, 2001; Rotte et al., 1998; Wagner et al., 1998b; see also Alkire et al., 1998; Brewer, Zhao, & Gabrieli, 1998). These findings provide a compelling example of the direct link between brain and behaviour in episodic memory encoding. Of particular theoretical interest, this relation between left frontal activity and subsequent memory for words has spanned a range of task contexts and even includes tasks involving episodic retrieval (Buckner et al., 2001).

In summary, the data described above suggest that the amount of activity within specific left frontal regions at the time of encoding correlates with later episodic memory performance for verbal materials. This consistent relation between encoding and frontal activity is perhaps one of the most ubiquitous in brain imaging studies of memory (see reviews by Buckner & Tulving, 1995;

Buckner et al., 1999; Fletcher, Frith, and Rugg, 1997; Nyberg, Cabeza, & Tulving, 1996a; Tulving, Kapur, Craik, Moscovitch, & Houle, 1994).

SPECIFIC REGIONS WITHIN FRONTAL CORTEX CONTRIBUTE TO EPISODIC ENCODING IN A DOMAIN-SPECIFIC MANNER

As highlighted earlier, activity within frontal cortex has been associated consistently with encoding of verbal materials into episodic memory. Frontal cortex, however, is a heterogeneous region that contains numerous anatomically distinct areas as defined by changes in the distribution of cell types and density, interconnections to other brain areas, and physiological properties (Goldman-Rakic, 1987). Based on these characteristics, multiple distinct areas have been well characterised in non-human primates and to a lesser extent, in humans (e.g. Barbas & Pandya, 1989; Brodmann, 1909/1994; Carmichael & Price, 1994; Petrides & Pandya, 1994; Preuss & Goldman-Rakic, 1991; Rajkowska & Goldman-Rakic, 1995a,b). Thus, it is a natural question to ask whether the relation between frontal activity and encoding demonstrates regional specificity that may derive from activity within distinct anatomic areas. The probable answer is yes.

There is considerable evidence to support two separate functional–anatomical dissociations in frontal cortex that relate to episodic encoding. The first is a dissociation between separate regions in left frontal cortex and the second is a dissociation between left and right frontal regions (see Buckner, 1996 for an early explication of this basic idea; see also Petrides & Panya, 1994; Petrides, Alivisatos, & Evans, 1995). The dissociation of left frontal regions will be discussed first.

Dissociation between left frontal regions

Activity within left frontal cortex associated with encoding has extended spatially from the dorsal extent of the inferior frontal gyrus to more ventral and anterior regions, encompassing classically defined Broca's area and portions of dorsolateral prefrontal cortex. The extent of the activation, in itself, suggests involvement of functionally heterogeneous areas. Of importance, two distinct left frontal regions have dissociated themselves functionally in a number of neuroimaging studies. The first region is located near the dorsal extent of inferior frontal gyrus (BA44/6), and the second is located more ventral and anterior extending into the middle frontal gyrus (near BA44/45/47). These two regions will be referred to here as the *dorsal* and *ventral* regions, but these labels should not be taken to reflect specific anatomic distinctions (such as a relation to dorsolateral prefrontal cortex; in other instances these same, or similar, regions have been labelled posterior and anterior, e.g. Kapur et al., 1996; Wagner, 1999; Wagner et al., 1998b). The approximate locations of the dorsal and ventral regions can be seen as the shaded areas in the topmost panel of Fig. 3.1 and have been directly disso-ciated in meta-analyses by considering their divergent behaviour across multiple task comparisons (Buckner, 1996; Buckner, Raichle, & Petersen, 1995; Poldrack et al., 1999).

It is possible to speculate upon the functional roles of these two regions. The dorsal region might provide access to lower-level, more generally utilised forms of representation, perhaps based on phonology or simple lexical access. Support for this possibility comes from the observation that elaborate verbal processing tasks almost universally activate this region independent of whether task demands require access to phonology or more elaborate meaning-based processing. That is, to the extent that a word or word-like representation is being elaborated upon, the dorsal extent of left inferior frontal cortex becomes active. Putatively non-verbal tasks have also activated (to a lesser degree) this dorsal region, suggesting either an extremely general role of this frontal region in elaborate processing or the tendency of humans to incorporate verbal codes across almost all tasks. The more ventral region might provide access to higher-level representations, perhaps based on mean-ing and related semantic associations, or selection among such representa-tions (Thompson-Schill et al., 1998). Evidence for this latter distinction comes from the finding that tasks requiring access to word meaning often activate ventral and anterior regions of prefrontal cortex in addition to more dorsal regions.

The relevance of the dissociation of these two regions is that the ventral region appears to be more selectively predictive of episodic encoding. In other words, in general, activity in the ventral region seems to be a better predictor of later memory performance. Considered from a functional per-spective, this could relate directly to the possibility that the ventral region is required to access and/or manipulate representations associated with word meaning (Buckner et al., 1995; Kapur et al., 1996). As noted earlier, tasks requiring meaning-based elaboration are usually those most conducive to forming robust episodic memories. A recent fMRI study by Logan and colleagues highlights the special role of the ventral region in episodic encoding.

Logan, Kelley, and Buckner (2000) presented subjects with words under one of two incidental encoding conditions that manipulated demands on semantic elaboration while holding constant overall time to respond (or time demands) (based on Demb et al., 1995). In the *deep encoding* condition, subjects decided whether words represented abstract or concrete entities—a task requiring access to word meaning. In the *shallow encoding* condition, subjects decided whether the beginning or ending letters of the words came earlier or later in the alphabet. Of critical importance, the shallow encoding task was quite difficult (as measured by time to respond) and required representation of phonological information but not access to meaning-based elaboration. In fact, the response times associated with the shallow encoding task were longer than those associated with the deep meaning-based encoding task.

Typical of such manipulations, the type of processing predicted subsequent memory, with deep encoding producing significantly better memory performance than shallow encoding. The key result in terms of functional brain anatomy was a significant interaction between dorsal and ventral frontal regions and encoding condition. Similar levels of activity were present in the dorsal frontal region for both encoding conditions, consistent with a more generic role of this region in verbal processing. That is, independent of whether the task required subjects to access word-meaning, dorsal frontal cortex was activated robustly yet subjects did not always remember those words encountered. By contrast, robust activation in the ventral region was present only during the deep encoding condition, where meaning-based semantic elaboration was required and memory performance was high. These results provide a further dissociation between dorsal and ventral regions of left frontal cortex, and also suggest that activity within the ventral prefrontal region, which correlates with meaning-based elaboration, is selectively predictive of verbal episodic encoding.

Dissociation between left and right frontal regions

The second prominent dissociation between frontal regions relates to differences in encoding verbal and non-verbal materials. Cognitive theories have long suggested that memory formation relies on multiple kinds of information, with one important (albeit heuristic) distinction being between verbal and non-verbal codes. Behavioural studies have shown that a picture of an object, such as a lion, is more likely to be remembered than the presentation of the word "lion" (a finding known as the picture superiority effect). The implication is that pictures are associated with both non-verbal (image-based) and verbal codes, whereas words (particularly abstract words) are associated predominantly with just a verbal code (Paivio, 1986; Paivio & Csapo, 1973). Moreover, patients with lateralised frontal lesions can show differences in memorisation of different material types (Riege, Metter, & Hanson, 1980; Whitehouse et al., 1981; but see also Milner et al., 1985) suggesting code-specific regional specialisation in frontal cortex.

Several recent brain-imaging studies have demonstrated that memorisation of materials associated with different verbal and non-verbal codes can activate distinct regions of left and right frontal cortex. As discussed earlier, encoding of verbal materials such as words is associated with activation in specific left frontal regions. By contrast, memorisation of unfamiliar faces

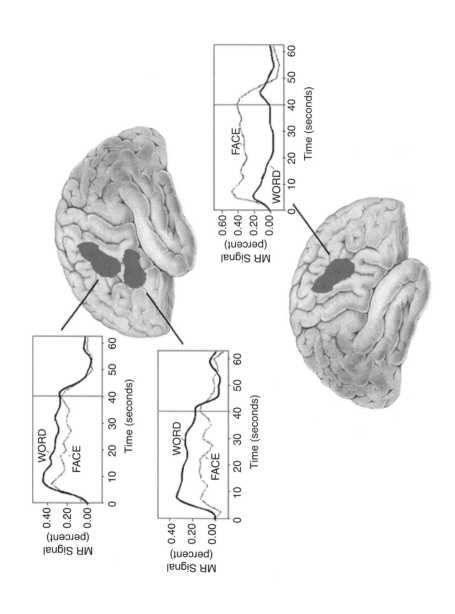

Figure 3.1. Heuristic representation of the three frontal regions most consistently implicated in episodic memory encoding. Two separate left frontal regions including dorsal (posterior) and ventral (anterior) regions are plotted (top lateral view of brain). The third region is located in the right dorsal (posterior) frontal cortex (bottom lateral view of brain). Importantly, these regions dissociate functionally across encoding paradigms. One dissociation is shown by plotting the response over an encoding block for each region, separately for word- and face-encoding conditions. Each time course (in seconds) shows the evolving fMRI signal over a 40s encoding epoch followed by a 24s control period (encoding epoch ends and control period begins at the vertical line in each plot). Data were averaged over 272 separate encoding epochs. FACE and WORD time course data are plotted separately. Three important points are worth noting: (1) there is increased involvement for WORD encoding in the left frontal regions and for FACE encoding in the right frontal regions; (2) within the left frontal regions, the ventral (anterior) region is most selective for WORD encoding; and (3) for those regions showing little or no sustained responses (e.g. the WORD-encoding condition in the right frontal region), there is none the less a transient increase at the beginning and end of the epoch, perhaps reflecting an initial recruitment of the region. See http://www.psypress.co.uk/brainscans-etc for a colour version of this figure.

(Kelley et al., 1998) and texture patterns (Wagner et al., 1998a), neither of which can be easily associated with a verbal label, strongly activates right frontal regions near the homologue to the left dorsal frontal region. The locations of the left and right frontal regions showing a dissociation between material types can be seen in Fig. 3.1. Several other studies using both PET and fMRI have also noted similar effects (e.g. Lee, Robbins, Pickard, & Owen, 2000; McDermott et al., 1999; but see Grady et al., 1995; Haxby et al., 1996).

To illustrate the robustness of the dissociation between these specific left and right frontal regions, Konishi, Donaldson, and Buckner (2001), performed a meta-analysis on data from 17 subjects who performed tasks involving intentional memorisation of words and faces (data were from Kelley et al., 1998, and McDermott et al., 1999). The data were combined such that the response to a single averaged encoding epoch could be observed. The epochs all involved a 40s period in which subjects attempted to memorise 16 individual items, followed by a 24s control period. In this manner, the evolution of the response to the encoding epochs could be observed in detail. In total, data were averaged across 272 separate data epochs resulting in extremely stable estimates of the responses (see Konishi et al., 2001). Results are shown in Fig. 3.1. The dorsal and ventral left frontal regions were both more active for word encoding than face encoding. Of interest, a hint of the dissociation discussed earlier in the context of separate left frontal regions is noted: the ventral region is modulated by material type to a larger degree than the dorsal region. Thus, verbal elaboration appears to recruit most selectively the left ventral frontal region. By contrast, right dorsal frontal cortex is activated robustly during face encoding and minimally, if at all, during word encoding. Clear specificity in these regions is thus observed in relation to whether words or faces are being memorised, which presumably derives from their differential ability to elicit verbal and nonverbal codes.

One further point arising from this meta-analysis stems from detailed examination of the temporal evolution of the responses within the encoding epochs. Quite surprisingly, those areas minimally active during the extended encoding epochs none the less sometimes show a transient activation at the beginning and end of the epochs (Konishi et al., 2001). This observation can best be observed in the word condition for the right dorsal frontal region. The word encoding condition shows almost no sustained activation within right dorsal frontal cortex yet there is a clear and significant transient activation at the beginning of the epoch. What could this mean? One possibility is that the regions are not recruited initially in an all-or-none manner. Rather, upon initiating a task epoch, multiple potentially useful regions begin to become active. Then a competition ensues, which results in the selective activation pattern most appropriate for processing and encoding the kind of material at hand. This idea is akin to biased-competition models in perception

(Desimone & Duncan, 1995) and could suggest a mechanism by which domain- (code-) specific frontal regions are recruited.

Taken collectively, these findings suggest that distinct regions of frontal cortex will process multiple kinds of verbal and non-verbal information and facilitate formation of episodic memory for those types of information. This interpretation is consistent with multiple-code models of human memory (Nelson, 1979; Paivio, 1986) and provides another example of a psychological phenomenon mapping onto specific aspects of brain function.

EPISODIC ENCODING IS A BY-PRODUCT OF ONLINE PROCESSING WITHIN FRONTAL CORTEX

A further point to consider is the relation between activity within the frontal regions described in the previous section and online task demands. Episodic encoding is a rather odd process in this regard; subjects need not attempt to remember, yet, as a consequence of performing task demands related to immediate goals, episodic memories will form (Craik & Lockhart, 1972; Craik & Tulving, 1975; Hyde & Jenkins, 1973; Postman, 1964;). It is notable that the frontal regions whose activity correlates so consistently with episodic memory formation have also been associated with verbal working memory and word generation tasks (tasks requiring elaboration, manipulation, and selection between verbal representations). A simple idea that could tie these findings to episodic encoding processes is that these activity correlates might reflect part of the neural substrate that maintains representations online (in working memory) while the representations are manipulated and used to guide and/or select further online events. At the same time, these representations might themselves be involved in encoding episodic memories. By this account, encoding processes necessary for episodic memory formation are a by-product or secondary effect of online processes.

This simple framework can account for a number of behavioural influences on episodic memory formation. For example, this notion might provide a cognitive neuroscientific explanation for the levels of processing effect (Craik & Lockhart, 1972; Craik & Tulving, 1975). Processing that requires verbal elaboration (deep processing) appears to activate specific regions of left frontal cortex, including the ventral regions near BA44/45/47 (discussed earlier), whereas well-automated language tasks and those based only on phonological processing (shallow tasks) do not. Shallow (surface-based) encoding tasks might not form episodic memories well because they do not require representation of information in these ventral prefrontal regions.

FRONTAL CORTEX PROVIDES AN INPUT TO
MEDIAL TEMPORAL REGIONS

Up to this point, one important question has been set aside; namely, exactly how does activity within frontal cortex interact with the medial temporal cortex to support episodic encoding? This question is important, because an extensive body of evidence supports an essential role for medial temporal structures in successful episodic memory formation. Damage to the medial temporal lobes is often associated with partial or near complete loss of the ability to remember new experiences (including episodic memories) in the presence of relatively intact cognitive functioning in other domains (Cohen & Eichenbaum, 1993; Corkin, 1984; Scoville & Milner, 1957; Squire, 1987). Non-human primate models of memory loss also suggest that lesions within hippocampus and adjacent cortex (within the medial temporal lobes) result in an impaired ability to remember new experiences (Murray, 1996; Zola-Morgan & Squire, 1993).

None the less, according to the ideas presented here episodic memory formation involves participation of both frontal and medial temporal regions. Specifically, we hypothesise that frontal cortex provides a source of information (an input or some form of modulatory influence) to medial temporal lobe structures (Buckner, 1999; Buckner et al., 1999; Moscovitch, 1992; Kapur et al., 1996). Such a notion fits well with the proposal that medial temporal lobe structures (including the hippocampus and adjacent cortex) play a role in the integration and cohesion (binding) of incoming information to form memories (Cohen & Eichenbaum, 1993; Johnson & Chalfonte, 1994; McClelland, McNaughton, & O'Reilly, 1995; Moscovitch, 1994; Schacter, Norman, & Koutstaal, 1998). Frontal cortex could provide a critical input to these medial temporal structures, supplying the necessary "ingredients" that must be bound together to form an enduring episodic memory. Thus, both frontal and medial temporal regions will be crucial to the formation of an episodic memory (Buckner et al., 1999).

The idea of frontal modulation of medial temporal cortex has previously received attention; we make no claim that this basic idea is novel. It is, in fact, noteworthy that investigators conducting their studies using different methodologies have converged to similar conclusions. For example, Squire (1987, p. 239) suggests that:

> Frontal cortex presumably performs its computations on many kinds of information, which are analyzed concurrently for other purposes by other regions of cortex. Frontal cortex allows information to be remembered in its appropriate context, that is, in the correct temporal coincident event. The medial temporal region then operates upon this information, allowing it to endure in the organized form it has achieved in neocortex.

Moscovitch (1994, p. 278) echoes a similar idea that the frontal lobes "are prototypical organization structures crucial for selecting and implementing encoding strategies that organize the input to the hippocampal component". Data more recently collected in the context of brain imaging studies support these earlier ideas as articulated here and as suggested by others.

One particularly insightful study by Parker and colleagues (1998) used a monkey lesion model to suggest that frontal/medial temporal interactions are required if certain kinds of memory are to form (Parker, Wilding, & Akerman, 1998). In their study, a disconnection procedure was used to damage portions of the frontal lobe in one hemisphere and the perirhinal cortex (within the medial temporal lobe) in the other hemisphere. Crucially, the white-matter tracts that allow cross-hemisphere communication between the frontal lobes were severed. By doing so, the monkeys were left with an intact frontal lobe in one hemisphere and an intact perirhinal cortex in the other, but no means for the two structures to interact (for more elaborate discussion of disconnection procedures see Ungerleider and Mishkin, 1982, pp. 551–552). Monkeys with disconnection lesions between perirhinal cortex and frontal cortex were impaired on a memory task that might tap processes similar to those underlying episodic memory in humans. Moreover, based on their results and findings from other lesion studies in monkeys, Parker et al. (1998) suggested an idea that parallels the human observations of domain specificity in encoding processes. They note that "Disconnection of the frontal lobe from other medial temporal areas may selectively influence the processing of different types of novel information and the attendant mnemonic processing" (Parker et al., 1998, p. 697).

It is important to point out that frontal lesions in humans produce episodic memory impairments, just not selectively so (Riege et al., 1980; Schacter, 1987; Shimamura, Janowsky, & Squire, 1991; Wheeler, Stuss, & Tulving, 1995; Whitehouse, 1981). One possible explanation for this observation is that, unlike medial temporal lobe contributions to episodic memory formation, frontal contributions arise as a secondary effect of their engagement to complete online task goals. If frontal activity plays both an immediate task-related role and a secondary role in providing an input to the medial temporal lobes, there might be inherent difficulties in trying to associate memory formation selectively with frontal injury. Lesions to frontal regions will produce speech and verbal fluency impairments if the lesion is in left frontal cortex (Geschwind, 1979), and visuospatial impairments if the lesion is localised to right frontal cortex (Milner, 1965), consistent with the role of frontal cortex in online processing associated with these functions.

None the less, frontal lesions might also have significant effects on episodic memory task performance. For example, patients with speech and fluency difficulties typical of left frontal damage do poorly on recognition tests of studied words (Riege et al., 1980; Whitehouse, 1981). These studies have also included patients with deficits likely arising from damage to similar right frontal regions. Consistent with the findings discussed above concerning multiple-code models of human memory, these patients were impaired at remembering non-verbal items, including pictures (Riege et al., 1980; White-house, 1981) and birdsongs (Riege et al., 1980). Newer studies with transcranial magnetic stimulation (TMS) will perhaps be able to generalise and extend these findings from patients with permanent lesions to healthy, normal subjects.

One notion implied by the title of this section is that the interaction between frontal and medial temporal regions is directional: frontal cortex is hypothesised to provide an input to, or influence on, medial temporal regions. Although there might well be interactions between the regions in ongoing cognitive operations, there is good reason to believe that the influence in the context of memory encoding is largely unidirectional. First, medial temporal lesions do not produce online information-processing impairments that would be associated with even mild frontal lesions. Second, and perhaps more important, two brain imaging studies of amnesic subjects have noted qualitatively normal frontal activity and task performance on incidental encoding tasks (Buckner & Koutstaal, 1998; Gabrieli, Poldrack, & Desmond, 1998). Yet, in these patients, consciously accessible memories did not form. The tentative conclusion is that, in the presence of medial temporal damage, frontal regions might be sending information to a silent set of brain areas critical for later stages of memory formation (Buckner, 1999).

FRONTAL CONTRIBUTIONS TO MEMORY ENCODING MIGHT UNDERLIE MEMORY DIFFICULTIES IN THE ELDERLY

As mentioned earlier, a question central to this chapter is why memories are formed for some episodes and not others. Exploring this question has direct implications for understanding why memory difficulties may arise. Older adults (60 years of age or older) consistently show declines in episodic memory performance compared with younger adults (e.g. Craik & Jennings, 1992; Light, 1991; Park, 2000). The frontal lobes, which, as discussed, are heavily implicated in episodic encoding, also appear to be particularly targeted by ageing. Raz, Gunning, et al. (1997) observed that, compared with other areas (such as limbic structures), prefrontal grey matter showed the most substantial age-related volumetric decline, suggesting that prefrontal cortex might be an anatomically selective site for deterioration in the ageing process (or at least one of the sites that shows age-related change). From a behavioural perspective, older adults often exhibit patterns similar to those observed in patients with frontal lesions. Moscovitch and Winocur (1995, p. 353) noted that "there is remarkable consistency between the memory deficits seen in human patients and experimental animals with frontal lesions and those seen in normal ageing". Thus, there appears to be general consensus that frontal dysfunction contributes to memory impairment in older adults. Findings from functional neuroimaging studies can lend insight into how age-related memory impairments arise from frontal dysfunction.

Several imaging studies of age-related memory impairments in older adults have demonstrated a failure to recruit frontal areas appropriately during memory encoding to the extent that they are recruited by younger adults (e.g, Cabeza et al., 1997; Grady et al., 1995, 1999; Madden et al., 1999). For instance, in a seminal study using PET, Grady and colleagues (1995) observed that older adults did not significantly activate left frontal regions activated in younger adults during an intentional encoding task involving faces. This region probably corresponded to the dorsal left frontal region described in an earlier section. The researchers interpreted this finding in older adults as part of the neural underpinnings for observed age-related memory impairments in behaviour (Grady et al., 1995). In a second important PET study, Cabeza and colleagues (1997), exploring intentional encoding of verbal materials, found that left prefrontal and occipitotemporal regions were more active during encoding for younger adults than older adults. Grady and colleagues (1999) found a similar pattern of results with episodic encoding of words and pictures, namely that older adults often did not show as extensive increases in activity as younger adults in prefrontal regions (among others) involved in intentional and deep encoding tasks.

These studies are examples of what seems to be a common principle emerging from functional neuroimaging studies of age-related memory impairments. Older adults often do not recruit areas related to successful encoding in younger adults as extensively as younger adults, and this might partly underlie age-related memory decline. An interesting open question is to what degree this underutilisation of frontal resources, which has been most often observed under conditions of intentional encoding where subjects must spontaneously initiate their own encoding strategies, reflects an inherent limitation in the available resources. An alternative is that resources are potentially available but not appropriately accessed when older adults must rely on self-initiated strategies. Further studies will be needed to explore this important issue.

Such results from brain imaging studies showing reductions in measured frontal activity levels should be interpreted cautiously, given potential age-related differences in the haemodynamic response that underlies PET and fMRI methods (Buckner et al., 2000; D'Esposito, Zarahn, Aguirre, & Rypma, 1999; Ross et al., 1997; Taoka et al., 1998). For example, Ross et al. (1997) noted that even responses to robust visual stimuli in or near primary visual cortex can show differences between age groups. There are, however, several additional observations that do not depend on reductions in activity in older adults that also suggest evidence for inappropriate activation of frontal regions in older adults. Several neuroimaging studies of encoding have reported that older adults activate frontal regions during encoding that are *not* activated (or less activated) by younger adults. A compelling recent example of such a phenomenon comes from a study conducted to explore short-term (working) memory. The principles derived from this study extend, as will be shown, to studies of long-term episodic encoding.

Reuter-Lorenz and colleagues (2000) examined younger and older adults in a PET study of verbal and spatial working memory. Similar to the findings of domain-specificity discussed earlier, prior studies using this paradigm have found that younger adults show lateralised activity for these two domains of working memory. Verbal working memory tasks usually show more left-lateralised activity, whereas spatial working memory tasks show more right-lateralised activity (e.g. Smith, Jonides, & Koepp, 1996). In the study by Reuter-Lorenz et al (2000), this pattern was observed to hold for younger adults but not for older adults. Older adults showed more bilateral activations in both verbal and spatial working memory tasks in more anterior regions recruited for the tasks, including some of the frontal regions that are consistently associated with episodic encoding.

Further findings from the study also demonstrate that older adults show "paradoxical laterality" and that younger adults do not. That is, whereas younger adults were observed to activate left prefrontal cortex more in verbal working memory tasks, and right prefrontal cortex more in spatial working memory tasks, older adults showed the opposite pattern: more right pre-frontal activity in verbal working memory tasks and more left prefrontal activity in spatial working memory tasks. The researchers interpret some of these additional or unexpected activations in older adults as evidence for a form of compensatory recruitment of regions to support task performance (such as has been observed in patients with unilateral frontal strokes, e.g. Buckner et al., 1996). The authors also suggest, however, that the paradoxical laterality observed in prefrontal cortex in older adults might be related to less efficient executive processing that hampers, rather than supports, task performance (Reuter-Lorenz et al., 2000).

Similar to bilateral activity shown in the study by Reuter-Lorenz et al. (2000), Madden et al. (1999) demonstrated that, in an encoding phase of a study with verbal materials, older adults were more likely to show bilateral activations in prefrontal cortex, compared to baseline, contrary to more common findings in younger adults, which often show more unilateral left prefrontal cortex activity. The authors note that these results could be indicative of some form of compensatory activity on the part of older adults, but also noted that it did not appear to compensate for an overall decrease in activation (Madden et al., 1999).

Finally, in the earlier study by Cabeza et al. (1997), although older adults were observed to show age-related decreases in activity in some frontal regions compared to younger adults, they were also observed to show age-related increases in activity in other regions, including bilateral activation of insular regions. The authors interpret this result as suggesting that the greater recruitment of regions by older adults, as compared to younger adults, might actually be inefficient and disruptive to encoding processes, and not necessarily serving a compensatory role in memory formation (Cabeza et al., 1997).

Two important principles emerge from these studies involving older adults. First, older adults fail to appropriately recruit frontal regions associated with encoding. Second, to the degree that frontal regions are recruited, older adults do so in a less selective manner than younger adults. Cabeza (2001) has recently expanded upon this second principle in a review noting that non-selective activation of frontal regions across the hemispheres is a widely observed phenomenon in ageing, labelling this principle "hemispheric asymmetry reduction in older adults" (Cabeza, 2001). Moreover, these principles are not limited to studies of episodic encoding and working memory. Reduced and non-selective activation of frontal regions have also been evident in studies investigating memory retrieval (Cabeza et al., 1997; Backman et al., 1999; Madden et al., 1999; Schacter, Savage, Alpert, Rauch, & Albert, 1996), implying that these principles might represent broader-based phenomena in cognitive ageing.

Whereas some researchers have suggested that older adults' recruitment of additional regions not observed in younger adults could be evidence of compensatory activation to support performance, others have raised the possibility that these additional activations are inappropriate for task performance. Activation of atypical regions might be related not to supporting older adults' performance but might actually be an underlying part of memory impairments (Cabeza et al., 1997; Reuter-Lorenz et al., 2000). Although the evidence for either side is far from conclusive, there are data that offer speculative support for the latter viewpoint. It might be that increased activity in some regions during encoding in older adults is a form of non-selective recruitment and reflects a breakdown in appropriate control of information processing rather than compensatory processing.

Evidence from analyses done by Konishi and colleagues, mentioned earlier, perhaps supports this. Konishi et al. (2001) observed significant transient activation at the beginning of extended intentional encoding epochs, suggesting the idea that activity becomes more selective and more appropriate for the task at hand after initial and transient activation of multiple, potentially useful regions. That is, competition among brain regions might commence when task performance is initiated and, in young adults, quickly resolve to select a specific set of brain regions most appropriate for task performance.

In this framework, the phenomenon of non-selective recruitment observed in imaging studies of older adults might be linked to a failure of older adults to become more selective in their recruitment of regions. In support of this idea, there is mounting evidence from behavioural studies to suggest that older adults exhibit breakdowns that might reflect inappropriate processing of unwanted information in a wide range of cognitive contexts (e.g. Zacks & Hasher, 1994).

Based on these imaging data, we thus, speculatively, propose that episodic memory formation takes a double hit from ageing, leading to declines in memory performance. The first hit is that older adults fail fully to recruit those frontal regions implicated in successful encoding in younger adults. The second hit is that the regions that *are* being recruited by older adults might be inappropriate and inefficient for the task at hand (Logan et al., 2002).

ACKNOWLEDGEMENTS

We thank Luigi Maccotta for providing detailed and thoughtful comments on an early version of this chapter. This work was supported by National Institute of Ageing grant AG05681, National Institute of Mental Health grant MH57506, and a James S. McDonnell Foundation Program in Cognitive Neuroscience grant (99–63/9900003). J. M. L. is supported by a National Science Foundation Graduate Research Fellowship.

REFERENCES

Alkire, M.T., Haier, R.J., Fallon, J.H., & Cahill, L. (1998). Hippocampal, but not amygdala, activity at encoding correlates with long-term, free recall of nonemotional information. *Proceedings of the National Academy of Science USA, 95*, 14506–14510.

Bäckman, L., Andersson, J.L., Nyberg, L., Winblad, B., Nordberg, A., & Almkvist, O. (1999). Brain regions associated with episodic retrieval in normal aging and Alzheimer's disease. *Neurology, 52*, 1861–1870.

Barbas, H., & Pandya, D.N. (1989). Architecture and intrinsic connections of the prefrontal cortex in the rhesus monkey. *Journal of Comparative Neurology, 286*, 353–375.

Brewer, J., Zhao, Z.H., & Gabrieli, J.D.E. (1998). Parahippocampal and frontal responses to single events predict whether those events are remembered or forgotten. *Science, 281*, 1185–1187.

Brodmann, K. (1909/1994). *Localisation in the cerebral cortex* (L.J. Garey, Transl.) London: Smith-Gordon.

Buckner, R.L. (1996). Beyond HERA: Contributions of specific prefrontal brain areas to long-term memory retrieval. *Psychonomic Bulletin and Review, 3*, 149–158.

Buckner, R.L. (1999). Dual effect theory of episodic encoding. In Tulving, E. (Ed.) *Memory, consciousness, and the brain* (pp. 278–292). Philadelphia, PA: Psychology Press.

Buckner, R.L., Bandettini, P.A., O'Craven, K.M., Savoy, R.L., Petersen, S.E., Raichle, M.E., & Rosen, B.R. (1996). Detection of cortical activation during averaged single trials of a cognitive task using functional magnetic resonance imaging. *Proceedings of the National Academy of Science USA, 93*, 14878–14883.

Buckner, R.L., Kelley, W.M., & Petersen, S.E. (1999). Frontal cortex contributes to human memory formation. *Nature Neuroscience, 2*, 1–4.

Buckner, R.L., & Koutstaal, W. (1998). Functional neuroimaging studies of encoding, priming, and explicit memory retrieval. *Proceedings of the National Academy of Science USA, 95,* 891–898.

Buckner, R.L., Raichle, M.E., & Petersen, S.E. (1995). Dissociation of human prefrontal cortical areas across different speech production tasks and gender groups. *Journal of Neurophysiology, 74,* 2163–2173.

Buckner, R.L., Snyder, A.Z., Sanders, A.L., Raichle, M.E., & Morris, J.C. (2000). Functional brain imaging of young, nondemented, and demented older adults. *Journal of Cognitive Neuroscience, 12* (Suppl. 2), 24–34.

Buckner, R.L., & Tulving, E. (1995). Neuroimaging studies of memory: Theory and recent PET results. In Boller, F., Grafman, J. (Eds.) *Handbook of neuropsychology* (pp. 439–466). Amsterdam: Elsevier.

Buckner, R.L., Wheeler, M., & Sheridan, M. (2001) Encoding processes during retrieval tasks. *Journal of Cognitive Neuroscience, 13,* 406–415.

Cabeza, R. (2001). Functional neuroimaging of cognitive ageing. In R. Cabeza & A. Kingstone (Eds.) *Handbook of functional neuroimaging of cognition.* Cambridge, MA: MIT Press.

Cabeza, R., Grady, C.L., Nyberg, L., McIntosh, A.R., Tulving, E., Kapur, S., Jennings, J.M., Houle, S., & Craik, F.I.M. (1997). Age-related differences in neural activity during memory encoding and retrieval: a positron emission tomography study. *Journal of Neuroscience, 17,* 391–400.

Carmichael, S.T., & Price, J.L. (1994). Architectonic subdivision of the orbital and medial pre-frontal cortex in the macaque monkey. *Journal of Comparative Neurology, 346,* 366–402.

Cohen, N.J., & Eichenbaum, H. (1993). *Memory, amnesia, and the hippocampal system.* Cambridge, MA: MIT Press.

Corkin, S. (1984). Lasting consequences of bilateral medial temporal lobe lobectomy: Clinical course and experimental findings in H.M. *Seminars in Neurology, 4,* 249–259.

Craik, F.I.M., Govoni, R., Naveh-Benjamin, M., & Anderson, N.D. (1996). The effects of divided attention on encoding and retrieval processes in human memory. *Journal of Experimental Psychology: General, 125,* 159 180.

Craik, F.I.M., & Jennings, J.M. (1992). Human memory. In F.I.M. Craik & T. Salthouse (Eds.) *Handbook of ageing and cognition* (pp. 51–110). Hillsdale, NJ: Lawrence Erlbaum Associates, Inc.

Craik, F.I.M., & Lockhart, R.S. (1972). Levels of processing: A framework for memory research. *Journal of Verbal Learning and Verbal Behavior, 11,* 671–684.

Craik, F.I.M., & Tulving, E. (1975). Depth of processing and the retention of words in episodic memory. *Journal of Experimental Psychology: General, 104,* 168–294.

Dale, A.M., & Buckner, R.L. (1997). Selective averaging of rapidly presented individual trials using fMRI. *Human Brain Mapping, 5,* 329–340.

Demb, J.B., Desmond, J.E., Wagner, A.D., Vaidya, C.J., Glover, G.H., & Gabrieli, J.D.E. (1995). Semantic encoding and retrieval in the left inferior prefrontal cortex: A functional MRI study of task difficulty and process specificity. *Journal of Neuroscience, 15,* 5870–5878.

Desimone, R., & Duncan, J. (1995). Neural mechanisms of selective visual attention. *Annual Review of Neuroscience, 18,* 193–222.

D'Esposito, M., Zarahn, E., Aguirre, G.K., & Rypma, B. (1999). The effect of normal ageing on the coupling of neural activity to the BOLD hemodynamic response. *Neuroimage, 10,* 6–14.

Dolan, R.J., & Fletcher, P.C. (1997). Dissociating prefrontal and hippocampal function in episodic memory encoding. *Nature, 388,* 582–585.

Fabiani, M., Karis, M., & Donchin, E. (1986). P300 and recall in an incidental memory paradigm. *Psychophysiology, 23,* 298–308.

Fisher, R.P., & Craik, F.I.M. (1977). Interaction between encoding and retrieval operations in cued recall. *Journal of Experimental Psychology: Human Learning and Memory, 3,* 701–711.

Fletcher, P.C., Frith, C.D, Grasby, P.M., Shallice, T., Frackokiak, R.S.J., & Dolan, R.J. (1995). Brain systems for encoding and retrieval of auditory–verbal memory: An *in vivo* study in humans. *Brain, 118*, 401–416.

Fletcher, P.C., Frith, C.D., & Rugg, M.D. (1997). The functional neuroanatomy of episodic memory. *Trends in Neuroscience, 20*, 213–218.

Gabrieli, J.D.E., Poldrack, R.A., & Desmond, J.E. (1998). The role of left prefrontal cortex in language and memory. *Proceedings of the National Academy of Science USA, 95*, 906–913.

Geschwind, N. (1979). Specializations of the human brain. *Scientific American, 241*, 180–199.

Goldman-Rakic, P.S. (1987). Circuitry of primate prefrontal cortex and regulation of behaviour by representational memory. In F. Plum (ed.) *Handbook of physiology, the nervous system, higher functions of the brain* (pp. 373–417). Bethesda, MD: American Physiological Society.

Grady, C.L., McIntosh, A.R., Horwitz, B., Maisog, J.M., Ungerleider, L.G., Mentis, M.J., Pietrini, P., Schapiro, M.B., & Haxby, J.V. (1995). Age-related reductions in human recognition memory due to impaired encoding. *Science, 269*, 218–221.

Grady, C.L., McIntosh, A.R., Rajah, M.N., Sania, B., & Craik, F.I.M. (1999). The effects of age on the neural correlates of episodic encoding. *Cerebral Cortex, 9*, 805–814.

Haxby, J.V., Ungerleider, L.G., Horwitz, B., Maisog, J.M., Rapoport, S.L., & Grady, C.L. (1996). Face encoding and recognition in the human brain. *Proceedings of the National Academy of Science USA, 93*, 922–927.

Hyde, T.S., & Jenkins, J.J. (1973). Recall of words as a function of semantic, graphic, and syntactic orienting tasks. *Journal of Verbal Learning and Verbal Behavior, 12*, 471–480.

Jacoby, L.L., & Craik, F.I.M. (1979). Effects of elaboration of processing at encoding and retrieval: Trace distinctiveness and recovery of initial context. In L.S. Cermak & F.I.M. Craik (Eds) *Levels of Processing in Human Memory* (pp. 1–21). Hillsdale, NJ: Lawrence Erlbaum Associates, Inc.

Johnson, M.K., & Chalfonte, B.L. (1994). Binding complex memories: The role of reactivation and the hippocampus. In Schacter, D.L., Tulving, E. (Eds.) *Memory systems.* Cambridge, MA: MIT Press (pp. 311–350).

Josephs, O., Turner, R., & Friston, K. (1997). Event-related fMRI. *Human Brain Mapping, 5*, 243–248.

Kapur, S., Craik, F.I.M., Tulving, E., Wilson, A.A., Houle, S., & Brown, G.M. (1994). Neuroanatomical correlates of encoding in episodic memory: Levels of processing effects. *Proceedings of the National Academy of Science USA, 91*, 2008–2011.

Kapur, S., Tulving, E., Cabeza, R., McIntosh, A.R., Houle, S., & Craik, F.I.M. (1996). The neural correlates of intentional learning of verbal materials: A PET study in humans. *Cognitive Brain Research, 4*, 243–249.

Kelley, W.M., Miezin, F.M., McDermott, K.B., Buckner, R.L., Raichle, M.E., Cohen, N.J., Ollinger, J.M., Akbudak, E., Conturo, T.E., Snyder, A.Z., & Petersen, S.E. (1998). Hemispheric specialization in human dorsal frontal cortex and medial temporal lobe for verbal and nonverbal encoding. *Neuron, 20*, 927–936

Kim, S.G., Richter, W., & Ugurbil, K. (1997). Limitations of temporal resolution in functional MRI. *Magnetic Resonance in Medicine, 37*, 631–636.

Konishi, S., Donaldson, D.I., & Buckner, R.L. (2001). Transient activation during block transition. *NeuroImage, 13*, 364–374.

Konishi, S., Yoneyama, R., Itagaki, H., Uchida, I., Nakajima, K., Kato, H., Okjima, K., Koizumi, H., & Miyashita, Y. (1996). Transient brain activity used in magnetic resonance imaging to detect functional areas. *Neuroreport, 8*, 19–23.

Lee, A.C.H., Robbins, T.W., Pickard, J.D., & Owen, A.M. (2000). Asymmetric frontal activation during episodic memory: The effects of stimulus type on encoding and retrieval. *Neuropsychologia, 38*, 677–692.

Light, L.L. (1991). Memory and ageing: Four hypotheses in search of data. *Annual Review of Psychology, 42*, 333–376.

Logan, J.M., Kelley, W.M., & Buckner, R.L. (2000). Inferior and dorsal frontal cortex play distinct roles in episodic memory formation. *Journal of Cognitive Neuroscience, Suppl., 34*.

Logan, J.M., Sanders, A.L., Snyder, A.Z., Morris, J.C., & Buckner, R.L. (2002). Under-recruitment and nonselective recruitment: Dissociable neural mechanisms associated with aging. *Neuron, 33*, 827–840.

Madden, D.J., Turkington, T.G., Provenzale, J.M., Denny, L.L., Hawk, T.C., Gottlob, L.R., & Coleman, R.E. (1999). Adult age differences in the functional neuroanatomy of verbal recognition memory. *Human Brain Mapping, 7*, 115–135.

McClelland, J.L., McNaughton, B.L., & O'Reilly, R.C. (1995). Why there are complementary learning systems in the hippocampus and neocortex: Insights from the successes and failures of the connectionist models of learning and memory. *Psychological Review, 102*, 419–457.

McDermott, K.B., Buckner, R.L., Pertersen, S.E., Kelley, W.M., & Sanders, A.L. (1999). Set- and code-specific activation in frontal cortex: an fMRI study of encoding and retrieval of faces and words. *Journal of Cognitive Neuroscience, 11*, 631–640.

Milner, B. (1965). Visually guided maze-learning in man: Effects of bilateral hippocampal, bilateral frontal, and unilateral cerebral lesions. *Neuropsychologia, 13*, 317–338.

Milner, B., Petrides, M., & Smith, M.L. (1985). Frontal lobes and the temporal organization of memory. *Human Neurobiology, 4* 137–142.

Morris, C.D., Bransford, J.D., & Franks, J.J. (1977). Levels of processing versus test-appropriate strategies. *Journal of Verbal Learning and Verbal Behaviour, 16*, 519–533.

Moscovitch, M. (1992). Memory and working-with-memory: A component process model based on modules and central systems. *Journal of Cognitive Neuroscience, 4*, 257–267.

Moscovitch, M. (1994). Memory and working with memory: Evaluation of a component process model and comparisons with other models. In D.L. Schacter & E. Tulving (Eds.) *Memory systems*. Cambridge, MA: MIT Press (pp. 269–310).

Moscovitch, M., & Winocur, G. (1995). Frontal lobes, memory, and ageing. In J. Grafman, K. Hollyoak, & F. Boller (eds.) *Structure and functions of the human prefrontal cortex. Annals of the New York Academy of Sciences*. New York: New York Academy of Science.

Murray, E.A. (1996). What have ablation studies told us about neural substrates of stimulus memory? *Seminars in the Neurosciences, 8*, 13–22.

Nelson, D.L. (1979). Remembering pictures and words: Appearance, significance, and name. In L.S. Cermak, F.I.M. Craik (Eds.) *Levels of processing in human memory* (pp. 45–76). Hillsdale, NJ: Lawrence Erlbaum Associates Inc.

Nyberg, L., Cabeza, R., & Tulving, E. (1996a). PET studies of encoding and retrieval: The HERA model. *Psychonomic Bulletin and Review, 3*, 135–148.

Nyberg, L., McIntosh, A.R., Cabeza, R., Habib, R., Houle, S., & Tulving, E. (1996b). General and specific brain regions involved in encoding and retrieval of events: What, where, and when. *Proceedings of the National Academy of Science USA, 93*, 11280–11285.

Paller, K.A. (1990). Recall and stem-completion priming have different electrophysiological correlates and are modified differentially by directed forgetting. *Journal of Experimental Psychology: Learning, Memory, and Cognition, 16*, 1021–1032.

Paivio, A. (1986). *Mental representations*. New York: Oxford University Press.

Paivio, A., & Csapo, K. (1973). Picture superiority in free recall: Imagery or dual coding? *Cognitive Psychology, 5*, 176–206.

Park, D.C. (2000). The basic mechanisms accounting for age-related decline in cognitive function. In D.C. Park & N. Schwarz (Eds.) *Cognitive ageing: A primer* (pp. 3–21). Philadelphia, PA: Psychology Press.

Parker, A., Wilding, E., & Akerman, C. (1998). The von Restorff effect in visual object recognition memory in humans and monkeys: The role of frontal/perirhinal interaction. *Journal of Cognitive Neuroscience, 10*, 691–703.

Petrides, M., Alivisatos, B., & Evans, A.C. (1995). Functional activation of the human vento-lateral frontal cortex during mnemonic retrieval of verbal information. *Proceedings of the National Academy of Science USA, 92*, 5803–5807.

Petrides, M., & Pandya, D.N. (1994) Comparitive architectonic analysis of the human and the macaque frontal cortex. In F. Boller & J. Grafman (Eds.) *Handbook of neuropsychology* (*Vol. 9*, pp. 17–58). Amsterdam: Elsevier.

Poldrack, R.A., Wagner, A.D., Prull, M.W., Desmond, J.E., Glover, G.H., & Gabrieli, J.D.E. (1999). Functional specialization for semantic and phonological processing in the left inferior prefrontal cortex. *NeuroImage, 10*, 15–35.

Postman, L. (1964). Short-term memory and incidental learning. In A.W. Melton (Ed.) *Categories of human learning* (pp. 146–201). New York: Academic Press.

Preuss, T.M., & Goldman-Rakic, P.S. (1991). Myelo- and cytoarchitecture of the granular frontal cortex and surrounding regions in the strepsirhine Galago and the anthropoid primate. *Macaca Journal of Comparative Neurology, 310*, 429–474.

Raichle, M.E., Fiez, J.A., Videen, T.O., MacLeod, A.-M.K., Pardo, J.V., Fox, P.T., & Petersen, S.E. (1994). Practice-related changes in human brain functional anatomy during nonmotor learning. *Cerebral Cortex, 4*, 8–26.

Rajkowska, G., & Goldman-Rakic, P.S. (1995a). Cytoarchitectonic definition of prefrontal areas in normal human cortex: I. Remapping of areas 9 and 46 using quantitative criteria. *Cerebral Cortex, 5*, 307–322.

Rajkowska, G., & Goldman-Rakic, P.S. (1995b). Cytoarchitectonic definition of prefrontal areas in normal human cortex: II. Variability in locations of 9 and 46 and relationship to the Talairach coordinate system. *Cerebral Cortex, 5*, 323–337.

Raz, N., Gunning, F.M., Head, D., Dupuis, J.H., McQuain, J., Briggs, S.D., Loken, W.J., Thornton, A.E., & Acker, J.D. (1997). Selective aging of the human cerebral cortex observed in vivo: Differential vulnerability of the prefrontal gray matter. *Crebral Cortex, 7*, 268–282.

Reuter-Lorenz, P.A., Jonides, J., Smith, E.E., Hartley, A., Miller, A., Marshuetz, C., & Koeppe, R.A. (2000). Age differences in the frontal lateralization of verbal and spatial working memory revealed by PET. *Journal of Cognitive Neuroscience, 12*, 174–187.

Riege, W.H., Metter, E.J., & Hanson, W.R. (1980). Verbal and nonverbal recognition memory in aphasic and nonaphasic stroke patients. *Brain and Language, 10*, 60–70.

Ross, M.H., Yurgelun-Todd, D.A., Renshaw, P.F., Maas, L.C., Mendelson, J.H., Mello, N.K., Cohen, M.D., & Levin, J.M. (1997). Age-related reduction in functional MRI response to photic stimulation. *Neurology, 48*, 173–176.

Rotte, M., Koustaal, W., Schacter, D.L., Wagner, A.D., Rosen, B.R., Dale, A.M., & Buckner, R.L. (1998). Left prefrontal activation correlates with the levels of processing during verbal encoding: An event-related fMRI study. *NeuroImage, 7*, S813.

Rugg, M.D. (1995). ERP studies of memory. In M.D. Rugg & M.G.H. Coles (Eds.) *Electrophysiology of mind: Event-related brain potentials and cognition*. Oxford: Oxford University Press.

Rypma, B., & D'Esposito, M. (2000). Isolating the neural mechanisms of age-related changes in human working memory. *Nature Neuroscience, 3*, 509–515.

Schacter, D.L. (1987). Memory, amnesia, and frontal lobe dysfunction. *Psychobiology, 15*, 21–36.

Schacter, D.L., Norman, K.A., & Koustaal, W. (1998). The cognitive neuroscience of constructive memory. *Annual Reviews of Psychology, 49*, 289–318.

Schacter, D.L., Savage, C.R., Alpert, N.M., Rauch, S.L., & Albert, M.S. (1996). The role of hippocampus and frontal cortex in age-related memory changes: a PET study. *Neuroreport, 7*, 1165–1169.

Scoville, W.B., & Milner, B. (1957). Loss of recent memory after bilateral hippocampal lesions. *Journal of Neurology, Neurosurgery, and Psychiatry, 20*, 11–21.

Shimamura, A.P., Janowsky, J.S., & Squire, L.R. (1991) What is the role of frontal lobe damage in memory disorders? In H.S. Levin, H.M. Eisenberg, & A.L. Benton (Eds.) *Frontal lobe function and dysfunction* (pp. 173–195). New York: Oxford University Press, New York.

Smith, E.E., Jonides, J., & Koepp, R.A. (1996). Dissociating verbal- and spatial-working memory using PET. *Cerebral Cortex, 6*, 11–20.

Squire, L.R. (1987). *Memory and brain.* New York: Oxford University Press.

Taoka, T., Iwasaki, S., Uchida, H., Fukusumi, A., Nakagawa, H., Kichikawa, K., Takayama, K., Yoshioka, T., Takewa, M., & Ohishi, H. (1998). Age correlation of the time lag in signal change on EPI-fMRI. *Journal of Computer-Assisted Tomography, 22*, 514–517.

Thompson-Schill, S.L., Swick, D., Farah, M.J., D'Esposito, M., Kan, I.P., & Knight, R.T. (1998). Verb generation in patients with focal frontal lesions: A neuropsychological test of neuroimaging findings. *Proceedings of the National Academy of Sciences USA, 95*, 876–882.

Tulving, E., Kapur, S., Craik, F.I.M., Moscovitch, M., & Houle, S. (1994). Hemispheric encoding/retrieval asymmetry in episodic memory: Positron emission tomography findings. *Proceedings of the National Academy of Science USA, 91*, 2016–2020.

Ungerleider, L.G., & Mishkin, M. (1982). Two cortical visual systems. In D.J. Engle, M.A. Goodale, & R.J. Mansfield (Eds.) *Analysis of visual behavior* (pp. 549–586). Cambridge, MA: MIT Press.

Wagner, A.D. (1999). Working memory contributions to human learning and remembering. *Neuron, 22*, 19–22.

Wagner, A.D., Koustaal, W., & Schacter, D.L. (1999). When encoding yields remembering: Insights from event-related neuroimaging. *Philosophical Transactions of the Royal Society of London, 354*, 1307–1324.

Wagner, A.D., Poldrack, R.A., Eldridge, L.L., Desmond, J.E., Glover, G.H., & Gabrieli, J.D.E. (1998a). Material-specific lateralization of prefrontal activation during episodic encoding and retrieval. *Neuroreport, 9*, 3711–3717.

Wagner, A.D., Schacter, D.L., Rotte, M., Koutstaal, W., Maril, A., Dale, A.M., Rosen, B.R., & Buckner, R.L. (1998b). Building memories: Remembering and forgetting of verbal experiences as predicted by brain activity. *Science, 281*, 1188–1191.

Wheeler, M.A., Stuss, D.T., & Tulving, E. (1995). Frontal lobe damage produces episodic memory impairment. *Journal of the International Neuropsychological Society, 1*, 525–536.

Whitehouse, P.J. (1981). Imagery and verbal encoding in left and right hemisphere damaged patients. *Brain and Language, 14*, 315–332.

Zacks, R.T., & Hasher, L. (1994). Directed ignoring: Inhibitory regulation of working memory. In D. Dagenbach & T.H. Carr (Eds.) *Inhibitory processes in attention, memory, and language* (pp. 242–264). San Diego, CA: Academic Press, Inc.

Zarahn, E., Aguirre, G., & D'Esposito, M. (1997). A trial-based experimental design for fMRI. *NeuroImage, 6*, 122–138.

Zola-Morgan, S., & Squire, L.R. (1993). Neuroanatomy of memory. *Annual Review of Neuroscience, 16*, 547–563.

CHAPTER FOUR

Prefrontal cortex and episodic memory: Integrating findings from neuropsychology and functional brain imaging

Charan Ranganath
Center for Neuroscience, University of California, Davis, USA

Robert T. Knight
Helen Wills Neuroscience Institute, University of California, Berkeley, USA

INTRODUCTION

Although it has been speculated for many years that the prefrontal cortex plays a role in long-term memory for events, or episodic memory, only recently have researchers made a concerted attempt to define this role. Most theories of prefrontal function suggest that this region implements "top-down" or "executive" processes that influence a variety of domains, including memory. For example, Luria (1966) postulated a role for the frontal lobes in the regulation of voluntary attention and the organisation of goal-directed behavior. Building on the work of Luria, Shallice (1982) argued that the frontal lobes are required for the attentional selection of schemes of action in novel situations. A complementary role suggested for the prefrontal cortex is the suppression of irrelevant or interfering stimuli (Brutkowski, 1965; Fuster, 1997; Knight, Staines, Swick, & Chao, 1999; Pribram, Ahumada, Hartog, & Roos, 1964; Shimamura, 1995). Teuber (1964) additionally proposed that the frontal lobes prepare sensory areas for environmental changes that will be induced by motor actions. This concept was later extended to include the generation of anticipatory behavioural sets (Fuster, 1997; Nauta, 1971). Several researchers have also postulated a central role for the prefrontal cortex in active, or working memory (Fuster, 1997; Goldman-Rakic, 1987).

It is conceivable that an impairment in any of these functions could contribute to poor performance on tests of episodic memory. What remains unclear, however, is whether the role of the prefrontal cortex in episodic memory is best characterised as an extension of the aforementioned "executive functions", or whether prefrontal cortex contributes to additional functions specific to the formation and retrieval of memories. Furthermore, it is unclear whether there is functional specialisation within prefrontal cortex, such that different subregions implement different functions relevant to episodic memory. In the following sections, we will review findings of neuropsychological data garnered from neurological patients, as well as neuroimaging studies of prefrontal activity associated with episodic memory in healthy volunteers. From these findings, we will present a model of how prefrontal cortex contributes to episodic memory.

NEUROPSYCHOLOGICAL STUDIES

Studies of verbal learning in patients with frontal lesions indicate that these patients, although impaired, do not demonstrate the same degree of global memory impairment seen in amnesic patients with damage to the diencephalon or medial temporal lobes (Janowsky, Shimamura, Kritchevsky, & Squire, 1989a). For example, several studies have shown that patients with prefrontal lesions can show normal performance on tests of recognition memory (Jetter, Poser, Freeman, & Markowitsch, 1986) and cued recall (Janowsky et al., 1989a; Swick & Knight, 1996). It should be noted that these studies had small sample sizes, and consequently might not have been sensitive enough to detect mild memory deficits. Indeed, a review of these studies by Wheeler, Stuss, and Tulving (1995) concluded that, across studies, patients with prefrontal lesions tend to show mild deficits on tests of recognition memory.

Unlike recognition and cued recall tasks that provide subjects with an external cue to drive retrieval processes, free recall tasks require subjects to initiate strategic processes to search for memory items (Moscovitch, 1992). Findings from two studies suggest that frontal lobe damage might impair the initiation of such processes (Gershberg & Shimamura, 1995; Jetter et al., 1986). In one study, patients with prefrontal lesions studied three lists of categorised words to learn (the categories from the three lists did not overlap), with the instruction that the words could be encoded by semantic category (Jetter et al., 1986). Subjects were tested on the three lists by free recall, cued recall, or recognition, after a 15min interval and then after a 1-day interval. Similarly, in experiments 2 and 3 of Gershberg and Shimamura's (1995) study, subjects were tested on immediate free recall of categorised lists. In both studies, patients showed a reduced tendency to report semantically related words together during recall. Importantly, in experiment 3 of Gershberg and Shimamura's (1995) study, patients who were given instructions to use a semantic organisational strategy (i.e. categorise the words) at encoding, retrieval, or both, showed significant improvements in free recall performance relative to patients who received no instructions. Furthermore, patients in Jetter et al.'s (1986) study performed at the same level as controls on cued recall and recognition, even at the 1-day delay. These findings suggest that patients with prefrontal lesions can perform at or near normal levels when given strategy instructions or retrieval cues.

Consistent with this idea, Incisa della Rochetta and Milner (1993) tested patients with unilateral frontal or hippocampal lesions and controls on recall of categorised lists. During the study phase, some categories of words were presented in blocks preceded by the name of the category, whereas others were intermixed. Next, subjects were either tested by free recall or category-cued recall. Patients with left frontal lesions were impaired in all encoding-retrieval conditions except for the blocked-category encoding, cued-recall condition. Thus, these patients were able to perform at normal levels only if given pre-organised material and presented with these organisational cues at retrieval. Collectively, the results obtained by Jetter and colleagues (1986), Gershberg and Shimamura (1995), and Incisa della Rochetta and Milner (1993) suggest strongly that patients with prefrontal lesions exhibit impairments in self-initiated organisational processes that are particularly relevant to free recall performance. Furthermore, these results demonstrate that even if these processes are not initiated at encoding, patients can still benefit from organisational cues at retrieval.

Patients with prefrontal lesions appear to show particular impairments remembering the context surrounding an event, termed *source memory* (Johnson, Hashtroudi, & Lindsay, 1993). For instance, Janowsky and colleagues (1989a) taught patients with prefrontal lesions, age-matched controls, and younger control participants a set of 20 trivia facts (e.g. "The last name of the actor who portrayed Dr Watson in the Sherlock Holmes series was Bruce"). Later, participants were asked to recall these facts (e.g. "What was the last name of the actor who portrayed Dr Watson in the Sherlock Holmes series?"), as well as 20 facts that were not presented during the study phase. For each correct response, each participant was then asked to recall the most recent time the fact was learned. Although patients showed normal recall and recognition for the facts, at retention intervals of either 2 hours or 1 week their ability to indicate when the fact was learned was significantly impaired relative to controls.

Results from several other studies support the notion that patients with prefrontal lesions have poor memory for the temporal context of events. For example, Shimamura and colleagues (Shimamura, Janowsky, & Squire, 1990) found that patients with prefrontal lesions exhibited intact recognition and only mildly impaired performance on free recall for words or historical events. These patients were disproportionately impaired, however, when asked to temporally order the information they had learned. Similarly, Milner and colleagues (Milner, Corsi, & Leonard, 1991) had patients with unilateral prefrontal lesions and controls study a series of easily visualised words, representational drawings, or abstract designs. Periodically, participants were shown cards with two previously studied stimuli, and were asked to decide which was seen more recently. Patients with left frontal lesions were impaired only on recency discrimination for words, whereas patients with right frontal lesions were impaired on all three recency tasks.

In a follow-up to this experiment, McAndrews and Milner (1991) examined whether providing salient cues as to when items occurred could help patients with prefrontal lesions overcome their deficits in temporal organisation. In this study, patients with unilateral frontal lesions and controls were presented with a series of objects, one at a time, with instructions to name each object. Interspersed among these were a number of "action items" that the participant was asked to manipulate as well as name. Later, they made three types of recency discriminations: between action items, between items that occurred before and after an action item, and between two items that were not separated by an action item. Patients with left and right frontal lesions were impaired at all recency discriminations except for discriminations between two action items. In contrast, healthy controls did not show any differences across the three types of tasks, despite the fact that they were performing below ceiling (approximately 80 per cent in all cases).

One explanation of these findings is that there were fewer action items than non-action items, so these findings might reflect an abnormal susceptibility to interference in the patients (Shimamura, 1995). Alternatively, it is possible that, because encoding in this task was intentional, control subjects used organisational strategies to distinguish the temporal position of all of the items, whereas the patients were able only to organise the salient and temporally distant action items from one another.

These explanations cannot account completely for the results of a subsequent study by Butters and colleagues (Butters, Kaszniak, Glisky, Eslinger, & Schacter, 1994). As in McAndrews and Milner's (1991) study, patients with prefrontal lesions and matched controls were given recency discrimination tasks with objects that were either named or named and manipulated. In other study conditions, participants either imaged the objects visually, watched the experimenter manipulate the objects, or elaborated verbally on the function of the objects. In accord with previous studies (McAndrews & Milner, 1991; Milner et al., 1991), patients exhibited intact recognition for the objects and impaired recency judgements for named objects, imaged objects, and described objects. Importantly, patients and controls performed equally well at making recency judgements for objects that they had manipulated.

It is unlikely that failure to control interference can explain the patients' pattern of performance in this experiment, because patients faced potentially equal levels of interference for all items but were only able to perform intact recency discriminations on manipulated objects. An alternate explanation is that the object manipulation task involved the encoding of motor and soma-tosensory information as well as visual and cognitive information, and that patients with prefrontal lesions can perform recency discrimination when they have several sources of such information to draw upon. One interpre-tation of these results is that whereas normal individuals have the ability to specify the source information required to make recency judgements, patients with prefrontal lesions are limited in what they can retrieve and, as a result, require representations in several modalities to make such judgements (Johnson et al., 1993).

Accordingly, these findings suggest that an important facet of memory deficits following prefrontal lesions is an inability to use and evaluate retrieved information to make memory judgements (Johnson & Raye, 1998; Moscovitch, 1989). Recent findings suggest that, in addition to contributing to poor source memory, such memory monitoring deficits can also contribute to memory distortions in patients with prefrontal damage.

For example, several studies of patients with damage to the ventromedial prefrontal cortex (following rupture of an aneurysm of the anterior com-municating artery) have revealed significantly elevated false alarm rates on recognition memory tests (Delbecq-Derouesne, Beauvois, & Shallice, 1990; Parkin, Yeomans, & Bindschaedler, 1994; Parkin, Bindschaedler, Harsent, & Metzler, 1996; Rapcsak et al., 1998; Rapcsak, Reminger, Glisky, Kaszniak, & Comer, 1999; Schnider, Gutbrod, Hess, & Schroth, 1996; Schnider & Ptak, 1999; Schnider, Ptak, von Daniken, & Remonda, 2000). A similar pattern was observed in a patient with a large right frontopolar lesion (Rapcsak et al., 1999), and a patient with a right ventrolateral prefrontal lesion (Curran, Schacter, Norman, & Galluccio, 1997; Schacter, Curran, Galluccio, Milberg, & Bates, 1996).

Further evidence of a memory-monitoring deficit following prefrontal damage comes from a recent study in which event-related potential (ERP: see Chapter 2) and behavioural measures of recognition memory were recorded from controls and from patients with prefrontal lesions (Swick & Knight, 1999). The majority of patients in this study had lesions of the left lateral prefrontal cortex caused by stroke. Patients and controls exhibited equivalent hit rates and both exhibited ERP differences between old and new items thought to index recollection (Ranganath & Paller, 1999a). However, patients with prefrontal lesions exhibited significantly higher false alarm rates than controls. Based on this pattern of results, Swick and Knight (1999) concluded that episodic recollection was intact in the patients, but patients were impaired in the evaluation of new words that may have elicited some degree of familiarity.

Altogether, the available neuropsychological evidence demonstrates that prefrontal cortex is essential for the implementation of strategic, goal-directed processes. These reflective processes are not essential for episodic memory but serve to enhance memory formation, facilitate retrieval, and aid in the evaluation of retrieved information (Johnson, 1992). But these findings provide little evidence for the idea that prefrontal cortex implements processes specific to episodic memory.

Nonetheless, there are reasons to believe that human neuropsychological studies might underestimate the importance of prefrontal cortical regions to episodic memory. For example, the studies reviewed earlier typically had small sample sizes and were unable to subdivide patients into damage in subregions of lateral and orbital prefrontal cortex. Thus, if prefrontal regions make differential contributions to episodic memory performance, such effects might be obscured by the variability of lesion locations in group analyses. Furthermore, most patients in these studies had unilateral lesions, so their memory performance may have been supported by compensatory activity in the nonlesioned hemisphere (Chao & Knight, 1998). Results from one study showed that when stimuli were presented to the left or right hemifields, patients exhibited recognition memory deficits and corresponding alterations in ERPs for stimuli presented contralateral to the lesioned hemisphere (Nielsen-Bohlman & Knight, 1999; Fig. 4.1).

NEUROIMAGING STUDIES

Another important source of evidence regarding the contributions of prefrontal regions to episodic memory has come from neuroimaging studies of

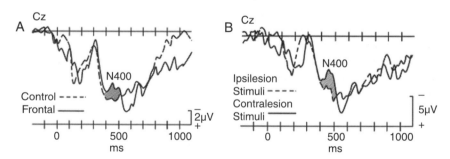

Figure 4.1. Results from an ERP study of recognition memory for objects in patients with lateral prefrontal lesions and matched controls. In this study, participants performed a continuous recognition task with objects presented to either the left or right hemifield. Behavioural results showed that, at short delays, patients exhibited recognition impairments relative to controls for objects presented to the contralesional hemifield. (A) Patients with prefrontal lesions exhibited an enhanced N400 component for these stimuli, relative to control subjects. (B) N400 amplitudes within patients with prefrontal lesions were greater for objects presented to the contralesional than the ipsilesional hemifield. These results suggest that, although patients with unilateral prefrontal lesions might exhibit intact recognition memory under most circumstances, impairments could be more apparent when stimuli are presented directly to the lesioned hemisphere.

healthy volunteers. Although neuroimaging results cannot reveal whether prefrontal regions are necessary for episodic memory, they can reveal insights into the functional organisation of the prefrontal cortex with a high degree of spatial resolution. Findings from these studies suggest that multiple prefrontal regions exhibit dissociable patterns of activity during episodic encoding and retrieval tasks (Buckner & Petersen, 1996; Nyberg, Cabeza, & Tulving, 1996; Tulving, Kapur, Craik, Moscovitch, & Houle, 1994; Wagner, 1999). Based on early findings from positron emission tomography (PET) studies of episodic memory, Tulving and colleagues proposed the Hemispheric Encoding Retrieval Asymmetry (HERA) model of episodic memory (Nyberg et al., 1996; Tulving et al., 1994). According to this model, left prefrontal cortex is more involved in semantic encoding of information into episodic memory, whereas right prefrontal cortex is more involved in episodic retrieval. Subsequent research, however, has revealed that both left and right prefrontal regions are active during encoding and retrieval (Buckner & Petersen, 1996; Wagner, 1999). These developments, in turn, have led to more specific hypotheses regarding functional contributions of prefrontal subregions to episodic memory processing. We will review findings of prefrontal activation during episodic encoding and retrieval and suggest how these findings might be integrated with the neuropsychological results reviewed earlier.

Several studies have reported activation in ventrolateral prefrontal cortex, including the inferior frontal gyrus (Brodmann's areas [BA] 44, 45, and 47) and precentral sulcus (BA6 and BA44) during intentional encoding (Buckner & Petersen, 1996; Wagner, 1999). Encoding activations in regions of dorsolateral prefrontal cortex in portions of the middle frontal gyrus (BA9 and BA46) have also been reported (Ranganath, Johnson, & D'Esposito, 2000). These results suggest that activation in ventrolateral prefrontal cortex tends to be lateralised according to the type of material that is encoded. For example, activation was greater in the right than the left inferior frontal and precentral gyri during encoding of faces or other non-verbal information; the opposite pattern was observed during encoding of words (Kelley et al., 1998; McDermott, Buckner, Petersen, Kelley, & Sanders, 1999; Wagner et al., 1998a). These findings are in agreement with prior neuropsychological findings (Milner, 1971) but no imaging studies have investigated what computational differences between the hemispheres might produce such specialisation (see Ivry & Robertson, 1998; Kosslyn, 1987; Marsolek, Kosslyn, & Squire, 1992, for discussion of some possibilities).

An important question regarding these activations is whether they are epiphenomenal or whether they actually reflect processes that contribute to memory encoding. Five recent event-related functional magnetic resonance imaging (fMRI) studies have reported that prefrontal activation during encoding actually predicts later memory (Aguirre, Zarahn, & D'Esposito, 1997; Brewer, Zhao, Desmond, Glover, & Gabrieli, 1998; Henson, Rugg,

Shallice, Josephs, & Dolan, 1999a; Kirchhoff, Wagner, Maril, & Stern, 2000; Wagner et al., 1998b). In these studies, participants were scanned during encoding of words (Aguirre et al., 1997; Henson et al., 1999a; Wagner et al., 1998b) or scenes (Brewer et al., 1998; Kirchhoff et al., 2000) and encoding activity was correlated with subsequent recognition judgements. Across these studies, encoding activation in the inferior frontal gyrus was greater for items that were subsequently remembered than for items that were forgotten. Furthermore, these subsequent memory effects were relatively right lateralised for visual scenes and left lateralised for words (Brewer et al., 1998; Henson et al., 1999a; Kirchhoff et al., 2000; Wagner et al., 1998b).

How does ventrolateral prefrontal cortex contribute to subsequent memory effects? One possibility is that these regions mediate "working memory" processes that act to enhance memory encoding (Aguirre et al., 1997; Wagner, 1999). For example, regions in the left inferior frontal gyrus have been associated with the selection and maintenance of semantic information (Thompson-Schill, D'Esposito, Aguirre, & Farah, 1997), associated with "deep" encoding (Craik & Lockhart, 1972). Another possibility is that ventrolateral prefrontal activity is sensitive to the novelty/familiarity of the item (Knight & Nakada, 1998) and that this information can be used to make recognition judgements (Yonelinas, Kroll, Dobbins, Lazzara, & Knight, 1998). Indeed, several studies have demonstrated enhanced ventrolateral PFC activation for novel relative to familiar stimuli (e.g. Buckner et al., 1998; Kirchhoff et al., 2000; Tulving, Markowitsch, Craik, Habib, & Houle, 1996), and patients with prefrontal lesions exhibit attenuated electrophysiological responses to novel stimuli (Knight, 1984, 1997; Yamaguchi & Knight, 1991; Fig. 4.2). Results from a recent study showed that intact monkeys exhibited enhanced memory for novel relative to familiar information, whereas monkeys with prefrontal lesions failed to show this effect (Parker, Wilding, & Akerman, 1998). These findings suggest that novelty-related modulations of ventrolateral prefrontal activity play a role in episodic memory encoding.

Although it is unclear precisely how ventrolateral prefrontal regions contribute to encoding, it is clear that these regions are also activated robustly during memory retrieval. For example, in one study, Ranganath et al. (2000; for additional discussion, see Chapter 1) used rapid presentation event-related fMRI to examine prefrontal activation during encoding and retrieval of objects. As shown in Fig. 4.3, the same regions of the inferior frontal gyrus were activated during both encoding and retrieval. Furthermore, a region in the right middle frontal gyrus was activated during both tasks. Although activation was more extensive and robust in the retrieval condition, these results suggest that dorsolateral and ventrolateral prefrontal regions implement cognitive processes that can be tapped by encoding and retrieval tasks.

In addition to dorsolateral and ventrolateral prefrontal cortex, results from several studies suggest that anterior prefrontal regions (BA10/46)

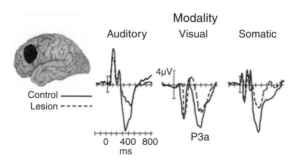

Figure 4.2. Electrophysiological evidence for attenuated responses to novel stimuli in patients with prefrontal damage (Knight, 1997). In these experiments, event-related brain potentials were recorded while patients with prefrontal damage, and matched controls, performed target detection tasks. In the auditory modality, targets and repeated non-target stimuli were pure tones, although irrelevant novel distractors (e.g. a dog bark, a ringing bell) were presented occasionally. In the visual modality, targets and repeated non-target stimuli were pure upright and inverted triangles; occasionally, irrelevant novel distractors (e.g. line drawings of objects or complex patterns) were presented. In the somatosensory modality, targets and repeated non-target stimuli were taps to the finger and occasional novel distractors consisted of brief random shocks to the median nerve. Novel stimuli across all modalities elicited a potential identifiable as the novelty P300, or the P3a. The magnitude of this potential was attenuated in patients with prefrontal damage, whereas electrophysiological responses to target and repeated non-targets were intact.

spanning the anterior middle, medial, and superior frontal gyri are particularly activated during retrieval tasks (Buckner & Petersen, 1996; Wagner, 1999). Unlike ventrolateral prefrontal regions, dorsolateral and anterior prefrontal cortex activation does not appear to reliably lateralise according to the type of material that is being processed (McDermott et al., 1999). Instead, the laterality of activation in these regions might be more dependent on the type of retrieval task that is being performed and the baseline against which this activity is compared (Nolde, Johnson, & D'Esposito, 1998a; Nolde, Johnson, & Raye, 1998b; Ranganath et al., 2000; Rugg, Fletcher, Chua, & Dolan, 1999).

For example, in their review of the neuroimaging literature, Nolde et al. (1998b) observed that relatively simple memory retrieval tasks revealed right-lateralised prefrontal activation, but that more demanding retrieval tasks were more likely to reveal left-lateralised or bilateral activation in dorsolateral and anterior prefrontal cortex (see Ranganath & Paller, 1999a,b, 2000, for relevant electrophysiological evidence). Interestingly, the types of retrieval tasks that elicited left-lateralised prefrontal activation bear strong resemblance to the types of source memory tests that are sensitive to prefrontal damage (Henson, Shallice, & Dolan, 1999b; Nolde et al., 1998a,b; Ranganath et al., 2000; Rugg et al., 1999). The findings of anterior prefrontal activation during blocked-trial studies of source memory could reflect a role for this region in the recollection of source information or in making the specific

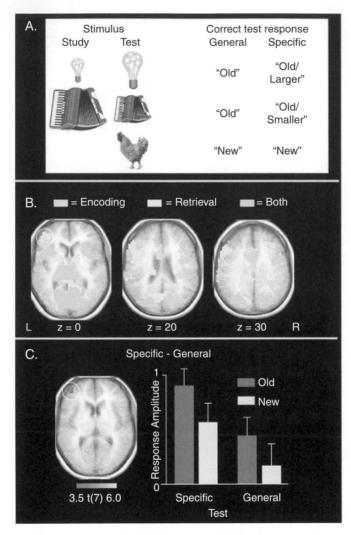

Figure 4.3. Results from a rapid presentation event-related fMRI study of episodic encoding and retrieval (Ranganath et al., 2000). (A) Examples of study and test stimuli and appropriate responses for each test condition. (B) Voxels were characterised according to whether they were activated reliably during encoding trials (blue), retrieval trials (yellow), or both (green). Bilateral regions in anterior and posterior inferior frontal gyri (BA44, BA45, and BA47), and right superior frontal gyrus (BA9) were active during both trial types. (C) The circled region in the left anterior prefrontal cortex was significantly more active during specific test trials than during general test trials. To the right, a bar graph shows response amplitudes within this region in response to old and new objects in each test condition. Activation in the left anterior hippo-campus (not shown) exhibited a similar pattern, suggesting that interactions between anterior prefrontal and hippocampal regions were crucial for the monitoring and evaluation of specific memory characteristics in the specific test (adapted from Ranganath, Johnson, & D'Esposito, 2000). See http://www.psypress.co.uk/brainscan-etc for a colour version of this figure.

memory attributions required by such tasks (Donaldson & Buckner, 1999; Ranganath & Paller, 1999a).

In one event-related fMRI study, Ranganath et al. (2000) examined prefrontal responses during item and source memory tests to differentiate between these explanations. Eight volunteers in this study were scanned during encoding of objects and during retrieval tests than included size-changed versions of studied objects and unstudied objects. During the "general test", instructions were to disregard the size changes and indicate whether each object was old or new. During the "specific test", instructions were to additionally specify whether each studied object was enlarged or reduced. Although test conditions were blocked, responses to old and new objects within each test block could be examined separately, because the sequence of old and new items in each test and the intertrial interval was randomised. Results showed that a region of the left anterior prefrontal cortex was more active during specific than general test trials, for both old and new objects. Because differences were seen for both old and new objects, it was unlikely that activation in this region solely reflected retrieval of learned information. Furthermore, because accuracy rates and response times for new objects were virtually identical between the two test conditions, this result could not be attributed to global difficulty or time-on-task differences. Instead, these results suggest that left anterior prefrontal cortex was implementing processes critical for the monitoring and evaluation of specific memory characteristics at retrieval.

NEUROPSYCHOLOGY AND NEUROIMAGING: INTEGRATING THE EVIDENCE

In summary, the neuropsychological and neuroimaging evidence we have reviewed converge on the idea that prefrontal cortex is not necessary for episodic encoding or retrieval. Instead, discrete prefrontal regions implement high level cognitive processes that can serve to enhance memory encoding and subsequent memory attributions. The degree to which these functions are tapped to perform the "Gestalt" functions that we refer to as episodic encoding or retrieval will depend on the task context. For example, ventrolateral prefrontal regions in the inferior frontal gyrus and precentral sulcus (BA6, BA44, BA45, and BA47) are activated robustly during both encoding and retrieval tasks, with the laterality of activation depending on the type of information that is being processed. Importantly, transient ventrolateral prefrontal activity has been observed during tasks that tax attentional selection or inhibition processes (Corbetta et al., 1998; D'Esposito, Postle, Jonides, & Smith, 1999), whereas more sustained activity in this region has been observed during working memory tasks (D'Esposito, Postle, & Rypma, 2000). In light of the attentional deficits observed in patients with ventrolateral prefrontal damage (Barcelo, Suwazono, & Knight, 2000; Knight, 1984, 1997; Knight, Scabini, & Woods, 1989; Knight et al., 1999), we propose that this region implements top-down control signals to bias processing in more posterior cortical regions (Knight et al., 1989, Barcelo et al., 2000; Miller, Erickson, & Desimone, 1996). Accordingly, activation of this region during episodic memory tasks may reflect selection and maintenance of relevant attributes of study items and test cues (Ranganath & D'Esposito, in press; Ranganath & Paller, 1999a,b, 2000)

Unlike ventrolateral prefrontal cortex, dorsolateral and anterior prefrontal cortex could be activated more reliably during episodic retrieval than encoding tasks. Furthermore, this activity can be reliably enhanced by increasing the specificity of memory judgements at retrieval. Interestingly, a similar pattern of dorsolateral prefrontal activation is evident in studies of working memory—that is, dorsolateral prefrontal cortex is sometimes active during working memory tasks that require simple maintenance, but activation in this region is further enhanced during tasks that require this information to be manipulated (D'Esposito, Postle, Ballard, & Lease, 1999; Postle, Berger, & D'Esposito, 1999). Accordingly, it has been suggested that dorsolateral prefrontal cortex acts to monitor and manipulate active memory representations (D'Esposito et al., 2000; Petrides, 1996), and that activity in this region might also exhibit a transient or sustained time course (D'Esposito et al., 2000; Ranganath & D'Esposito, in press; Ranganath et al., 2000), depending on task demands. These processes might be essential when specific attributes of retrieval cues must be compared with information retrieved from memory (Nolde et al., 1998b; Ranganath et al., 2000; Ranganath & Paller, 1999a, 2000).

Our review also suggests important directions for new research regarding prefrontal contributions to memory. For example, although left and right dorsolateral and anterior prefrontal regions exhibit different patterns of activation across episodic retrieval tasks (Nolde et al., 1998b), it is unclear precisely what these differences reflect. Another unresolved question is whether anterior and dorsolateral prefrontal regions make distinct contributions to episodic retrieval (Ranganath et al., 2000).

Finally, perhaps the most important unresolved question in the literature is how regions in orbital prefrontal cortex (BA11, BA12, BA13, and BA14) contribute to episodic memory. Unfortunately, little systematic work has been done to address this question in either the neuroimaging or neuropsychological literature. Given that this area of prefrontal cortex has extensive interconnections with medial and anterior temporal and retrosplenial cortical regions thought to be essential for memory formation, there is reason to believe this region also plays a special role in mnemonic processing—perhaps more so for emotionally charged material. Furthermore, some neuropsychological results suggest that amnesic patients with orbital prefrontal damage exhibit memory distortions, including spontaneous confabulation (Johnson, Hayes, D'Esposito, & Raye, 2001; Moscovitch & Melo, 1997; Schnider, 2000; Schnider & Ptak, 1999; Schnider, von Daniken, & Gutbrod, 1996). Evidence from PET studies also suggests that orbital prefrontal cortex is active during episodic memory tasks (Cabeza & Nybcrg, 2000), particularly when previously relevant information retrieved from memory must be suppressed (Schnider, Treyer, & Buck, 2000). Unfortunately, most of the fMRI studies reviewed earlier were insensitive to orbital frontal activity, most likely because of signal loss caused by susceptibility artefact. Recent fMRI methods have been developed, however, to image this region (Sobel et al., 1997). Application of these methods to event-related fMRI studies of episodic memory will undoubtedly help to identify the functional characteristics of this region.

In conclusion, neuropsychological and neuroimaging findings offer complementary and convergent perspectives on prefrontal contributions episodic memory. There is no module for episodic encoding or retrieval in prefrontal cortex. Instead, results suggest that anterior, dorsolateral, and ventrolateral prefrontal regions implement strategic operations at encoding and retrieval. Depending on the experimental context, different subregions of prefrontal cortex are engaged to enable successful memory performance.

NOTE

Address correspondence to cranganath@ucdavis.edu. Supported by NIH grants NS21135 (RTK) and AG08563 (CR), and by a grant from the McDonnell–Pew Program in Cognitive Neuroscience (CR).

REFERENCES

Aguirre, G.K., Zarahn, E., & D'Esposito, M. (1997). A test of the relationship between hippocampal activity and correct word recognition with trial-based fMRI. *Cognitive Neuroscience Society Abstracts, 4*, 63.

Barcelo, P., Suwazono, S., & Knight, R.T. (2000). Prefrontal modulation of visual processing in humans. *Nature Neuroscience, 3*(4), 399–403.

Brewer, J.B., Zhao, Z., Desmond, J.E., Glover, G.H., & Gabrieli, J.D. (1998). Making memories: brain activity that predicts how well visual experience will be remembered [see comments]. *Science, 281*(5380), 1185–1187.

Brutkowski, S. (1965). Functions of prefrontal cortex in animals. *Physiological Review, 45*, 721–746.

Buckner, R.L., Goodman, J., Burock, M., Rotte, M., Koutstaal, W., Schacter, D., Rosen, B., & Dale, A.M. (1998). Functional–anatomic correlates of object priming in humans revealed by rapid presentation event-related fMRI. *Neuron, 20*(2), 285–296.

Buckner, R.L., & Petersen, S.E. (1996). What does neuroimaging tell us about the role of prefrontal cortex in memory retrieval? *Seminars in the Neurosciences, 8*, 47–55.

Butters, M.A., Kaszniak, A.W., Glisky, E.L., Eslinger, P.W., & Schacter, D.L. (1994). Recency discrimination deficits in frontal patients. *Neuropsychology, 8*, 343–353.

Cabeza, R., & Nyberg, L. (2000). Imaging cognition II: An empirical review of 275 PET and fMRI studies. *Journal of Cognitive Neuroscience, 12*(1), 1–47.

Chao, L.L., & Knight, R.T. (1998). Contribution of human prefrontal cortex to delay performance. *Journal of Cognitive Neuroscience, 10*(2), 167–177.

Corbetta, M., Akbudak, E., Conturo, T.E., Snyder, A.Z., Ollinger, J.M., Drury, H.A., Linenweber, M.R., Petersen, S.E., Raichle, M.E., Van Essen, D.C., & Shulman, G.L. (1998). A common network of functional areas for attention and eye movements. *Neuron, 21*(4), 761–773.

Craik, F., & Lockhart, R. (1972). Levels of processing: A framework for memory research. *Journal of Verbal Learning and Verbal Behaviour, 11*, 671–684.

Curran, T., Schacter, D.L., Norman, K.A., & Galluccio, L. (1997). False recognition after a right frontal lobe infarction: Memory for general and specific information. *Neuropsychologia, 35*(7), 1035–1049.

Delbecq-Derouesne, J., Beauvois, M.F., & Shallice, T. (1990). Preserved recall versus impaired recognition. *Brain, 113*, 1045–1074.

D'Esposito, M., Postle, B.R., Ballard, D., & Lease, J. (1999). Maintenance and manipulation of information held in working memory: An event-related fMRI study. *Brain & Cognition, 41*, 66–86.

D'Esposito, M., Postle, B.R., Jonides, J., & Smith, E.E. (1999). The neural substrate and temporal dynamics of interference effects in working memory as revealed by using event related fMRI. *Proceedings of the National Academy of Sciences USA, 96*(13), 7514–7519.

D'Esposito, M., Postle, B.R., & Rypma, B. (2000). Prefrontal cortical contributions to working memory: Evidence from event-related fMRI studies. *Experimental Brain Research, 133*(1), 3–11.

Donaldson, D.I., & Buckner, R.L. (1999). Trying versus succeeding: event-related designs dissociate memory processes. *Neuron, 22*(3), 412–414.

Fuster, J. (1997). *The prefrontal cortex: Anatomy, physiology, and neuropsychology of the frontal lobes* (3rd ed.). New York: Raven Press.

Gershberg, F.B., & Shimamura, A.P. (1995). Impaired use of organizational strategies in free recall following frontal lobe damage. *Neuropsychologia, 33*(10), 1305–1333.

Goldman-Rakic, P.S. (1987). Circuitry of the prefrontal cortex and the regulation of behavior by representational memory. In F. Plum & V. Mountcastle (Eds.) *Handbook of physiology. Section 1. The nervous system.* (Vol. section I, vol. V, part 1, pp. 373–417). Bethesda, MD: Americal Physiological Society.

Henson, R.N.A., Rugg, M.D., Shallice, T., Josephs, O., & Dolan, R.J. (1999a). Recollection and familiarity in recognition memory: An event-related functional magnetic resonance imaging study. *Journal of Neuroscience, 19*(10), 3962–3972.

Henson, R.N.A., Shallice, T., & Dolan, R.J. (1999b). Right prefrontal cortex and episodic memory retrieval: A functional MRI test of the monitoring hypothesis. *Brain, 122*(Pt 7), 1367–1381.

Incisa della Rochetta, A., & Milner, B. (1993). Strategic search and retrieval initiation: the role of the frontal lobes. *Neuropsychologia, 31*, 503–524.

Ivry, R., & Robertson, L.C. (1998). *The two sides of perception.* Cambridge, MA: MIT Press.

Janowsky, J.S., Shimamura, A.P., Kritchevsky, M., & Squire, L.R. (1989a). Cognitive impairment following frontal lobe damage and its relevance to human amnesia. *Behavioral Neuroscience, 103*(3), 548–560.

Janowsky, J.S., Shimamura, A.P., & Squire, L.R. (1989b). Source memory impairment in patients with frontal lobe lesions. *Neuropsychologia, 27*(8), 1043–1056.

Jetter, W., Poser, U., Freeman, R.B., & Markowitsch, H.J. (1986). A verbal long-term memory deficit in frontal lobe damaged patients. *Cortex, 22*, 229–242.

Johnson, M.K. (1992). MEM: Mechanisms of recollection. *Journal of Cognitive Neuroscience, 4*(3), 268–280.

Johnson, M.K., Hashtroudi, S., & Lindsay, D.S. (1993). Source monitoring. *Psychological Bulletin, 114*, 3–28.

Johnson, M.K., Hayes, S.M., D'Esposito, M., & Raye, C.L. (2001). Confabulation. In F. Boller & J. Grafman (Eds.), *Handbook of neuropsychology* (Vol. 4, 2nd ed.). Amsterdam: Elsevier Science.

Johnson, M.K., & Raye, C.L. (1998). False memories and confabulation. *Trends in Cognitive Sciences, 2*, 137–145.

Kelley, W.M., Miezin, F.M., McDermott, K.B., Buckner, R.L., Raichle, M.E., Cohen, N.J., Ollinger, J.M., Akbudak, E., Conturo, T.E., Snyder, A.Z., & Petersen, S.E. (1998). Hemispheric specialization in human dorsal frontal cortex and medial temporal lobe for verbal and nonverbal memory encoding. *Neuron, 20*(5), 927–936.

Kirchhoff, B.A., Wagner, A.D., Maril, A., & Stern, C.E. (2000). Prefrontal–temporal circuitry for episodic encoding and subsequent memory. *Journal of Neuroscience, 20*(16), 6173–6180.

Knight, R.T. (1984). Decreased response to novel stimuli after prefrontal lesions in man. *Electroencephalography and Clinical Neurophysiology, 59*(1), 9–20.

Knight, R.T. (1997). Distributed cortical network for visual attention. *Journal of Cognitive Neuroscience, 9*(1), 75–91.

Knight, R.T., & Nakada, T. (1998). Cortico-limbic circuits and novelty: A review of EEG and blood flow data. *Reviews in Neuroscience, 9*(1), 57–70.

Knight, R.T., Scabini, D., & Woods, D.L. (1989). Prefrontal cortex gating of auditory transmission in humans. *Brain Research, 504*(2), 338–342.

Knight, R.T., Staines, W.R., Swick, D., & Chao, L.L. (1999). Prefrontal cortex regulates inhibition and excitation in distributed neural networks. *Acta Psychol (Amst), 101*(2–3), 159–178.

Kosslyn, S. (1987). Seeing and imagining in the cerebral hemisphere: A computational approach. *Psychological Review, 94*, 148–175.

Luria, A.R. (1966). *The working brain*. New York: Penguin.

Marsolek, C.J., Kosslyn, S.M., & Squire, L.R. (1992). Form-specific visual priming in the right cerebral hemisphere. *Journal of Experimental Psychology: Learning, Memory & Cognition, 18*(3), 492–508.

McAndrews, M.P., & Milner, B. (1991). The frontal cortex and memory for temporal order. *Neuropsychologia, 29*(9), 849–859.

McDermott, K.B., Buckner, R.L., Petersen, S.E., Kelley, W.M., & Sanders, A.L. (1999). Set- and code-specific activation in frontal cortex: An fMRI study of encoding and retrieval of faces and words. *Journal of Cognitive Neuroscience, 11*(6), 631–640.

Miller, E.K., Erickson, C.A., & Desimone, R. (1996). Neural mechanisms of visual working memory in prefrontal cortex of the macaque. *Journal of Neuroscience, 16*(16), 5154–5167.

Milner, B. (1971). Interhemispheric differences in the localization of pyschological processes in man. *British Medical Bulletin, 27*, 272–277.

Milner, B., Corsi, P., & Leonard, G. (1991). Frontal-lobe contribution to recency judgements. *Neuropsychologia, 29*(6), 601–618.

Moscovitch, M. (1989). Confabulation and the frontal systems: Strategic versus associative retrieval in neuropsychological theories of memory. In H.L.I. Roediger (Ed.), *Varieties of memory and consciousness: Essays in honour of Endel Tulving* (pp. 133–160). Hillsdale, NJ: Lawrence Erlbaum Associates, Inc.

Moscovitch, M. (1992). Memory and working-with-memory: A component process model based on modules and central systems. *Journal of Cognitive Neuroscience, 4*(3), 257–267.

Moscovitch, M., & Melo, B. (1997). Strategic retrieval and the frontal lobes: Evidence from confabulation and amnesia. *Neuropsychologia, 35*(7), 1017–1034.

Nauta, W.J.H. (1971). The problem of the frontal lobe: A reinterpretation. *Journal of Psychiatric Research, 8*, 167–187.

Nielsen-Bohlman, L., & Knight, R.T. (1999). Prefrontal cortical involvement in visual working memory. *Brain Research. Cognitive Brain Research, 8*(3), 299–310.

Nolde, S.F., Johnson, M.K., & D'Esposito, M. (1998a). Left prefrontal activation during episodic remembering: An event-related fMRI study. *Neuroreport, 9*(15), 3509–3514.

Nolde, S.F., Johnson, M.K., & Raye, C.L. (1998b). The role of prefrontal regions during tests of episodic memory. *Trends in Cognitive Sciences, 2*, 399–406.

Nyberg, L., Cabeza, R., & Tulving, E. (1996). PET studies of encoding and retrieval: The HERA model. *Psychonomic Bulletin and Review, 3*, 135–148.

Parker, A., Wilding, E.L., & Akerman, C. (1998). The Von Restorff effect in visual object recognition memory in humans and monkeys. The role of frontal/perirhinal interaction. *Journal of Cognitive Neuroscience, 10*, 691–703.

Parkin, A., Yeomans, J., & Bindschaedler, C. (1994). Further characterization of the executive memory impairment following frontal lobe lesions. *Brain and Cognition, 26*, 23–42.

Parkin, A.J., Bindschaedler, C., Harsent, L., & Metzler, C. (1996). Pathological false alarm rates following damage to left frontal cortex. *Brain and Cognition, 32*, 14–27.

Petrides, M. (1996). Lateral frontal cortical contribution to memory. *Seminars in the Neurosciences, 8*, 57–63.

Postle, B.R., Berger, J.S., & D'Esposito, M. (1999). Functional neuroanatomical double dissociation of mnemonic and nonmnemonic processes contributing to working memory. *Proceedings of the National Academy of Sciences USA, 96*, 12959–12964.

Pribram, K.H., Ahumada, A., Hartog, J., & Roos, L. (1964). A progress report on the neurological processes disturbed by frontal lesions in primates. In J.M. Warren & K. Akert (Eds.) *The frontal granular cortex and behavior* (pp. 28–55). New York: McGraw-Hill Book Company.

Ranganath, C., & D'Esposito, M. (in press). Prefrontal activity associated with working memory and episodic long-term memory. *Neuropsychologia.*

Ranganath, C., Johnson, M.K., & D'Esposito, M. (2000). Left anterior prefrontal activation increases with demands to recall specific perceptual information. *Journal of Neuroscience, 20, RC108*, 1–5.

Ranganath, C., & Paller, K.A. (1999b). Frontal brain activity during episodic and semantic retrieval: insights from event-related potentials. *Journal of Cognitive Neuroscience, 11*(6), 598–609.

Ranganath, C., & Paller, K.A. (1999b). Frontal brain potentials during recognition are modulated by requirements to retrieve perceptual detail. *Neuron, 22*(3), 605–613.

Ranganath, C., & Paller, K.A. (2000). Neural correlates of memory retrieval and evaluation. *Brain Research. Cognitive Brain Research, 9*(2), 209–222.

Rapcsak, S.Z., Kaszniak, A.W., Reminger, S.L., Glisky, M.L., Glisky, E.L., & Comer, J.F. (1998). Dissociation between verbal and autonomic measures of memory following frontal lobe damage. *Neurology, 50*, 1259–1265.

Rapcsak, S.Z., Reminger, S.L., Glisky, E.L., Kaszniak, A.W., & Comer, J.F. (1999). Neuropsychological mechanisms of false facial recognition following frontal lobe damage. *Cognitive Neuropsychology, 16*, 267–292.

Rugg, M.D., Fletcher, P.C., Chua, P.M., & Dolan, R.J. (1999). The role of the prefrontal cortex in recognition memory and memory for source: An fMRI study. *Neuroimage, 10*(5), 520–529.

Schacter, D.L., Curran, T., Galluccio, L., Milberg, W.P., & Bates, J.F. (1996). False recognition and the right frontal lobe: A case study. *Neuropsychologia, 34*(8), 793–808.

Schnider, A. (2000). Spontaneous confabulations, disorientation, and the processing of 'now'. *Neuropsychologia, 38*(2), 175–185.

Schnider, A., Gutbrod, K., Hess, C.W., & Schroth, G. (1996). Memory without context: amnesia with confabulations after infarction of the right capsular genu. *Journal of Neurology, Neurosurgery and Psychiatry, 61*(2), 186–193.

Schnider, A., & Ptak, R. (1999). Spontaneous confabulators fail to suppress currently irrelevant memory traces. *Nature Neuroscience, 2*(7), 677–681.

Schnider, A., Ptak, R., von Daniken, C., & Remonda, L. (2000). Recovery from spontaneous confabulations parallels recovery of temporal confusion in memory. *Neurology, 55*(1), 74–83.

Schnider, A., Treyer, V., & Buck, A. (2000). Selection of currently relevant memories by the human posterior medial orbitofrontal cortex. *Journal of Neuroscience, 20*(15), 5880–5884.

Schnider, A., von Daniken, C., & Gutbrod, K. (1996). The mechanisms of spontaneous and provoked confabulations. *Brain, 119*(Pt 4), 1365–1375.

Shallice, T. (1982). Specific impairments of planning. *Philosophical Transactions of the Royal Society London B, 298*, 199–209.

Shimamura, A.P. (1995). Memory and frontal lobe function. In M.S. Gazzaniga (Ed.) *The cognitive neurosciences* (pp. 803–813). Cambridge, MA: MIT Press.

Shimamura, A.P., Janowsky, J.S., & Squire, L.R. (1990). Memory for the temporal order of events in patients with frontal lobe lesions and amnesic patients. *Neuropsychologia, 28*(8), 803–813.

Sobel, N., Prabhakaran, V., Desmond, J.E., Glover, G.H., Sullivan, E.V., & Gabrieli, J.D. (1997). A method for functional magnetic resonance imaging of olfaction. *Journal of Neuroscience Methods, 78*(1–2), 115–123.

Swick, D., & Knight, R.T. (1996). Is prefrontal cortex involved in cued recall? A neuropsychological test of PET findings. *Neuropsychologia, 34*(10), 1019–1028.

Swick, D., & Knight, R.T. (1999). Contributions of prefrontal cortex to recognition memory: Electrophysiological and behavioral evidence. *Neuropsychology, 13*(2), 155–170.

Teuber, H.-L. (1964). The riddle of frontal lobe function in man. In J.M. Warren & K. Akert (Eds.) *The frontal granular cortex and behavior* (pp. 410–444). New York: McGraw Hill.

Thompson-Schill, S.L., D'Esposito, M., Aguirre, G.K., & Farah, M.J. (1997). Role of left inferior prefrontal cortex in retrieval of semantic knowledge: A reevaluation. *Proceedings of the National Academy of Sciences USA, 94*(26), 14792–14797.

Tulving, E., Kapur, S., Craik, F.I., Moscovitch, M., & Houle, S. (1994). Hemispheric encoding/ retrieval asymmetry in episodic memory: positron emission tomography. *Proceedings of the National Academy of Sciences USA, 91*, 2016–2020.

Tulving, E., Markowitsch, H.J., Craik, F.E., Habib, R., & Houle, S. (1996). Novelty and familiarity activations in PET studies of memory encoding and retrieval. *Cerebral Cortex, 6*(1), 71–79.

Wagner, A.D. (1999). Working memory contributions to human learning and remembering. *Neuron, 22*, 19–22.

Wagner, A.D., Poldrack, R.A., Eldridge, L.L., Desmond, J.E., Glover, G.H., & Gabrieli, J.D. (1998a). Material-specific lateralization of prefrontal activation during episodic encoding and retrieval. *Neuroreport, 9*(16), 3711–3717.

Wagner, A.D., Schacter, D.L., Rotte, M., Koutstaal, W., Maril, A., Dale, A.M., Rosen, B.R., & Buckner, R.L. (1998a). Building memories: Remembering and forgetting of verbal experiences as predicted by brain activity. *Science, 281*(5380), 1188–1191.

Wheeler, M.A., Stuss, D.T., & Tulving, E. (1995). Frontal lobe damage produces episodic memory impairment. *Journal of the International Neuropsychological Society, 1*(6), 525–536.

Yamaguchi, S., & Knight, R.T. (1991). Anterior and posterior association cortex contributions to the somatosensory P300. *Journal of Neuroscience, 11*(7), 2039–2054.

Yonelinas, A.P., Kroll, N.E., Dobbins, I., Lazzara, M., & Knight, R.T. (1998). Recollection and familiarity deficits in amnesia: convergence of remember-know, process dissociation, and receiver operating characteristic data. *Neuropsychology, 12*(3), 323–339.

PART TWO

Non-human primate studies

CHAPTER FIVE

Memory and the medial temporal lobe: Differentiating the contribution of the primate rhinal cortex

Mark G. Baxter
Department of Psychology, Harvard University, USA

INTRODUCTION

Neural structures in the primate medial temporal lobe are known to play a critical role in memory formation. The involvement of these structures in memory was discovered as a result of the severe amnesia in the patient H.M. following bilateral resection of the medial temporal lobes, in an attempt to treat his intractible epilepsy (Corkin, 1984; Scoville & Milner, 1957). Subsequent experimental studies have attempted to resolve the contribution of different structures within the medial temporal lobe to particular aspects of memory function.

This research, conducted primarily through experimental lesion studies in non-human primates, has established the importance of the medial temporal lobe in the formation of new memories; for instance, monkeys with medial temporal lobe damage are profoundly impaired in tests of recognition memory (Alvarez, Zola-Morgan, & Squire, 1994; Gaffan, 1974; Mishkin, 1978). These monkeys demonstrate normal memory at very brief retention intervals, but a profound impairment is manifested if the delay between study and test is extended beyond tens of seconds. The particular involvement of specific medial temporal lobe structures in memory, however, continues to be a subject of debate. This controversy revolves mainly around the relative importance of cortical and subcortical temporal lobe structures in memory: the entorhinal and perirhinal cortex (referred to together as the rhinal cortex) on the one hand, and the amygdala and hippocampus on the other.

This controversy originated, in part, because the method used to produce lesions of subcortical temporal lobe structures (the amygdala and hippocampus) also resulted in damage to other components of the temporal lobe, a topic reviewed in greater detail elsewhere (Baxter & Murray, 2000; Murray, 1992). The initial finding was that macaque monkeys with bilateral lesions of the amygdala and hippocampus, produced by direct surgical aspiration, demonstrated a severe impairment in stimulus recognition memory that extended at least to the visual and tactual modalities (Mishkin, 1978; Murray & Mishkin, 1984). The first indication that this deficit might not arise (exclusively) from damage to the amygdala and hippocampus, however, was the finding that lesions of the amygdala and hippocampus in which an effort was made to spare the overlying rhinal cortex produced a less severe impairment in recognition memory (Murray, Bachevalier, & Mishkin, 1985). Subsequent experiments demonstrated that damage limited to the rhinal cortex was sufficient to produce a severe impairment in visual recognition memory, one that was nearly as severe as that following the original aspiration lesions of amygdala and hippocampus (Meunier, Bachevalier, Mishkin, & Murray, 1993). Indeed, selective lesions of the amygdala and hippocampus with MRI-guided injections of ibotenic acid, sparing the rhinal cortex completely, were without effect on visual or spatial recognition memory (Murray & Mishkin, 1998).

Because lesions of rhinal cortex in monkeys impair visual recognition memory, as well as tactual–visual cross-modal associations, and visual paired-associate learning, it has been hypothesised that the rhinal cortex forms the core of a system for knowledge about objects (Murray, 2000; Murray & Bussey, 1999). The rhinal cortex is anatomically well-situated to perform such a role; it receives highly processed visual input from temporal cortical area TE, as well as input from other unimodal and polymodal sensory areas (for review see Murray, 2000; Suzuki, 1996). The first goal of this chapter is to discuss what functions in memory are performed by the rhinal cortex, versus those that involve the hippocampus and amygdala, structures that are heavily interconnected with the rhinal cortex and have traditionally been thought to serve particular roles in memory function. Specifically, the amygdala has been thought to play a role in stimulus–reward association, and the hippocampus has been thought to be involved in object and spatial memory, among other things. Recent technical advances in stereotaxic neurosurgery in non-human primates, which permit selective neurotoxic lesions of the amygdala or hippocampus without damage to subjacent cortical areas, have shed new light on the functions of these structures. The second goal of this chapter is to consider how different functions attributed to the rhinal cortex, including both perception and memory (Buckley & Gaffan, 1998a; Murray & Bussey, 1999) might be related to one another.

STIMULUS–REWARD ASSOCIATIONS: THE RHINAL CORTEX VERSUS THE AMYGDALA

Damage to the amygdala is associated with impairments in stimulus–reward learning (Gaffan & Harrison, 1987; Gaffan, Gaffan, & Harrison, 1988; Spiegler & Mishkin, 1981). The idea that the amygdala might serve a general role in associating neutral stimuli with an affective valence has been invoked to explain the bizarre effects of temporal lobe damage that includes the amygdala on emotional behaviour in primates, including the Klüver–Bucy syndrome (Brown & Schäfer, 1888; Iwai, Nishio, & Yamaguchi, 1986; Klüver & Bucy, 1938, 1939; Mishkin & Aggleton, 1981). Of course, most studies of stimulus–reward learning in amygdalectomised monkeys were based on amygdala lesions that would have damaged fibres of passage en route through or nearby the amygdala, the overlying temporal cortex, or both (reviewed by Baxter & Murray, 2000).

Recent experiments in macaque monkeys have suggested that the rhinal cortex plays a role in stimulus–reward learning, but probably only to the extent that it is required for identifying or discriminating the objects to be associated with reinforcement. That is, the psychological function of "stimulus–reward learning" is not a unique property of the rhinal cortex, but appears to be distributed throughout the rhinal cortex and the laterally adjacent temporal cortical area TE (at least for stimulus–reward learning with visual stimuli). The amygdala, on the other hand, does not appear to be required for basic stimulus–reward learning. However, the amygdala *does* appear to be required to adjust choice behaviour in response to changes in the value of a reinforcer, a function performed via interaction with the orbital prefrontal cortex.

Comparison of amygdala and rhinal cortex lesion effects on stimulus–reward association learning

Málková, Gaffan and Murray (1997) tested monkeys with neurotoxic amygdala lesions on visual discrimination for auditory secondary reinforcement. In this task, the monkey must learn which stimulus of a pair is correct based only on auditory feedback; touching the correct stimulus produces an auditory secondary reinforcer, whereas touching the incorrect stimulus produces an auditory secondary non-reinforcer. Four correct choices in a row results in delivery of primary (food) reinforcement, followed by presentation of a new problem. Monkeys with aspiration lesions of the amygdala are severely impaired in performance of this task (Gaffan & Harrison, 1987). By contrast, neurotoxic amygdala lesions produced no impairment in performance (Málková et al., 1997).

In an attempt to understand the origin of the deficit in stimulus–reward learning that had been observed in monkeys with amygdala aspiration lesions, Baxter et al. (1999) tested monkeys with lesions of the rhinal or perirhinal cortex on this task. These lesions produced an impairment in performance, but one that was relatively mild. Extension of the lesion to include area TE in one monkey produced a deficit comparable in magnitude to that originally observed in monkeys with amygdala aspiration lesions (Baxter, Hadfield, & Murray, 1999). The data from these studies are summarised in Fig. 1. The conclusion from these experiments was that association of visual stimuli with reward does not require the amygdala, but rather is a function that is distributed throughout the temporal cortex, including the rhinal cortex.

Additional data on the representation of objects in rhinal cortex come from a study by Thornton, Rothblat, and Murray (1997), who trained rhesus monkeys on sets of object discrimination problems 16 weeks and 1 week before surgery to remove the rhinal cortex bilaterally. These monkeys were dramatically impaired at postoperative retention of preoperatively learned

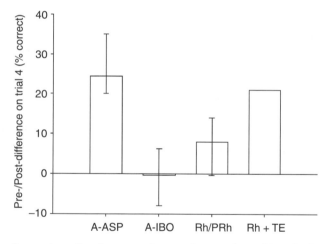

Figure 5.1. Comparison of performance of cynomolgus monkeys with aspiration lesions of the amygdala (A-ASP, $N = 3$, Gaffan & Harrison, 1987), rhesus monkeys with ibotenic acid lesions of the amygdala (A-IBO, $N = 4$, Málková et al., 1997), and rhesus monkeys with lesions of rhinal or perirhinal cortex (Rh/PRh, $N = 6$, Baxter et al., 1999) on visual discrimination learning for auditory secondary reinforcement. The height of each bar represents the group mean difference in trial 4 performance of problems given pre- and postoperatively. The vertical bars show the range of scores within each group. A severe impairment is evident in the monkeys with aspiration lesions of the amygdala, but there is no impairment in monkeys with ibotenic acid lesions of the amygdala and only a mild (but statistically significant) impairment in monkeys with lesions of rhinal or perirhinal cortex. Additional data is included for one rhesus monkey (Rh + TE) tested in this task, who received a rhinal cortex lesion that was deliberately extended more laterally to include cortical area TE (Baxter and Murray, unpublished observations). This monkey showed an impairment comparable to that observed in the monkeys with aspiration lesions of the amygdala in the original study by Gaffan and Harrison (1987).

object discriminations, but new postoperative acquisition of object discriminations, and retention of those discriminations, was at levels equivalent to those of unoperated control subjects. These observations provide further support for the notion that the association of objects with reward does not necessarily require the rhinal cortex. However, the finding that monkeys demonstrated retrograde amnesia for preoperatively acquired discriminations indicates that when the rhinal cortex is present, it is involved in storage of stimulus–reward associations.

An apparent contradiction in these sets of findings is that Baxter et al. (1999) observed an impairment (albeit mild) in learning of new discrimination problems in their monkeys with rhinal cortex lesions, whereas Thornton et al. (1998, 1997) observed no impairment in postoperative acquisition of new object discrimination problems. So is the rhinal cortex required, at least to some degree, in the acquisition of new stimulus–reward associations? This might be explained because the monkeys in Baxter et al. (1999) were learning object discrimination problems for a secondary reinforcer of a different sensory modality, rather than for primary reinforcement, as in Thornton et al. (1997, 1998). However, Baxter and Murray (2001a) observed an impairment of similar magnitude in monkeys with rhinal cortex lesions learning discrimination problems for primary reinforcement, so a difference in the type or modality of reinforcer probably does not account for the discrepancy. What seems more likely is a difference in the nature of the discriminanda in the different studies: two-dimensional computer graphic stimuli in Baxter et al. (1999) and Baxter and Murray (2001a), and three-dimensional objects in Thornton et al. (1997, 1998). This notion is generally supported by data from other studies of object discrimination learning in monkeys with rhinal (or perirhinal) cortex lesions; these data are summarised in Table 1.

Other experiments suggest a role for rhinal cortex, particularly perirhinal cortex, in object identification (Buckley & Gaffan, 1998a; Bussey, Saksida, & Murray, 1999; Murray & Bussey, 1999; Saksida, Bussey, & Murray, 1999). Indeed, deficits in new learning of stimulus–reward associations seem to be exacerbated by extensive preoperative training on similar discrimination problems, perhaps placing a particular burden on object identification capacity (Easton & Gaffan, 2000). A tentative summary of these findings would be that rhinal cortex damage produces a deficit in stimulus–reward association learning, only to the extent that the rhinal cortex is required to perceptually identify the discriminanda. Object representations formed in the presence of an intact rhinal cortex are stored at least partially in that structure, but the rhinal cortex is not necessarily required for new stimulus–reward learning.

TABLE 5.1

Postoperative performance on object discrimination tasks in monkeys following lesions of rhinal or perirhinal cortex.

Study	Lesion type	Discriminanda	Discrimination task	Magnitude of impairment
Gaffan & Murray (1992)	Rhinal	3-D junk objects	10-pair concurrent	None*
Thornton et al. (1997)	Rhinal	3-D junk objects	10-pair concurrent	None*
			Single pair	None
Buckley & Gaffan (1997)	Perirhinal	2-D computer graphic (ASCII)	Concurrent (20, 40, 80 pair)	Moderate*
			Concurrent with multiple foils	Greater impairment with more foils
Thornton et al. (1998)	Rhinal	3-D junk objects	60-pair concurrent	None
Buckley & Gaffan (1998b)	Perirhinal	3-D junk objects	10-pair concurrent	Moderate
		2-D computer (digital photographs of objects)	10-pair concurrent	Moderate
Baxter et al. (1999)	Rhinal or perirhinal	2-D computer graphic (ASCII)	Single pair for auditory secondary reinforcement	Mild
Buffalo et al. (1999)	Perirhinal	3-D junk objects	Single pair	Mild
			8-pair concurrent	None (?)
Easton & Gaffan (2000)	Perirhinal	2-D computer graphic (ASCII)	10-pair concurrent	Severe**
Baxter & Murray (2001a)	Rhinal (neurotoxic)	2-D computer graphic (ASCII)	Single pair	Mild
			8-pair concurrent	None

Notes:

* Impaired retention of preoperatively acquired discrimination problems; ** discrimination learning was overtrained preoperatively, no apparent deficit in retention of preoperatively acquired discriminations.

Access of object representations to reinforcer value

The same monkeys with neurotoxic amygdala lesions that were tested by Málková et al. (1997) on visual discrimination learning for auditory secondary reinforcement were subsequently tested on a reinforcer devaluation task. In this procedure, monkeys learned a set of 60 object discrimination problems. Half of the positive (rewarded) objects were consistently rewarded with one particular foodstuff (Food-1), and the other half were rewarded with a different, approximately equally preferred foodstuff (Food-2). After acquiring the discrimination problems, monkeys were confronted with sessions of critical trials in which the rewarded objects were paired with each other, Food-1 objects with Food-2 objects. Before some of these critical test sessions, the monkey was allowed to eat its fill of one of the two foods in the home cage before beginning the test session. Hence, because the monkey was satiated on that reinforcer, its value was decreased. In the critical test sessions following satiation, monkeys tended to avoid objects baited with the devalued (satiated) reinforcer, compared to baseline sessions (that are not preceded by satiation). Neurotoxic amygdala lesions abolish this effect (Málková et al., 1997). This effect requires interaction between the amygdala and orbital prefrontal cortex: monkeys with crossed unilateral lesions of these structures, combined with forebrain commissurotomy, showed a similar abolition of reinforcer devaluation effects (Fig. 2; Baxter, Parker, Lindner, Izquierdo, & Murray, 2000).

These results indicate that although the amygdala is not required for the formation of stimulus–reward associations, its presence is required if behaviour is to be adjusted in response to a change in the value of a reinforcer, or for representations of objects to gain access to the current value of a particular reinforcer. Remarkably, monkeys with rhinal cortex lesions do not display an impairment on the reinforcer devaluation task, avoiding objects paired with the devalued reinforcer just as control monkeys do (Thornton et al., 1998). Hence, the presence of the rhinal cortex is not required for adjustment of behaviour in response to a change in reinforcer value, or for access of object representations to the current value of a particular reinforcer.

Findings from these two tasks (visual discrimination learning for auditory secondary reinforcement, and the reinforcer devaluation task) represent a double dissociation of function between the amygdala and rhinal cortex, providing a basis for differentiating the roles of these structures in stimulus–reward association learning. Additional data from rats implicates the amygdala (specifically the basolateral amygdala) in the acquisition of reinforcing value by previously neutral stimuli (Hatfield, Han, Conley, Gallagher, & Holland, 1996). Hence, in the absence of the amygdala, stimulus representations seem to be unable to acquire reinforcing properties, nor do they have access to

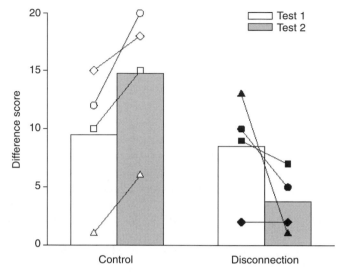

Figure 5.2.   The effects of reinforcer devaluation carried out before (test 1) and after (test 2) surgical disconnection of amygdala and orbital prefrontal cortex had been completed (Baxter et al., 2000). Rhesus monkeys received unilateral neurotoxic lesions of the amygdala, or unilateral aspiration lesions of orbital frontal cortex, with section of the anterior commissure and corpus callosum, before training on object discrimination problems and test 1. The complementary surgery was performed in the opposite hemisphere to complete the disconnection between test 1 and test 2. Difference scores (devaluation – baseline) for the control and disconnection group means are shown as bars, with the symbols representing scores of individual monkeys. Higher scores indicate a greater devaluation effect, evinced by avoidance of objects covering the devalued (satiated) food. Normal monkeys showed an enhancement of the devaluation effect in the second test, whereas operated monkeys showed a significant reduction of this effect in the second test.

information about the qualities of associated reinforcers. None the less, the association of these stimuli with reward is possible.

RHINAL CORTEX AND HIPPOCAMPUS IN RECOGNITION MEMORY

The study of the role of the hippocampus in stimulus recognition memory has a long and varied history. Initial experimental studies of the role of the hippocampus in memory in nonhuman primates met with a certain degree of failure, because monkeys with hippocampal lesions demonstrated relatively intact memory (e.g. Correll & Scoville, 1965), unlike the human amnesic patient H.M. An apparent resolution to this problem was proposed by Mishkin (1978), who suggested that conjoint damage to amygdala and hippocampus was required to produce amnesia. (H.M.'s surgery included removal of the amygdala.) However, other investigators observed a reliable effect of hippocampal damage alone on recognition memory (Mahut, Zola-Morgan, & Moss, 1982; Zola-Morgan & Squire, 1986). An apparent resolution of this conflict was provided by Ringo (1988), who suggested that the differences between studies could be accounted for by differences in the baseline performance of control subjects between the different studies, related to the degree of training they had received on the recognition memory tasks.

Studies of monkeys with lesions limited to the hippocampus have done little to elucidate the question of whether the hippocampus is essential for stimulus recognition memory. These experiments have focused primarily on recognition memory as assessed in the visual trial-unique delayed non-matching-to-sample (DNMS) procedure, a "benchmark" test of recognition memory function in monkeys. Varied effects of selective hippocampal damage on DNMS have been reported, ranging from no effect (Murray & Mishkin, 1998), to a mild deficit (Zola et al., 2000), to a more severe impairment (Beason-Held, Rosene, Killiany, & Moss, 1999).

A possible resolution of these disparate findings became apparent in a meta-analysis of these data (Baxter & Murray, 2001b), which also has implications for differentiating the contributions of the hippocampus and rhinal cortex to visual recognition memory (as measured by DNMS). The meta-analysis was performed by transforming percentage correct scores in DNMS into a d'metric, to permit comparison of results from different studies despite differences in performance of unoperated controls (Ringo, 1988). This meta-analysis had two main findings. First, when combined across the three studies, lesions limited to the hippocampus had a reliable effect on DNMS, but this impairment was significantly smaller than the DNMS impairment produced by lesions limited to perirhinal cortex (a loss in d', relative to controls, of 0.29 following hippocampal lesions, compared with 0.51 for perirhinal cortex lesions). Lesions that included the perirhinal cortex and at least one other component of the medial temporal lobe (entorhinal cortex, parahippocampal cortex, or hippocampus) produced an even larger deficit, a loss in d', relative to controls, of 0.89 on average; lesions of rhinal cortex produced the largest deficit, a loss in d' of 1.13 relative to controls. This result suggests that the perirhinal cortex makes a greater contribution to DNMS performance than does the hippocampus, and that lesions of rhinal cortex produce an even more severe DNMS impairment.

The second, and most surprising, finding concerned the relationship between the amount of hippocampal damage and the magnitude of the DNMS impairment. Typically, it would be expected that if a structure is essential for a particular behaviour, then behavioural impairment would increase as damage to that structure increases. This analysis for DNMS impairment and hippocampal damage found precisely the opposite pattern of results: the correlation between volume of hippocampal damage and

DNMS impairment was large and *negative*. That is, the larger the hippo-campal lesion, the smaller the behavioural impairment relative to controls. This result did not seem to be an artefact of combining data across the three studies: the correlation between hippocampal damage and DNMS impairment within each of the three studies individually was also negative. In contrast, when a similar analysis was performed on data from monkeys with lesions limited to the rhinal cortex, a significant correlation was again observed, this time large and positive. These relationships are illustrated in Fig. 5.3.

A number of possible explanations for this finding exist, and of course any conclusions drawn from the meta-analysis must remain tentative, pending the outcome of additional investigations that are aimed explicitly at testing the hypothesis that subtotal hippocampal lesions are more deleterious to DNMS performance than complete ones (see also Zola & Squire, 2001; Baxter & Murray, 2001c). The opposite relationship between amount of hippocampal or rhinal cortex damage and DNMS impairment suggests that these two structures make fundamentally different contributions to performance in the DNMS task. A speculative account of this result is that these two structures are employing different strategies in memory encoding, and that these strategies are competing for control of behavioural performance: the hippocampus uses an "episodic" strategy, whereas the rhinal cortex uses a "semantic" encoding strategy (Aggleton & Brown, 1999; Mishkin, Suzuki, Gadian, & Vargha-Khadem, 1997; Mishkin, Vargha-Khadem, & Gadian, 1998; Vargha-Khadem et al., 1997). By this view, DNMS might be solved based on an episodic recollection of the event of choosing the sample, or by relative familiarity of the objects on the choice trial (a property that can be encoded by inferotemporal cortex; Miller, Li, & Desimone, 1991, 1993). If these strategies are in competition with one another (e.g. Eichenbaum, Otto, & Cohen, 1994), a partially damaged hippocampus might still be able to compete for control of behaviour, providing a defective episodic recollection; this competition would diminish as the extent of hippocampal damage increases, providing the observed negative correlation.

Whatever the explanation, these findings (if borne out by further experiments aimed at directly verifying the existence of this inverse correlation) signal that the hippocampus and rhinal cortex must be playing very different roles in recognition memory, as least as indexed by the DNMS task. This finding is at odds with the view that medial temporal lobe structures, including the rhinal cortex and hippocampus, are jointly involved in a unitary form of memory processing (Squire & Knowlton, 2000; Zola-Morgan, Squire, & Ramus, 1994).

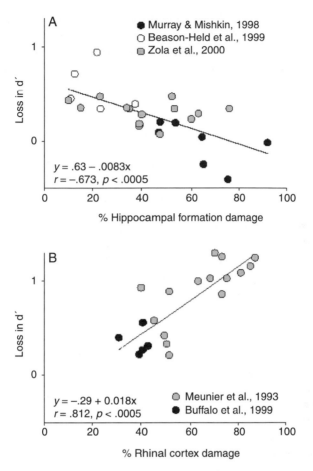

Figure 5.3. (A) Relationship between the magnitude of DNMS impairment (loss in d') and percent damage to the hippocampal formation (hippocampus, dentate gyrus, and subicular complex) for monkeys with selective hippocampal lesions ($N = 26$) from 3 studies (Murray & Mishkin, 1998; Beason-Held et al., 1999; Zola et al., 2000). Higher scores reflect greater DNMS impairment. Greater hippocampal damage is associated with smaller impairment on DNMS. (B) Relationship between DNMS impairment (loss in d') and percent damage to the rhinal (i.e. entorhinal and perirhinal) cortex for monkeys with lesions limited to the rhinal cortex ($N = 20$) from 2 studies (Meunier et al., 1993; Buffalo et al., 1999). Greater rhinal cortex damage is associated with greater impairment on DNMS.

OBJECT AND SPATIAL MEMORY: THE RHINAL CORTEX VERSUS THE HIPPOCAMPUS

One attempt to differentiate between the functions of the rhinal cortex and hippocampus might be made based on the modality of information processing. Specifically, hippocampal damage is associated with impairments in spatial cognition, and certain spatial navigation tasks activate the hippocampus in humans (Angeli, Murray, & Mishkin, 1993; Maguire et al., 1998; Maguire, Burke, Phillips, & Staunton, 1996; Morris, Garrud, Rawlins, & O'Keefe, 1982; Parkinson, Murray, & Mishkin, 1988). The hippocampus does not appear to be essential for stimulus recognition memory (Murray & Mishkin, 1998), although this conclusion is somewhat controversial (see the preceding section). As mentioned earlier, damage to the rhinal cortex is associated with impairments in stimulus recognition memory and stimulus–stimulus associative memory (Meunier et al., 1993; Murray, Gaffan, & Mishkin, 1993). Some experiments have reported a double dissociation between damage to the hippocampal system (by fornix transection) and damage to the perirhinal cortex, on tests of spatial and object memory, respectively (Gaffan, 1994). Most data from non-human primates, however, are somewhat difficult to interpret, owing to the less specific lesion methods used to damage the hippocampus in these studies.

As was the case for the amygdala, the use of MRI-guided stereotaxic neurosurgery to produce selective neurotoxic hippocampal lesions has permitted a more direct examination of the contribution of the hippocampus to memory in primates, facilitating differentiation of hippocampal function from rhinal cortex function in learning and memory. The few experiments to date, however, have not provided evidence for a clear dissociation of function between hippocampus and rhinal cortex, at least with regard to the functional domains that have been examined. Lesions of either hippocampus or rhinal cortex produce impairment in object reversal learning, although the impairment produced by rhinal cortex lesions is more severe (Murray, Baxter, & Gaffan, 1998); selective hippocampal lesions have also been reported to produce an impairment on rapid acquisition of single-pair object discrimination problems, although this effect was extremely mild and restricted to the first few trials of training (Teng, Stefanacci, Squire, & Zola, 2000). Selective hippocampal damage also appears to impair the ability to learn to use contextual information to solve visual discrimination problems (Doré, Thornton, White, & Murray, 1998). Lesions of the rhinal cortex and hippocampus produced impairments of equivalent magnitude on a spatial scene learning task (Fig. 5.4; Murray et al., 1998); indeed, a study using a related object-in-place learning task found that interaction between the fornix and perirhinal cortex was required for efficient learning of new scene problems (Gaffan & Parker, 1996).

The different contributions of the rhinal cortex and hippocampus to object and spatial memory remain to be elucidated. It is tempting to speculate that these structures interact in memory for complex scenes and places, by virtue of object representations held in rhinal cortex that are bound together into a representation of a scene or place in the hippocampus. Experiments with spatial navigation tasks in freely-moving monkeys (e.g. Rapp, Kansky, & Roberts, 1997) might shed further light on this question.

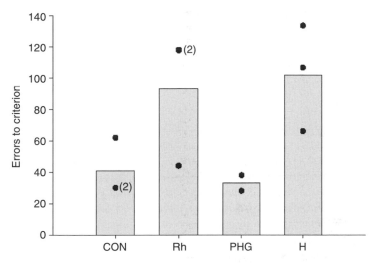

Figure 5.4.   Spatial scene learning in monkeys with lesions of hippocampus (H), rhinal cortex (Rh), or parahippocampal gyrus (PHG) (Murray et al., 1998). The height of the bars shows the mean errors to criterion (averaged across three sets of problems consisting of eight scenes each) for each group; the circles show the scores of individual monkeys in each group. "(2)" indicates that 2 data points overlap. Groups Rh and H are significantly impaired relative to controls.

OBJECT IDENTIFICATION AND RECOGNITION MEMORY FUNCTIONS OF THE RHINAL CORTEX

At least two roles of the rhinal cortex in memory formation can be identified on the basis of the extant data: object identification ("the knowledge that a particular object or class of objects is one and the same across the different instances in which it is experienced"; Murray & Bussey, 1999; Murray, Bussey, Hampton, & Saksida, 2000), and object recognition memory (literally "knowing the stimulus again"; Mishkin & Murray, 1994). On the one hand, these two functions must be intimately connected: it would not be possible to accurately recognise that one has seen a particular stimulus before if it could not be identified accurately. On the other hand, memories of objects based on individual features of the objects, rather than a representation of the object as a conjunction of features (Murray & Bussey, 1999; Saksida & Bussey, 1998), should be more susceptible to decay or interference. Conversely, being unable to remember a stimulus across multiple episodes of experience with it would also seem to preclude learning to identify a particular stimulus.

However, data already exist that suggest that these two functions of rhinal cortex must, at some level, be separable: visual recognition memory for three-dimensional objects is dramatically impaired by rhinal cortex lesions (Meunier et al., 1993) although learning of discrimination problems involving such objects is relatively normal after rhinal cortex damage (Thornton et al., 1998, 1997). Although different memory systems can subserve these different forms of learning and memory (memory versus habit, declarative versus procedural, and so forth), such data question the notion that there might be a unitary perceptual (object identification) and mnemonic (object recognition) function that can be ascribed to rhinal (or perirhinal) cortex (Murray & Bussey, 1999).

Testing of monkeys with rhinal cortex lesions on both object discrimination and recognition memory tasks also provides some insight into this question. Monkeys with neurotoxic lesions of rhinal cortex, studied by Baxter and Murray (2001a), were impaired on both object discrimination and delayed matching-to-sample. However, the magnitude of impairment on these tasks was uncorrelated; that is, the monkey that performed most poorly on object discrimination was not the most impaired on delayed matching-to-sample, and vice versa. Other recent data suggest that monkeys with perirhinal damage exhibit impairments in recognition memory even when their perceptual identification of the stimuli to be remembered is equated with controls (Hampton & Murray, 2000), providing further evidence for the separability of these functions.

An existing computational model of perirhinal cortex function can fully account for the effects of these lesions on discrimination learning (Bussey & Saksida, 2002), and make testable (and experimentally verified) predictions about the effects of these lesions on various discrimination tasks (Bussey et al., 1999; Saksida et al., 1999). Unfortunately, however, this model cannot describe effects of perirhinal lesions on recognition memory, because it is not a real-time model. Hence, a rapprochement of these views must await further computational modelling and experimental tests. It seems clear based on the present data that the effects of damage to perirhinal and rhinal cortex in monkeys cannot be exclusively classified as mnemonic; on the other hand, it is not apparent that a deficit in perceptual processing can necessarily explain the deficits either. The discovery that object identification and object recognition memory functions of rhinal cortex might be controlled by separable neural substrates or mechanisms would explain the dual effects of lesions of this structure. Furthermore, investigation of these mechanisms might give further insight into how cortical areas involved in higher-order visual processing interact both with information from other sensory systems (in the service of object identification) and with temporal lobe structures involved in memory.

REFERENCES

Aggleton, J.P., & Brown, M.W. (1999). Episodic memory, amnesia, and the hippocampal-anterior thalamic axis [with commentary]. *Behavioral and Brain Sciences, 22*, 425–489.
Alvarez, P., Zola-Morgan, S., & Squire, L.R. (1994). The animal model of human amnesia:

Long-term memory impaired and short-term memory intact. *Proceedings of the National Academy of Sciences, USA, 91*, 5637–5641.

Angeli, S.J., Murray, E.A., & Mishkin, M. (1993). Hippocampectomized monkeys can remember one place but not two. *Neuropsychologia, 31*, 1021–1030.

Baxter, M.G., Hadfield, W.S., & Murray, E.A. (1999). Rhinal cortex lesions produce mild deficits in visual discrimination learning for an auditory secondary reinforcer in rhesus monkeys. *Behavioral Neuroscience, 113*, 243–252.

Baxter, M.G., & Murray, E.A. (2000). Reinterpreting the behavioural effects of amygdala lesions in nonhuman primates. In J.P. Aggleton (Ed.) *The amygdala: A functional analysis* (pp. 545–568). Oxford: Oxford University Press.

Baxter, M.G., & Murray, E.A. (2001a). Impairments in visual discrimination learning and recognition memory produced by neurotoxic lesions of rhinal cortex in rhesus monkeys. *European Journal of Neuroscience, 13*, 1228–1238.

Baxter, M.G., & Murray, E.A. (2001b). Opposite relationship of hippocampal and rhinal cortex damage to delayed nonmatching-to-sample deficits in monkeys. *Hippocampus, 11*, 61–71.

Baxter, M.G., & Murray, E.A. (2001c). Effects of hippocampal lesions on delayed nonmatching-to-sample in monkeys: A reply to Zola and Squire (2ed). *Hippocampus, 11*, 201–203.

Baxter, M.G., Parker, A., Lindner, C.C.C., Izquierdo, A.D., & Murray, E.A. (2000). Control of response selection by reinforcer value requires interaction of amygdala and orbital prefrontal cortex. *Journal of Neuroscience, 20*, 4311–4319.

Beason-Held, L.L., Rosene, D.L., Killiany, R.J., & Moss, M.B. (1999). Hippocampal formation lesions produce memory impairment in the rhesus monkey. *Hippocampus, 9*, 562–574.

Brown, S., & Schäfer, E.A. (1888). An investigation into the functions of the occipital and temporal lobes of the monkey's brain. *Philosophical Transactions of the Royal Society of London Series B, 179*, 303–327.

Buckley, M.J., & Gaffan, D. (1997). Impairment of visual object–discrimination learning after perirhinal cortex ablation. *Behavioral Neuroscience, 111*, 467–475.

Buckley, M.J., & Gaffan, D. (1998a). Perirhinal cortex ablation impairs visual object identification. *Journal of Neuroscience, 18*, 2268–2275.

Buckley, M.J., & Gaffan, D. (1998b). Learning and transfer of object–reward associations and the role of the perirhinal cortex. *Behavioral Neuroscience, 112*, 15–23.

Buffalo, E.A., Ramus, S.J., Clark, R.E., Teng, E., Squire, L.R., & Zola, S.M. (1999). Dissociation between the effects of damage to perirhinal cortex and area TE. *Learning & Memory, 6*, 572–599.

Bussey, T.J., & Saksida, L.M. (2002). The organization of visual object representations: A connectionist model of effects of lesions in perirhinal cortex. *European Journal of Neuroscience, 15*, 355–364.

Bussey, T.J., Saksida, L.M., & Murray, E.A. (1999). Overgeneralization in monkeys with perirhinal cortex lesions. *Society for Neuroscience Abstracts, 25*, 789.

Corkin, S. (1984). Lasting consequences of bilateral medial temporal lobectomy: Clinical course and experimental findings in H.M. *Seminars in Neurology, 4*, 249–259.

Correll, R.E., & Scoville, W.B. (1965). Performance on delayed match following lesions of medial temporal lobe structures. *Journal of Comparative and Physiological Psychology, 60*, 360–367.

Doré, F.Y., Thornton, J.A., White, N.M., & Murray, E.A. (1998). Selective hippocampal lesions yield nonspatial memory impairments in rhesus monkeys. *Hippocampus, 8*, 323–329.

Easton, A., & Gaffan, D. (2000). Comparison of perirhinal cortex ablation and crossed unilateral lesions of the medial forebrain bundle from the inferior temporal cortex in the rhesus monkey: Effects on learning and retrieval. *Behavioral Neuroscience, 114*, 1041–1057.

Eichenbaum, H., Otto, T., & Cohen, N.J. (1994). Two functional components of the hippocampal memory system [with commentary]. *Behavioral and Brain Sciences, 17*, 449–518.

Gaffan, D. (1974). Recognition impaired and association intact in the memory of monkeys after transection of the fornix. *Journal of Comparative and Physiological Psychology*, *86*, 1100–1109.

Gaffan, D. (1994). Dissociated effects of perirhinal cortex ablation, fornix transection and amygdalectomy: Evidence for multiple memory systems in the primate temporal lobe. *Experimental Brain Research*, *99*, 411–422.

Gaffan, D., & Harrison, S. (1987). Amygdalectomy and disconnection in visual learning for auditory secondary reinforcement by monkeys. *Journal of Neuroscience*, *7*, 2285–2292.

Gaffan, D., & Murray, E.A. (1992). Monkeys (*Macaca fascicularis*) with rhinal cortex ablations succeed in object discrimination learning despite 24-hr intertrial intervals and fail at matching to sample despite double sample presentations. *Behavioral Neuroscience*, *106*, 30–38.

Gaffan, D., & Parker, A. (1996). Interaction of perirhinal cortex with the fornix–fimbria: Memory for objects and "object-in-place" memory. *Journal of Neuroscience*, *16*, 5864–5869.

Gaffan, E.A., Gaffan, D., & Harrison, S. (1988). Disconnection of the amygdala from visual association cortex impairs visual reward–association learning in monkeys. *Journal of Neuroscience*, *8*, 3144–3150.

Hampton, R.R., & Murray, E.A. (2000). Deficits following perirhinal cortex lesions: Representation or retention? *Society for Neuroscience Abstracts*, *26*, 545.

Hatfield, T., Han, J.-S., Conley, M., Gallagher, M., & Holland, P. (1996). Neurotoxic lesions of basolateral, but not central, amygdala interfere with Pavlovian second-order conditioning and reinforcer devaluation effects. *Journal of Neuroscience*, *16*, 5256–5265.

Iwai, E., Nishio, T., & Yamaguchi, K. (1986). Neuropsychological basis of a K-B sign in Klüver-Bucy syndrome produced following total removal of inferotemporal cortex of macaque monkeys. In Y. Oomura (Ed.) *Emotion – neural and chemical control* (pp. 299–311). Tokyo: Japan Scientific Society Press.

Klüver, H., & Bucy, P.C. (1938). An analysis of certain effects of bilateral temporal lobectomy in the rhesus monkey, with special reference to "psychic blindness". *Journal of Psychology*, *5*, 33–54.

Klüver, H., & Bucy, P.C. (1939). Preliminary analysis of functions of the temporal lobes in monkeys. *Archives of Neurology and Psychiatry*, *42*, 979–1000.

Maguire, E.A., Burgess, N., Donnett, J.G., Frackowiak, R.S., Frith, C.D., & O'Keefe, J. (1998). Knowing where and getting there: A human navigation network. *Science*, *280*, 921–924.

Maguire, E.A., Burke, T., Phillips, J., & Staunton, H. (1996). Topographical disorientation following unilateral temporal lobe lesions in humans. *Neuropsychologia*, *34*, 993–1001.

Mahut, H., Zola-Morgan, S., & Moss, M. (1982). Hippocampal resections impair associative learning and recognition memory in the monkey. *Journal of Neuroscience*, *2*, 1214–1220.

Málková, L., Gaffan, D., & Murray, E.A. (1997). Excitotoxic lesions of the amygdala fail to produce impairments in visual learning for auditory secondary reinforcement but interfere with reinforcer devaluation effects in rhesus monkeys. *Journal of Neuroscience*, *17*, 6011–6020.

Meunier, M., Bachevalier, J., Mishkin, M., & Murray, E.A. (1993). Effects on visual recognition of combined and separate ablations of the entorhinal and perirhinal cortex in rhesus monkeys. *Journal of Neuroscience*, *13*, 5418–5432.

Miller, E.K., Li, L., & Desimone, R. (1991). A neural mechanism for working and recognition memory in inferior temporal cortex. *Science*, *254*, 1377–1379.

Miller, E.K., Li, L., & Desimone, R. (1993). Activity of neurons in anterior inferior temporal cortex during a short-term memory task. *Journal of Neuroscience*, *13*, 1460–1478.

Mishkin, M. (1978). Memory in monkeys severely impaired by combined but not by separate removal of amygdala and hippocampus. *Nature*, *273*, 297–298.

Mishkin, M., & Aggleton, J. (1981). Multiple functional contributions of the amygdala in the monkey. In Y. Ben-Ari (Ed.) *The amygdaloid complex* (pp. 409–420). Amsterdam: Elsevier/North-Holland Biomedical Press.

Mishkin, M., & Murray, E.A. (1994). Stimulus recognition. *Current Opinion in Neurobiology*, *4*, 200–206.

Mishkin, M., Suzuki, W.A., Gadian, D.G., & Vargha-Khadem, F. (1997). Hierarchical organization of cognitive memory. *Philosophical Transactions of the Royal Society of London Series B*, *352*, 1461–1467.

Mishkin, M., Vargha-Khadem, F., & Gadian, D.G. (1998). Amnesia and the organization of the hippocampal system. *Hippocampus*, *8*, 212–216.

Morris, R.G.M., Garrud, P., Rawlins, J.N.P., & O'Keefe, J. (1982). Place navigation impaired in rats with hippocampal lesions. *Nature*, *297*, 681–683.

Murray, E.A. (1992). Medial temporal lobe structures contributing to recognition memory: The amygdaloid complex versus the rhinal cortex. In J.P. Aggleton (Ed.) *The Amygdala: Neurobiological aspects of emotion, memory, and mental dysfunction* (pp. 453–470). New York: Wiley-Liss.

Murray, E.A. (2000). Memory for objects in nonhuman primates. In M.S. Gazzaniga (Ed.) *The New cognitive neurosciences* (pp. 753–763). Cambridge, MA: MIT Press.

Murray, E.A., Bachevalier, J., & Mishkin, M. (1985). Rhinal cortex: A third temporal-lobe component of the limbic memory system. *Society for Neuroscience Abstracts*, *11*, 461.

Murray, E.A., Baxter, M.G., & Gaffan, D. (1998). Monkeys with rhinal cortex damage or neurotoxic hippocampal lesions are impaired on spatial scene learning and object reversals. *Behavioral Neuroscience*, *112*, 1291–1303.

Murray, E.A., & Bussey, T.J. (1999). Perceptual–mnemonic functions of the perirhinal cortex. *Trends in Cognitive Sciences*, *3*, 142–151.

Murray, E.A., Bussey, T.J., Hampton, R.R., & Saksida, L.M. (2000). The parahippocampal region and object identification. *Annals of the New York Academy of Sciences*, *911*, 166–174.

Murray, E.A., Gaffan, D., & Mishkin, M. (1993). Neural substrates of visual stimulus–stimulus association in rhesus monkeys. *Journal of Neuroscience*, *13*, 4549–4561.

Murray, E.A., & Mishkin, M. (1984). Severe tactual as well as visual memory deficits follow combined removal of the amygdala and hippocampus in monkeys. *Journal of Neuroscience*, *4*, 2565–2580.

Murray, E.A., & Mishkin, M. (1998). Object recognition and location memory in monkeys with excitotoxic lesions of the amygdala and hippocampus. *Journal of Neuroscience*, *18*, 6568–6582.

Parkinson, J.K., Murray, E.A., & Mishkin, M. (1988). A selective mnemonic role for the hippocampus in monkeys: Memory for the location of objects. *Journal of Neuroscience*, *8*, 4159–4167.

Rapp, P.R., Kansky, M.T., & Roberts, J.A. (1997). Impaired spatial information processing in aged monkeys with preserved recognition memory. *Neuroreport*, *8*, 1923–1928.

Ringo, J.L. (1988). Seemingly discrepant data from hippocampectomized macaques are reconciled by detectability analysis. *Behavioral Neuroscience*, *102*, 173–177.

Saksida, L.M., Bussey, T.J., & Murray, E.A. (1999). Perirhinal cortex and stimulus overgeneralization: Predictions of a neural network model. *Society for Neuroscience Abstracts*, *25*, 789.

Scoville, W.B., & Milner, B. (1957). Loss of recent memory after bilateral hippocampal lesions. *Journal of Neurology, Neurosurgery, and Psychiatry*, *20*, 11–21.

Spiegler, B.J., & Mishkin, M. (1981). Evidence for the sequential participation of inferior temporal cortex and amygdala in the acquisition of stimulus–reward associations. *Behavioural Brain Research*, *3*, 303–317.

Squire, L.R., & Knowlton, B.J. (2000). The medial temporal lobe, the hippocampus, and the memory systems of the brain. In M.S. Gazzaniga (Ed.) *The new cognitive neurosciences* (pp. 765–779). Cambridge, MA: MIT Press.

Suzuki, W.A. (1996). The anatomy, physiology and functions of the perirhinal cortex. *Current Opinion in Neurobiology*, *6*, 179–186.

Teng, E., Stefanacci, L., Squire, L.R., & Zola, S.M. (2000). Contrasting effects on discrimination learning after hippocampal lesions and conjoint hippocampal–caudate lesions in monkeys. *Journal of Neuroscience, 20*, 3853–3863.

Thornton, J.A., Málková, L., & Murray, E.A. (1998). Rhinal cortex ablations fail to disrupt reinforcer devaluation effects in rhesus monkeys (*Macaca mulatta*). *Behavioral Neuroscience, 112*, 1020–1025.

Thornton, J.A., Rothblat, L.A., & Murray, E.A. (1997). Rhinal cortex removal produces amnesia for preoperatively learned discrimination problems but fails to disrupt postoperative acquisition and retention in rhesus monkeys. *Journal of Neuroscience, 17*, 8536–8549.

Vargha-Khadem, F., Gadian, D.G., Watkins, K.E., Connelly, A., Van Paesschen, W., & Mishkin, M. (1997). Differential effects of early hippocampal pathology on episodic and semantic memory. *Science, 277*, 376–380.

Zola, S.M., & Squire, L.R. (2001). Relationship between magnitude of damage to the hippocampus and impaired recognition memory in monkeys. *Hippocampus, 11*, 92–98.

Zola, S.M., Squire, L.R., Teng, E., Stefanacci, L., Buffalo, E.A., & Clark, R.E. (2000). Impaired recognition memory in monkeys after damage limited to the hippocampal region. *Journal of Neuroscience, 20*, 451–463

Zola-Morgan, S., & Squire, L.R. (1986). Memory impairment in monkeys following lesions limited to the hippocampus. *Behavioral Neuroscience, 100*, 155–160.

Zola-Morgan, S., Squire, L.R., & Ramus, S.J. (1994). Severity of memory impairment in monkeys as a function of locus and extent of damage within the medial temporal lobe memory system. *Hippocampus, 4*, 483–495.

CHAPTER SIX

A role for extraperirhinal cortices in recognition memory? Evidence from neuronal recording and immunohistochemical imaging studies

E.C. Warburton and M.W. Brown
MRC Centre for Synaptic Plasticity, Department of Anatomy,
University of Bristol, UK

INTRODUCTION

In recent years considerable advances have been made in understanding the neural substrates of recognition memory. These advances have been possible because recognition memory can be studied in rats and monkeys as well as humans. This chapter concerns studies of brain regions in rats and monkeys that are involved in recognition memory processes. It presents a review of evidence chiefly from recording and immunohistochemical imaging studies of possible contributions to recognition memory of different cortical regions.

The core decision in recognition memory is a judgement of prior occurrence (Mandler, 1980). Such judgement is a common feature of everyday human life and can involve individual items or whole constellations of items; for example, have I met this person before or have I been in this room before? The judgement can involve more than an all-or-none decision (is it novel or familiar?); for example, it might also include information about the relative familiarity or recency of occurrence of a previously experienced stimulus. Moreover, when we recollect a previous experience, the successful remembrance of that experience implies its prior occurrence and thereby implicitly entails recognition memory. For example, recollecting where and when a person has been encountered previously provides convincing evidence for you having met that person previously. Additionally, such recollection supplies information concerning the context and associations of a stimulus beyond that of a simple judgement of the prior occurrence of that stimulus.

Given these considerations, it is not surprising that there is much evidence suggesting that, under appropriate conditions, subprocesses of recognition memory can be identified (Brown & Aggleton, 2001). Differing subprocesses necessarily have differing neural substrates. Thus, although recognition memory can commonly operate as an integrated entity, it has been possible to provide strong arguments that a system centred on the perirhinal cortex of the temporal lobe is responsible for the judgement of prior occurrence (familiarity discrimination) for individual items, whereas such judgement concerning arrangements of stimuli or recollective aspects of recognition memory is likely to involve the hippocampus (Brown & Xiang, 1998; Aggleton & Brown, 1999; Brown & Aggleton, 2001).

As evidence concerning the role of the perirhinal cortex in recognition memory has been recently reviewed elsewhere (Brown & Xiang, 1998; Murray & Bussey, 1999; Brown, 2000; Brown & Aggleton, 2001), this chapter will present only briefly electrophysiological findings concerning perirhinal cortex. It will chiefly review what is known concerning processing related to judgement of prior occurrence in structures that are anatomically connected to the perirhinal cortex. Although the perirhinal cortex has connections with many different structures, in this chapter only five cortical regions of particular interest will be considered: sensory association cortex afferent to perirhinal cortex, prefrontal cortex, the hippocampus, entorhinal cortex and the postrhinal cortex. The review centres on what can be deduced from single neuronal recording studies of prefrontal cortex and immunohistochemical studies of the hippocampus and postrhinal cortex. The great majority of the data comes from studies of visual recognition memory.

ANATOMICAL RELATIONS

As classically defined, perirhinal cortex (Brodmann's area 35) is polymodal. More recently, perirhinal cortex has been redefined to include area 36, and this broader definition is that chiefly used in experimental studies of the neural basis of recognition memory, and is that used in this chapter (Fig. 6.1) (Burwell, Witter, & Amaral, 1995). Information of all modalities is fed into perirhinal cortex from sensory association areas (Burwell & Amaral, 1998; Jones & Powell, 1970; Shi & Cassell, 1997; Witter et al., 2000). In particular, afferents come from high-level visual association cortex, area TE in the monkey and Te2 in the rat, but there are feedback connections as well (Burwell & Amaral, 1998) (Fig. 6.2). In turn, perirhinal cortex supplies inputs to entorhinal cortex and thence to the hippocampus, again receiving reciprocating connections from these structures (Witter et al., 2000). Postrhinal cortex in the rat has been suggested to be a homologue of parts (areas TF and TH) of the parahippocampal gyrus in the monkey: there are again inputs from many parts of sensory association cortex and reciprocal connections with the

(A) Monkey brain, ventral view

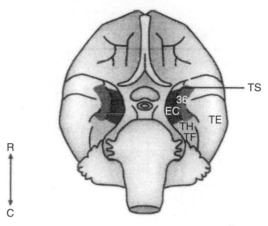

(B) Rat brain, lateral view

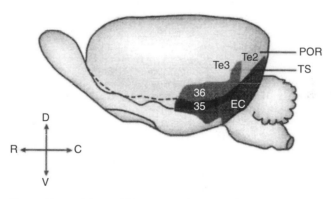

Figure 6.1. The positions of the perirhinal, entorhinal, parahippocampal, and postrhinal cortices are shown in the monkey (macaque) brain (A) and rat brain (B). The perirhinal cortex as defined here includes both Brodmann's areas 35 and 36. EC, entorhinal cortex; POR, postrhinal cortex; rs, rhinal sulcus; STG, superior temporal gyrus (reproduced from Burwell et al., 1995, "Perirhinal and postrhinal cortices of the rat: A review of the neuroanatomical literature and comparison with findings from the monkeybrain", *Hippocampus*, 5, 390–408, Copyright © 1995 Wiley-Liss, Inc. Reprinted by permission of Wiley-Liss Inc., a subsidiary of John Wiley & Sons, Inc.)

hippocampal formation. The perirhinal and postrhinal cortices seem to participate in parallel but somewhat independent anatomical circuits through the hippocampal formation (Witter, Groenewegen, Lopes da Silva, & Lohman 1989). In addition, parts of the prefrontal cortex are closely interconnected

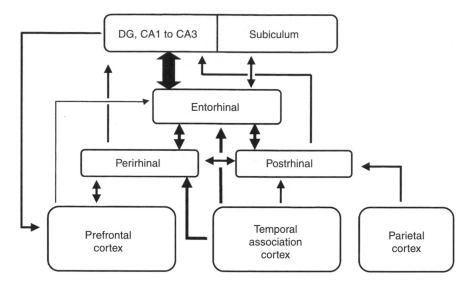

Figure 6.2. Connectional diagram showing the parallel routes by which sensory information from the temporal association cortex and parietal cortex reaches the perirhinal and postrhinal cortices, and from there reaches the hippocampus Also shown are the routes by which the prefrontal cortex can interact with the perirhinal cortex and the hippocampus. The thickness of the arrows signifies the size of the projection.

with the perirhinal cortex and adjacent temporal cortical regions by corticocortical fibres, although information from these regions can also reach prefrontal cortex via the thalamus.

PERIRHINAL NEURONAL RESPONSES AND THEIR RELATION TO JUDGEMENTS OF PRIOR OCCURRENCE

Recordings made in monkey anterior inferior temporal cortex, including perirhinal cortex, have established that the responses of ~25 per cent of the neurons in this region are reduced if a visual stimulus has been seen previously (Brown, Wilson, & Riches, 1987; Desimone, 1996, Ringo, 1996; Brown & Xiang, 1998; Xiang and Brown, 1998a). The response reduction carries information concerning the prior occurrence of stimuli. This information is sufficient to potentially allow solution of many recognition memory tasks (Brown & Xiang, 1998, Brown, 2000). Thus the response changes carry information concerning the relative familiarity and recency of occurrence of specific stimuli (Fahy, Riches, & Brown, 1993; Li, Miller, & Desimone, 1993; Miller, Li, & Desimone, 1993; Xiang & Brown, 1998a). They demonstrate single trial learning that is not disrupted by distracting intervening stimulus presentations and, in many cases, signal information concerning prior occurrences that happened the previous day (Fahy et al., 1993; Brown & Xiang, 1998; Xiang & Brown, 1998a) so that the information has been retained for 24 hours or more. As a population, the responses signal prior occurrence very fast (population latency ~75ms) and have a very large storage capacity (Brown & Xiang, 1998; Xiang & Brown, 1998a). It has been possible to develop a neural network model based on such changes in neuronal responses (Bogacz, Brown, & Giraud-Carrier, 1999, 2001). The model uses biologically plausible parameters and Hebbian learning to achieve very fast and efficient familiarity discrimination with very high storage capacity (Bogacz et al., 1999, 2001). The existence of such a model establishes that such responses can potentially be used to effect familiarity discrimination (although it does not establish that the brain uses the precise parameters or architecture of the model). Such response changes can also be found in rats (Zhu, Brown, McCabe, & Aggleton, 1995a). Moreover, in rats the population changes in responsiveness to novel and familiar stimuli have been demonstrated using immunohistochemistry for a marker of neuronal activation, the protein products Fos of the immediate early gene c-*fos*. Again, this method shows that novel visual stimuli produce greater neuronal activation in perirhinal cortex than do familiar stimuli (Zhu et al., 1995a, 1996; Wan, Aggleton, & Brown, 1999).

In spite of numerous recording studies in perirhinal and adjacent anterior inferior temporal cortices, such response reductions are the only known potential substrate of general familiarity discrimination (Brown, 2000; Brown & Xiang, 1998; Xiang & Brown, 1998a). There are four other activity changes observed during specific recognition memory tasks—delay activity, response enhancements, match–mismatch differences, and correlated firing— but none of these has yet been shown to satisfy the requirements of a general as opposed to a particular familiarity discrimination substrate. The first three have been demonstrated in tasks that are most readily solved using short-term memory or attentive mechanisms. Thus delay activity between sample and choice presentations (Fuster & Jervey, 1981; Miller and Desimone, 1994; Miyashita & Chang, 1988;) and increased responses to repeated target stimuli (Miller & Desimone, 1994) have not been shown for situations where more than one stimulus has to be held in mind at a time or in situations other than the specific trained procedure. Such activity changes might well be important to the judgement of prior occurrence when one stimulus must be remembered until it recurs or the repeated occurrence of a distracter differentiated from that of a target. However, in everyday life, recognition memory more commonly involves stimuli whose eventual recurrence is not at all predictable. Similarly, differences in neuronal responses on match and mismatch trials of delayed matching or non-matching tasks with small stimulus sets (Brown, 1996; Gross, Rochamiranda, & Bender, 1972; Li et al., 1993; Riches, Wilson, & Brown, 1991; Ringo, 1996; Wood, Didchenko, & Eichenbaum, 1999), and hence frequently repeating stimuli, can be distinguished from the response reductions seen to infrequently repeated stimuli (Riches et al., 1991): these match–mismatch differences do not encode the relative familiarity of stimuli; thus they cannot provide a substrate for general familiarity discrimination (Brown & Aggleton, 2001; Brown & Xiang, 1998, Riches et al., 1991), although they are likely to be important for the solution of repetitious recency discrimination tasks (Young, Otto, Fox, & Eichenbaum, 1997). Correlated neuronal firing is likely to contribute to information processing, but it has not yet been shown to provide information additional to or at as early a latency as that provided by firing rate changes (Xiang & Brown, 1997a, b; Brown & Xiang, 1998). By contrast, neuronal response reductions are found in all investigated situations where infrequently presented stimuli are repeated, even when there are many presentations of other stimuli between sample and choice and many stimuli have to be remembered simultaneously (Brown and Xiang, 1998; Xiang and Brown, 1998a). Such response reductions are found in rats as well as monkeys, and also in human imaging studies (Brewer, Zhao, Desmond, Glover, & Gabrieli, 1998; Brown & Xiang, 1998; Cho et al., 2000a; Duzel, Yonelinas, Mangun, Heinze, & Tulving, 1997; Fernandez et al., 1999; Henson, Rugg, Shallice, Josephs, & Dolan, 1999; Zhu, Brown, & Aggleton, 1995b). They also occur whether or not an animal is performing a recognition memory task and, indeed, even if the animal has never been trained in a recognition memory task (Brown and Xiang, 1998; Fahy et al., 1993; Riches et al., 1991; Zhu et al., 1995b).

The synaptic changes responsible for such response reductions are not known. Possible candidates might be provided by studying processes underlying long-term depression (LTD) or long-term potentiation (LTP) (Brown, 2000, Brown, & Xiang, 1998). Both types of long-term synaptic plastic change can be found in slices of perirhinal cortex maintained *in vitro* (Cho et al., 2000b; Ziakopoulos, Brown, & Bashir, 1999), but attempts have only recently begun to investigate links between such synaptic plastic changes and processes underlying recognition memory (Brown, 2000; Brown, & Xiang, 1998; Brown, Warburton, & Duguid, 2000).

COMPARISON OF NEURONAL RESPONSIVENESS IN SENSORY ASSOCIATION CORTICES WITH THAT IN PERIRHINAL CORTEX

Sensory association areas are found adjacent to perirhinal cortex and are reciprocally connected to it (Burwell et al., 1995). The visual association areas adjacent to perirhinal cortex are area TE in the monkey and area Te2 in the rat. This visual association cortex in both the rat and the monkey contains neurons whose responses signal the prior occurrence of visual stimuli (Brown & Xiang, 1998; Riches et al., 1991; Zhu et al., 1995b).

In the monkey, for which more data are available, neuronal response characteristics for visual stimuli in anterior TE are similar to those in perirhinal cortex, an exception being a greater incidence of certain response changes demonstrating evidence of very long memory for prior occurrence in perirhinal cortex (Xiang & Brown, 1998a). Thus, as in perirhinal cortex, the responses of individual neurons signal information concerning the relative familiarity or recency of occurrence of visual stimuli by response reductions for previously encountered stimuli. Population measures of the latencies of response changes on repetition of visual stimuli indicate that the changes are first generated in anterior TE (although the longer memory spans of neurons in perirhinal cortex indicate that changes might additionally be generated in perirhinal cortex) (Brown & Xiang, 1998; Xiang & Brown, 1998a). The changes occur in anterior TE so soon after the onset of a stimulus that it is not possible for these initial changes to be fed back from distant regions such as the hippocampus or prefrontal cortex (Brown & Xiang, 1998; Miller & Desimone, 1993; Xiang & Brown, 1998a), although this does not exclude later parts of these responses being under such influences. Again, in Te2 in the rat the reduced neuronal responsiveness for familiar compared to novel visual stimuli can be demonstrated using Fos immunohistochemistry (Wan et al., 1999; Zhu et al., 1995a; Zhu, McCabe, Brown, & Aggleton, 1996).

More posteriorly in area TE of the monkey, response reductions on stimulus repetition are also found, but the reductions fade faster than those produced more anteriorly (Bayliss & Rolls, 1987; Fahy et al., 1993). Similarly, response reductions have also been described in more posterior visual cortices, but do not appear to span time intervals of more than a few seconds (Maunsell, Sclar, Nealey, & DePriest, 1991; Vogels, Sary, & Orban, 1995). These results indicate that lasting response changes are not initially generated in earlier parts of the visual pathway than anterior TE. Indeed, there are grounds for not expecting such response changes to be first generated in early parts of the visual pathway. To make judgements of the prior occurrence of any individual member of the theoretically huge numbers of complex stimuli that might be encountered in a lifetime, it is necessary to be able to discriminate accurately amongst the physical features of all these stimuli. It is unlikely that such high-level visual discrimination can be completed before processing that involves area TE. Accordingly, judgement of prior occurrence for such stimuli is unlikely to be possible before the level of processing occurring in TE has been achieved. Moreover, individual physical features are likely to occur with increasing frequency as they become simpler and hence possessed by increasingly large classes of stimuli. Thus, such individual features are likely to be encountered frequently (as belonging to many different whole items). Accordingly, judging the prior occurrence of such simple individual features in isolation will provide correspondingly less useful information concerning the prior occurrence of whole items not encountered in the very recent past.

Recent work on the auditory system has demonstrated a critical role for auditory association cortex in judging the prior occurrence of sounds (Kowalska, 2000). In contrast to the results using visual stimuli, the integrity of perirhinal cortex seems not to be crucial in the dog or the monkey (Kowalska & Kuśmierek, 1997; Kowalska, Kuśmierek, & Kosmal, 1998; Saunders, Fritz, & Miskin, 1998). Using the Fos immunohistochemical imaging technique in the rat, significantly greater neuronal activation was evoked by novel than by familiar sounds in auditory association cortex (area Te3), but not in perirhinal cortex (Wan, Warburton, Kowalska, & Brown, 2001). These findings for auditory stimuli raise the possibility that the involvement of perirhinal cortex depends on the nature of the stimuli whose familiarity must be judged. For multimodal stimuli it would seem plausible that perirhinal cortex would be involved, as this region receives inputs from all the sensory systems so allowing cross-modal information to be processed there; by contrast, the sensory association cortices are likely to be dominated by information from a single modality. However, the involvement of perirhinal cortex in judging the prior occurrence of multimodal stimuli remains to be investigated. It has also been argued that perirhinal cortex has a specific role in the processing and hence perception of objects as entities rather than as a number of individual features (Buckley & Gaffan, 1997; 1998; Murray & Bussey, 1999). With such a view it might be supposed that the sensory association cortices would contribute to the judgement of prior occurrence of a stimulus by providing information through their neuronal responsiveness to the relative familiarity of the stimulus's complex individual features: perirhinal cortex would judge the familiarity of the stimulus as an entire object. In such cases, the difference between the involvement of the perirhinal cortex in auditory and visual recognition memory process might relate to the nature of the stimuli used and the way these are processed. However, alternatively, it is possible that, for the auditory system, other parahippocampal brain regions play a role corresponding to that of the perirhinal cortex in the visual system (Wan et al., unpublished observations).

COMPARISON OF NEURONAL RESPONSIVENESS IN PREFRONTAL CORTEX WITH THAT IN PERIRHINAL CORTEX

Both recording and lesion studies suggest an important involvement of prefrontal cortex in recognition memory processes, although both sets of data suggest that perirhinal processes are not wholly dependent on prefrontal cortex. Thus prefrontal lesions have smaller effects on delayed matching-to-sample than do perirhinal lesions (Bachevalier & Mishkin, 1986; Meunier, Bachevalier, & Mishkin, 1997). In addition, there is evidence of an interaction between the perirhinal cortex and the frontal cortex in recognition memory processes. A series of disconnection studies have showed that crossed lesions of the perirhinal cortex and frontal lobe produce a large deficit in visual object recognition memory (Parker & Gaffan, 1998).

What is known about prefrontal neuronal responses signalling information of potential use to recognition memory? There have been a number of studies of prefrontal neuronal responses during the performance of recognition memory tasks by monkeys (Fuster, 1973; Fuster & Alexander, 1971; Kojima & Goldman-Rakic, 1982; Miller, Erickson, & Desimone, 1996; Ramus & Eichenbaum, 2000; Rainer, Asaad, & Miller, 1998a,b; Wilson, Scalaidhe, & Goldman-Rakic, 1993). The studies agree in finding little evidence in dorsolateral prefrontal cortex of neuronal responses carrying information concerning discrimination of the familiarity of individual stimulus items. However, many neurons (~50 per cent of the visually responsive neurons) in ventral and medial prefrontal areas, as well as in the anterior cingulate gyrus, do signal such information (Miller et al., 1996; Xiang & Brown, 1998b).

The most striking difference from the findings in anterior inferior temporal cortex is that response changes, in prefrontal neurons, when infrequently occurring stimuli are repeated are more commonly increases than decreases (Miller et al., 1996; Xiang & Brown, 1998b). Thus, novel stimuli typically evoke smaller responses than do familiar stimuli. In anterior inferior temporal cortex, the incidence of responses that increase with stimulus repetition is less than the chance expectation (Miller et al., 1996; Xiang & Brown, 2000) except after specialised training (Miller & Desimone, 1994). In perirhinal cortex, if both highly familiar and novel stimuli are used in a serial recognition task in which a decision about the prior occurrence of an individual stimulus has to be made on each trial, three types of neuronal response change are commonly found (Xiang and Brown, 1998a). These types of response change have been named after the type of information they signal under these circumstances as "novelty", "familiarity", and "recency" responses, and make up over 90 per cent of the observed response changes (Xiang & Brown, 1998a). Response changes in prefrontal cortex can be similarly categorised (Xiang & Brown, 1998b). In prefrontal cortex, novelty neurones respond only weakly to first presentations of a novel stimulus but more strongly when that stimulus is repeated or when a highly familiar stimulus is shown, i.e. the inverse pattern to that found in anterior inferior temporal cortex. Similarly inverted from the anterior inferior temporal cortex pattern, familiarity responses are stronger to both the first and repeat presentations of highly familiar stimuli but weaker to the first or second presentation of an initially novel stimulus, and recency responses are stronger to the second than to the first presentations of both novel and highly familiar stimuli (Fig. 6.3). In monkey anterior inferior temporal cortex, there are no descriptions of inhibitory responses (i.e. ones where the activity is reduced rather than enhanced on stimulus presentation) that change with stimulus

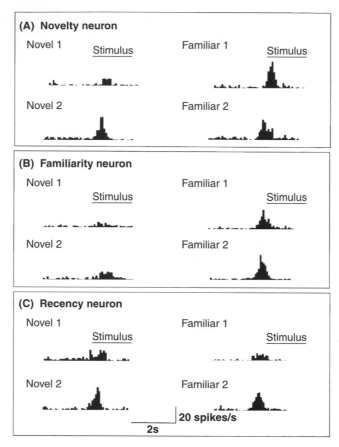

Figure 6.3. Repetition-related neuronal responses of neurons in the prefrontal cortex. (A) Novelty neuron; (B) familiarity neuron; (C) recency neuron. Note the stronger response of the novelty and familiarity neurones to the second presentation of the stimulus compared to the first.

repetition (Sobotka & Ringo, 1994; Brown & Xiang, 1998). However, such changes have been found in prefrontal cortex, again the response (the decrease in activity) being greater for familiar than novel stimuli.

It has been argued that the reason responses are larger for novel than for familiar stimuli in perirhinal cortex is because novel stimuli should attract greater attention and also require greater processing (Brown & Xiang, 1998; Desimone, 1996; Fahy et al., 1993). They also provide an increased signal that can be used by mechanisms effecting the storage of the novel occurrence (Bogacz et al., 1999, 2001). The speed of the response changes in anterior inferior temporal cortex potentially provides a very early signal of the occurrence of novelty to attentional, behavioural, and further processing mechanisms (Bogacz et al., 2001; Brown & Xiang, 1998; Xiang & Brown, 1998a). In contrast, a possible reason why familiar stimuli evoke greater responses than novel stimuli in prefrontal cortex might be that such activity in prefrontal cortex is related to activation of recollective processes concerning the previously encountered stimuli. Human imaging studies have established the involvement of prefrontal cortex in recollective processes (Buckner & Petersen, 1996; Ranganath, Johnson, & D'Esposito, 2000). Perhaps prefrontal cortex is not so strongly activated during acquisition (i.e. for the first presentations of stimuli) as encoding and registration is automatic under the conditions of the recording experiments, in which contextual or associational encoding of stimuli conveys no behavioural advantage.

The latency before responses to novel stimuli differ from those to familiar stimuli is typically longer (~135–195ms) in prefrontal cortex than in either anterior TE (~75ms) or perirhinal cortex (~75–135ms). Unless shorter latencies are found in future work, this difference precludes the initial response changes in anterior inferior temporal cortex being passive reflections of responses in prefrontal cortex, though the latency difference is potentially sufficient to allow the reverse to be true.

The incidence of neurons with memory spans of at least 24h is lower in prefrontal cortex than in perirhinal cortex. Indeed, if response change is plotted as a function of the number of intervening trials since a stimulus was last seen across the population of neurons that change their response, the memory span of the population is only a few minutes (Fig. 6.4), whereas that in perirhinal cortex is at least 24h. This finding has relevance to imaging studies based on activity of the whole neuronal population in the area, and

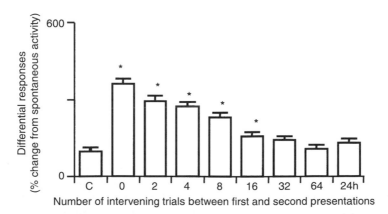

Figure 6.4. Memory spans of recognition-related neurons in prefrontal (orbital) cortex–population 24h memory span. The mean (+S.E.M.) responses of recency neurons recorded in monkey prefrontal (orbital) cortex to the first presentation of novel stimuli (C) and to the second presentations of such stimuli after varying intervening intervals either after the indicated numbers of intervening trials or after 24h.

emphasises that population changes can mask or fail to register important changes in smaller proportions of neurons.

Neuronal responses in the prefrontal cortex, which signal information concerning the prior occurrence of both object and location stimuli, have been shown in monkeys and in rats performing a variety of tasks. Using a delayed matching-to-sample task, the neural activity cells in the prefrontal cortex were found to correspond to at least one, if not several, of the task parameters (Miller et al., 1996). One-quarter of cells measured were found to respond to the visual stimuli, half of the cells showed heightened activity during the delay period, and more than half the visually responsive cells showed either enhanced or suppressed responses to the repetition of the sample stimulus.

Prefrontal responses related to prior occurrence are not confined to the visual modality. Rat orbitofrontal neurones display response changes in a continuous delayed non-matching to sample (DNMS) task using a set of eight odours (Ramus & Eichenbaum, 2000). In this task, reward is contingent on whether the next odour is the same or different from that last presented. Under these conditions, 48% of orbitofrontal neurons code for the match or non-match contingency, with both odour-specific enhancements and reductions in response being found on stimulus repetition. Additionally, as in visual working memory tasks (Fuster, 1991), stimulus-selective delay activity occurred during the period between odour presentations. These findings contrast with those in perirhinal cortex, where only 15% of the neurons coded for the match/non-match contingency (Young et al., 1997). The difference might be related to the finding that, whereas damage to the orbitofrontal cortex in rats results in an impairment in acquisition of the DNMS rule, rats with damage to the perirhinal cortex are able to acquire the rule. However, rats with the latter lesion show an impairment in performance at longer delays, suggesting an impairment in memory (or attentive) function (Eacott, Gaffan, & Murray, 1994; Gaffan, 1994a; Gaffan and Murray, 1992; Meunier, Bachevalier, Mishkin, & Murray, 1993; Mumby & Pinel, 1994; Otto & Eichenbaum, 1992a; Suzuki, Zola-Morgan, Squire, & Amaral, 1993; Zola-Morgan, Squire, Amaral, & Suzuki, 1989; Zola-Morgan, Squire, & Ramus, 1994).

In monkeys, delay activity is found in a visual delayed matching task in which a target stimulus is followed by a series of up to four distracter stimuli before the target is repeated: the animal must respond once the target stimulus reappears (Miller et al., 1996). In anterior inferior temporal cortex, delay activity is disrupted by a single intervening stimulus occurring before the reappearance of the target stimulus. In contrast, prefrontal delay activity persists in spite of the occurrence of more than one such distracter stimulus. This difference could reflect a more sustained short-term memory or attentive process in prefrontal than anterior inferior temporal cortex (Desimone, 1996).

There is experimental evidence from lesion studies to suggest that the prefrontal cortex is involved in spatial tasks as well as in object recognition memory. In particular, lesions of the dorsolateral prefrontal cortex have been shown to impair a spatial working memory task (Kesner, 1989; Levy & Goldman-Rakic, 1999; Seamans, Floresco, & Phillips, 1995).

Electrophysiological studies have also provided evidence that the dorso-lateral prefrontal cortex contains neurons that are involved in short-term spatial memory processes (Rao, Rainer, & Miller, 1997; Wilson et al., 1993). In particular, delay activity has been recorded in the prefrontal cortex of monkeys performing a delayed matching-to-sample task combined with a delayed matching-to-position task (Rao et al., 1997). In the first part of the task, the animal had to remember the sample object (the "what" information). After a delay, the sample was re-presented together with a non-matching item and the animal had to make a saccade to the remembered location of the match (the "where" information). Certain neurons showed differential delay neuronal activity related to the object, whereas others responded to the location, but most (52%) were tuned to both the location and the object (Rao et al., 1997). Consistent with this argument, many prefrontal neurons convey object information only within highly localised memory fields (Rainer et al., 1998a). These results suggest that prefrontal neurons play a role in integrating both location and object information. However, there is also evidence that the prefrontal cortex contains separate processing mechanisms for remembering what and where an object is (Wilson et al., 1993).

Thus there is evidence from recording and lesion studies that the pre-frontal cortex contributes to recognition memory processes for both individual items and for spatial information, but this evidence suggests that its role might be concerned with modulation or elaboration of temporal lobe processing, the basic processing being carried out in temporal lobe structures.

COMPARISON OF NEURONAL RESPONSIVENESS IN THE HIPPOCAMPUS WITH THAT IN PERIRHINAL CORTEX

The involvement of the hippocampal formation (defined as hippocampal fields CA1–4, the dentate gyrus and subiculum) in familiarity discrimination of infrequently encountered individual items in standard tests of monkey recognition memory is controversial. There is dispute concerning the effects of hippocampal lesions on recognition memory (Alvarez, Zola-Morgan, & Squire, 1995; Beason-Held, Rosene, Killiany, & Moss, 1999; Murray & Mishkin, 1998; Zola et al., 2000), although any impairment is agreed to be less than that following perirhinal lesions. Importantly, a recent meta-analysis of such reports has established that memory impairment increases as perirhi-nal damage increases but, counterintuitively, increases as hippocampal damage decreases (Baxter & Murray, 2001). The latter finding is consistent with a malfunctioning hippocampus being more disruptive to familiarity discrimination than a non-existent one, as was suggested by studies in the rat (Mumby, Wood, & Pinel, 1992).

These results for recognition memory tasks using infrequently repeating ("trial unique") stimuli can be contrasted with those using small stimulus sets. In such tasks the stimuli rapidly all become highly familiar so that recency rather than familiarity mechanisms are favoured. Moreover, typically in such tasks only one target stimulus must be remembered at a time so that short-term- or working-memory-based mechanisms provide the optimum strategy for task solution. Perirhinal lesions do not prevent performance of such tasks (Eacott et al., 1994).

The results of recording studies parallel those of ablation work. Thus, on the one hand, they indicate that the incidence of hippocampal neurons carrying information concerning the familiarity or recency of presentation of individual, infrequently repeating stimuli is low (~1 per cent) (Brown, Wilson, & Riches, 1987; Miyashita, Rolls, Cahusac, Niki, & Feigenbaum, 1989; Rolls, Cahusac, Feigenbaum, & Miyashita, 1993; Xiang & Brown, 1998a). This figure compares with 25 per cent found in perirhinal cortex under the same conditions. Moreover, for those hippocampal neurons that do change response on stimulus repetition, their latencies to signal a difference between novel and familiar stimuli are not as short and their memory spans have not been demonstrated to be as long as those of many such neurons in anterior inferior temporal, including perirhinal cortex (Rolls et al., 1993; Xiang & Brown, 1998a). Thus, electrophysiological evidence for a hippocampal basis for long-term familiarity discrimination of individual items is weak. Additionally, these data indicate that it is unlikely that neuronal responses in perirhinal cortex are dependent upon hippocampal inputs.

On the other hand, both delay activity and match–mismatch differences have been reported at high incidence in the hippocampus when small stimulus sets have been used in tasks where short-term- or working-memory-based mechanisms might be used (Brown, 1982; Hampson, Simeral, & Deadwyler, 1999; Otto and Eichenbaum, 1992b; Riches et al., 1991, Wiebe & Staubli, 1999). Such activity changes have been found using odours as well as visual stimuli, and in rats as well as monkeys (Otto & Eichenbaum, 1992b; Wood et al., 1999). However, unlike perirhinal cortex, these activity changes do not appear to signal information that is to do with novelty or familiarity of a particular stimulus as opposed to the type of trial in which it occurs (match/mismatch) (Brown, 1990; Brown & Aggleton, 2001, Otto & Eichenbaum, 1992b; Riches et al., 1991). Thus, as in perirhinal cortex, these match/mismatch activity changes, although probably important for solving repetitious recognition memory tasks, do not provide a possible substrate for general, long-term familiarity discrimination.

In contrast to a still equivocal role in familiarity discrimination for individual items, the importance of the hippocampal formation to allocentric spatial processing is well established (Aggleton, Hunt, & Rawlins, 1986; Gaffan, 1994b; Morris, Garrud, Rawlins, & O'Keefe, 1982; O'Keefe & Nadel, 1978). In contradistinction, lesion studies have shown that damage to the perirhinal cortex has relatively little or no effect on spatial memory tasks, and thus perirhinal cortex is relatively unimportant in the processing of spatial stimuli (Bussey, Muir, & Aggleton, 1999; Ennaceur, Neave, & Aggleton, 1996; Gaffan, 1994a; but see Bilkey & Liu, 2000; Liu & Bilkey, 1998a,b,c).

Although the hippocampus has been shown to contain a much lower proportion of neurons that signal the prior presentation of infrequently occurring individual stimuli than perirhinal cortex, many studies show that the hippocampus contains many neurons that respond to the position or arrangement of stimuli in the environment (Eichenbaum, Schoenbaum, Young, & Bunsey, 1996; Muller, 1996; O'Keefe, 1993; O'Keefe, Burgess, Donnett, Jeffery, & Maguire, 1998; Rolls et al., 1989; Wiener, 1996). For example, individual neurons in the rat respond to particular spatial positions in the environment, described as place fields (Muller, 1996; O'Keefe & Nadel, 1978). In the monkey, increases in the firing of hippocampal neurons have been shown when the animal directs its gaze to a particular position in the environment, and these neurons have been described as spatial view cells (Rolls, Treves, Robertson, Georges-François, & Panzeri, 1998). The responses of perirhinal cortex neurons to the presentation of spatial stimuli have been little studied (Burwell, Shapiro, O'Malley, & Eichenbaum, 1998).

Recent experiments have provided evidence that the hippocampus is involved in judging prior occurrence when spatial information is involved (Vann, Brown, Erichsen, & Aggleton, 2000; Wan et al., 1999). Such evidence further supports a dissociation between the contributions of the perirhinal cortex and hippocampus to recognition memory. Moreover, the hippocampal involvement provides a potential link to the episodic memory impairment found in humans with hippocampal damage as episodic memories normally include spatial information (the location of the episode). The recent experimental evidence comes from a series of immunohistochemical studies. In these studies the expression of the immediate early gene c-*fos* (measured by quantitative immunohistochemistry for its protein products, Fos) has been used to map patterns of neuronal activation produced by different types of visual stimuli (Herdegen, 1996; Herrera & Robertson, 1996). This technique has some advantages over electrophysiological and lesion studies, as comparisons can be made in the intact animal between activities in different brain regions of whole populations of neurons when presented with different types of stimuli.

In an initial study, levels of neuronal activation were measured in animals presented with novel stimuli in a familiar environment compared with animals presented with novel objects in a novel environment (Zhu, McCabe, Aggleton, & Brown, 1997). It was found that levels of neuronal activity were significantly higher in the hippocampus of the group of rats for whom the environment was novel compared to the hippocampal activity of the group of rats for whom the environment was familiar. In contrast, levels of activation in the perirhinal cortex did not differ, but were high in both groups, presumably reflecting the novelty of the objects presented. In this study, however, differences in levels of attention and arousal between the two rat groups might have accounted for, or contributed to, the different levels of hippocampal activation observed. Thus, in a second experiment the experimental design was modified so that two different stimuli, one novel and one familiar, were presented simultaneously to a rat (Wan et al., 1999). The stimuli were presented in such a way that one eye saw only the novel picture, and the other eye saw only the familiar picture (Fig. 6.5). By presenting a series of such paired stimuli, the amount of neuronal activation evoked by novel and familiar stimuli could be assessed in the same rat by comparing the levels of c-*fos* activation in the two hemispheres; one hemisphere having chiefly processed the information from the familiar stimuli, and the other hemisphere having processed the information from the novel stimuli. Thus,

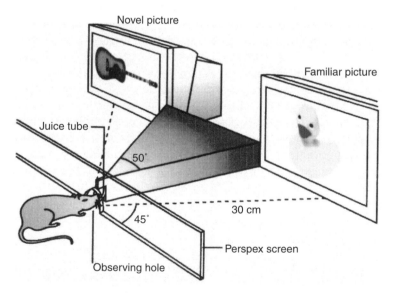

Figure 6.5.   Paired viewing procedure for simultaneously presenting novel and familiar stimuli. In the paired viewing procedure, a rat views two pictures simultaneously, one novel and the other seen many times previously, while its head is in a hole in a perspex screen. A central divider ensures that each picture is seen by only one eye and is processed initially by the opposite cerebral hemisphere. In this way, novel and familiar stimuli can be shown under the same conditions of alertness, motivation, and with similar eye movements (reproduced from Brown & Aggleton, 2001 in *Nature Reviews Neuroscience*, Copyright 2001, Macmillan Magazines Ltd).

any non-specific differences produced by the presentation of the novel com-pared to the familiar stimuli were controlled: both types of stimuli were presented under the same conditions of movement, arousal and motivation, and with similar eye movements.

Using this paired-viewing experimental design, the levels of neuronal acti-vation evoked by a series of novel and familiar spatial stimuli were assessed. Pictures that each contained three individual items and in which the arrangements of the individual items rather than the items themselves were either novel or familiar, were presented (Fig. 6.6). Indeed, all the individual items were equally familiar. This type of stimulus was found to produce different levels of activation in various parts of the hippocampus, although not all regions showed the same pattern of activation. In subfield CA1 of the hippocampus, presentation of the novel arrangements produced greater neur-onal activation than for the familiar arrangements. By contrast, there was significantly less neuronal activation to the novel compared to the familiar stimuli in the dentate gyrus and subiculum. The perirhinal cortex and area TE were not differentially affected by the presentation of the novel and famil-iar arrangements, which is consistent with previous findings as the individual items in the arrangements were equally familiar; it was the spatial configur-ation of the items that was either novel or familiar. These findings suggest that recognition memory for spatial arrangements of stimuli might depend on a neural system involving the hippocampus, rather than the perirhinal cortex.

The observed increases in activation produced by the familiar spatial stimuli in the dentate gyrus and subiculum were found primarily outside the principal cell layers and could reflect increased activity in inhibitory inter-neurones. The differential activity of inhibitory neurons could explain the reversed directions of the differences in activation for novel and familiar stimuli as the information passed from one region to the next through the hippocampal formation (Wan et al., 1999). Another possibility, that the changes in activation reflected differences in processing between the dorsal and ventral hippocampal formation, was excluded in further (unpublished) work in which samples of both subfield CA1 and the dentate gyrus were made at both dorsal and the ventral levels. However, these data did indicate greater activation in the dorsal than the ventral hippocampus. This finding is consistent with lesion and electrophysiological studies indicating that the dorsal hippocampal formation is more important than the ventral for learning about the arrangements of spatial stimuli (Moser, Moser, & Aggleton, 1993; Moser, Moser, Forrest, Andersen, & Morris, 1995). Thus dorsal hippocampal lesions impair spatial memory performance in the water maze whereas ventral hippocampal lesions have no effect (Moser et al., 1993, 1995), and the ventral hippocampus has fewer place cells with larger and less selective place fields than the dorsal hippocampus (Jung, Wiener, & McNaughton, 1994).

Figure 6.6. Example pictures of arrangements of the same items, in the same spatial locations, on the computer screen.

The importance of the hippocampus and postrhinal cortex in processing novel arrangements of items (Vann et al., 2000) has been highlighted by further studies using Fos imaging, this time in rats performing a spatial memory task. In these experiments, two groups of rats were trained in a standard eight-arm radial arm maze. One group was trained in one room and then subsequently tested in a different, novel room containing new spatial cues. The second group were both trained and tested in the same room so that the room cues were highly familiar at test. A significant increase in the levels of neuronal activation in the hippocampus was found in both groups when compared to a control group that had been trained to run down only one arm of a radial arm maze, i.e. to obtain the same amount of reward but without the need to use spatial information. In the group of rats exposed to the novel room cues, all parts of the dorsal hippocampus showed a significantly greater enhancement in neuronal activation compared with the ventral hippocampus. In this same group of rats, i.e. those tested in the novel room, one would have predicted that the perirhinal cortex would also show increased neuronal activation reflecting the presence of novel visual cues in the room. However, although there was a slight increase in the number of Fos-stained nuclei in the perirhinal cortex of this group, the difference did not reach significance, possibly because the number of novel stimuli was insufficient to produce a sufficiently great increase in neuronal activation.

These immunohistochemical findings indicate that the hippocampal formation is crucially involved in processing not only perceptual aspects of spatial information, but also in its prior occurrence (Vann et al., 2000; Wan et al., 1999). Further, they confirm that the hippocampal formation is less important than the perirhinal cortex in familiarity discrimination for individual items. Thus, hippocampal involvement mirrors that of the perirhinal cortex, which is crucial to judging the prior occurrence of individual items but is less important than the hippocampal formation when the judgement concerns spatial information. Hence the hippocampal formation seems to become involved where recognition memory involves spatial (and possibly other) relationships or associations between items (Brown, 1990; Brown & Aggleton, 2001; Eichenbaum, Otto, & Cohen, 1994). The inference is that the familiarity discrimination system centred on the perirhinal cortex is not sufficient to solve judgements concerning prior occurrence when the judgement cannot be made on the basis of individual items taken in isolation. Where both the spatial position and the identity of an individual item is crucial to task performance, then both the perirhinal cortex and the hippocampal formation appear to be crucial to its performance (Parker & Gaffan, 1998). In such situations it is clear that there must be an interchange of information between the two structures. However, where the information is solely spatial or solely concerns individual items, it seems that the systems involving the two structures can operate independently. Accordingly, information concerning prior occurrence is not transferred between perirhinal cortex and the hippocampus under all circumstances and the contributions of perirhinal cortex and the hippocampus to recognition memory processes are potentially separable (Aggleton & Brown, 1999; Brown & Aggleton, 2001; Brown & Xiang, 1998).

COMPARISON OF NEURONAL RESPONSIVENESS IN THE ENTORHINAL CORTEX WITH THAT IN PERIRHINAL CORTEX

The entorhinal cortex has also been shown to contain neurons that signal information concerning the prior occurrence of stimuli (Fahy et al., 1993, Suzuki, Miller, & Desimone 1997; Xiang & Brown, 1998a; Young et al., 1997; Zhu et al., 1995b). In a study that looked at monkey entorhinal as well as perirhinal neuronal responses to infrequently repeating visual stimuli, a high incidence of neurons that changed response on stimulus repetition was found, similar to that in perirhinal cortex (Xiang & Brown, 1998a). Moreover, the patterns of response change also paralleled those in perirhinal cortex. However, the mean differential latencies of the recency, novelty, and familiarity neurons were all longer than the corresponding latencies in the perirhinal cortex and memory spans tended to be shorter. Thus, such responses of entorhinal neurons could be explained as passive reflections of those generated in perirhinal cortex and area TE. Consistent differences in Fos staining for novel and familiar individual stimuli have not been found for entorhinal cortex (Zhu et al., 1995a, 1996).

There is evidence that, like the perirhinal cortex, the entorhinal cortex is also involved in recognition memory for odours (Young et al., 1997). Using a continuous delayed non-matching-to-sample task, many neurons were active during the sampling of an odour and such odour-responsive cells showed an odour-selective enhancement or suppression of activity upon stimulus repetition (Young et al., 1997). Again, however, it needs to be noted that these response differences have been found in a task with frequently repeating stimuli and where only one stimulus needs to be remembered at a time.

Cells in the entorhinal cortex show differential activity in response not only to pictures of objects, but also to spatial stimuli (Suzuki et al., 1997). Neurons in the entorhinal cortex were recorded while monkeys were tested on both a delayed non-matching-to-sample and delayed non-matching-to-place task. The neurons did show response increases or decreases on repetition of the sample stimulus; however, in this study, the proportion of such cells was lower than in the perirhinal cortex. Conversely, the entorhinal cortex had a higher incidence than perirhinal cortex of cells that showed delay activity in the interval between sample and test presentations, possibly suggesting that the entorhinal cortex is specialised for modulating activity during working memory and is less involved in the analysis and coding of object features than the perirhinal cortex. A further indication that entorhinal cortex is involved in recognition memory for spatial stimuli is that Fos counts in this brain region were higher in rats that had performed in a radial maze in a novel rather than a familiar room (Vann et al., 2000).

Thus there is evidence that neurons of the entorhinal cortex are involved both in judgements about the prior occurrence of individual items and recognition memory processes involving spatial information. This conjunction of properties suggests that the entorhinal cortex might act in the way suggested by its anatomical relationships. Anatomically, it provides an interface between the perirhinal cortex and the hippocampal formation (Steward, 1976; Suzuki & Amaral, 1994; Swanson & Köhler, 1986; Witter et al., 1989). The recording data indicate that it might act as a junctional region, making contributions to both the hippocampally and the perirhinally centred systems involved in recognition memory. However, excitotoxic lesions of the entorhinal cortex have no effect on either a non-spatial working-memory task (Yee & Rawlins, 1998) or on a spatial delayed non-matching-to-position task in rats (Marighetto, Yee, & Rawlins, 1998). Moreover, in monkeys, only a temporary delayed non-matching-to-sample deficit has been found following lesions of the entorhinal cortex (Meunier et al., 1993, Leonard, Amaral, Squire, & Zola-Morgan, 1995). Thus although entorhinal cortex might contribute to these processes, it is not essential for them.

COMPARISON OF NEURONAL RESPONSIVENESS IN THE POSTRHINAL CORTEX WITH THAT IN PERIRHINAL CORTEX

A further region to show differential patterns of activation following the presentation of novel and familiar spatial stimuli is the postrhinal cortex. The postrhinal cortex lies caudal to the perirhinal cortex. It can be differentiated from the perirhinal cortex on cytoarchitectonic criteria (for a more comprehensive description, see Burwell et al., 1995) and on the different anatomical connections of the two regions (Burwell et al., 1995; Witter et al., 2000). It has been proposed that the postrhinal cortex in the rat has homologies with areas TF and TH of the parahippocampal cortex in the monkey (Burwell et al., 1995), and both behavioural and anatomical studies have suggested that the parahippocampal cortex plays an important role in spatial memory processing (Burwell et al., 1995).

Increased neuronal activation for novel compared to familiar stimuli in this area was found both in the radial arm maze task and for spatial arrangements of individual items, i.e. both when animals were using the novel spatial information to guide behaviour and when they were not required to make any behavioural response. Thus, as with perirhinal cortex, the differential activation appears to be automatic and endogenous rather than being dependent on or induced by behavioural training. Additionally, as for perirhinal cortex, the differential activation is also available when such information is likely to be valuable for task performance.

Although pictures of novel arrangements of familiar items produced significantly greater activation than familiar arrangements of these items in postrhinal cortex, this region was not differentially affected by the presentation of individual items (Wan et al., 1999). Moreover, consistent with this result, no differences in neuronal responses to novel and familiar individual stimuli were found in area TF/TH in the monkey (Riches et al., 1991). Thus the perirhinal cortex and the postrhinal cortex seem to be differentially involved in recognition memory processing, with the postrhinal cortex appearing to be part of the hippocampal system. The different contributions of these two regions to recognition memory for spatial stimuli is consistent with their different anatomical connections. For example, the postrhinal cortex receives a stronger input from parietal cortical areas processing visuospatial stimuli than does the perirhinal cortex (Naber, Caballero-Bleda, Jorritsma-Byham, & Witter, 1997). The two regions also project to distinct areas of the entorhinal cortex, the postrhinal cortex projects to the medial entorhinal cortex whereas fibres originating in the perirhinal cortex preferentially target the lateral entorhinal cortex. These two regions of the entorhinal cortex then project to distinct regions of the CA1 and subiculum (Naber et al., 1997, 1999; Witter et al., 2000).

As yet, the likely functional differences between these peri- and postrhinal anatomical pathways have not received support from corresponding differences in Fos or neuronal recording studies of entorhinal cortex or the hippocampal formation. Thus, despite the strong anatomical interconnections between the perirhinal cortex, lateral entorhinal cortex, and the hippocampus, the increased neuronal activation in the perirhinal cortex to novel individual stimuli is not paralleled by an increase in neuronal activation in the hippocampus lateral entorhinal cortex (Wan et al., 1999). This finding suggests that not all of the perirhinal information is passed on to hippocampal neurons. Surprisingly, no significant differences in neuronal activation in the lateral entorhinal cortex were found following the presentation of novel arrangements of stimuli, although a significant increase was found in the animals that performed the radial arm maze task in the novel room, in both the lateral and medial entorhinal cortex.

The demonstration that both the hippocampus and the postrhinal cortex show differential neuronal activation to the presentation of novel spatial stimuli prompts the question of whether the activation in the hippocampus depends upon the postrhinal cortex or whether responses seen in the postrhinal cortex depend on the hippocampus? First, previous studies have shown that excitotoxic lesions of the postrhinal cortex have no effect on spatial memory tasks, which are known to be disrupted by lesions of the hippocampus or disconnection of hippocampal connections by transection of the fornix (Bussey et al., 1999). Second, excitotoxic lesions of the hippocampus attenuate the increase in activation in the postrhinal cortex seen following presentation of novel visuospatial information (Warburton, Fry, Winstone, Aggleton, & Brown, 2000). Together the behavioural and Fos results suggest that the processing of spatial information by the postrhinal cortex might be dependent upon information coming from the hippocampus (i.e. fed-back), rather than the hippocampus being dependent on feed-forward perirhinal information. In this respect, therefore, the processing of information in the postrhinal cortex might differ in kind from that in the perirhinal cortex. As previously mentioned, the evidence suggests that the processing in the perirhinal cortex is independent of the hippocampal information. First, there is a low incidence of decremental neuronal responses in the hippocampus and the memory spans of hippocampal neurons with such responses are insufficiently long to explain those found in perirhinal cortex. Second, the shortest reported latencies of hippocampal response decrements are longer than those in the perirhinal cortex and area TE. Third, excitotoxic lesions of the hippocampus do not impair delayed non-matching to sample, whereas perirhinal lesions do. Thus, it has been shown consistently in the immunohistochemical and recording studies that there is a dissociation between the effects of novel stimuli and novel arrangements of stimuli on the perirhinal cortex and hippocampus.

CONCLUSIONS

Recording and immunohistochemical studies support the conclusion that systems based on the perirhinal cortex and hippocampus make different contributions to recognition memory processes (Brown & Aggleton, 2001). The perirhinal cortex is key to a system responsible for familiarity discrimination involving individual objects, whereas the hippocampus is key to a system responsible for recognition memory processes involving spatial (and probably other associative) information. There is strong evidence that parts of the temporal sensory association cortices contribute to the perirhinal cortical system's judgements of the prior occurrence of individual stimuli. In contrast, the postrhinal cortex appears to be part of the hippocampal system that is involved in judging the prior occurrence of spatial arrangements, and probably more general associations between constellations of items. The entorhinal cortex appears to have an involvement in both these systems, as its anatomical connections would predict. Additionally, studies of prefrontal cortex suggest that it might be involved with the retrieval and further elaboration of information concerning both individual items and constellations of items that have occurred previously. Thus, although there is still much to discover concerning the precise information processing operations of different brain regions involved in judging prior occurrence, there are already clear indications of the types of information that are dealt with in several cortical areas associated with the perirhinal cortex.

ACKNOWLEDGEMENTS

The authors gratefully acknowledge the financial support of the Medical Research Council (UK), the Wellcome Trust and the BBSRC.

REFERENCES

Aggleton, J.P. & Brown, M.W. (1999). Episodic memory, amnesia and the hippocampal–anterior thalamic axis. *Behavioural Brain Sciences, 22,* 425–489.

Aggleton, J.P., Hunt, P.R., & Rawlins, J.N.P. (1986). The effects of hippocampal lesions upon spatial and non-spatial tests of working memory. *Behavioural Brain Research, 19,* 133–146.

Alvarez, P., Zola-Morgan, S., & Squire, L.R. (1995). Damage limited to the hippocampal region produces long-lasting memory impairment in monkeys. *Journal of Neuroscience, 15,* 3796–3807.

Bachevalier, J., & Mishkin, M. (1986). Visual recognition impairment follows ventromedial but not dorsolateral prefrontal lesions in monkeys. *Behavioural Brain Research, 20,* 249–261.

Baxter, M.G., & Murray, E.A. (2001). Opposite relationship of hippocampal and rhinal cortex damage to delayed nonmatching-to-sample deficits in monkeys. *Hippocampus, 11,* 61–71.

Bayliss, G.C., & Rolls, E.T. (1987). Responses of neurons in the inferior temporal cortex in short-term and serial recognition memory tasks. *Experimental Brain Research, 65,* 614–622.

Beason-Held, L.L., Rosene, D.L., Killiany, R.J., & Moss, M.B. (1999). Hippocampal formation lesions produce memory impairment in the rhesus monkey. *Hippocampus, 9,* 562–574.

Bilkey, D.K., & Liu, P. (2000). The effects of separate and combined perirhinal and prefrontal cortex lesions on spatial memory tasks in the rat. *Psychobiology, 28,* 12–20.

Bogacz, R., Brown, M.W., & Giraud-Carrier, C. (1999). High capacity neural networks for familiarity discrimination. *Proceedings of the International Conference in Artificial Neural Networks,* 773–776.

Bogacz, R., Brown, M.W. & Giraud-Carrier, C. (2001). Model of familiarity discrimination in the perirhinal cortex. *Journal of Computational Neuroscience, 10,* 5–23.

Brewer, J.B., Zhao, Z., Desmond, J.E., Glover, G.H., & Gabrieli, J.D.E. (1998). Making memories: Brain activity that predicts how well visual experience will be remembered. *Science, 281,* 1185–1187.

Brown, M.W. (1982). Effect of context on the responses of single units recorded from the hippocampal region of behaviourally trained monkeys. In C. Ajmone-Marsan & H. Matthies (Eds.) *Neuronal plasticity and memory formation. IBRO Monograph Series* (Vol. 9, pp. 557–573). New York: Raven Press.

Brown, M.W. (1990). Why does the cortex have a hippocampus? In M. Gabriel & J. Moore (Eds.) *Learning and computational neuroscience: Foundations of adaptive networks* (pp. 233–282). New York: MIT Press.

Brown, M.W. (1996). Neuronal responses and recognition memory. *Seminars in the Neurosciences, 8,* 23–32.

Brown, M.W. (2000). Neuronal correlates of recognition memory. In J.J. Bolhuis (Ed.) *Brain perception and memory.* Oxford: Oxford University Press.

Brown, M.W. & Aggleton, J.P. (2001). Recognition memory: What are the roles of the perirhinal cortex and hippocampus? *Nature Reviews Neuroscience, 2,* 51–61.

Brown, M.W., Warburton, E.C., & Duguid, G.L. (2000). Scopolamine disrupts both differential fos expression in perirhinal cortex and spontaneous object recognition in rats. *European Journal of Neuroscience, 12*, 437–437.

Brown, M.W., Wilson, F.A.W., & Riches, I.P. (1987). Neuronal evidence that inferotemporal cortex is more important than hippocampus in certain processes underlying recognition memory. *Brain Research, 409*, 158–162.

Brown, M.W., & Xiang, J.Z. (1998). Recognition memory: Neuronal substrates of the judgement of prior occurrence. *Progress in Neurobiology, 55*, 149–189.

Buckley, M.J., & Gaffan, D. (1997). Impairment of visual object-recognition learning after perirhinal cortex ablation. *Behavioral Neuroscience, 111*, 467–475.

Buckley, M.J., & Gaffan, D. (1998). Perirhinal cortex ablation impairs visual object identification. *Journal of Neuroscience, 18*, 2268–2275.

Buckner, R.L. & Petersen, S.E. (1996). What does neuroimaging tell us about the role of prefrontal cortex in memory. *Seminars in the Neurosciences, 8*, 47–55.

Burwell, R.D., & Amaral, D.G. (1998). Cortical afferents of the perirhinal, postrhinal and entorhinal cortices of the rat. *Journal of Comparative Neurology, 398*, 179–205.

Burwell, R.D., Shapiro, M.L., O'Malley, M.T., & Eichenbaum, H. (1998). Positional firing properties of perirhinal cortex neurons. *NeuroReport, 9*, 3013–3018.

Burwell, R.D., Witter, M.P., & Amaral, D.G. (1995). Perirhinal and postrhinal cortices of the rat: A review of the neuroanatomical literature and comparison with findings from the monkey brain. *Hippocampus, 5*, 390–408.

Bussey, T.J., Muir, J.L., & Aggleton, J.P. (1999). Functionally dissociating aspects of event memory: The effects of combined perirhinal and postrhinal cortex lesions on object place memory in the rat. *Journal of Neuroscience, 19*, 495–502.

Cho, K., Kemp, N., Noel, J., Aggleton, J.P., Brown, M.W., & Bashir, Z.I. (2000b). A new form of long-term depression in the perirhinal cortex. *Nature Neuroscience, 3*, 150–156.

Cho, K., Lim, M.K., Choi, K.H., Suh, C.H., Suh, C.K., & Brown, M.W. (2000a). An fMRI study of differential perirhinal and prefrontal activation during familiarity/recency discrimination. *European Journal of Neuroscience, 12*, 42.13.

Desimone, R. (1996). Neural mechanisms for visual memory and their role in attention. *Proceedings of the National Academy of Sciences USA, 93*, 13494–13499.

Duzel, E., Yonelinas, A.P., Mangun, G.R., Heinze, H.J., & Tulving, E. (1997). Event related potential correlates of two states of conscious awareness in memory. *Proceedings of the National Academy of Sciences, USA, 94*, 5973–5978.

Eacott, M.J., Gaffan, D., & Murray, E.A. (1994). Preserved recognition memory for small sets, and impaired stimulus identification for large sets following rhinal cortex ablations in monkeys. *European Journal of Neuroscience, 6*, 1466–1478.

Eichenbaum, H., Otto, T., & Cohen, N.J. (1994). Two functional components of the hippocampal memory system. *Behavioural Brain Sciences, 17*, 449–518.

Eichenbaum, H., Schoenbaum, G., Young, B., & Bunsey, M. (1996). Functional organization of the hippocampal memory system. *Proceedings of the National Academy of Sciences, USA, 93*, 13500–13507.

Ennaceur, A., Neave, N., & Aggleton, J.P. (1996). Neurotoxic lesions of the perirhinal cortex do not mimic the behavioural effects of fornix transection in the rat. *Behavioural Brain Research, 80*, 9–25.

Fahy, F.L., Riches, I.P., & Brown, M.W. (1993). Neuronal activity related to visual recognition memory: Long-term memory and the encoding of recency and familiarity information in the primate anterior and medial inferior temporal and rhinal cortex. *Experimental Brain Research, 96*, 457–472.

Fernandez, G., Effern, A., Grunwald, T., Pezer, N., Lehnertz, K., Dümpelmann, M., Van Roost, D., & Elger, C.E. (1999). Real-time tracking of memory formation in the human rhinal cortex and hippocampus. *Science, 285*, 1582–1585.

Fuster, J.M. (1973). Unit activity in prefrontal cortex during delayed response performance: neuronal correlates of transient memory. *Journal of Neurophysiology*, *36*, 61–78.

Fuster, J.M. (1991). The prefrontal cortex and its relation to behavior. *Progress in Brain Research*, *87*, 201–211.

Fuster, J.M., & Alexander, G.E. (1971). Neuron activity related to short term memory. *Science*, *173*, 652–654.

Fuster, J.M., & Jervey, J.P. (1981). Inferotemporal neurons distinguish and retain behaviourally relevant features of visual stimuli. *Science*, *212*, 952–955.

Gaffan, D. (1994a). Dissociated effects of perirhinal cortex ablation, fornix transection and amygdalectomy: Evidence for multiple memory systems in the primate temporal lobe. *Experimental Brain Research*, *99*, 411–422.

Gaffan, D. (1994b). Scene specific memory for objects: A model of episodic memory impairment in monkeys with fornix transection. *Journal of Cognitive Neuroscience*, *6*, 305–320.

Gaffan, D., & Murray, E.A. (1992). Monkeys (*Macaca fascicularis*) with rhinal cortex ablations succeed in object discrimination learning despite 24hr intervals and fail at matching to sample despite double sample presentations. *Behavioural Neuroscience*, *106*, 30–38.

Gross, C.G., Rochamiranda, C.E., & Bender, D.B. (1972). Visual properties of neurons in inferotemporal cortex of the macaque. *Journal of Neurophysiology*, *35*, 96–111.

Hampson, R.E., Simeral, J.D., & Deadwyler, S.A. (1999). Distribution of spatial and nonspatial infromation in dorsal hippocampus. *Nature*, *402*, 610–614.

Henson, R.N.A., Rugg, M.D., Shallice, T., Josephs, O., & Dolan, R.J. (1999). Recollection and familiarity in recognition memory: An event-related functional magnetic imaging study. *Journal of Neuroscience*, *19*, 3962–3972.

Herdegen, T. (1996). Jun, Fos and CREB/ATF transcription factors in the brain: Control of gene expression under normal and pathophysiological conditions. *The Neuroscientist*, *2*, 153–161.

Herrera, D.G., & Robertson, H.A. (1996). Activation of c-fos in the brain. *Progress in Neurobiology*, *50*, 83–107.

Jones, E.G., & Powell, T.P.S. (1970). Parahippocampal/primate. *Brain*, *93*, 793–820.

Jung, M.W., Wiener, S.I., & McNaughton, B.L. (1994). Comparison of spatial firing characteristics of units in dorsal and ventral hippocampus of the rat. *Journal of Neuroscience*, *14*, 7347–7356.

Kesner, R.P. (1989). Retrospective and prospective coding of information: Role of the medial prefrontal cortex. *Experimental Brain Research*, *74*, 63–167.

Kojima, S., & Goldman-Rakic, P.S. (1982). Delay activity of prefrontal neurons in rhesus monkeys performing delayed response. *Brain Research*, *248*, 43–49.

Kowalska, D.M. (2000). Cognitive functions of the temporal lobe in the dog: A review. *Progress in Neuro-Psychopathology*, *24*, 855–880.

Kowalska, D.M., & Kuśmierek, P. (1997). Rhinal cortex as well as hippocampus removals do not impair auditory recognition memory in dogs. *Society for Neuroscience Abstracts*, *23*, 623.6.

Kowalska, D.M., Kuśmierek, P., & Kosmal, A. (1998). The effects of auditory association areas lesions on the sound recognition memory in dogs. *Society for Neuroscience Abstracts*, *24*, 518.6.

Leonard, B.W., Amaral, D.G., Squire, L.R., & Zola-Morgan, S. (1995). Transient memory impairment in monkeys with bilateral lesions of the entorhinal cortex. *Journal of Neuroscience*, *15*, 5637–5659.

Levy, R., & Goldman-Rakic, P.S. (1999). Association of storage and processing functions in dorsolateral prefrontal cortex of the nonhuman primate. *Journal of Neuroscience*, *19*, 5149–5158.

Li, L., Miller, E.K., & Desimone, R. (1993). The representation of stimulus familiarity in anterior inferior temporal cortex. *Journal of Neurophysiology*, *69*, 1918–1929.

Liu, P., & Bilkey, D.K. (1998a). Excitotoxic lesions centered on perirhinal cortex produce delay-dependent deficits in a test of spatial memory. *Behavioral Neuroscience*, *112*, 512–524.

Liu, P., & Bilkey, D.K. (1998b). Lesions of perirhinal cortex produce spatial memory deficits in the radial maze. *Hippocampus, 8*, 114–121.

Liu, P., & Bilkey, D.K. (1998c). Perirhinal cortex contributions to performance in the Morris water maze. *Behavioral Neuroscience, 112*, 304–315.

Mandler, G. (1980) Recognizing the judgement of previous occurrence. *Psychological Review, 87*, 252–271.

Marighetto, A., Yee, B.K., & Rawlins, J.N.P. (1998). The effects of cytotoxic entorhinal lesions and electrolytic medial septal lesions on the acquisition and retention of a spatial working memory task. *Experimental Brain Research, 119*, 517–528.

Maunsell, J.H.R., Sclar, G., Nealey, T.A., & DePriest, D.D. (1991). Extraretinal representations in area V4 in the macaque monkey. *Visual Neuroscience, 7*, 561–573.

Meunier, M., Bachevalier, J. Mishkin, M., & Murray, E.A. (1993). Effects on visual recognition of combined and separate ablations of entorhinal and perirhinal cortex in rhesus monkeys. *Journal of Neuroscience, 13*, 5418–5432.

Meunier, M., Bachevalier, J., & Mishkin, M. (1997). Effects of orbital frontal and anterior cingulate lesions on object and spatial memory in rhesus monkeys. *Neuropsychologia, 35*, 999–1015.

Miller, E.K., & Desimone, R. (1994). Parallel neuronal mechanisms for short term memory. *Science, 263*, 520–522.

Miller, E.K., Erickson, C.A., & Desimone, R. (1996). Neural mechanisms of visual working memory in prefrontal cortex of the macaque. *Journal of Neuroscience, 16*, 5154–5167.

Miller, E.K., Li, L., & Desimone, R. (1993). Activity of neurons in anterior inferior temporal cortex during a short-term memory task. *Journal of Neuroscience, 13*, 1460–1478.

Miyashita, Y., & Chang, H.S. (1988). Neuronal correlate of pictorial short-term memory in the primate temporal cortex. *Nature, 331*, 68–70.

Miyashita, Y., Rolls, E.T., Cahusac, P.M.B., Niki, H., & Feigenbaum, J.D. (1989). Activity of hippocampal-formation neurons in the monkey related to a conditional spatial response task. *Journal of Neurophysiology, 61*, 669–678.

Morris, R.G.M., Garrud, P., Rawlins, J.N.P., & O'Keefe, J. (1982). Place navigation impaired in rats with hippocampal lesions. *Nature, 297*, 681–683.

Moser, E., Moser, M.B., & Andersen, P. (1993). Spatial-learning impairment parallels the magnitude of dorsal hippocampal-lesions, but is hardly present following ventral lesions. *Journal of Neuroscience, 13*, 3916–3925.

Moser, M.B., Moser, E.I., Forrest, E., Andersen, P., & Morris, R.G.M (1995). Spatial-learning with a minislab in the dorsal hippocampus. *Proceedings of the National Academy of Sciences, USA, 92*, 9697–9701.

Muller, R. (1996). A quarter of a century of place cells. *Neuron, 17*, 813–822.

Mumby, D.G., & Pinel, J.P. (1994). Rhinal cortex lesions and object recognition in rats. *Behavioral Neuroscience, 108*, 11–18.

Mumby, D.G., Wood, E.R., & Pinel, J.P. (1992). Object recognition memory is only mildly impaired in rats with lesions of the hippocampus and amygdala. *Psychobiology, 20*, 18–27.

Murray, E.A., & Bussey, T.J. (1999). Perceptual-mnemonic functions of the perirhinal cortex. *Trends in Cognitive Neurosciences, 3*, 142–151.

Murray, E.A. & Mishkin, M. (1998). Object recognition and location memory in monkeys with excitotoxic lesions of the amygdala and hippocampus. *Journal of Neuroscience, 18*, 6568–6582.

Naber, P.A., Caballero-Bleda, B., Jorritsma-Byham, B., & Witter, M.P. (1997). Parallel input to the hippocampal memory system through perirhinal and postrhinal cortices. *Neuroreport, 8*, 2617–2621.

Naber, P.A., Witter, M.P., & Lopes da Silva, F.H (1999). Perirhinal cortex input to the hippocampus in the rat: Evidence for parallel pathways, both direct and indirect. A combined physiological and anatomical study. *European Journal of Neuroscience, 11*, 4119–4133.

O'Keefe, J. (1993). Hippocampus, theta rhythms and spatial memory. *Current Opinion in Neurobiology*, *3*, 917–924.

O'Keefe, J., Burgess, N., Donnett, J.G., Jeffery, K.J., & Maguire, E.A. (1998). Place cells, navigational accuracy, and the human hippocampus. *Philosophical Transactions of the Royal Society, London (Biology)*, *353*, 1333–1340.

O'Keefe, J., & Nadel, L. (1978). *The hippocampus as a cognitive map*. Oxford: Clarendon Press, Oxford.

Otto, T., & Eichenbaum, H. (1992a). Complementary roles of orbital prefrontal cortex and the perirhinal-entorhinal cortices in an odor-guided delayed non-matching to sample task. *Behavioral Neuroscience*, *106*, 763–776.

Otto, T., & Eichenbaum, H. (1992b). Neuronal activity in the hippocampus during delayed non-match to sample performance in rats: Evidence for hippocampal processing in recognition memory. *Hippocampus*, *2*, 323–334.

Parker, A., & Gaffan, D. (1998). Interaction of frontal and perirhinal cortices in visual object recognition memory in monkeys. *European Journal of Neuroscience*, *10*, 3044–3057.

Rainer, G., Asaad, W.F., & Miller, E.K. (1998a). Memory fields of neurons in the primate prefrontal cortex. *Proceedings of the National Academy of Sciences*, *95*, 15008–15013.

Rainer, G., Asaad, W.F., & Miller, E.K. (1998b). Selective representation of relevant information by neurones in the primate prefrontal cortex. *Nature*, *393*, 577–579.

Ramus, S.J., & Eichenbaum, H. (2000). Neural correlates of olfactory recognition memory in the rat orbitofrontal cortex. *Journal of Neuroscience*, *20*, 8199–8208.

Ranganath, C., Johnson, M.K., & D'Esposito, M. (2000). Left prefrontal activation increases with demands to recall specific perceptual information. *Journal of Neuroscience*, *20*, U11–U15.

Rao, S.C., Rainer, G., & Miller, E.K. (1997). Integration of what and where in the primate prefrontal cortex. *Science*, *276*, 821–824.

Riches, I.P., Wilson, F.A.W., & Brown, M.W. (1991). The effects of visual stimulation and memory on neurones of the hippocampal formation and the neighbouring parahippocampal gyrus and inferior temporal cortex of the primate. *Journal of Neuroscience*, *11*, 1763–1779.

Ringo, J.L. (1996). Stimulus specific adaptation in inferior temporal and medial temporal cortex of the monkey. *Behavioural Brain Research*, *76*, 191–197.

Rolls, E.T., Cahusac, P.M.B., Feigenbaum, J.D., & Miyashita, Y. (1993). Responses of single neurons in the hippocampus of the macaque related to recognition memory. *Experimental Brain Research*, *93*, 299–306.

Rolls, E.T., Miyashita, Y., Cahusac, P.M.B., Kesner, R.P, Niki, H., Feigenbaum, J.D., & Bach, L. (1989). Hippocampal neurons in the monkey with activity related to the place in which a stimulus is shown. *Journal of Neuroscience*, *9*, 1835–1845.

Rolls, E.T., Treves, A., Robertson, R.G., Georges-François, P., & Panzeri, S. (1998). Information about spatial view in an ensemble of primate hippocampal cells. *Journal of Neurophysiology*, *79*, 1797–1813.

Saunders, R.C., Fritz, J.B., & Mishkin, M. (1998). The effects of rhinal cortical lesions on auditory short-term memory in the rhesus monkey. *Society for Neuroscience Abstracts*, *28*, 757.14.

Seamans, J.K., Floresco, S.B., & Phillips, A.G. (1995). Functional differences between the prelimbic and anterior cingulate regions of rat prefrontal cortex. *Behavioral Neuroscience*, *109*, 1063–1073.

Shi, C.J., & Cassel, M.D. (1997). Cortical, thalamic, and amygdaloid projections of rat temporal cortex. *Journal of Comparative Neurology*, *382*, 153–175.

Sobotka, S., & Ringo, J.L. (1994). Stimulus-specific adaptation in excited but not in inhibited cells in inferotemporal cortex of macaque. *Brain Research*, *646*, 95–99.

Steward, O. (1976). Topographical organization of the projections from the entorhinal area to the hippocampal formation of the rat. *Journal of Comparative Neurology*, *167*, 285–314.

Suzuki, W.A., & Amaral, D.G. (1994). Topographical organization of the reciprocal connections between the monkey, cortical afferents. *Journal of Comparative Neurology, 350,* 497–533.

Suzuki, W.A., Miller, E.K., & Desimone, R. (1997). Object and place memory in the macaque entorhinal cortex. *Journal of Neurophysiology, 78,* 1062–1081.

Suzuki, W.A., Zola-Morgan, S., Squire, L.A., & Amaral, D.G. (1993). Lesions of the perirhinal and parahippocampal cortices in the monkey produce long-lasting memory impairment in the visual and tactual modalities. *Journal of Neuroscience, 13,* 2430–2451.

Swanson, L.W., & Köhler, C. (1986). Anatomical evidence for direct projections from the entorhinal cortex to the entire cortical mantle in the rat. *Journal of Neuroscience, 6,* 3010–3023.

Vann, S.D., Brown, M.W., Erichsen, J.T., & Aggleton, J.P. (2000). Fos imaging reveals differential patterns of hippocampal and parahippocampal subfield activation in rats in response to different spatial memory tasks. *Journal of Neuroscience, 20,* 2711–2718.

Vogels, R., Sary, G., & Orban, G.A. (1995). How task-related are the responses of inferior temporal neurons? *Visual Neuroscience, 12,* 207–214.

Wan, H., Aggleton, J.P., & Brown, M.W. (1999). Different contributions of the hippocampus and perirhinal cortex to recognition memory. *Journal of Neuroscience, 19,* 1142–1148.

Wan, H., Warburton, E.C., Kowalska, D.M., & Brown, M.W. (2001). Involvement of the temporal lobe in auditory recognition memory. *European Journal of Neuroscience, 14,* 118–124.

Warburton, E.C., Fry, B., Winstone, J., Aggleton, J.P., & Brown, M.W. (2000). *Effects of hippocampal damage on the processing of visuo-spatial information in the perirhinal and postrhinal cortices.* Abstract presented at 'The nature of hippocampal–cortical interactions: Theoretical and experimental perspectives' conference. Dublin, Trinity College.

Wiebe, S.P., & Staubli, U.V. (1999). Dynamic filtering of recognition memory codes in the hippocampus. *Journal of Neuroscience, 19,* 10562–10574.

Wiener, S.I. (1996). Spatial, behavioral and sensory correlates of hippocampal CA1 complex spike cell activity: Implications for information processing functions. *Progress in Neurobiology, 49,* 335–361.

Wilson, F.A.W., Scalaidhe, S.P.O., & Goldman-Rakic, P.S. (1993). Dissociation of object and spatial processing domains in primate prefrontal cortex. *Science, 260,* 1955–1958.

Witter, M.P., Groenewegen, H.J., Lopes da Silva, F.H., & Lohman, A.H.M. (1989). Functional organization of the extrinsic and intrinsic circuitry of the parahippocampal region. *Progress in Neurobiology, 33,* 161–253.

Witter, M.P., Naber, P.A., van Haeften, T., Machielsen, W.C.M., Rombouts, S.A.R.B., Barkhof, F., Scheltens, P., & Lopes da Silva, F.H. (2000). Cortico-hippocampal communication by way of parallel parahippocampal-subicular pathways. *Hippocampus, 10,* 398–410.

Wood, E.R., Didchenko, P.A., & Eichenbaum, H. (1999). The global record of memory in hippocampal neuronal activity. *Nature, 397,* 613–616.

Xiang, J.Z., & Brown, M.W. (1997a). Processing visual familiarity and recency information: neuronal interactions in area TE and rhinal cortex. *Brain Research Abstracts, 14,* 69.

Xiang, J.Z., & Brown, M.W. (1997b). Neuronal encoding of the prior occurrence of visual stimuli in rhinal cortex and area TE of the monkey. *Brain Research Abstracts, 14,* 42.

Xiang, J.Z., & Brown, M.W. (1998a). Differential neuronal encoding of novelty, familiarity and recency in regions of the anterior temporal lobe. *Neuropharmacology, 37,* 657–676.

Xiang, J.Z., & Brown, M.W. (1998b). Encoding of relative familiarity and recency information in orbital ventromedial and dorsolateral prefrontal cortices and anterior cingulate gyrus. *Society for Neuroscience Abstracts, 28,* 561.20.

Xiang, J.Z., & Brown, M.W. (2000). Interactions between simultaneously recorded neurons in anterior cingulated, orbital, dorsolateral, and ventromedial prefrontal cortex. *European Journal of Neuroscience, 12,* 318–318.

Yee, B.K., & Rawlins, J.N.P. (1998). A comparison between the effects of medial septal lesions and entorhinal cortex lesions on performance of nonspatial working memory tasks and reversal learning. *Behavioural Brain Research, 94*, 281–300.

Young, B.J., Otto, T., Fox, G.D. & Eichenbaum, H. (1997). Memory representation within the parahippocampal region. *Journal of Neuroscience, 17*, 5183–5195.

Zhu, X.O., Brown, M.W., McCabe, B.J., & Aggleton, J.P. (1995a). Effects of novelty or familiarity of visual stimuli on the expression of the immediate early gene c-fos in the rat brain. *Neuroscience, 69*, 821–829.

Zhu, X.O., Brown, M.W., & Aggleton, J.P. (1995b). Neuronal signalling of information important to visual recognition memory in rat rhinal and neighbouring cortices. *European Journal of Neuroscience, 7*, 753–765.

Zhu, X.O., McCabe, B.J., Brown, M.W., & Aggleton, J.P. (1996). Mapping visual recognition through expression of the immediate early gene c-fos. *Neuroreport, 7*, 1871–1875.

Zhu, X.O., McCabe, B.J., Aggleton, J.P., & Brown, M.W. (1997). Differential activation of the hippocampus and perirhinal cortex by novel visual stimuli and a novel environment. *Neuroscience, 229*, 141–143.

Ziakopoulos, Z., Brown, M.W., & Bashir, Z.I. (1999). Input dependent short and long term synaptic plasticity in the rat perirhinal cortex in vitro. *Neuroscience, 92*, 459–472.

Zola, S.M., Squire, L.R., Teng, E., Stefanacci, L., Buffalo, E.A., & Clark, R.E. (2000). Impaired recognition memory in monkeys after damage limited to the hippocampal region. *Journal of Neuroscience, 20*, 451–463.

Zola-Morgan, S.M., Squire, L.R., Amaral, D.G., & Suzuki, W.A. (1989). Lesions of perirhinal and parahippocampal cortex that spare the amygdala and hippocampal formation produce severe impairment. *Journal of Neuroscience, 9*, 4355–4370.

Zola-Morgan, S.M., Squire, L.R., & Ramus, S.J. (1994). Severity of memory impairment in monkeys as a function of locus and extent of damage within the medial temporal lobe memory system. *Hippocampus, 4*, 483–495.

CHAPTER SEVEN

Memory encoding in the primate brain: The role of the basal forebrain

Amanda Parker, Alex Easton
School of Psychology, University of Nottingham, UK

David Gaffan
Department of Experimental Psychology, Oxford University, UK

INTRODUCTION

The neural structures underlying the encoding of memories have long been a subject of investigation. Studies in human patients in the mid-1950s indicated that damage to structures in the medial temporal lobe resulted in a severe memory impairment that did not affect other cognitive abilities. The early focus of investigation in these patients was the hippocampus, but more recent work has suggested that the role of the hippocampus is limited primarily to the encoding of episodic memories. Further patient groups, with damage to other structures of the brain but with similar severe amnesia, can help shed light on the structures that interact to allow encoding of memories. These investigations have given rise to several different explanations about the cause of severe anterograde amnesia in humans. Similarly, lesion studies in animals have shown that there are multiple memory systems in the brain, underlying different aspects of memory, and consensus is not yet reached over the relative importance of either structures or systems. In this chapter, we review the literature and then our recent work, which suggests that none of the brain areas that store the elements of memories are able to encode information without modulation of their activity by the cholinergic cells of the basal forebrain.

THE HIPPOCAMPAL HYPOTHESIS OF AMNESIA

The effects of medial temporal lobe surgery in human patients (Scoville & Milner, 1957) highlighted the importance of medial temporal lobe structures in learning and memory. The severity of the amnesia in the patients appeared to correlate with the amount of damage that the surgeon believed to have occurred to the hippocampus (Scoville & Milner, 1957). The hypothesis that damage to the hippocampus was the cause of the severe anterograde amnesia, however, faced immediate problems. Attempts in monkeys to recreate the surgical approach used in the amnesic patients failed to show the severe impairments that would be expected from these patients (Correll & Scoville, 1965a,b; Orbach, Miller, & Rasmussen, 1960). However, human patients with severe amnesia and damage to the hippocampal system continued to be reported (Delay & Brion, 1969; Oxbury et al., 1997; Warrington & Duchen, 1992; Zola-Morgan, Squire, & Amaral, 1986).

Selective damage to the hippocampus is rare in humans. Whereas in monkeys excitotoxic lesions of the hippocampus can lead to a selective cell loss without damaging fibres of passage, damage to the hippocampus in humans is often associated with damage to fibres of passage and adjacent structures. However, one group of patients that might be of importance in studying the effects of hippocampal damage alone in humans are those who suffer anoxic damage to the hippocampus early in life (Vargha-Khadem et al., 1997) or damage to the fornix alone (Aggleton et al., 2000; Gaffan, Gaffan, & Hodges, 1991; McMackin, Cockburn, Anslow, & Gaffan, 1995; for a review see Gaffan & Gaffan, 1991). Findings from the patients suggest that the role of the hippocampus in memory is much more selective. Typically, these patients show a clinical amnesia, especially for events, but can show normal recognition memory and those children with early anoxic damage can develop a nearly normal level of semantic knowledge. Similarly, monkeys with bilateral section of the fornix are impaired at a scene memory task that might be considered as a primate model of episodic memory (Gaffan, 1994), but are unimpaired at tasks of recognition memory (Gaffan, Gaffan, & Harrison, 1984; for a review, see Gaffan, 1992). This has led to the hypothesis that the hippocampus is part of a system that is specifically adapted for episodic memory and which includes the mamillary bodies and anterior thalamus (Aggleton & Brown, 1999; Delay & Brion, 1969; Parker & Gaffan, 1997a,b).

THE AMYGDALO-HIPPOCAMPAL THEORY OF SEVERE ANTEROGRADE AMNESIA

As the hippocampal damage alone in patient H.M. does not appear able to explain his severe and global memory impairments, alternative ideas had to be considered. H.M.'s medial temporal lobe damage was not confined to the hippocampus but also included the amygdala (Scoville & Milner, 1957). Experiments in the monkey suggested that complete bilateral removals of both the hippocampus and amygdala resulted in a very severe deficit in visual recognition memory (Mishkin, 1978; Zola-Morgan, Squire, & Mishkin, 1982). It was also demonstrated that impairments in visual recognition memory could be created in monkeys with damage to only the fibre tracts of both these structures, the fornix and the ventral amygdalo-fugal pathway (Bachevalier, Parkinson, & Mishkin, 1985; but see also Parker & Gaffan, 1998a). The proposal was that these structures, through their fibre pathways, would influence the activity of two memory pathways, one projecting to the mediodorsal nucleus of the thalamus via the amygdala and projecting on then to frontal cortex, and a second projection through hippocampus and fornix to the mamillary bodies and then on to the anterior nucleus of the thalamus (Mishkin, 1982). Thus memory formation relied upon communication between temporal cortex and the diencephalon via structures of the medial temporal lobe.

Densely amnesic patients, however, are impaired not only at the tests of visual recognition memory seen in non-human primates with lesions of medial temporal lobe structures, but also at object discrimination learning (Aggleton, Nicol, Huston, & Fairburn, 1988; Hood, Postle, & Corkin, 1996; Oscar-Berman & Zola-Morgan, 1980). Therefore, any animal model of severe anterograde amnesia should include an impairment in object discrimination learning. Gaffan (1996) showed that object discrimination learning could be seen to be reliant on limbic structures if the difficulty of the task was raised to be of a similar level to trial-unique match-to-sample or non-match-to-sample, by increasing the number of concurrent discriminations being learnt. Similarly, Dore, Thornton, White, & Murray (1998) demonstrated that monkeys with selective hippocampal lesions could be impaired at visual discrimination learning if the discriminations were made dependent on visual context.

THE RHINAL CORTEX THEORY OF SEVERE
ANTEROGRADE AMNESIA

Another major problem faced by the amygdalo-hippocampal hypothesis was that the surgical approach used to make these lesions in monkey and humans involved incidental damage to surrounding cortical areas (Murray, 1996). However, damage to the rhinal cortex (entorhinal plus perirhinal cortex) was found to be very important in the visual recognition deficits seen after medial temporal lobe surgery in monkey (Buckley, Gaffan, & Murray, 1997; Gaffan & Murray, 1992; Meunier, Bachevalier, Mishkin, & Murray, 1993; Murray, 1996; Zola-Morgan, Squire, Amaral, & Suzuki, 1989). Focus on the role of the rhinal cortex in learning began in earnest with the observation that the perirhinal cortex extended more laterally and more rostrally than was previously thought (Amaral, Insausti, & Cowan, 1987; Insausti, Amaral, & Cowan, 1987; Suzuki & Amaral, 1994). This led to a re-examination of the histology of animals that had received medial temporal lobe ablations, to measure the amount of rhinal cortex damage that had been produced by the surgeries. Studies of the rhinal cortex in those animals that were severely impaired at object recognition memory showed that there had been some damage to this cortical area in those lesions (Murray, 1996).

Electrophysiological studies in the monkey had shown that there were cells in the inferior temporal cortex, most notably the perirhinal cortex, that showed activity based on the novelty or familiarity of a visual object (see Chapter 6 for a review). Such cells suggest a role for the perirhinal cortex in object recognition, where such novelty and familiarity judgements can allow an animal to determine if an object has been seen before. This again supports the argument that disruption of normal rhinal cortex function by medial temporal lobe ablations would result in a recognition memory impairment (Murray, 1996; Zola-Morgan et al., 1989; Gaffan & Murray, 1992; Meunier et al., 1993; Buckley et al., 1997). By contrast, large bilateral excitotoxic lesions of the amygdala and hippocampus do not produce an impairment in recognition memory (Murray & Mishkin, 1998), again supporting the idea that the impairments seen after medial temporal lobe ablations can be attributed to rhinal cortex damage. (For discussion of a recent meta-analysis of studies in monkeys looking at recognition memory in monkeys with lesions of either the hippocampus or the perirhinal cortex, see Chapter 5.)

If ablation of the medial temporal lobe in monkeys produces memory deficits that are the result of damage to rhinal cortex, does the same hold true in patients with severe anterograde amnesia? An anatomical study of patient H.M.'s lesion using magnetic resonance imaging (MRI) (Corkin et al., 1997) showed that, indeed, there was damage to rhinal cortex bilaterally, almost completely removing entorhinal cortex, but sparing the ventrocaudal extent of the perirhinal cortex. Could this damage, then, underlie the severe anterograde amnesia? First, we must ask whether the effects of rhinal cortex lesions in monkey are similar to the memory impairments in densely amnesic patients? Rhinal or perirhinal cortex ablations in the monkey are seen to impair recognition memory and the recall of object discriminations, but not always the postoperative learning of new object discriminations (Buckley & Gaffan, 1997; Buckley et al., 1997; Gaffan & Murray, 1992; Thornton, Rothblat, & Murray, 1997). However, animals with perirhinal lesions are impaired at the new learning of discriminations if those discriminations are made perceptually more difficult. This can be done by increasing the number of distracting, non-rewarded objects (Buckley & Gaffan, 1997), by presenting two objects in different views on each trial (Buckley & Gaffan, 1998a) or within a complex background (Buckley & Gaffan, 1998b), or by increasing the number of similar stimuli that the animal has learnt in the past, making discriminations of these similar stimuli more difficult (Easton & Gaffan, 2000a).

One recent explanation of these findings is that the perirhinal cortex has both mnemonic and perceptual functions (Buckley & Gaffan, 1998c; Murray & Bussey, 1999) and that the learning impairments seen after perirhinal lesions closely resemble the impairments in semantic memory seen in humans after inferior temporal lobe lesions (Murray, 1996; Murray & Bussey, 1999). Rhinal cortex lesioned monkeys are unimpaired at a visual recognition task that has non-trial-unique object presentations (Eacott, Gaffan, & Murray, 1994) and at colour discrimination (Buckley et al., 1997), but they are impaired at paired associate learning and configural learning to a similar degree (Buckley & Gaffan, 1998c). Also, monkeys with lesions of the peri-rhinal cortex are impaired at recognising the odd-one-out of six stimuli where five are images of the same object from different views and the sixth is an image of a different object (Buckley, Booth, Rolls, & Gaffan, 1998). The pattern of impairments after rhinal cortex ablations in monkeys, then, does not appear to support the hypothesis that such damage produces severe anterograde amnesia in man.

DIENCEPHALIC THEORIES OF SEVERE ANTEROGRADE AMNESIA

Damage to the diencephalon can result in severe anterograde amnesia in humans (Dusoir et al., 1990; Graff-Radford, Tramel, Van Hoesen, & Brandt, 1990; Kopelman 1995; Mair, Warrington, & Weiskrantz, 1979). Two possible routes through the diencephalon have been considered important in memory, either alone or in combination. The first is a route from hippocampus through the fornix to the mamillary bodies and then on to the anterior thal-amus and cingulate cortex (Aggleton & Brown, 1999; Delay & Brion, 1969). The second is a route from inferior temporal cortex to the mediodorsal nucleus of the thalamus (MD) and then on to frontal cortex (Aggleton and Mishkin, 1983a,b; Mishkin, 1982).

There is now much evidence that the hippocampal–anterior-thalamic cir-cuit is of importance in human episodic memory (for a review, see Aggleton & Brown, 1999). In monkeys, a scene-based object-in-place task can be con-sidered as in some ways analogous to human episodic memory because of its combination of spatial and object knowledge, rapid learning, and unique background scenes for every problem (Gaffan, 1994, 1998). Lesions at any point of this hippocampal–anterior-thalamic circuit in monkeys impair nor-mal learning in this scene task (Gaffan, 1994; Gaffan & Parker, 1996; Parker & Gaffan, 1997a,b). This impairment, however, does not extend to lesions of the cingulate cortex (Parker & Gaffan, 1997a), which was considered to be the final projection of the circuit, as originally proposed by Delay and Brion (1969). In humans too, lesions within this pathway lead to a significant impairment in episodic memory (Aggleton & Sahgal, 1993; Aggleton et al., 2000; Delay & Brion, 1969; Dusoir et al., 1990; Gaffan & Gaffan, 1991; Mair et al., 1979).

Although lesions at any point in this pathway can lead to an impairment in episodic memory in humans, not all patients with such lesions are densely amnesic, as recognition memory can be spared (Aggleton & Brown, 1999; Gaffan & Gaffan, 1991). Patient R.B. (Zola-Morgan et al., 1986) had anoxic damage that, at pathology, appeared to be localised within the CA1 region of the hippocampus. The more significant amnesia in this patient than in those with damage to the fornix alone calls into question the extent to which the hippocampal–anterior-thalamic circuit can be considered as a single functional circuit. However, anoxic damage in monkeys, which like R.B. can result in pathology apparently limited to the CA1 region of the hippocampus, can produce more severe memory impairments than excitotoxic hippocampal lesions (Bachevalier & Meunier, 1996). This suggests that although anoxic pathology appears limited to the CA1 region of the hippocampus, other areas might also be affected. Therefore, R.B.'s amnesia might result from undetected pathology outside of the hippocampus. The hippocampal–anterior-thalamic circuit, then, might underlie some aspects of episodic memory but cannot explain the severe anterograde amnesia seen after medial temporal lobe surgery (Scoville & Milner, 1957) where hippocampectomy will disrupt this hippocampal–anterior-thalamic circuit.

In contrast to this hippocampal–anterior-thalamic circuit, the circuit from inferior temporal cortex to nucleus MD of the thalamus and on to the frontal cortex allows communication between two separate cortical areas essential for learning. Bilateral ablations of either inferior temporal or frontal cortex in monkeys results in an inability to learn new visual discriminations (Gross, 1973; Mishkin, 1954; Parker & Gaffan, 1998b), or perform recognition memory tasks (Bachevalier & Mishkin, 1986; Gaffan & Murray, 1992; Meunier, Bachevalier, & Mishkin, 1997; Mishkin, 1982). Similarly, lesions of nucleus MD of the thalamus in monkeys also lead to impairments in these tasks (Aggleton & Mishkin, 1983a,b; Zola-Morgan & Squire, 1985). Inferior temporal cortex can project to nucleus MD of the thalamus either directly (passing close to the amygdala and so likely to be disrupted by medial temporal lobe surgery; Goulet, Dore, & Murray, 1998) or via the amygdala. The afferents to nucleus MD of the thalamus from these structures, however, project only to the medial portion of the magnocellular division of nucleus MD (Russchen, Amaral, & Price, 1987) whereas the entire nucleus MD of the thalamus has reciprocal connections with the frontal cortex (Goldman-Rakic & Porrino, 1985; Russchen et al., 1987). If nucleus MD of the thalamus is acting as a relay between inferior temporal and frontal cortex, then lesions restricted to this medial portion of the magnocellular division of nucleus MD should have the same effects on learning as lesions removing the entire magnocellular division of nucleus MD. This has been tested in monkeys performing delayed match-to-sample in an automated apparatus, where lesions confined to this medial portion of the magnocellular division of MD have a very mild effect on this task (Parker, Eacott, & Gaffan, 1997) while lesions removing the entire magnocellular division have a much greater effect (Gaffan & Parker, 2000).

That the larger lesions of nucleus MD of the thalamus produce a larger impairment than lesions restricted to the medial portion of the magnocellular division indicates that the impairment is not entirely a result of disrupting the flow of information from inferior temporal to frontal cortex via nucleus MD, as this should be equally affected by both the large and small lesions of MD. Instead, Gaffan and Parker (2000) proposed that the effect of the large MD lesion is to disrupt the normal activity of the frontal cortex to which it projects. A smaller lesion of MD (affecting only the medial portion of the magnocellular division) produces a smaller impairment because it disrupts frontal activity to a lesser extent. In amnesic patients with medial thalamic damage, the lesion is rarely so localised as to be specific to those regions receiving limbic afferents (i.e. the medial portion of the magnocellular division of MD). Therefore, lesions of MD (where they exist) in humans tend to be large and might have their amnestic effect by disruption of frontal cortical activity. This also fits with observations that amnesic patients with damage to nucleus MD of the thalamus can have impairments in tasks sensitive to frontal cortex function (Daum & Ackermann, 1994; Kopelman, 1995). If disruption of frontal cortex activity is the amnestic effect of MD lesions in man, then the disruption of projections to MD from inferior temporal cortex cannot be the explanation for the severe anterograde amnesia seen after medial temporal lobe surgery as previously proposed (Mishkin, 1978, 1982).

THE TEMPORAL STEM THEORY OF SEVERE ANTEROGRADE AMNESIA

An alternative explanation of the severe anterograde amnesia following medial temporal lobe surgery was put forward by Horel (1978), who proposed that damage to the white matter of the anterior temporal stem was the cause of severe anterograde amnesia. The temporal stem is the band of white matter at the base of the temporal lobe, dorsolateral to the amygdala and hippocampus. In humans it contains many fibres, including the uncinate fascicle, inferior occipitofrontal fascicle, Meyer's loop, anterior commissure, and the inferior thalamic bundle (Ebeling & Cramon, 1992). Horel proposed that the anterior portion of the temporal stem would be damaged in medial temporal lobe ablations that successfully removed the amygdala and part of the hippocampus. Horel and colleagues demonstrated that lesions of this white matter tract in monkeys produced severe deficits in visual recognition memory (Cirillo, Horel, & George, 1989), and in some cases also profound deficits in visual discrimination learning (Horel & Misantone, 1976; Cirillo et al., 1989; Zola-Morgan et al., 1982). Indeed, Correll & Scoville (1965a,b) showed some evidence, with their medial temporal lobe ablations in monkeys, that the impairment on their visual tasks was most severe in those animals with some involvement of the temporal stem. However, the lesions of Horel and colleagues were not generally consistent and, especially on visual discrimination learning, not all animals showed the same lesion effects. Although the results of Zola-Morgan et al. (1982) demonstrated that lesions of the temporal stem did not have the effect on visual recognition memory that combined lesions of the hippocampus and amygdala lesions did, the temporal stem sections in these animals were more posterior than that discussed by Horel (1978). Also, as discussed above, the effects of the combined ablation of the hippocampus and amygdala was more likely to be the result of rhinal cortex damage (Murray, 1996).

In the anatomical study of patient H.M.'s lesion (Corkin et al., 1997) the temporal stem was specifically studied and found to be intact. The temporal stem in this study, however, was defined as being "immediately dorsal to the hippocampal formation" (Corkin et al., 1997, p. 3977). This correlates to the temporal stem as sectioned by Zola-Morgan et al. (1982) and not that discussed by Horel (1978), which is specifically the anterior portion of the temporal lobe white matter. Indeed, the anterior portion of the temporal lobe white matter is substantially damaged in H.M. (Corkin et al., 1997, p. 3975 and Figures 2H, I, and J). A more recent MRI scan of another severely amnesic patient with damage in the medial temporal lobe (patient E.P.) also shows significant bilateral damage to the temporal stem white matter (Stefanaci, Buffalo, Schmolck, & Squire, 2000). Also, as will be discussed later, many important fibres through the temporal stem, that might be involved in learning, run close to the amygdala and so are unlikely to be spared by a complete ablation of the grey matter of the amygdala.

A variety of explanations for the effect of temporal stem section in monkeys have been put forward. Horel himself discussed the temporal stem section as disrupting communication between temporal and frontal lobes (Horel, 1978). This could either be by direct corticocortical communication, as in the uncinate fascicle, or by indirect communication via the thalamus. The uncinate fascicle is the major monosynaptic corticocortical projection route of fibres between area TE and the frontal lobe (Ungerleider, Gaffan, & Pelak, 1989). Section of the uncinate fascicle bilaterally has no effect on visual recognition memory, or visual discrimination learning (Gaffan & Eacott, 1995; Gutnikov, Ma, Buckley, & Gaffan, 1997a), although it does impair specific types of conditional learning (Eacott & Gaffan, 1992).

Therefore, damage to the uncinate fascicle alone is not the cause of the impairments seen in monkeys after section of the temporal stem.

Cortico-thalamic projections from area TE and perirhinal cortex to nucleus MD of the thalamus have been shown to be disrupted by aspiration amygdala lesions, although not excitotoxic amygdala lesions (Goulet et al., 1998). It is possible that the route for these fibres is within the temporal stem white matter close to the amygdala and so is affected by temporal stem sections in monkeys (Goulet et al., 1998). However, as discussed above, the main role of the medial thalamus in memory appears to be the modulation of normal frontal cortical activity, not the relay of information arriving from temporal cortex and amygdala. One other group of fibres to project through the temporal stem white matter are those from the basal forebrain, and recent work in the monkey has indicated that this projection may be vital to new memory formation (Gaffan, Parker, & Easton, 2001; Easton & Gaffan, 2000a,b; 2001; Easton, Ridley, Baker, & Gaffan, 2002; Easton, Parker, & Gaffan, 2001).

ANATOMY OF THE BASAL FOREBRAIN

The basal forebrain consists of the substantia innominata, nucleus basalis of Meynert, nucleus of the diagonal band, the septal nuclei, and the hypothalamus. The hypothalamus has the largest projection to cortex of any structure after the thalamus, suggesting a modulatory role (Saper, 1990). Much attention has been paid to the cholinergic cells of the basal forebrain, but many cells not expressing acetylcholine also exist. The cells of the monkey basal forebrain were divided by Mesulam, Mufson, Levey, & Wainer (1983) into distinct groups. The cholinergic cells of the basal forebrain were divided into four groups, Ch1–4 and have become known as the cholinergic basal forebrain (Mesulam, 1995).

Group Ch1 constitutes approximately 10 per cent of the medial septal nucleus that projects to the hippocampus. Group Ch2 corresponds to a large proportion (about 70 per cent) of the vertical limb of the nucleus of the diagonal band. This is a major source of basal forebrain afferents to the hippocampus, and also innervates the hypothalamus. Group Ch3 is a very small group (about 1 per cent of all the cells), which projects mainly to the olfactory bulb. The major cholinergic projection to cortex arises from group Ch4, which corresponds to approximately 90 per cent of the nucleus basalis of Meynert. These cells project to almost the entire cortical mantle, as well as the amygdala. It has been proposed that these cholinergic cells allow a route for selected cortical and limbic areas to influence the entire cortical mantle (Mesulam & Mufson, 1984). Despite the widespread projection from the cholinergic cells of group Ch4 to the cortex (Mesulam et al., 1983), they receive input from only a few select cortical areas. These afferents to Ch4 cells arise from orbitofrontal cortex, the temporal pole, entorhinal cortex, and medial temporal cortex (Mesulam & Mufson, 1984). Mesulam and Mufson argue that this limited set of afferents and diverse efferents allows areas such as the frontal cortex to modulate the cholinergic activity to the entire cortical mantle.

The projections of the basal forebrain to inferior temporal cortex and medial temporal lobe structures pass through the fornix, amygdala and anterior temporal stem. Kitt et al. (1987) studied the projection of cells from Ch2, Ch3, and Ch4 to the entire cortical mantle using autoradiography and immunohistochemical techniques to show the pathways of the fibres. These findings in monkey have been supported by more recent work with human brains showing a very similar pattern of projections to cortex from the basal forebrain (Seldon et al., 1998).

RELATIONSHIP BETWEEN THE BASAL FOREBRAIN AND THE TEMPORAL STEM THEORY OF SEVERE ANTEROGRADE AMNESIA

As discussed above, fibres from the basal forebrain reach structures of the temporal and medial temporal lobe through three main routes, the ventral pathway, the lateral pathway, and the fornix. We proposed (Gaffan et al., 2001) that some of the variability in the results of Horel and others (Horel, 1978; Horel & Misantone, 1976; Cirillo et al., 1989) could be due to only partial disruption of these fibres. Transection of the anterior temporal stem alone would leave fibres in the fornix and those in the ventral pathway running through, or near to, the amygdala intact. Gaffan et al. (2001) more completely isolated the temporal lobe from these basal forebrain inputs by making a combined section of the white matter tracts of the fornix, amygdala, and anterior temporal stem. These animals were tested on a variety of new learning tasks with various combinations of lesions. In agreement with the variable effects after temporal stem sections alone (Cirillo et al., 1989), it was seen that animals with lesions of temporal stem alone were only partially impaired at visual discriminations, improving significantly over three sets of ten concurrent discriminations postoperatively. Addition of either an amygdala section or a fornix transection to these animals made no significant difference, but a combined lesion of all three white matter tracts resulted in a substantial and persistent impairment in the learning of concurrent visual discrimination problems (Gaffan et al., 2001). Also, in agreement with the temporal stem alone sections (Cirillo et al., 1989), we showed that sections of the temporal stem and amygdala, even with fornix intact, produced a very severe impairment in postoperative performance of a delayed match-to-sample task (Gaffan et al., 2001).

Dense amnesia is characterised by a deficit in encoding memories of a variety of types, so we also measured performance on a scene-based object-in-place task that, as discussed above, can be considered a useful model of episodic memory in the monkey (Gaffan, 1994, 1998). After section of the anterior temporal stem and amygdala bilaterally, these animals showed a significant impairment in this task, similar in severity to that seen after fornix section alone (Gaffan, 1994; Gaffan et al., 2001). Addition of a fornix section to this lesion, however, resulted in a very severe impairment in performance, with animals showing no improvement from chance within a session where preoperatively they were performing at nearly 90 per cent correct after one presentation of each scene. This effect of adding the fornix section to the amygdala and anterior temporal stem section was very much greater than the additive effects of fornix section and amygdala and anterior temporal stem section separately. This led us to propose that the complete isolation of the temporal lobe from its basal forebrain afferents resulted in a severe anterograde amnesia in the monkey.

Importantly, and in contrast to previous results obtained with rhinal cortex ablations, although these animals with combined white matter lesions were severely impaired at new visual learning, their postoperative retention of preoperatively learnt material was relatively preserved (Gaffan et al., 2001). One animal was taught 100 visual discrimination problems preoperatively and tested on its postoperative retention. Although this animal did not perform at preoperative levels on the very first presentation of the problems postoperatively, it was significantly above chance. Also, it rapidly relearnt these 100 problems postoperatively (within four presentations it was performing at over 90 per cent correct), although it was severely impaired at learning very much fewer new problems postoperatively. This rapid relearning, then, is an effect of retention of preoperatively learnt material, which resembles the relative sparing of retrograde memory in densely amnesic patients despite their severe impairment in new learning (Dusoir et al., 1990; Kapur et al., 1996; Milner, Corkin, & Teuber, 1968; Scoville & Milner, 1957; Teuber, Milner, & Vaughan, 1968).

EVIDENCE FOR THE IMPORTANCE OF THE BASAL FOREBRAIN IN MEMORY

The basal forebrain has been implicated in human amnesia both through lesions resulting in amnesia after anterior communicating artery aneurysms (Abe, Inokawa, Kashiwagi, & Yanagihara, 1998; Damasio et al., 1985) and penetrating injuries through the nostril (Dusoir et al., 1990; Teuber et al., 1968). Damage from aneurysms of the anterior communicating artery often cause widespread damage of basal forebrain regions such as the substantia innominata, septal nuclei, nucleus basalis of Meynert, and the hypothalamus. Penetrating injuries, on the other hand, produce much more localised lesions that are typically in the region of the mamillary bodies in the hypothalamus (Dusoir et al., 1990; Squire et al., 1989), although alterations of the patient's pituitary system and emotional responses suggest that other regions of the hypothalamus are also compromised (Dusoir et al., 1990). Indeed, relatively localised damage to the region of the ventromedial hypothalamus has been shown in humans to lead to an abnormal behavioural pattern that can include significant anterograde amnesia (Flynn, Cummings, & Tomiyasu, 1988). It should be noted, though, that the amnesia in these patients was not formally tested, and was part of a much wider behavioural impairment including emotional and motivational problems.

There are also changes in the cells of the basal forebrain in Alzheimer's disease, with significant loss of acetylcholine (Whitehouse et al., 1982). Although as the disease progresses many other transmitter systems change, the reduction in basal forebrain acetylcholine is the change best correlated with the severity of the dementia (Bierer et al., 1995). Also, the acetylcholinesterase-staining non-cholinergic cells of the hypothalamus are among the first cells in the brain to develop neurofibrillary tangles typical of Alzheimer's disease (Saper & German, 1987). If this functional system of cholinergic and non-cholinergic cells of the basal forebrain are among the first to show signs of disease, and the loss of these cells is correlated with the severity of dementia in Alzheimer's, then this too supports the proposal that the basal forebrain is important in learning and memory in humans.

The basal forebrain damage in humans from anterior communicating artery aneurysms or nasal penetration injuries, however, is not very specific and damages many areas outside of the basal forebrain. Even in those fairly localised lesions such as reported by Abe et al. (1998) where damage does not appear to extend beyond the basal forebrain, the number of fibre tracts and transmitter systems in this area confuse any interpretation of the results. Similarly, in Alzheimer's disease the loss of acetylcholine might best correlate with the severity of the dementia, but so many areas and transmitter systems of the brain are disrupted by this disease, as are so many cognitive functions, that again any interpretation in terms of the role of basal forebrain in learning and memory is difficult. It is therefore important to consider specific and localised basal forebrain lesions in animals and examine how these correlate with learning and memory impairments.

ROLE OF BASAL FOREBRAIN IN LEARNING IN NON-HUMAN SPECIES

Excitotoxic lesions of the basal forebrain in monkeys have been used to spare fibres of passage through the region but to lesion the cells that project to cortex, including the cholinergic cells of the nucleus basalis of Meynert (group Ch4). These lesions have typically resulted in impairments in learning and reversal of visual discriminations and recognition memory (Aigner et al., 1991; Irle & Markowitsch, 1987; Ridley, Murray, Johnson, & Baker, 1986). Voytko et al. (1994) found, however, that combined excitotoxic lesions of groups Ch1–4 in monkeys did not produce learning impairments in a variety of discrimination tasks. However, staining for AChE (a marker for acetylcholine) was normal in the hippocampus of these animals, implying that the lesion, especially of groups Ch1 and Ch2, might have been incomplete. It should also be noted that these excitotoxic lesions would also have affected cells in the basal forebrain outside of the cholinergic cell groups. Aigner et al. (1991) noted that only combined lesions of groups Ch1–4 gave consistent reductions in markers for acetylcholine and a behavioural impairment; any lesions that spared some of these cholinergic cell groups did not. This could indicate that either a very large loss of acetylcholine must be obtained to produce an effect or that significant damage to non-cholinergic cells of the basal forebrain must also be important in learning and memory. The excitotoxic lesions used in these studies will destroy both cholinergic and non-cholinergic cells, and so any effect of the lesion can be ascribed only to the basal forebrain, and not to the cholinergic system implicated by its association with Alzheimer's disease.

Administration of scopolamine (an antagonist of the cholinergic muscarinic receptor) in monkeys leads to an impairment in a number of tasks, such as discrimination learning (Aigner & Mishkin, 1993; Harder, Baker, & Ridley, 1998) and recognition memory (Tang, Mishkin, & Aigner, 1997). This effect is specific to the cholinergic system and implies an important role for this system in learning. Recently a technique has been developed for producing lesions of only the cholinergic cells of the basal forebrain. Selective destruction of cholinergic basal forebrain cells in New World monkeys (marmosets) have been shown to produce behavioural effects, impairing visuospatial conditional discriminations (Ridley et al., 1999a,b), and difficult visual discriminations (Fine et al., 1997). More recently, lesions using this immunotoxin in macaque monkeys has shown a severe anterograde learning impairment (Easton et al., 2000), which is similar in extent to that following bilateral ablation of the temporal stem, amygdala and fornix (Gaffan et al., 2001). This is in contrast to some studies in rats using a similar selective toxin.

These studies in rats have failed to find impairments in spatial learning (Baxter et al., 1995, 1996). By contrast, some studies have found impairments in spatial learning in rats after lesions localised to the Ch4 group (Berger-Sweeney et al., 1994). Where impairments are found after cholinergic lesions in rats, there is some indication that the impairments are more attentional than mnemonic, affecting delayed match-to-position in a non-delay-dependent manner (Baxter et al., 1995) or preventing latent inhibition (Baxter, Holland, & Gallagher, 1997). Such inconsistencies in the results of the same lesions in monkeys and rats might have a physiological foundation.

The cholinergic system in primates has several anatomical and pharmaco-
logical differences to that of the rat (Mesulam 1995). Also, although in all the
selective cholinergic lesion studies described above, the saporin is conjugated
with an antibody for the p75 receptor, it is found that the antibody to the rat
p75 receptor does not bind in the monkey brain (Fine et al., 1997). Therefore,
in monkey studies the saporin is conjugated to the antibody for the human
p75 receptor (Fine et al., 1997; Mrzljak, Levey, Belcher, & Golman-Rakic,
1998). This implies that the cholinergic cells being destroyed in both species
are different, and this difference could be the origin of the species difference
seen after these lesions.

Whether or not the cholinergic cells alone play an important part in the
role played by the basal forebrain in learning requires further study. Indeed,
the work using the immunotoxin in macaques suggests that isolation of the
inferior temporal cortex and medial temporal lobe from their cholinergic
afferents might not be sufficient to produce a severe anterograde amnesia
(Easton et al., 2000). Instead, Easton et al. showed that the most severe
deficits came when the cholinergic cells of the basal forebrain were lesioned in
combination with a fornix section (Easton et al., 2000). However, it appears
from this evidence in monkeys that the cholinergic system has a role to play in
learning and memory. That the sections of fornix, amygdala, and anterior
temporal stem in monkeys (Gaffan et al., 2001) isolate the inferior temporal
cortex from its basal forebrain afferents, resulting in a dense anterograde
amnesia, also supports this hypothesis. Gaffan et al. (2001) proposed the
basal forebrain to be a site of corticocortical communication between frontal
and inferior temporal cortex, and that this is the basis of the role it plays in
learning.

BASAL FOREBRAIN AS A ROUTE OF CORTICO-
CORTICAL COMMUNICATION BETWEEN FRONTAL
AND INFERIOR TEMPORAL CORTEX

As described earlier, both frontal and inferior temporal cortex are required
for new learning in tasks such as recognition memory tasks, or visual discriminations. In tasks such as visual discrimination where lesions of frontal
cortex in one hemisphere and inferior temporal cortex in the opposite hemisphere have no effect on learning (Parker & Gaffan, 1998b) this communication must be interhemispheric and subcortical. The basal forebrain is ideally
suited for such communication. The entire basal forebrain receives projections from the frontal cortex (Mesulam & Mufson, 1984; Ongur, An, & Price,
1998; Rempel-Clower & Barbas, 1998) and, in turn, projects to the inferior
temporal cortex (Mesulam et al., 1983; Webster, Bachevalier, & Ungerleider,
1993). The communication within the basal forebrain between hypothalamus
and the cholinergic cells of more anterior areas can be bilateral (Cullinan &

Zaborszky, 1991), and this in combination with the connections of the basal forebrain with midbrain areas (Russchen et al., 1987) (which themselves receive afferents from both hemispheres), allows the basal forebrain to be part of a bilateral communication between these cortical areas.

The cells of the basal forebrain are responsive to reward, and also to predictors of reward (Rolls, Sanghera, & Roper-Hall, 1979; Fukuda, Ono, Nishino, & Nakamura, 1986; Fukuda, Masuda, Ono, & Tabuchi, 1993; Wilson & Rolls, 1990). One way in which the basal forebrain might contribute to the communication between frontal and inferior temporal cortex, then, is the signalling of reinforcement. If the frontal cortex sets the current goals of the task, then this can be signalled to the basal forebrain. If the basal forebrain then receives a signal of reward that corresponds to the current goal, as determined by the frontal cortex, then it can signal this to the inferior temporal cortex to reinforce the representation of the correct object. This can explain the limited afferents to basal forebrain in comparison to the widespread efferents (Mesulam & Mufson, 1984) in that the afferents set the currently appropriate condition while the reinforcement can be signalled to any appropriate cortical area.

Recent work in the monkey has shown that lesions of the medial forebrain bundle (which communicates between midbrain reward centres and the basal forebrain) in one hemisphere and inferior temporal cortex in the opposite hemisphere impairs learning of object discriminations (Easton & Gaffan, 2000a; 2001), scenes (Easton & Gaffan, 2000a), and recognition memory (Easton et al., 2001) to a similar extent as lesions of the temporal stem, amygdala, and fornix (Gaffan et al., 2001) or the cholinergic basal forebrain (Easton et al., 2000). Interestingly, crossed lesions of the medial forebrain bundle in one hemisphere and frontal cortex in the opposite hemisphere result in a similar level of impairment in these tasks to the disconnections from inferior temporal cortex (Easton & Gaffan, 2001; Easton et al., 2001).

We have proposed a model of frontotemporal interactions via the basal forebrain based on these results (Easton et al., 2001). In this model, the frontal cortex determines the current goal of the animal. This goal is then signalled to the midbrain reward centres where peripheral signals of reward are integrated with the goal signal. In this way, the animal can determine whether it has succeeded in achieving its goal. This integrated signal of reward and goal is then sent to the cholinergic basal forebrain via the medial forebrain bundle. The cholinergic basal forebrain then signals the information to the structures involved in encoding the memory (such as the hippocampal–anterior-thalamic circuit for episodic memories, or perirhinal cortex for visual memories) where the event or object is then reinforced if it coincides with the animal's goals.

CONCLUSIONS

Where early work on the neuroanatomy of amnesia focused on the hippocampus, it now appears that this structure is essential only for episodic memories. In this type of learning, it is a part of a unified system that includes the mamillary bodies and anterior thalamus. By contrast, the perirhinal cortex appears to be required for the type of learning that can be classed as semantic learning. Damage to the mediodorsal nucleus of the thalamus also appears to have an amnestic effect through disruption of frontal cortical function. Despite there being this variety of memory structures in the brain, each with a different function, recent work is indicating that the cholinergic basal forebrain acts to modulate these different systems. In modulating these systems they allow normal memory formation, although do not affect memories once they are encoded in these structures. Future work must examine the specific role of the cholinergic cells in this modulation, and also test the model proposed here that the basal forebrain is not required for the retrieval of memories that are already encoded. The interactions of memory structures in the retrieval of encoded memories is examined further in Chapter 8.

REFERENCES

Abe, K., Inokawa, M., Kashiwagi, A., & Yanagihara, T. (1998). Amnesia after a discrete basal forebrain lesion. *Journal of Neurology, Neurosurgery and Psychiatry*, *65*, 126–130.

Aggleton, J.P., & Brown, M.W. (1999). Episodic memory, amnesia and the hippocampal–anterior thalamic axis. *Behavioral and Brain Sciences*, *22*, 425–444.

Aggleton, J.P., & Mishkin, M. (1983a). Memory impairments following restricted medial thalamic lesions in monkeys. *Experimental Brain Research*, *52*, 199–209.

Aggleton, J.P., & Mishkin, M. (1983b). Visual recognition impairment following medial thalamic lesions in monkeys. *Neuropsychologia*, *21*, 189–197.

Aggleton, J.P., McMackin, D., Carpenter, K., Hornak, J., Kapur, N., Halpin, S., Wiles, C.M., Kamel, H., Brennan, P., Carton, S., & Gaffan, D. (2000). Differential cognitive effects of colloid cysts in the third ventricle that spare or compromise the fornix. *Brain*, *123*, 800–815.

Aggleton, J.P., Nicol, R.M., Huston, A.E., & Fairburn, A.F. (1988). The performance of amnesic subjects on tests of experimental amnesia in animals: Delayed matching-to-sample and concurrent learning. *Neuropsychologia*, *26*, 265–272.

Aggleton, J.P., & Sahgal, A. (1993). The contribution of the anterior thalamic nuclei to anterograde amnesia. *Neuropsychologia*, *31*, 1001–1019.

Aigner, T.G., & Mishkin, M. (1993). Scopolamine impairs recall of one-trial stimulus–reward association in monkeys. *Behavioural Brain Research*, *54*, 133–136.

Aigner, T.G., Mitchell, S.J., Aggleton, J.P., DeLong, M.R., Struble, R.G., Price, D.L., Wenk, G.L., Pettigrew, K.D., & Mishkin, M. (1991). Transient impairment of recognition memory following ibotenic-acid lesions of the basal forebrain in macaques. *Experimental Brain Research*, *86*, 18–26.

Amaral, D.G., Insausti, R., & Cowan, W.M. (1987). The entorhinal cortex of the monkey; 1. Cytoarchitectonic organization. *Journal of Comparative Neurology*, *264*, 326–355.

Bachevalier, J., & Meunier, M. (1996). Cerebral ischemia: Are the memory deficits associated with hippocampal cell loss? *Hippocampus*, *6*, 553–560.

Bachevalier, J., & Mishkin, M. (1986). Visual recognition impairment follows ventromedial but not dorsolateral prefrontal lesions in monkeys. *Behavioural Brain Research, 20*, 249–261.

Bachevalier, J., Parkinson, J.K., & Mishkin, M. (1985). Visual recognition in monkeys: Effects of separate vs combined transection of fornix and amygdalafugal pathways. *Experimental Brain Research, 57*, 554–561.

Baxter, M.G., Bucci, D.J., Gorman, L.K., Wiley, R.G., & Gallagher, M. (1995). Selective immunotoxic lesions of basal forebrain cholinergic cells: Effects on learning and memory in rats. *Behavioral Neuroscience, 109*, 714–722.

Baxter, M.G., Bucci, D.J., Sobel, T.J., Williams, M.J., Gorman, L.K., & Gallagher, M. (1996). Intact spatial learning following lesions of basal forebrain cholinergic neurons. *Neuroreport, 7*, 1417–1420.

Baxter, M.G., Holland, P.C., & Gallagher, M. (1997). Disruption of decrements in conditioned stimulus processing by selective removal of hippocampal cholinergic input. *Journal of Neuroscience, 17*, 5230–5236.

Berger-Sweeney, J., Heckers, S., Mesulam, M.-M., Wiley, R.G., Lappi, D.A., & Sharma, M. (1994). Differential effects on spatial navigation of immunotoxin-induced cholinergic lesions of the medial septal area and nucleus basalis magnocellularis. *Journal of Neuroscience, 14*, 4507–4519.

Bierer, L.M., Haroutunian, V., Gabriel, S., Knott, P.J., Carlin, L.S., Purohit, D.P., Perl, D.P., Schmeidler, J., Kanof, P., & Davis, K.L. (1995). Neurochemical correlates of dementia severity in Alzheimer's disease: Relative importance of the cholinergic deficits. *Journal of Neurochemistry, 64*, 749–760.

Buckley, M.J., Booth, M.C.A., Rolls, E.T., & Gaffan, D. (1998). Selective visual perceptual deficits following perirhinal cortex ablation in the macaque. *Society for Neuroscience Abstracts, 24*, 18.

Buckley, M.J., & Gaffan, D. (1997). Impairment of visual object-discrimination learning after perirhinal cortex ablation. *Behavioral Neuroscience, 111*, 467–475.

Buckley, M.J., & Gaffan, D. (1998a). Learning and transfer of object-reward associations and the role of the perirhinal cortex. *Behavioral Neuroscience, 112*, 15–23.

Buckley, M.J., & Gaffan, D. (1998b). Perirhinal cortex ablation impairs visual object identification. *Journal of Neuroscience, 18*, 2268–2275.

Buckley, M.J., & Gaffan, D. (1998c). Perirhinal cortex ablation impairs configural learning and paired-associate learning equally. *Neuropsychologia, 36*, 535–546.

Buckley, M.J., Gaffan, D., & Murray, E.A. (1997). Functional double-dissociation between two inferior temporal cortical areas: Perirhinal cortex vs middle temporal gyrus. *Journal of Neurophysiology, 97*, 587–598.

Cirillo, R.A., Horel, J.A., & George, P.J. (1989). Lesions of the anterior temporal stem and the performance of delayed match-to-sample and visual discriminations in monkeys. *Behavioural Brain Research, 34*, 55–69.

Corkin, S., Amaral, D.G., Gonzalez, R.G., Johnson, K.A., & Hyman, B.T. (1997). H.M.'s medial temporal lobe lesion: Findings from magnetic resonance imaging. *Journal of Neuroscience, 17*, 3964–3979.

Correll, R.E., & Scoville, W.B. (1965a). Effects of medial temporal lobe lesions on visual discrimination performance. *Journal of Comparative and Physiological Psychology, 60*, 175–181.

Correll, R.E., & Scoville, W.B. (1965b). Performance on delayed match following lesions of medial temporal lobe structures. *Journal of Comparative and Physiological Psychology, 60*, 360–367.

Cullinan, W.E., & Zaborszky, L. (1991). Organization of ascending hypothalamic projections to the rostral forebrain with spatial reference to the innervation of cholinergic projection neurons. *Journal of Comparative Neurology, 306*, 631–667.

Damasio, A.R., Graff-Radford, N.R., Eslinger, P.J., Damasio, H., & Kassell, N. (1985). Amnesia following basal forebrain lesions. *Archives of Neurology, Chicago, 42*, 263–271.

Daum, I., & Ackermann, H. (1994). Frontal-type memory impairment associated with thalamic damage. *International Journal of Neuroscience, 77,* 187–198.

Delay, J., & Brion, S. (1969). *Le Syndrome de Korsakoff.* Paris: Masson.

Dore, F.Y., Thornton, J.A., White, N.M., & Murray, E.A. (1998). Selective hippocampal lesions yield nonspatial memory impairments in rhesus monkeys. *Hippocampus, 8,* 323–329.

Dusoir, H., Kapur, N., Byrnes, D.P., McKinstry, S., & Hoare, R.D. (1990). The role of diencephalic pathology in human memory disorder: Evidence from a penetrating paranasal brain injury. *Brain, 113,* 1695–1706.

Eacott, M.J., & Gaffan, D. (1992). Inferotemporal–frontal disconnection: The uncinate fascicle and visual associative learning in monkeys. *European Journal of Neuroscience, 4,* 1320–1332.

Eacott, M.J., Gaffan, D., & Murray, E.A. (1994). Preserved recognition memory for small sets, and impaired stimulus identification for large sets, following rhinal cortex ablation in monkeys. *European Journal of Neuroscience, 6,* 1466–1478.

Easton, A., & Gaffan, D. (2000a). Comparison of perirhinal cortex ablation and crossed unilateral lesions of medial forebrain bundle from inferior temporal cortex in the Rhesus monkey: Effects on learning and retrieval. *Behavioral Neuroscience, 114,* 1041–1057.

Easton, A., & Gaffan, D. (2000b). Amygdala and the memory of reward: The importance of fibres of passage from the basal forebrain. In J.P. Aggleton (Ed.) *The amygdala: A functional analysis* (2nd ed., pp. 569–586). Oxford: Oxford University Press.

Easton, A., & Gaffan, D. (2001). Crossed unilateral lesions of the medial forebrain bundle and either inferior temporal or frontal cortex impair object–reward association learning in Rhesus monkeys. *Neuropsychologia, 39,* 71–82.

Easton, A., Parker, A., & Gaffan, D. (2001). Crossed unilateral lesions of medial forebrain bundle and either inferior temporal or frontal cortex impair object recognition memory in Rhesus monkeys. *Behavioural Brain Research, 121,* 1–10.

Easton, A., Ridley, R.M., Baker, H.F., & Gaffan, D. (2002). Lesions of the cholinergic basal forebrain and fornix in one hemisphere and inferior temporal cortex in the opposite hemisphere produce severe learning impairments in Rhesus monkeys. *Cerebral Cortex, 12,* 729–736.

Ebeling, U., & Cramon, D.V. (1992). Topography of the uncinate fascicle and adjacent temporal fibre tracts. *Acta Neurochirurgica, 115,* 143–148.

Fine, A., Hoyle, C., Maclean, C.J., Levatte, T.L., Baker, H.F., & Ridley, R.M. (1997). Learning impairments following injection of a selective cholinergic immunotoxin, ME20.4 IgG-Saporin, into the basal nucleus of Meynert in monkeys. *Neuroscience, 81,* 331–343.

Flynn, F.G., Cummings, J.L., & Tomiyasu, U. (1988). Altered behavior associated with damage to the ventromedial hypothalamus: A distinctive syndrome. *Behavioural Neurology, 1,* 49–58.

Fukuda, M., Masuda, R., Ono, T., & Tabuchi, E. (1993). Responses of monkey basal forebrain neurons during a visual discrimination task. *Progress in Brain Research, 95,* 359–369.

Fukuda, M., Ono, T., Nishino, H., & Nakamura, K. (1986). Neuronal responses in monkey lateral hypothalamus during operant feeding behaviour. *Brain Research Bulletin, 17,* 879–884.

Gaffan, D. (1992). The role of the hippocampus-fornix-mamillary system in episodic memory. In L.R. Squire & N. Butters (Eds.) *Neuropsychology of memory* (2nd ed., pp. 336–346). New York: Guilford Press.

Gaffan, D. (1994). Scene-specific memory for objects: A model of episodic memory impairment in monkeys with fornix transection. *Journal of Cognitive Neuroscience, 6,* 305–320.

Gaffan, D. (1996). Memory, action and the corpus striatum: Current developments in the memory–habit distinction. *Seminars in the Neurosciences, 8,* 33–38.

Gaffan, D. (1998). Idiothetic input into object–place configuration as the contribution to memory of the monkey and human hippocampus: A review. *Experimental Brain Research, 123,* 201–209.

Gaffan, D., & Eacott, M.J. (1995). Uncinate fascicle section leaves delayed matching-to-sample intact, both with large and small stimulus sets. *Experimental Brain Research, 105,* 175–180.

Gaffan, D., & Gaffan, E.A. (1991). Amnesia in man following transection of the fornix: A review. *Brain*, *114*, 2611–2618.

Gaffan, D., Gaffan, E.A., & Harrison, S. (1984). Effects of fornix transection on spontaneous and trained non-matching by monkeys. *Quarterly Journal of Experimental Psychology*, *36B*, 285–303.

Gaffan, E.A., Gaffan, D., and Hodges, J.R. (1991). Amnesia following damage to the left fornix and to other sites: a comparative study. *Brain*, *114*, 1297–1313.

Gaffan, D., & Murray, E.A. (1992). Monkeys (*Macaca fascicularis*) with rhinal cortex ablations succeed in object discrimination learning despite 24-hr intertrial intervals and fail at matching to sample despite double sample presentations. *Behavioral Neuroscience*, *106*, 30–38.

Gaffan, D., & Parker, A. (1996). Interaction of perirhinal cortex with the fornix-fimbria: Memory for objects and "object-in-place" memory. *Journal of Neuroscience*, 16, 5864–5869.

Gaffan, D & Parker, A. (2000) Mediodorsal thalamic function in scene memory in the Rhesus monkey. *Brain*, *123*, 816–827.

Gaffan, D., Parker, A., & Easton, A. (2001). Dense amnesia in the monkey after transection of fornix, amygdala and anterior temporal stem. *Neuropsychologia*, *39*, 51–70.

Goldman-Rakic, P.S., & Porrino, L.J. (1985). The primate mediodorsal (MD) nucleus and its projections to the frontal lobe. *Journal of Comparative Neurology*, *242*, 535–560.

Goulet, S., Dore, F.Y., & Murray, E.A. (1998). Aspiration lesions of the amygdala disrupt the rhinal corticothalamic projection system in rhesus monkeys. *Experimental Brain Research*, *119*, 131–140.

Graff-Radford, N.R., Tramel, N., Van Hoesen, G.W., & Brandt, J.P. (1990). Diencephalic amnesia. *Brain*, *113*, 1–25.

Gross, C.G. (1973). Inferotemporal cortex and vision. *Progress in Physiological Psychology*, *5*, 77–123.

Gutnikov, S.A., Ma, Y., Buckley, M.J., & Gaffan, D. (1997). Monkeys can associate visual stimuli with reward delayed by 1 s even after perirhinal cortex ablation, uncinate fascicle section or amygdalectomy. *Behavioural Brain Research*, *87*, 85–96.

Harder, J.A., Baker, H.F., & Ridley, R.M. (1998). The role of the central cholinergic projections in cognition: Implications of the effects of scopolamine on discrimination learning by monkeys. *Brain Research Bulletin*, *45*, 319–326.

Hood, K.L., Postle, B.R., & Corkin, S. (1996). Habit learning in H.M.: Results from a concurrent discrimination task. *Society for Neuroscience Abstracts*, *22*, 732.18.

Horel, J.A. (1978). The neuroanatomy of amnesia: A critique of the hippocampal memory hypothesis. *Brain*, *101*, 403–445.

Horel, J.A., & Misantone, L.G. (1976). Visual discrimination impaired by cutting temporal lobe connections. *Science*, *193*, 336–338.

Insausti, R., Amaral, D.G., & Cowan, W.M. (1987). The entorhinal cortex of the monkey: II. Cortical afferents. *Journal of Comparative Neurology*, *264*, 356–395.

Irle, E., & Markowitsch, H.J. (1987). Basal forebrain-lesioned monkeys are severely impaired in tasks of association and recognition memory. *Annals of Neurology*, *22*, 735–743.

Kapur, N., Thompson, S., Cook, P., Lang, D., & Brice, J. (1996). Anterograde but not retrograde memory loss following combined mamillary body and medial thalamic lesions. *Neuropsychologia*, *34*, 1–8.

Kitt, C.A., Mitchell, S.J., DeLong, M.R., Wainer, B.H., & Price, D.L. (1987). Fiber pathways of basal forebrain cholinergic neurons in monkeys. *Brain Research*, *406*, 192–206.

Kopelman, M.D. (1995). The Korsakoff syndrome. *British Journal of Psychiatry*, *166*, 154–173.

Mair, W.G.P., Warrington, E.K., & Weiskrantz, L. (1979). Memory disorder in Korsakoff's psychosis: a neuropathological and neuropsychological investigation of two cases. *Brain*, *102*, 749–783.

McMackin, D., Cockburn, J., Anslow, P., & Gaffan, D. (1995). Correlation of fornix damage with memory impairment in six cases of colloid cyst removal. *Acta Neurochirurgica*, *135*, 12–18.

Mesulam, M.-M. (1995). Cholinergic pathways and the ascending reticular activating system of the human brain. *Annals of New York Academic Sciences, 757,* 169–179.

Mesulam, M.-M., & Mufson, E.J. (1984). Neural inputs into the nucleus basalis of the substantia innominata (Ch4) in the rhesus monkey. *Brain, 107,* 253–274.

Mesulam, M.-M., Mufson, E.J., Levey, A.I., & Wainer, B.H. (1983). Cholinergic innervation of cortex by the basal forebrain: Cytochemistry and cortical connections of the septal area, diagonal band nuclei, nucleus basalis (substantia innominata), and hypothalamus in the rhesus monkey. *Journal of Comparative Neurology, 214,* 170–197.

Meunier, M., Bachevalier, J., Mishkin, M., & Murray, E.A. (1993). Effects on visual recognition of combined and separate ablations of the entorhinal and perirhinal cortex in rhesus monkeys. *Journal of Neuroscience, 13,* 5418–5432.

Meunier, M., Bachevalier, J., & Mishkin, M. (1997). Effects of orbital frontal and anterior cingulate lesions on object and spatial memory in rhesus monkeys. *Neuropsychologia, 35,* 999–1015.

Milner, B., Corkin, S., & Teuber, H.-L. (1968). Further analysis of the hippocampal amnesic syndrome: 14-year follow-up study of H.M. *Neuropsychologia, 6,* 215–234.

Mishkin, M. (1954). Visual discrimination performance following partial ablations of the temporal lobe: II. Ventral surface vs. hippocampus. *Journal of Comparative and Physiological Psychology, 47,* 187–193.

Mishkin, M. (1978). Memory in monkeys severely impaired by combined but not by separate removal of amygdala and hippocampus. *Nature, 273,* 297–298.

Mishkin, M. (1982). A memory system in the monkey. *Philosophical Transactions of the Royal Society, London, B 298,* 85–95.

Mrzljak, L., Levey, A.I., Belcher, S., & Goldman-Rakic, P.S. (1998). Localization of the m2 muscarinic acetylcholine receptor protein and mRNA in cortical neurons of the normal and cholinergically deafferented rhesus monkey. *Journal of Comparative Neurology, 390,* 112–132.

Murray, E.A. (1996). What have ablation studies told us about the neural substrates of recognition memory? *Seminars in the Neurosciences, 8,* 13–22.

Murray, E.A., & Bussey, T.J. (1999). Perceptual-mnemonic function of the perirhinal cortex. *Trends in Cognitive Sciences, 3,* 142–151.

Murray, E.A., and Mishkin, M. (1998). Object recognition and location memory in monkeys with excitotoxic lesions of the amygdala and hippocampus. *Journal of Neuroscience, 18,* 6568–6582.

Ongur, D., An, X., & Price, J.L. (1998). Prefrontal cortical projections to the hypothalamus in macaque monkeys. *Journal of Comparative Neurology, 401,* 480–505.

Orbach, J., Milner, B., & Rasmussen, T. (1960). Learning and retention in monkeys after amygdala–hippocampus resection. *Archives of Neurology, Chicago, 3,* 230–251.

Oscar-Berman, M., & Zola-Morgan, S. (1980). Comparative neuropsychology and Korsakoff's syndrome. II – two-choice visual discrimination learning. *Neuropsychologia, 18,* 513–525.

Oxbury, S., Oxbury, J., Renowden, S., Squier, W., & Carpenter, K. (1997). Severe amnesia: An unusual late complication after temporal lobectomy. *Neuropsychologia, 35,* 975–988.

Parker, A., & Gaffan, D. (1997a). The effect of anterior thalamic and cingulate cortex lesions on object-in-place memory in monkeys. *Neuropsychologia, 35,* 1093–1102.

Parker, A., & Gaffan, D. (1997b). Mamillary body lesions in monkeys impair object-in-place memory: functional unity of the fornix–mamillary system. *Journal of Cognitive Neuroscience, 9,* 512–521.

Parker, A., & Gaffan, D. (1998a). Interaction of frontal and perirhinal cortices in visual object recognition memory in monkeys. *European Journal of Neuroscience, 10,* 3044–3057.

Parker, A., & Gaffan, D. (1998b). Memory after frontal-temporal disconnection in monkeys: Conditional and nonconditional tasks, unilateral and bilateral frontal lesions. *Neuropsychologia, 36,* 259–271.

Parker, A., Eacott, M.J., & Gaffan, D. (1997). The recognition memory deficit caused by mediodorsal thalamic lesion in non-human primates: A comparison with rhinal cortex lesion. *European Journal of Neuroscience, 9*, 2423–2431.

Rempel-Clower, N.L., & Barbas, H. (1998). Topographic organization of connections between the hypothalamus and prefrontal cortex in the rhesus monkey. *Journal of Comparative Neurology, 398*, 393–419.

Ridley, R.M., Barefoot, H.C., Maclean, C.J., Pugh, P., & Baker, H.F. (1999a). Different effects on learning ability after injection of the cholinergic immunotoxin ME20.4IgG-Saporin into the diagonal band of Broca, basal nucleus of Meynert, or both in monkeys. *Behavioral Neuroscience, 113*, 303–315.

Ridley, R.M., Murray, T.K., Johnson, J.A., & Baker, H.F. (1986). Learning impairment following lesion of the basal nucleus of Meynert in the marmoset: Modification by cholinergic drugs. *Brain Research, 376*, 108–116.

Ridley, R.M., Pugh, P., Maclean, C.J., & Baker, H.F. (1999b). Severe learning impairment caused by combined immunotoxic lesion of the cholinergic projections to the cortex and hippocampus in monkeys. *Brain Research, 836*, 120–138.

Rolls, E.T., Sanghera, M.K., & Roper-Hall, A. (1979). The latency of activation of neurones in the lateral hypothalamus and substantia innominata during feeding in the monkey. *Brain Research, 164*, 121–135.

Russchen, F.T., Amaral, D.G., & Price, J.L. (1987). The afferent input to the magnocellular division of the mediodorsal thalamic nucleus in the monkey, *Macaca fascicularis. Journal of Comparative Neurology, 256*, 175–210.

Saper, C.B. (1990). Hypothalamus. In G. Paxinos (Ed.) *The human nervous system* (pp. 389–411). London: Academic Press.

Saper, C.B., & German, D.C. (1987). Hypothalamic pathology in Alzheimer's disease. *Neuroscience Letters, 74*, 364–370.

Scoville, W.B., and Milner, B. (1957). Loss of recent memory after bilateral hippocampal lesions. *Journal of Neurology, Neurosurgery and Psychiatry, 20*, 11–21.

Seldon, N.R., Gitelman, D.R., Salamon-Murayama, N., Parrish, T.B., & Mesulam, M.-M. (1998). Trajectories of cholinergic pathways within the cerebral hemispheres of the human brain. *Brain, 121*, 2249–2257.

Squire, L.R., Amaral, D.G., Zola-Morgan, S., Kritchevsky, M., & Press, G. (1989). Description of brain injury in the amnesic patient N.A. based on magnetic resonance imaging. *Experimental Neurology, 105*, 23–35.

Stefanacci, L., Buffalo, E.A., Schmolck, H., & Squire, L.R. (2000). Profound amnesia after damage to the medial temporal lobe: A neuroanatomical and neuropsychological profile of patient E.P. *Journal of Neuroscience, 20*, 7024–7036.

Suzuki, W.A., & Amaral, D.G. (1994). Perirhinal and parahippocampal cortices of the macaque monkey: Cortical afferents. *Journal of Comparative Neurology, 350*, 497–533.

Tang, Y., Mishkin, M., & Aigner, T.G. (1997). Effects of muscarinic blockade in perirhinal cortex during recognition. *Proceedings of the National Academy of Science (USA), 94*, 12667–12669.

Teuber, H.-L., Milner, B., & Vaughan, H.G.J. (1968). Persistent anterograde amnesia after stab wound of the basal brain. *Neuropsychologia, 6*, 267–282.

Thornton, J.A., Rothblat, L.A., & Murray, E.A. (1997). Rhinal cortex removal produces amnesia for preoperatively learned discrimination problems but fails to disrupt postoperative acquisition and retention in rhesus monkey. *Journal of Neuroscience, 17*, 8536–8549.

Ungerleider, L.G., Gaffan, D., and Pelak, V.S. (1989). Projections from inferior temporal cortex to prefrontal cortex via the uncinate fascicle in Rhesus monkeys. *Experimental Brain Research, 76*, 473–484.

Vargha-Khadem, F., Gadian, D.G., Watkins, K.E., Connelly, A., Paesschen, W.V., & Mishkin, M. (1997). Differential effects of early hippocampal pathology on episodic and semantic memory. *Science, 277*, 376–380.

Voytko, M.L., Olton, D.S., Richardson, R.T., Gorman, L.K., Tobin, J.R., & Price, D.L. (1994). Basal forebrain lesions in monkeys disrupt attention but not learning and memory. *Journal of Neuroscience*, *14*, 167–186.

Warrington, E.K., & Duchen, L.W. (1992). A re-appraisal of a case of persistent global amnesia following right temporal lobectomy: A clinico-pathological study. *Neuropsychologia*, *30*, 437–450.

Webster, M.J., Bachevalier, J., & Ungerleider, L.G. (1993). Subcortical connections of inferior temporal areas TE and TEO in macaque monkeys. *Journal of Comparative Neurology*, *335*, 73–91.

Whitehouse, P.J., Price, D.L., Struble, R.G., Clark, A.W., Coyle, J.T., & DeLong, M.R. (1982). Alzheimer's disease and senile dementia: Loss of neurons in the basal forebrain. *Science*, *215*, 1237–1239.

Wilson, F.A., & Rolls, E.T. (1990). Learning and memory is reflected in the reponses of reinforcement-related neurons in the primate basal forebrain. *Journal of Neuroscience*, *10*, 1254–1267.

Zola-Morgan, S., & Squire, L.R. (1985). Amnesia in monkeys after lesions of the mediodorsal nucleus of the thalamus. *Annals of Neurology*, *17*, 558–564.

Zola-Morgan, S., Squire, L.R., & Amaral, D.G. (1986). Human amnesia and the medial temporal region: enduring memory impairment following a bilateral lesion limited to field CA1 of the hippocampus. *Journal of Neuroscience*, *6*, 2950–2967.

Zola-Morgan, S., Squire, L.R., Amaral, D.G., & Suzuki, W.A. (1989). Lesions of perirhinal and parahippocampal cortex that spare the amygdala and hippocampal formation produce severe memory impairment. *Journal of Neuroscience*, *9*, 4355–4370.

Zola-Morgan, S., Squire, L.R., & Mishkin, M. (1982). The neuroanatomy of amnesia: amygdala-hippocampus versus temporal stem. *Science*, *218*, 1337–1339.

CHAPTER EIGHT

Memory encoding and retrieval: The nature of the interactions between the primate frontal lobe and posterior cortex

Alexander Easton, Amanda Parker
School of Psychology, University of Nottingham, UK

David Gaffan
Department of Experimental Psychology, Oxford University, UK

INTRODUCTION

In Chapter 7 we discussed experimental work in monkeys that has shown that both the frontal and inferior temporal cortex are essential for the new learning of visual tasks. We also stressed the importance of the basal forebrain in encoding. This theme is developed further here, as we consider whether the basal forebrain also has a role in retrieval. We will also review the way frontal cortical areas operate corticocortically to enable the retrieval of memories laid down in posterior cortical areas.

The way that cortical areas interact in retrieval and performance of memory tasks is related to the nature of the task and the nature of the material to be retrieved. Direct interaction between the frontal and inferior temporal cortex is essential in tasks that require memory for visual properties of objects and scenes, but interaction through the uncinate fascicle, the direct corticocortical pathway between them, appears to be required only for the learning of visually cued conditional tasks. A much wider range of tasks rely upon interaction between frontal and inferior temporal cortices within the same hemisphere. However, some tasks appear able to be performed normally even when these two structures can no longer communicate within the same hemisphere. In this chapter we shall first describe some different routes by which frontal and inferior temporal cortex can interact, and then consider ways in which these routes can be disrupted surgically. We shall then consider the tasks that have been studied with these different frontotemporal disconnections. The pattern of impairments with different types of lesions will be explained by a model in which the frontal and inferior temporal cortices can interact via corticocortical pathways when performing actions based upon previously learnt material.

PATHWAYS FOR FRONTOTEMPORAL INTERACTIONS AND SURGICAL DISRUPTIONS OF THOSE PATHWAYS

Monosynaptic corticocortical communication: Bilateral transection of the uncinate fascicle

The uncinate fascicle is the direct monosynaptic corticocortical communication between frontal and inferior temporal cortex. Surgical transection of the uncinate fascicle can be achieved by an approach via the cortex of the lower bank of the lateral sulcus (which is not essential for the learning of any of the visual tasks described below). Bilateral transection of the uncinate fascicle prevents the monosynaptic corticocortical communication between frontal and inferior temporal cortex (Ungerleider, Gaffan, & Pelak, 1989). As we outline below, despite the monosynaptic nature and large size of this projection, bilateral uncinate fascicle transection has been found to produce impairments in very few learning tasks, namely conditional tasks with a visual cue.

Multisynaptic corticocortical communication: Crossed unilateral lesions of frontal and inferior temporal cortex

Frontal and inferior temporal cortex can also communicate within the same hemisphere via multisynaptic corticocortical routes. One way in which the function of these routes can be studied is by crossed unilateral lesions of frontal cortex in one hemisphere and inferior temporal cortex in the opposite hemisphere. After these crossed unilateral lesions, all intrahemispheric communication between these cortical areas is lost. This includes all corticocortical communication, including that via the uncinate fascicle. Although not transected in these crossed unilateral lesions, communication via the uncinate fascicle is prevented, as in each hemisphere one of the cortical termination sites of this pathway has been removed. With crossed unilateral lesions of frontal and inferior temporal cortex, however, all the intrahemispheric communication between these structures is lost, including subcortical intrahemispheric routes such as via the corpus striatum.

Multisynaptic communication via the basal forebrain: Transection of the fornix, amygdala and anterior temporal stem

Frontal and inferior temporal cortex can also communicate via multisynaptic pathways through the basal forebrain. As discussed in Chapter 7, the basal forebrain is ideally suited for multisynaptic subcortical communication between these two cortical areas, receiving a strong projection from frontal cortex (Mesulam & Mufson, 1984; Ongur, An, & Price, 1998; Rempel-Clower & Barbas, 1998) and in turn projecting to inferior temporal cortex (Mesulam, Mufson, Levey, & Wainer, 1983; Webster, Bachevalier, & Ungerleider, 1993). There are also projections from lateral hypothalamic cells to contralateral cells of the substantia innominata (Cullinan & Zaborszky, 1991). These crossed projections, along with the strong interconnection of basal forebrain with midbrain areas (Russchen, Amaral, & Price, 1985) which are themselves bilaterally integrated, allow the basal forebrain to be a route of communication between frontal lobe and inferior temporal cortex both within the same hemisphere and between hemispheres.

These basal forebrain projections to inferior temporal cortex project through three routes, the fornix, amygdala and anterior temporal stem (Gaffan, Parker, & Easton, 2001; Kitt et al., 1987; Seldon et al., 1998). The white matter of the anterior temporal stem includes the uncinate fascicle and is approached surgically from the same approach as uncinate fascicle section. Ventral to the uncinate fascicle, however, lie many more white matter tracts (Ebeling & Cramon, 1992) which are all included in a section of the temporal stem, but are not damaged by uncinate fascicle section. In combined surgical sections of fornix, amygdala, and anterior temporal stem, the amygdala is sectioned following the temporal stem section that exposes the amygdala itself. Fornix section is then added by a midline approach.

Multisynaptic communication via the basal forebrain: Crossed unilateral lesions of medial forebrain bundle and cortex

Another way to interrupt the circuit via the basal forebrain is to disrupt the basal forebrain and midbrain activity without damaging cortical white matter (as happens in surgery of the anterior temporal stem). One way to disrupt the basal forebrain activity is to make a heat lesion of the medial forebrain bundle, through which run many fibres controlling the activity of the basal forebrain cells (Cullinan & Zaborszky, 1991). This medial forebrain bundle lesion is made in one hemisphere, and then either inferior temporal cortex or frontal cortex in the opposite hemisphere. In this case, then, the communication between the basal forebrain and the removed cortical area is disrupted bilaterally.

Multisynaptic communication via the basal forebrain: Crossed unilateral lesions of the cholinergic basal forebrain and cortex

The role of the basal forebrain can also be more specifically tested by use of the immunotoxin IgG-saporin, which acts to selectively kill cholinergic cells in the basal forebrain. Lesions of the cholinergic cells in one hemisphere, and inferior temporal cortex in the opposite hemisphere, can help us to understand further the role of basal forebrain interactions with cortex, as well as identifying the role of a specific transmitter system (acetylcholine) in this interaction.

SUMMARY OF BEHAVIOURAL TASKS AND THE EFFECTS OF DIFFERENT FRONTOTEMPORAL DISCONNECTIONS

Having described these different types of frontotemporal disconnection, we now summarise the results from behavioural tasks where the effects of these disconnections have been investigated. The pattern of impairments from the different lesion types discussed below are summarised in Table 8.1.

Visual object–reward association learning

Object–reward association learning is one of the most simple and widely used tests of visual learning. For each problem, two visual objects are presented to the animal, of which the animal chooses one. One of the objects is rewarded and the other is unrewarded. On every subsequent trial in which the same problem is presented, the same object remains rewarded and the same object remains unrewarded. The animal must simply learn to choose the rewarded object on each trial. New learning in this task is severely impaired either by bilateral removals of inferior temporal cortex (Gaffan, Harrison, & Gaffan, 1986) or bilateral removals of frontal cortex (Parker & Gaffan, 1998). By contrast, learning of new object-reward associations is unimpaired after bilateral section of the uncinate fascicle (Eacott & Gaffan, 1992) or crossed unilateral lesions of frontal and inferior temporal cortex (Parker & Gaffan, 1998). Therefore, it is apparent that the frontal and inferior temporal cortex, in this task, can communicate between hemispheres. We have previously proposed, and outlined in Chapter 7, that the route for such interhemispheric communication is the basal forebrain (Easton & Gaffan, 2000a, 2001; Gaffan et al., 2001).

TABLE 8.1
Summary of effects of different surgeries on performance of various tasks in monkeys

Task	Lesion				
	FxIT	*UF*	*Basal forebrain disconnections*		
			TS + Fx + Am	*MFBxIT*	*AChxIT*
vORA	Y	Y	N	N	N
Scenes	n	—	N	N	N
Strategy	N	Y	Y	—	—
V-V Con	N	N	—	—	—
V-M Con	—	N	—	—	—
R-V Con	N	Y	—	—	—
T-V Con	—	Y	—	—	—
V-V BiCon	Y	—	—	—	—

Notes:
N, impairment; n, milder impairment; Y, unimpaired. FxIT, crossed unilateral lesions of frontal and inferior temporal cortex; UF, uncinate fascicle section; TS + Fx + Am, section of the temporal stem, fornix, and amygdala; MFBxIT, crossed unilateral lesions of medial forebrain bundle and inferior temporal cortex; AChxIT, crossed unilateral lesions of the cholinergic basal forebrain and inferior temporal cortex; vORA, visual object reward association; V-V Con, visuovisual conditional task; V-M Con, visuomotor conditional task. R-V Con, reward–visual conditional task; T-V Con, time–visual conditional task; V-V BiCon, concurrent biconditional task.

Object–reward association is one of the tasks which is severely impaired by disrupting frontotemporal communication via the basal forebrain, either by section of the fornix, amygdala, and anterior temporal stem (Gaffan et al., 2001), crossed unilateral lesions of the medial forebrain bundle and frontal or inferior temporal cortex (Easton & Gaffan, 2001), or by crossed unilateral lesions of the cholinergic basal forebrain and inferior temporal cortex (Easton et al., 2002). This has led us to propose that after crossed unilateral lesions of frontal and inferior temporal cortex in object–reward association learning, the intact frontal cortex can still communicate with the intact inferior temporal cortex by means of interhemispheric communication via the basal forebrain

This route via the basal forebrain in object-reward association learning is shown in Fig. 8.1A. The objective properties of a specific reward event, which could be a primary reward like a small food pellet or a secondary reward that is associated with food, are shown as an afferent input to the basal forebrain ("reward" in the figure). In addition, frontal cortex input to the basal forebrain modulates the response of the basal forebrain to this specific reward event according to the current goals of the animal ("goal"). If the reward event is relevant to current goals, it produces a general arousal signal

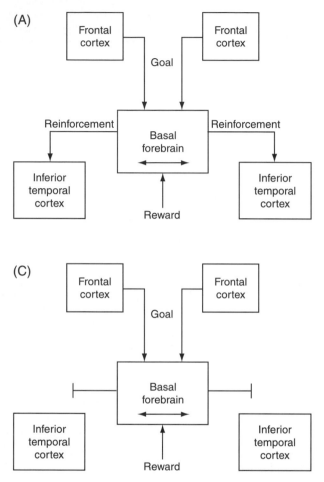

Figure 8.1. Model of frontal influence on inferior temporal cortex via the basal forebrain in object-reward association learning. (A) model of the interactions in a normal brain. Frontal cortex signals the current goal to basal forebrain, which also receives peripheral reward signals. In turn, reinforcement is signalled from basal forebrain to the inferior temporal cortex to set the visual memory. (B) Model of the interactions in the case of crossed unilateral lesions of frontal and inferior temporal cortex. Lesions are indicated by shading. The interhemispheric communication of reinforcement by the basal forebrain allows the intact frontal lobe to communicate with the intact inferior temporal cortex in the case of crossed unilateral lesions of these structures. (C) Model of the interactions in the case of section of the fornix, amygdala, and anterior temporal stem. The lesion is indicated by a blocked line. The reinforcement signal from the basal forebrain is now prevented from reaching inferior temporal cortex in both hemispheres. (D) Model of the interactions in the case of crossed unilateral lesions of basal forebrain and inferior temporal cortex (either by medial forebrain bundle section or cholinergic immunotoxin). The communication between frontal cortex in both hemispheres and the intact inferior temporal cortex is now prevented by the basal forebrain lesion. As a result, no reinforcement signal reaches the intact inferior temporal cortex.

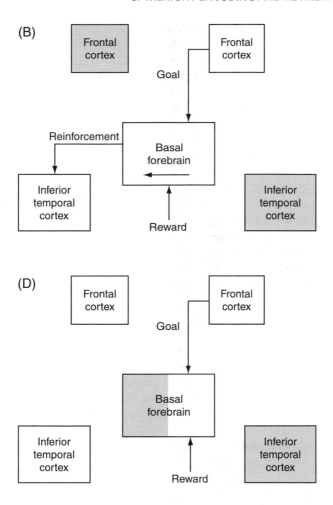

("reinforcement") that is sent to temporal cortex and facilitates the formation of an associative memory. Similarly, the absence of a food reward can be a memorable event when an animal is seeking food, and memory of non-reward is modulated by cortical interaction with the basal forebrain in the same way (not shown in the figure).

The case of crossed unilateral lesions of frontal and inferior temporal cortex in object–reward association learning is shown in Fig. 8.1B, with shaded areas representing lesions. It can be seen that the intact frontal cortex can still signal "goal" to the basal forebrain, which is receiving "reward" information. Because of the bilateral integration within the basal forebrain, the achievement of a reward related to the current goal can be communicated between hemispheres, so that in this case, the intact inferior temporal cortex can still receive the "reinforcement" signal. Therefore, the learning of object–reward associations is not impaired by crossed unilateral lesions of frontal or inferior temporal cortex.

The case of section of the fornix, amygdala, and temporal stem is shown in Fig. 8.1C, with a blocked line representing the effects of the lesion. It can be seen that frontal lobes can still signal "goal" to the basal forebrain, which still receives the "reward" information. However, section of the projections to inferior temporal cortex prevent the signalling of "reinforcement" to the inferior temporal cortex. Therefore, the setting of visual memories in inferior temporal cortex is prevented by this lesion.

Fig. 8.1D shows the case of either crossed unilateral lesions of medial forebrain bundle or cholinergic basal forebrain and inferior temporal cortex. In the hemisphere with the intact or properly functioning basal forebrain the frontal lobe cannot communicate with inferior temporal cortex, as inferior temporal cortex is removed in that hemisphere. Nor can reinforcement signals reach the intact inferior temporal cortex, as the basal forebrain in that hemisphere is removed or not functioning normally. Therefore, the reinforcement of visual memories within the intact inferior temporal cortex is prevented.

Importantly, what is discussed in the model above is the encoding of new object–reward associations. Once these memories are encoded in the inferior temporal cortex, their retrieval is independent of the basal forebrain. Whereas sections of the fornix, amygdala, and anterior temporal stem severely impair new learning of object–reward associations, they do not impair the retention of a large number of such problems taught preoperatively (Gaffan et al., 2001). Similarly, disruption of the basal forebrain circuit by medial forebrain bundle section does not cause a significant impairment in retention of preoperatively taught material, although it does severely impair new learning of the same material (Easton & Gaffan, 2000b).

Interaction of the inferior temporal cortex and posterior cortical areas

One issue that needs to be addressed from the model outlined above is the reinforcement of visual memories within the inferior temporal cortex by basal forebrain. In our present model, the inferior temporal cortical cells that encode object identity are postsynaptic to the basal forebrain cells that encode reward and non-reward. This is the wrong way round for the Hebb model of learning, in which the events to be recalled (in this case reward or non-reward) are encoded in the depolarisation of the postsynaptic cell, whereas, by contrast, the retrieval cue (here an object) is encoded in the depolarisation of the presynaptic cell (Hebb, 1949). That model could still perhaps be applied if the basal forebrain input into temporal cortex elicited powerful activity reflecting reward or non-reward in the temporal cortex cells themselves, but there is no evidence that reward and non-reward are power-fully encoded in inferior temporal cortical action potentials (Rolls, Judge, & Sanghera, 1977). Instead, we propose that the basal forebrain input to inferior temporal cortex acts to facilitate the synaptic plasticity of corticocortical synapses, as discussed in the models below where posterior cortical areas (parietal and prestriate cortex) interact with inferior temporal cortex to activate the appropriate object representations in inferior temporal cortex. The inferior temporal cortical cells which encode object identity, then, provide the retrieval cue for representations of reward and non-reward events that are encoded, for example, in the prestriate, parahippocampal, or parietal cortex (Brown, Desimone, & Mishkin, 1995; Gaffan & Hornak 1997a; Platt & Glimcher, 1999).

Cells in the parietal cortex of monkey have been shown to respond to the rewards that can be expected on a given trial, and these responses are directly related to the relative reinforcement value of different motor responses (Platt & Glimcher, 1999). This is the kind of posterior cortical signal that, in the models below, can represent the current condition of the task and activate the representation of the correct choice in inferior temporal cortex. The current condition of the task, in these models, is the condition that makes an object choice appropriate. In a conditional task the current condition is determined by the instruction cue and provides the information as to which choice is appropriate. In the scene-based object-in-place task described below, the current condition is more closely related to context, representing the spatial background that makes the correct object choice more readily identifiable.

In the model proposed here, the corticocortical projections between posterior cortical areas and inferior temporal cortex are strengthened in learning, and not the projection from basal forebrain to inferior temporal cortex. This distribution of processing between cortical areas and the subsequent convergence in inferior temporal cortex of the object identification and current condition is an example of the type of integrated competition theory put forward by Duncan (1996). In the tasks described below this corticocortical interaction is seen to be the determining factor in how different tasks are affected by different frontotemporal disconnections. The link between an attentional competition and memory encoding and retrieval suggested by this model is an extension of the idea that these two cognitive functions are closely linked. For example, one cannot learn about something without attending to it first, and one cannot determine what is important to attend to without having learnt about these items first. Indeed, some descriptions of learning have included a specific link between attention and learning (Mackintosh, 1975).

Conditional learning

Conditional learning tasks are another commonly used test of visual learning in the monkey. These tasks take the form of the presentation of an instruction cue (which might be a visual object, an auditory stimulus, or some other event) followed by a choice between two visual objects or motor behaviours. Only one of these objects or behaviours is appropriate on any given trial, and is dependent on the cue presented on that trial. Let us first consider visuo-visual conditional learning, where the correct choice between two visual objects is determined by a visual instruction cue. Eacott and Gaffan (1992) found that uncinate fascicle section severely impaired the learning of a visuo-visual conditional task. On the first trials presented postoperatively, animals that preoperatively performed at 90 per cent correct on a retention test now performed, on average, at just over 60 per cent correct. Some limited learning was observed over 4000 postoperative trials but no animal reattained pre-operative performance levels. This result after uncinate fascicle section implies that the task must rely on this monosynaptic corticocortical pathway between frontal and inferior temporal cortex.

Our model of the interactions in this visuovisual conditional task is outlined in Fig. 8.2A. The frontal influence on basal forebrain remains, as for object–reward association learning, allowing interhemispheric communication of reinforcement to the inferior temporal cortex. The "goal" signalled via this route, however, is the general goal of the current situation, i.e. to achieve small food rewards. However, trial by trial, the way to achieve the food reward is predicted by the visual cue, which indicates the correct object choice on that trial. This cue (in this case "A") is represented in inferior temporal cortex. This visual cue information is then signalled to frontal cortex, where the representation of the current condition is maintained and communicated back to posterior cortical areas such as parietal and prestriate cortex (see earlier) where the current condition ("X CONDITION") is represented. The current condition provides the information as to which choice object is appropriate on that trial. In turn these posterior cortical areas project to inferior temporal cortex to activate the representation of the appropriate choice object (in this case "X"). Therefore, trial by trial goal selection is controlled by the frontal lobes but is communicated via corticocortical pathways between frontal and inferior temporal cortex.

The effect of bilateral uncinate fascicle section, then, is outlined in Fig. 8.2B. The visual cue information can now no longer reach frontal cortex. In the absence of this visual cue information to frontal cortex, the frontal cortical projection of the current condition to posterior cortical areas is disrupted (as indicated by a dashed line). As the representation of the current condition within the posterior cortical areas is now without frontal cortical influence it no longer can activate the correct object representation in inferior temporal cortex (as indicated by the absence of a line, compare Fig. 8.2A with 8.2B). Therefore, uncinate fascicle section is seen to impair learning of this visuo-visual conditional task (Eacott & Gaffan, 1992). The reason for considering the signal from frontal cortex indicating the current condition as being independent of the uncinate fascicle and via posterior cortical areas is discussed below.

Eacott and Gaffan (1992) also found that visuomotor conditional learning (i.e. a visual cue with a choice between two motor behaviours) was impaired by uncinate fascicle section, with more than doubling of errors postoperatively. This fully supports our proposal for visuovisual conditional learning in that the uncinate fascicle section prevents the "visual cue" information from the representation of the cue in inferior temporal cortex from reaching frontal cortex (Fig. 8.2B). The frontal lobe activation of the condition in posterior cortical areas will then be disrupted by the uncinate fascicle section. The posterior cortical areas will not then be able to activate the correct choice of either an object (in visuovisual conditional learning) or motor response (in visuo-motor conditional learning).

In this model, then, any conditional task with a visual instruction cue will be impaired by uncinate fascicle section. If the signal from frontal cortex to activate the representation of the correct choice object in inferior temporal cortex also came through the uncinate fascicle, then any conditional task that had visual choice objects would be impaired by uncinate fascicle section. This is not the case, however, as conditional tasks without a visual instruction cue but with visual choice objects (e.g. a reward-visual or a time-visual conditional task) were unimpaired by uncinate fascicle section (Eacott & Gaffan, 1992). For example, in the reward-visual conditional task, the presence or absence of a small food reward before the start of the trial indicates which of the two subsequently presented visual objects is correct. Such a task uses visual choice objects but is unimpaired by uncinate fascicle section. In Fig. 8.2A we propose that the current condition signal from frontal lobes is communicated within the same hemisphere to posterior cortical areas that in turn activate the correct object representation in inferior temporal cortex. This model is supported by the observation that although the reward-visual conditional task is not impaired by uncinate fascicle section (Eacott & Gaffan, 1992), it is severely impaired by crossed unilateral lesions of frontal and inferior temporal cortex (Parker & Gaffan, 1998). As described earlier, the latter combination of lesions prevents all intrahemispheric communication between frontal and inferior temporal cortex and so disrupts the multi-synaptic corticocortical route that we propose as being involved in the communication of the current condition in the task from frontal to posterior cortex.

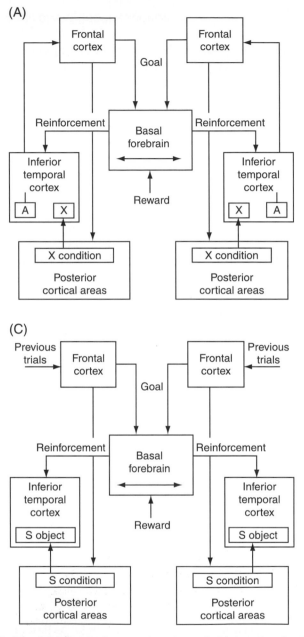

Figure 8.2. Models of the proposed routes of corticocortical interactions in visuovisual conditional learning and a complex strategy task. In all cases the reinforcement signalled by the basal forebrain is as outlined in Fig. 8.1. (A) Visuovisual conditional learning in a normal brain. The conditional instruction cue "A" is represented in inferior temporal cortex, which signals this information to the frontal cortex. The frontal cortex then signals the current condition back to posterior cortical areas (such as parietal and prestriate cortex) to activate the representation of the appropriate condition ("X CONDITION"). These posterior cortical areas in turn activate "X" in the inferior temporal cortex. (B) The same interactions for the visuovisual conditional task but, in the case of the uncinate fascicle section, the representation of the correct object shown by a blocked line. Information about the visual cue cannot now reach the frontal cortex and so the subsequent activation of the correct condition and object representation are

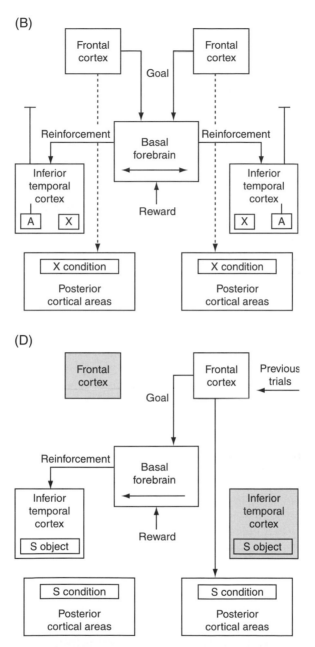

disrupted. (C) Strategy task performance in a normal brain. The events of the previous trials are signalled to frontal cortex, which in turn signals the current condition to posterior cortical areas. In this case, the "S CONDITION" condition is signalled and represented. Connections between these posterior cortical areas and inferior temporal cortex then activate the representation of the appropriate object ("S OBJECT"). (D) The same strategy task connections in the case of crossed unilateral lesions of frontal and inferior temporal cortex. In the hemisphere of the intact frontal cortex the "S CONDITION" representation cannot activate the "S OBJECT" representation because the inferior temporal cortex is removed in that hemisphere. In the hemisphere with the intact inferior temporal cortex the "S CONDITION" activation of the "S OBJECT" representation is impaired because it has no frontal cortical guidance.

Visual strategy learning

Gaffan, Easton, and Parker (2002) discuss the mechanism by which frontal and inferior temporal cortices interact in a visual object strategy task that can be considered in some ways as a complex conditional task. In this task the monkey learns a series of pairs of visual objects. Of each pair, one object requires a persistent (P) strategy to be applied to it whereas the other requires a sporadic (S) strategy. Touching a P object on four consecutive trials results in the delivery of a small food reward. Once this reward has been delivered the animal can obtain another reward by touching the S object on any trial. Once an S reward has been achieved, however, the animal must return to consecutive P choices. Therefore, the animals can attain a specified number of rewards in a variety of ways, but the most efficient strategy is to choose four P objects followed by an S object followed by four P objects, and so on. This strategy will result in an average of 2.5 responses per reward obtained, and at the end of preoperative training animals performed very close to this maximally efficient strategy.

Unilateral ablation of either frontal or inferior temporal cortex had little effect on the animal's performance of the strategy task, but crossed unilateral lesions of frontal and inferior temporal cortex severely impaired performance, with animals now making on average more than three times as many responses per reward as preoperatively. Gaffan, Easton, and Parker (2002) also examined the effects of isolating inferior temporal cortex from basal forebrain by combined section of the fornix, amygdala, and anterior temporal stem on this strategy task. Although this basal forebrain disconnection impairs object–reward association learning (Gaffan et al., 2001; Gaffan, Easton, & Parker, 2002) only the new learning of objects was seen to be impaired by this pattern of lesions, not the implementation of the strategy with preoperatively learned objects.

We propose that the route by which frontal cortex influences inferior temporal cortex, within the same hemisphere, in the performance of this task is by means of a multisynaptic corticocortical pathway, outlined in Fig. 8.2C. Frontal cortex determines the currently appropriate strategy (for example, choice of an "S OBJECT") on the basis of factors occurring on the previous trials (such as which class of object was touched and what the reward outcome was). The frontal projections, within the same hemisphere, to posterior cortical areas (parietal and prestriate cortex) then activate a representation of the currently appropriate strategy ("S CONDITION"), as they were seen to do for the current condition in conditional learning (Fig. 8.2A). The reciprocal connections between these posterior cortical areas and inferior temporal cortex then activate representations of the appropriate object for that trial ("S OBJECT"). In this case, then, frontal cortex influences object representations within the inferior temporal cortex by means of intrahemispheric communication and so performance is severely impaired after crossed unilateral lesions of frontal and inferior temporal cortex (Gaffan, Easton, & Parker, 2002). This effect of crossed unilateral lesions is shown in Fig. 8.2D. On the side of the intact inferior temporal cortex, where the "S OBJECT" representation can be activated, the "S CONDITION" representation in posterior cortical areas is no longer influenced by frontal cortex. The signal from posterior cortical areas to inferior temporal cortex, then, is disrupted (as indicated now by the absence of a signal) and cannot accurately activate the correct object representation.

The role of the basal forebrain remains the same as in object–reward association, in sending reinforcement signals to the object representations in inferior temporal cortex based on the current goal (achievement of food reward). In this case, however, such interhemispheric transfer of information is not sufficient to control the object choices from trial to trial, only the learning of the visual objects in the first instance (which is seen to be affected by section of the fornix, amygdala and anterior temporal stem; Gaffan et al., 2002).

Scene-based object-in-place learning

This scene task is very similar to object–reward association in that pairs of visual objects are presented concurrently, and only one of each pair is correct. However, the visual objects are presented on each trial within the context of a problem-specific spatial background. As a result, the task is not learnt purely by spatial or object–reward association mechanisms (Gaffan, 1994). Learning of new scenes in this task is severely impaired by crossed unilateral lesions of frontal and inferior temporal cortex (Easton & Gaffan, 1999). The spatial background scene, we propose, acts as a contextual conditional cue, i.e. if spatial background A then choose object B in position C. In our model of frontotemporal interactions, then, the spatial conditional information is signalled to the frontal cortex and, in turn, the frontal cortex signals the current spatial condition to posterior cortical areas representing the appropriate position within the current background. This spatial representation promotes the representation in inferior temporal cortex of the appropriate visual object. Therefore, crossed unilateral lesions of frontal and inferior temporal cortex prevent this intrahemispheric control of the spatial conditional aspect of this task in the same way that they prevent the communication of other conditional information in the conditional tasks described above.

Performance on the scene task, however, although severely impaired, is not as badly impaired after crossed unilateral lesions of frontal and inferior temporal cortex as it is after section of the fornix, amygdala, and anterior temporal stem (Gaffan et al., 2001). This observation implies that the subcortical interhemispheric communication of reinforcement via the basal forebrain remains after crossed unilateral lesions of frontal and inferior temporal cortex, and is sufficient to allow some learning of the task, much as in normal object–reward association learning. Scene learning is slowed dramatically after crossed unilateral lesions of frontal and inferior temporal cortex, though, as the spatial conditional component of the task allows the rapid learning of each problem (Gaffan, 1994). In contrast, the combined fornix, amygdala, and temporal stem lesions prevent learning of both the object and spatial aspects of the task, and performance is very severely impaired (Gaffan et al., 2001).

Concurrent biconditional discrimination

Using the model of frontotemporal interactions presented earlier, we can explain an unexpected result from a study using a concurrent visuovisual biconditional task (Easton & Gaffan, in press). This task was a modification of experiments in the rat on conditional learning with different reward outcomes (Trapold, 1970; Carlson & Weilkiewicz, 1972). There were two visually cued conditions, one of which indicated the availability of an immediate food reward, whereas the other indicated the availability of a delayed food reward. Only one reward type was available on each trial. Each trial began with the presentation of a visual instruction cue and, when the monkey touched it, the cue disappeared from the screen and was replaced by two visual choice objects. In the course of the experiment each monkey learnt many instruction cues and choice objects and all objects fell into one of two classes. The pattern of each trial is outlined in Fig. 8.3. An instruction cue from the class IN (Instruction, No delay of reward) indicated that a choice object from the class CN (Choice, No delay of reward) was rewarded (with immediate delivery of reward) on that trial. An instruction cue from the class ID (Instruction, Delayed reward) indicated that a choice object from the class CD (Choice, Delayed reward) was rewarded (with delayed delivery of reward) on that trial. On each type of trial, the wrong choice (i.e. CD following IN or CN following ID) was unrewarded. All the choice objects were learned in the early stages of training and remained the same throughout the experiment. The remainder of the experiment consisted of the learning of new instruction cues introduced in pairs, one new ID and one new IN. To show that the monkeys had used the difference in reward outcome to learn the new instruction cues, we conducted transfer tests. The classes of choice objects were now split into two subsets. One subset consisted of half the choice objects, CD1 and CN1, whereas the other subset consisted of the remaining choice objects, CD2 and CN2. When a new ID and IN pair of instruction cues was learned, the initial training with these cues was with only one subset of the choice objects, say CD1 and CN1. After a criterion level of performance was attained the same pair of instruction cues was now presented with the other subset of choice objects, CD2 and CN2. Good transfer of the

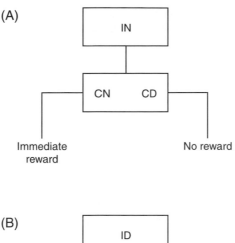

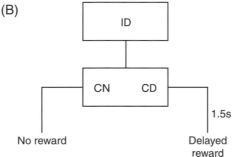

Figure 8.3. Pattern of possible reward outcomes in the concurrent conditional discrimination test. (A) Instruction cue IN (instruction, No delay of reward) is presented in the centre of the touchscreen and the animal responds to it. It is removed from the touchscreen and replaced by two choice objects (CN (Choice, No delay of reward) and CD (Choice, Delay of reward)) in the left and right positions on the touchscreen. Instruction cue IN indicates that on this trial a response to choice object CN is correct and rewarded by an immediate food reward. A response to choice object CD is unrewarded. (B) Instruction cue ID is presented in the centre of the touchscreen and the animal responds to it. It is removed from the touchscreen and replaced by two choice objects (CN and CD) in the left and right positions on the touchscreen. Instruction cue ID indicates that on this trial a response to choice object CD is correct and rewarded by a food reward after a 1.5s delay period. A response to choice object CN is unrewarded.

instruction cues at this stage indicated that the initial learning of the new pair of instruction cues with CD1 and CN1 was not by visuovisual associative learning, but instead by the expectation of a specific reward type.

Surprisingly, this task is unimpaired by crossed unilateral lesions of frontal and inferior temporal cortex, whether testing new learning of instruction cues, or transfer of those cues to other choice objects. In this task, however, the choice of the correct choice object on each trial is determined not by frontal cortex, but by the visual instruction cue which is represented in inferior temporal cortex. This pattern of connections and object choice for the appropriate reward condition is shown in Fig. 8.4A for the case of the delay condition. Once again the posterior cortical areas (such as parietal and prestriate cortex) represent the current strategy (in this case "D CONDITION"), but this representation is not activated by frontal lobe influence as in the previous tasks. Instead, the representation is activated by the reciprocal connections with inferior temporal cortex where the visual instruction cue is represented ("ID"). As with the other tasks discussed above, this representation of the correct reward condition on that trial can then activate the correct representation choice object within the inferior temporal cortex ("CD"). Frontal cortex, then, has no influence on the activation of the visual choice object memory in inferior temporal cortex in this task, and as a result crossed unilateral lesions of frontal and inferior temporal cortex do not impair the learning or transfer of new instruction cues. This case is outlined in Fig. 8.4B. On the side of the intact inferior temporal cortex, where the object representations will occur, the "D CONDITION" signal from posterior cortical areas remains under the control of the visual cue from the intact inferior temporal cortex, and so the absence of frontal cortex in that hemisphere plays no part in the performance of the task.

In this concurrent biconditional task, the difference in reward conditions allows the representation of the current goal in posterior visual cortical areas rather than in the frontal cortex, and so intra-hemispheric communication between frontal and inferior temporal cortex is not required for the normal performance of this task. Removal of the different reward conditions for each choice object would have returned the task to frontal cortex control as in the visuo-visual conditional task of Eacott and Gaffan (1992). The model does predict, however, that basal forebrain disconnection from inferior temporal cortex would again impair the learning of new instruction cues and choice objects, but not the performance with those objects once they are learnt.

CONCLUSIONS

The pattern of results we have reviewed makes it clear that no simple hypothesis can account for the effects of all the different kinds of surgical temporal–frontal disconnection in learning and memory tasks. It is not the case, for example, that all visual tasks that rely on temporal and frontal cortex rely also on the monosynaptic projection between temporal and frontal cortex in the uncinate fascicle. Nor is it the case that the different kinds of disconnection can be ranked simply in terms of the severity of their functional effect, regardless of the task studied. Rather, the different kinds of disconnection have qualitatively different effects on different kinds of memory performance. Therefore, study of these effects can shed light on the specific roles that frontal cortex plays in these different kinds of memory performance.

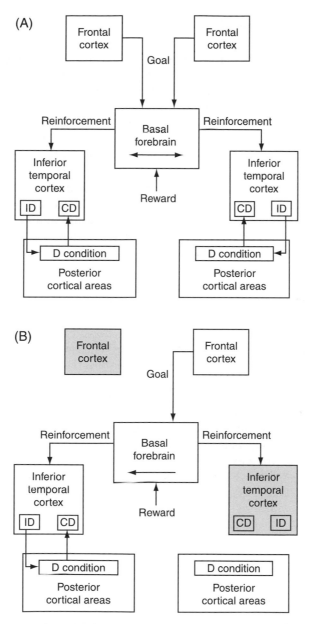

Figure 8.4. Models of the proposed routes of corticocortical interactions in the concurrent conditional task. (A) The instruction cue (in this case "ID") is represented in inferior temporal cortex and signalled to posterior cortical areas where the current reward condition ("D CONDITION") is represented. This "D CONDITION" representation activates the representation in inferior temporal cortex of the appropriate choice object ("CD"). (B) The connections for the concurrent conditional discrimination task in the case of crossed unilateral lesions of frontal and inferior temporal cortex. The "D CONDITION" representation in posterior cortical areas is outside the control of frontal cortex and so removal of frontal cortex in the hemisphere of the intact inferior temporal cortex does not disrupt the normal control of object representation in inferior temporal cortex.

The results indicate that for the acquisition of new learning, the inter-action of the frontal cortex with the basal forebrain and of the basal fore-brain with the temporal cortex is essential. However, this necessary influence of the frontal cortex on temporal cortex via the basal forebrain in memory acquisition is much less important in memory retrieval. Performance with preoperatively learned objects in the strategy task of Gaffan et al. (2002) was not impaired by bilateral section of fornix, amygdala, and anterior tem-poral stem, which interrupts basal forebrain inputs to temporal lobe. Equally, retrieval of preoperatively acquired object–reward associations and scene problems was relatively well preserved after crossed unilateral lesions of basal forebrain and temporal cortex in the study by Easton and Gaffan (2000b). Bilateral section of fornix, amygdala, and anterior temporal stem also had little effect on retrieval of preoperatively acquired object–reward associations (Gaffan et al., 2001).

Furthermore, crossed unilateral temporal and frontal cortical ablations had no effect on the learning and retrieval of object–reward associations (Parker & Gaffan, 1998), and this result rules out an important contribution of within-hemisphere temporofrontal interactions, either exclusively corti-cocortical or mediated by corticostriatal loops (Alexander, Delong, & Strick, 1986), in this kind of memory retrieval. Taken together with negative results from selective amygdala lesions in object–reward associative memory (Malkova, Gaffan, & Murray, 1997), and evidence that memories retrieved by objects are spatially organised (Gaffan & Hornak 1997b, Hornak et al., 1997), these findings suggest that retrieval of simple non-conditional object–reward associations is effected by the direct influence of inferior temporal cortex on posterior, parietal, and prestriate cortex. Retrieval in the concur-rent conditional task shows the same independence of within-hemisphere temporofrontal interaction as does the simple object–reward association learning task (Figs 8.4A and 8.1A), and we therefore propose that memory retrieval in the concurrent conditional task is also effected by the influence of inferior temporal cortex on posterior cortex, as shown in Fig. 8.4A.

In simple object–reward association learning the association between an object and a reward outcome (reward or non-reward) is a predictive associ-ation: choice of a positive object is consistently followed by reward and not by non-reward. In the same way, in the concurrent biconditional task, the association between an instruction cue and a reward outcome (in this case, delayed reward or immediate reward) is a predictive association: there is a direct association between a cue object and a reward type, and similarly between the choice objects and their respective reward types. For example, an instruction cue ID is sometimes followed by a delayed reward for object choice, but never followed by an immediate reward for object choice. How-ever, in many other conditional tasks there is no predictive relationship of this kind for the instruction cues. In the case of visuovisual conditional learning, the visual cue determines a specific condition in that only one of the choice objects presented will be rewarded, and which object is rewarded is determined by the visual cue. The cue is not associated with any particular type of reward and the choice objects are all associated with the same type of reward. What is needed for correct choice in this visuovisual conditional task is a prediction based on the configuration of a particular instruction cue with a particular object: object X after cue A predicts a choice reward, object Y after cue B predicts a choice reward. The other configurations of objects and cues predict no reward for choice. In this visuovisual conditional task, unlike the concurrent biconditional task with unique reward types for each condition, frontotemporal interactions had to occur within the same hemisphere, the performance of the task being severely impaired after bilateral section of the uncinate fascicle (Eacott & Gaffan, 1992). We therefore propose that, in learning tasks of this kind, frontal cortex is able to learn the configural association between choice object identity and instruction cue identity that is necessary for performance. This configural association is then able to activate representations of the current condition within posterior cortical areas that can then, in turn, activate the appropriate choice object representation within inferior temporal cortex.

Several previous authors have emphasised the role of prefrontal cortex in conditional learning tasks (Gaffan & Harrison, 1989; Petrides, 1991; Passingham, 1993; Wise, Murray, & Gerfen, 1997). The concurrent biconditional task, however, has helped to clarify that role by showing that conditional relationships can be expressed normally in the absence of frontal–temporal within-hemisphere interaction, specifically in the case where the conditional relationship between an instruction cue and a choice is mediated by the simple association of each of them with a particular reward outcome, immediate or delayed (Easton & Gaffan, in press). This indicates that, in those conditional tasks that are impaired by crossed unilateral ablations of frontal and temporal cortex, the important feature of those tasks is not one of those that is shared with the concurrent conditional task, such as the need to switch choices back and forth between choice objects on a trial-by-trial basis. Rather, the important feature of those tasks is the need for configural processing of stimuli or their attributes by the frontal cortex. If a task can be solved by simple associations between these stimuli and the outcome then the task is independent of the frontal cortex. However, if the same outcome can occur with equal likelihood for different stimuli, where the reward condition is defined by a cue, then there must be a configural association between the cue and the stimulus, which is then associated with reward. It is this need for a configural association to solve the task that places reliance on the frontal cortex. Many real-world situations, such as interacting socially with groups, short-term decision making, or the construction of long-term plans, require such complex configural associations to be formed. The model proposed in this paper, then, has direct relevance to these complex behaviours, and mirrors other recent hypotheses of the role of frontal cortex in such situations (e.g. Miller & Cohen, 2001). A full understanding of the processes and structures involved in memory retrieval will require clear delineation of the complete set of subprocesses and routes of interaction involved.

REFERENCES

Alexander, G.E., Delong, M.R., & Strick, P.L. (1986). Parallel organization of functionally segregated circuits linking basal ganglia and cortex. *Annual Review of Neuroscience, 9,* 357–381.

Brown, V.J., Desimone, R., & Mishkin, M. (1995). Responses of cells in the tail of the caudate nucleus during visual discrimination learning. *Journal of Neurophysiology, 74,* 1083–1094.

Carlson, J.G., & Wielkiewicz, R.M. (1972). Delay of reinforcement in instrumental discrimination learning in rats. *Journal of Comparative and Physiological Psychology, 81,* 365–370.

Cullinan, W.E., & Zaborszky, L. (1991). Organization of ascending hypothalamic projections to the rostral forebrain with spatial reference to the innervation of cholinergic projection neurons. *Journal of Comparative Neurology, 306,* 631–667.

Duncan, J. (1996). Cooperating brain systems in selective perception and action. In T. Inui & J.L. McClelland (Eds.) *Attention and performance XVI* (pp. 549–578). Cambridge, MA: MIT Press.

Eacott, M.J., & Gaffan, D. (1992). Inferotemporal–frontal disconnection: The uncinate fascicle and visual associative learning in monkeys. *European Journal of Neuroscience, 4,* 1320–1332.

Easton, A., & Gaffan, D. (1999). Interaction of frontal lobe and inferior temporal cortex in object-in-place memory. *Society for Neuroscience Abstracts, 25,* 316.10.

Easton, A., & Gaffan, D. (2000a). Amygdala and the memory of reward: The importance of fibres of passage from the basal forebrain. In J.P. Aggleton (Ed.) *The amygdala: A functional analysis* (pp. 569–586). Oxford: Oxford University Press.

Easton, A., & Gaffan, D. (2000b) Comparison of perirhinal cortex ablation and crossed unilateral lesions of medial forebrain bundle from inferior temporal cortex in the Rhesus monkey: Effects on learning and retrieval. *Behavioral Neuroscience, 114,* 1041–1057.

Easton, A., & Gaffan, D. (2001). Crossed unilateral lesions of the medial forebrain bundle and either inferior temporal or frontal cortex impair object–reward association learning in Rhesus monkeys. *Neuropsychologia, 39,* 71–82.

Easton, A., & Gaffan, D. (in press). Insights into the nature of fronto-temporal interactions from a biconditional discrimination task in the monkey. *Behavioral Brain Research.*

Easton, A., Ridley, R.M., Baker, H.F., & Gaffan, D. (2002). Unilateral lesions of the cholinergic basal forebrain in one hemisphere and inferior temporal cortex in the opposite hemisphere produce severe learning impairments in Rhesus monkeys. *Cerebral Cortex, 12,* 729–736.

Ebeling, U., & Cramon, D.V. (1992). Topography of the uncinate fascicle and adjacent temporal fibre tracts. *Acta Neurochirurgica, 115,* 143–148.

Gaffan, D. (1994). Scene-specific memory for objects: A model of episodic memory impairment in monkeys with fornix transection. *Journal of Cognitive Neuroscience, 6,* 305–320.

Gaffan, D., & Harrison, S. (1989). A comparison of the effects of fornix transection and sulcus principalis ablation upon spatial learning by monkeys. *Behavioural Brain Research, 31,* 207–220.

Gaffan, E.A., Harrison, S., & Gaffan, D. (1986). Single and concurrent discrimination learning by monkeys after lesions of inferotemporal cortex. *Quarterly Journal of Experimental Psychology, 38B,* 31–51.

Gaffan, D., & Hornak, J. (1997a). Amnesia and neglect: Beyond the Delay–Brion system and the Hebb synapse. *Philosophical Transactions of the Royal Society, London, B352*, 1481–1488.

Gaffan, D., & Hornak, J. (1997b). Visual neglect in the monkey: representation and disconnection. *Brain, 120*, 1647–1657.

Gaffan, D., Easton, A., & Parker, A. (2002). Interaction of inferior temporal cortex with frontal cortex and basal forebrain: double dissociation in strategy implementation and associative learning. *Journal of Neuroscience, 22*, 7288–7296.

Gaffan, D., Parker, A., & Easton, A. (2001). Dense amnesia in the monkey after transection of fornix, amygdala and anterior temporal stem. *Neuropsychologia, 39*, 51–70.

Hebb, D.O. (1949). *Organization of behavior*. New York: Wiley.

Hornak, J., Oxbury, S., Oxbury, J., Iversen, S.D., & Gaffan, D. (1997). Hemifield-specific visual recognition memory impairments in patients with unilateral temporal lobe removals. *Neuropsychologia, 35*, 1311–1315.

Kitt, C.A., Mitchell, S.J., DeLong, M.R., Wainer, B.H., and Price, D.L. (1987). Fiber pathways of basal forebrain cholinergic neurons in monkeys. *Brain Research, 406*, 192–206.

Mackintosh, N.J. (1975). A theory of attention: Variations in the associability of stimulus with reinforcement. *Psychological Review, 82*, 276–298.

Malkova, L., Gaffan, D., & Murray, E.A. (1997). Excitotoxic lesions of the amygdala fail to produce impairment in visual learning for auditory secondary reinforcement but interfere with reinforcer devaluation effects in rhesus monkeys. *Journal of Neuroscience, 17*, 6011–6020.

Mesulam, M.-M., & Mufson, E.J. (1984). Neural inputs into the nucleus basalis of the substantia innominata (Ch4) in the rhesus monkey. *Brain, 107*, 253–274.

Mesulam, M.-M., Mufson, E.J., Levey, A.I., & Wainer, B.H. (1983). Cholinergic innervation of cortex by the basal forebrain: Cytochemistry and cortical connections of the septal area, diagonal band nuclei, nucleus basalis (substantia innominata), and hypothalamus in the rhesus monkey. *Journal of Comparative Neurology, 214*, 170–197.

Miller, E.K., & Cohen, J.D. (2001). An integrative theory of prefrontal cortex function. *Annual Review of Neuroscience, 24*, 167–202.

Ongur, D., An, X., & Price, J.L. (1998). Prefrontal cortical projections to the hypothalamus in macaque monkeys. *Journal of Comparative Neurology, 401*, 480–505.

Parker, A., & Gaffan, D. (1998). Memory after frontal-temporal disconnection in monkeys: Conditional and nonconditional tasks, unilateral and bilateral frontal lesions. *Neuropsychologia, 36*, 259–271.

Passingham, R.E. (1993). *The frontal lobes and voluntary action*. Oxford: Oxford University Press.

Petrides, M. (1991). Learning impairments following excisions of the primate frontal cortex. In H.S. Levin, H.M. Eisenberg, & A.L. Benton (Eds.) *Frontal lobe function and dysfunction* (pp. 256–272). New York: Oxford University Press.

Platt, M.L., & Glimcher, P.W. (1999). Neural correlates of decision variables in parietal cortex. *Nature, 400*, 233–238.

Rempel-Clower, N.L., & Barbas, H. (1998). Topographic organization of connections between the hypothalamus and prefrontal cortex in the rhesus monkey. *Journal of Comparative Neurology, 398*, 393–419.

Rolls, E.T., Judge, S.J., & Sanghera, M.K. (1977). Activity of neurones in the inferior temporal cortex of the alert monkey. *Brain Research, 130*, 2229–2238.

Russchen, F.T., Amaral, D.G., & Price, J.L. (1985). The afferent connections of the substantia innominata in the monkey, *Macaca fascicularis. Journal of Comparative Neurology, 242*, 1–27.

Seldon, N.R., Gitelman, D.R., Salamon-Murayama, N., Parrish, T.B., & Mesulam, M.-M. (1998). Trajectories of cholinergic pathways within the cerebral hemispheres of the human brain. *Brain, 121*, 2249–2257.

Trapold, M.A. (1970). Are expectancies based upon different positive reinforcing events discriminably different? *Learning and Motivation, 1,* 129–140.

Ungerleider, L.G., Gaffan, D., & Pelak, V.S. (1989). Projections from inferior temporal cortex to prefrontal cortex via the uncinate fascicle in Rhesus monkeys. *Experimental Brain Research, 76,* 473–484.

Webster, M.J., Bachevalier, J., & Ungerleider, L.G. (1993). Subcortical connections of inferior temporal areas TE and TEO in macaque monkeys. *Journal of Comparative Neurology, 335,* 73–91.

Wise, S.P., Murray, E.A., & Gerfen, C.R. (1997). The frontal cortex–basal ganglia system in primates. *Critical Reviews in Neurobiology, 10,* 317–356.

PART THREE

Rat studies

Brain mechanisms of declarative memory: The fundamental role of the hippocampus as revealed by studies on rodents

Howard Eichenbaum
Department of Psychology, Boston University, USA

INTRODUCTION

The observations from studies on amnesia in humans have provided a unique window into brain mechanisms of memory, focusing attention both on declarative memory as a special form of memory representation and on structures of the medial temporal lobe as critical to this kind of memory processing. However, this work by itself, even when complemented by observations for brain imaging in normal human subjects, offers only a preliminary insight into the brain mechanisms of memory. It tells us what kind of memory processing is accomplished by the medial temporal region, but it does not tell us *how* this kind of processing is accomplished in fundamental coding mechanisms and neural algorithms. To seek a deeper understanding of the cognitive and neurobiological mechanisms that underlie memory function, we need valid animals models of memory, and approaches that offer more detailed characterisations of the functional circuitry in the critical brain structures.

This chapter begins with an overview of the characteristics of amnesia in humans with damage to the medial temporal lobe, with the aim of identifying key properties of memory dependent on that region of the brain. In particular, I will discuss evidence demonstrating the selective role of the medial temporal lobe in memory, and its selective role to a particular domain of memory. I will argue that the hippocampal region mediates declarative memory, characterised by a combination of episodic and semantic memory processing, and by the capacity consciously to recollect and flexibly to express memories. I will then focus on developments in my laboratory, and in related research, towards an animal model of amnesia that seeks to improve our understanding of the fundamental cognitive mechanisms of that kind of memory processing, and to identify the particular role of the hippocampus, as well as that of other structures with which it is connected. This work involves studies on rats with damage to the hippocampus, and suggests a specific role for the hippocampus in the organisation and flexible expression of memories. Finally, I will outline a theoretical model of how the hippocampus encodes information in the service of memory. I will provide evidence for this model from observations on the firing patterns of hippocampal neurons in behaving animals. The emerging evidence suggests that the hippocampus might encode episodic memories as sequences of events and the places where they occur, and represents events and places that are common between related episodes. The combination of these aspects of memory representation provides insights into the fundamental properties of declarative memory processing by the hippocampus. More detailed and comprehensive discussions of this material can be found in other recent publications (Eichenbaum & Cohen, 2000; Eichenbaum et al., 1999, 2000; Eichenbaum, 2000).

CHARACTERISTICS OF AMNESIA IN HUMANS WITH DAMAGE IN THE MEDIAL TEMPORAL LOBE

Most of our preliminary insights came from observations by Milner and colleagues on the patient H.M., who became severely amnesic following removal of the medial temporal lobe region in an attempt to ameliorate epilepsy that was refractory to other medial treatment (Scoville & Milner, 1957; Milner, Corkin & Teuber, 1968; Corkin, 1984). The amnesia in this case was particulary remarkable in both its severity and its selectivity. H.M. could remember almost no new facts or events. Memories of the people he meets, and of the circumstances of the meetings and the specific experiences during those events, are lost as soon as they leave his immediate attention. He has acquired almost no new factual information about public events or personalities, new words that have entered the lexicon, or general information about his immediate circumstances or about the world. Despite the overall severity of his deficit in new learning, H.M. has retained some information that has been introduced since his operation. However, those items he remembers typically involve material with which he has been exposed repetitively. He has learned the meaning of the word "astronaut" and a few other very common words that have come into usage since his operation. He knows who Elvis Presley and John Kennedy were, although they came into fame after his operation. However, his memories on these and other facts are fragmentary and often confused, lacking appropriate connections to the general framework in which they occurred and the other events or persons to which one ordinarily ties our knowledge.

In formal memory testing H.M. typically scores near zero memory capacity on a very broad variety of tests for information across perceptual and response modalities. Even with repeated testing he fails to recall logical facts from a story, arbitrary word associations (verbal paired associates), and recently seen pictures. The combined results from these and many other conventional tests of learning and memory have shown that H.M.'s memory deficit is "global" in that he is impaired in every conventional stimulus modality. His delayed recall is impaired whether the items are stories, words, digits, new vocabulary words, drawings, songs, common objects, object locations, or simple mazes. Thus the early studies indicated that his impairment is both nearly absolute and seems to pervade all kinds of memory.

H.M.'s impairment is also remarkable in its selectivity to memory function. He has normal visual fields, visual adaptation, and other commonly tested visual–perceptual functions and visuospatial perception, and can recognise and name common objects. Aside from some signs of peripheral neuropathy and loss of fine motor coordination, his somatosensory function and motor coordination are normal. H.M.'s intelligence as measured by conventional IQ scales was above average prior to the operation and, after the surgery, actually rose somewhat, perhaps because of the alleviation of his seizures. H.M.'s language capacities are also largely within the normal range and communicates spontaneously and successfully. Indeed, one of the major breakthroughs in the early observations on H.M. was the finding that memory could be isolated as a cognitive function.

Even within his memory functions, H.M.'s amnesic disorder is selective to particular domains of learning and memory. H.M. can remember both factual material and specific experiences learned remotely prior to his operation. His memory for the English language seems fully intact. He retains and can relate many childhood memories. However, H.M. does have a retrograde amnesia, that is a loss of memories acquired prior to his surgery. The extent of retrograde amnesia was first estimated as the 2 years preceding the surgery, based on the postoperative interviews. Later objective tests revealed a longer period of lost recent memory, and indicate some loss extending back several years, approaching the onset of his epilepsy. In addition, H.M.'s short-term or working memory is intact. He can immediately reproduce a list of numbers as long as that of control subjects and he can briefly retain pictorial material. His decay of short-term memory is normal in both recognition and recall tests. However, his memory deficit becomes evident as soon as his immediate memory span is exceeded or after a delay with distraction.

In addition to these spared domains of remote memory and short-term memory, the early studies on H.M. also revealed two "exceptions" to his otherwise profound deficit. One of these involved the acquisition of sensori-motor skill, the ability to reproduce a drawing from a mirror image view. The other involved strikingly good performance by H.M. on a perceptual learning in a task, called the Gollins partial pictures task, in which subjects improve with repetition in the recognition of fragmented line drawings of common objects and words.

In the succeeding decades, many studies have shown that these successes are merely examples of a large domain of spared learning and memory capacity in amnesic patients with damage to the medial temporal lobe region (for a review see Eichenbaum & Cohen, 2000). Successes include examples from a broad domain of general skill learning, including acquisition of the ability to read mirror-reversed words, learning to manually track a position on a slowly revolving disk (rotary pursuit), the acquisition of an artificial "grammar" that specifies rules for sequencing and length of the letter strings, and learning to categorise dot patterns that correspond to a set of hidden prototypes. Another domain of spared learning involves many examples of success in the acquisition of habits or stimulus–response sequences, including a serial reaction time task where subjects become faster in responding to a repetitive sequence of stimuli, improvement in speed in reading repeated text (using either real or fake words), and learning to classify combinations of stimuli according to outcomes they predict in a probabilistic way. In addition, yet another domain of spared memory in amnesia involves examples of intact Pavlovian conditioning, including eyeblink conditioning and emotional response conditioning, and normal "priming" of response speed or selection with repetition of previously experienced stimulus elements.

Two examples of these will be briefly summarised here, to illustrate the robustness of spared memory capacities in amnesia. One involves probabilistic classification learning in an experiment performed by Knowlton, Mangels, and Squire (1996). In this task subjects are presented repeatedly with a number of cues that predict one of two arbitrary outcomes, but the prediction is probabilistic in that each stimulus configuration determines the outcome on only a specific percentage of trials. Learning is measured as increasing performance in matching the predicted outcome based on any set of cues. For example, Knowlton et al. (1996) presented subjects with one to four playing-card cues on a computer monitor and asked them, based on these cues, to predict whether the "outcome" would be rain or shine. Each cue was associated with a different predictive value. For example, one card predicted "sun" on 75 per cent of the trials, and other cards 40 per cent, 60 per cent, or 25 per cent of the trials. Card combinations predicted the weather according to their joint probabilities. Because it is very difficult to remember the many specific combinations of cards presented, and because memory for specific trials can be contradicted in repetitions because of the probabilistic nature of the regularities, the benefit of remembering specific trials is minimised. Nevertheless, after 50 training trials both normal subjects and amnesic patients had improved gradually, reaching a level of well over that predicted by chance. In a subsequent debriefing the same amnesics were impaired in remembering specific facts about the testing sessions, illustrating a clear dissociation between their intact capacity for acquisition of the associations between responses and particular stimulus-compounds versus their impairment in memory for facts and events about performing the task. Knowlton and colleagues compared the performance of amnesic subjects to that of patients in the early stages of Parkinson's disease, associated with degeneration of neurons in the substantia nigra resulting in a major loss of input to the neostriatum. The Parkinson's patients showed the opposite pattern of the amnesics, severely impaired acquisition of the probabilistic associations but intact memory for facts and events about the training.

My other example is a study by Bechara and colleagues (1995) that examined emotional learning in three patients with selective damage to the hippocampus or amygdala. Their report focused on a form of autonomic conditioning involving an association between a neutral stimulus and a loud sound. The conditioning stimulus (CS+) was either a monochrome colour slide or a pure tone. Subjects were initially habituated to the CS+ as well as to several like stimuli (different colours or tones) that would be presented as CS− stimuli. Subsequently, during conditioning the CSs were presented in random order for 2s each. Each presentation of the CS+ was terminated with the unconditioned stimulus (US), a loud boat horn that was sounded briefly. Autonomic responses to these stimuli were measured as skin conductance changes through electrodermal recordings. Normal control subjects showed skin conductance changes to the US, and robust conditioning to the CS+, with smaller responses to the CS− stimuli. A patient with selective hippocampal damage showed robust skin conductance changes to the US and normal conditioning to the CS+ stimuli. This patient also showed responsiveness to the CS− stimuli, but clearly differentiated these from the CS+s. By contrast, a patient with selective damage to the amygdala showed normal unconditioned responses to the US but failed to develop conditioned responses to the CS+ stimuli. Finally, a subject with combined amygdala and hippocampal damage failed to condition, even though he responded to the US. After the conditioning sessions, the subjects were debriefed with several questions about the stimuli and their relationships. Control subjects and the patient with selective amygdala damage answered most of these questions correctly, but both patients with hippocampal damage were severely impaired in recollecting the task events.

The findings in these studies demonstrate two major points about the memory deficit associated with hippocampal region damage in humans. First, the memory disorder associated with medial temporal lobe damage is selective to a particular type of memory that involves the capacity to recall specific events and facts. Second, as shown by clear double dissociations, forms of habit learning and emotional conditioning are disrupted by damage to other brain systems (the neostriatum and amygdala, respectively). The finding that different forms of memory for the identical stimuli and associations are differentially affected by localised brain damage supports the notion that there are multiple memory systems in the brain and that the hippocampus and associated structures of the medial temporal lobe region is involved in only one of them. Furthermore, recent studies have shown that damage to the hippocampus itself is sufficient to result in the pattern of deficits described above, indicating a specific and critical role for the hippocampus in this particular type of memory (Rempel-Clower, Zola, Squire, & Amaral, 1996, Vargha-Khadem et al., 1997; Zola-Morgan, Squire, & Amaral, 1986).

WHAT IS DECLARATIVE MEMORY?

The findings from studies on amnesia in humans point to a critical role for the hippocampus itself in "declarative memory", our ability to recollect everyday events and factual knowledge. To understand this role it is important to reconsider the fundamental properties of this kind of memory and how it breaks down as revealed in the studies of amnesia discussed above. We acquire our declarative memories through everyday personal experiences, and the ability to retain and recall these "episodic" memories. But the full scope of declarative memory also extends to semantic memory, the body of general knowledge about the world that is accrued from linking multiple experiences that share some of the same information. For example, a typical episodic memory about your breakfast this morning would contain specific information about the events and places associated with your breakfast. Your general knowledge about where people eat breakfast, about what time of day breakfast is taken, about typical breakfast foods, and several other facts about breakfast, comes in great part from a synthesis of the representations of many breakfast episodes and other experiences in which breakfasts are observed or discussed. In addition, declarative memory for both the episodic and semantic information is special in that the contents of these memories are accessible through various routes. Most commonly in humans, declarative memory is expressed through conscious, effortful recollection. This means that one can access and express declarative memories to solve novel problems by making inferences from memory. For example, even without ever explicitly studying a list of common breakfast items, one can infer such a list from the set of episodic memories about breakfasts.

It is the capacity to connect multiple experiences and to use this information flexibly and inferentially that distinguishes the critical involvement of the hippocampus. Even though the variety of hippocampal-independent learning is broad, all the forms of skill, habit, conditioning, and priming spared in amnesia share the common feature that memory is expressed by reperformance of some kind of processing experienced during an initial learning event. Whenever the demands for memory exceed a reperformance and instead require the organisation and flexible expression of memories, the hippocampus becomes requisite.

AN ANIMAL MODEL OF DECLARATIVE MEMORY

These properties of declarative memory have recently been investigated in animals, and the findings serve to show a commonality of hippocampal function in fundamental properties of declarative memory (Squire, 1992; Eichenbaum & Cohen, 2000). The critical experiments include initial training on multiple distinct experiences that share common elements, and then testing whether these experiences have been linked in memory to solve new problems, that is, to make inferences from memory. The following presents some examples that serve to elucidate these properties. In some of these experimental protocols, the requirement to distinguish multiple overlapping experiences is sufficient to require hippocampal function, and even when this demand is eliminated memory expression is not flexible. In other protocols, initial learning of different specific events is accomplished in the absence of normal hippocampal function, but flexible expression that requires linking distinct episodes is impaired. In yet other protocols, initial learning involving only a single episode is intact, but flexible expression is impaired. Selected examples of each of these protocols follows.

Water-maze learning: Linking distinct spatial learning episodes and showing a capacity for flexible memory expression in navigation from new locations

One of the most commonly used assays of hippocampal function is spatial learning in the Morris water maze. In the standard version of this task, rats are released into the water at different starting points on successive trials, a manipulation that presents the animal with four distinct experiences in swimming to escape and requires the animal to link together information about these experiences across trials (Morris, Garrud, Rawlins, & O'Keefe, 1982). The procedure of presenting the four different swim paths demands an organised respresentation of all of the different swim paths, to disentangle otherwise conflicting associations of the separate views seen from each starting point. Eichenbaum, Stewart, and Morris (1990) assessed the importance of this demand in standard water-maze learning by training rats on a version of the task where rats were gradually trained to swim to a hidden platform when released into the maze from a constant start position on each trial. Initially, animals were trained to approach a visible black-and-white striped platform. Then the visibility of the platform was gradually diminished using a series of training stages that involved a large, visible, white platform, then smaller platforms, and finally sinking the platform below the water surface. With this gradual training procedure, rats with hippocampal damage (fornix lesions) showed suprisingly successful learning. Thus, in contrast to their complete failure on the standard version of this task, animals with hippocampal damage were able to learn the location of the escape platform, and standard "transfer" tests indicated that they could identify the place of escape by the same set of available extra-maze cues rather than solely by the approach trajectory.

Our interpretation of these results was that the comparison between different kinds of trial episodes while concurrently learning all four swim paths in the water-maze situation necessarily requires hippocampal function. However, in related experiments Whishaw and colleagues (1995, 1997) have extended our gradual approach to demonstrate intact water-maze learning with all four types of trials in rats with fornix transections. They trained rats initially using a visible platform, placing them on the platform, then in the water farther from the platform in each of the different start directions. By this method of gradual training using a visible platform, rats with fornix transections learned the task as well as normal rats, and showed normal patterns of swimming trajectories throughout. Then a hidden platform was substituted at the same location and training continued. During this phase, the escape latencies of rats with hippocampal damage were initially much higher than those of normal rats, and they continued to show more near misses throughout training. However, their escape latencies converged on those of normal rats after several sessions, and they showed a strong bias for the former platform quadrant when the platform was subsequently removed. These findings show that even the variable start version of the water maze can be learned by animals with hippocampal damage, under highly regimented conditions. Whishaw and colleagues (1995) have also further analysed the limitations of rats with hippocampal damage. After successful hidden platform training, the same rats were tested on a variant of the task in which the platform location was moved each day and training proceeded for four trials from different starting points. Normal rats showed shorter escape latencies across the four trials within each day, and generally improved on the task across test session. By contrast rats with fornix transections were impaired and showed no general improvement across days. In a follow-up study, Whishaw and Tomie (1997) replicated the success on initial place learning by rats with fornix transection, and the poor performance on reversal. In addition, they found that the deficit during reversal was related to the tendency by rats with fornix transections to return to the originally learned platform location. This perseveration of an initially learned escape location was taken as further evidence for successful place learning, albeit clearly mediated by a different strategy than that used by normals, one that did not support rapid reversal learning.

In a second part of their study, Eichenbaum et al. (1990) asked whether, having successfully acquired a constant-start-point variant of this place learning task, the animals could use this information to solve new related navigational problems. In this test, the platform was left in its normal place but the start position was moved to various novel locations. When the start position was the same as that used during instruction trials, both normal rats and rats with hippocampal damage had short escape latencies. On the trials with novel starting positions, normal rats also swam directly to the platform regardless of the starting position. By contrast, rats with hippocampal damage rarely swam directly to the escape platform and sometimes went far astray, subsequently had abnormally long average escape latencies on these probe trials. This striking deficit was demonstrated by close examination of their individual swim trajectories. All the normal rats nearly always swam directly to the platform regardless of their starting point. But rats with hippocampal damage swam in various directions, occasionally leading them straight to the platform, but more often in the wrong direction, and they sometimes never found the platform in this highly familiar environment.

Combining the results of these studies, the findings indicate a remarkable preserved capacity for spatial learning even when guided by distal spatial cues. But this preserved learning does not involve an organisation of distinctive experiences, and instead appears to rely on separate representations for each successful swim path. In addition, even when animals with hippocampal damage can acquire specific swim paths with repetition, they show no capacity to use this information flexibly, either in the normal capacity to navigate from new start locations or to learn to swim to new escape loci.

Transitive inference: Acquisition of separate discrimination problems but failure to inferentially express memory for links across different experiences

In several other experimental protocols, animals with hippocampal damage successfully acquire a set of overlapping experiences, often at a rate not substantially different than that of normal subjects. But they fail to express their memories of the experience in novel situations that require an inference based on linking the distinct experiences in memory. In one of these studies, rats were trained on sets of odour "paired associates" with shared elements, then tested to determine if they could infer an association between elements that were only indirectly related (Bunsey & Eichenbaum, 1996). The task involved an odour-guided version of the paired associate task for rodents, and extended the learning requirement to include multiple stimulus–stimulus associations with overlapping stimulus elements. In this task, animals were initially trained to associate pairs of odour stimuli with one another (e.g. A–B). Then they were trained on a second set of paired associates, but this time each association involved an element that overlapped with one of those in the previous pairings (e.g. B–C). Subsequently, they were given two probe tests to determine whether they had learned the arbitrary associations and could use them flexibly to make inferences from memory. In the critical test for *associative transitivity*, subjects were asked to recognise the appropriate relations between indirectly associated elements (e.g. A–C). In the test for *symmetry*, subjects were asked to recognise appropriate pairings in the reverse order of that used in training (e.g. C–B).

Exploiting rodents' natural foraging strategies that employ olfactory cues, animals were trained with stimuli that consisted of distinctive odours added to a mixture of ground rat chow and sand through which they dug to obtain buried cereal rewards. On each paired associate trial, one of two sample odours initially presented was followed by two choice odours, each assigned as the "associate" of one of the samples and baited only when preceded by that sample. Intact rats learned paired associates rapidly, and selective damage to the hippocampus (using neurotoxic lesions) did not affect acquisition rate on either of the two training sets, consistent with recent reports on stimulus–stimulus association learning in rats and monkeys (Murray, Gaffan, & Mishkin, 1993; Saunders & Weiskrantz, 1989). Intact rats also showed strong transitivity across the sets, reflected in a preference for items indirectly associated with the presented sample. By contrast, rats with selective hippocampal lesions were severely impaired, showing no evidence of transitivity. In the symmetry test, intact rats again showed the appropriate preference in the direction of the symmetrical association. By contrast, rats with selective hippocampal lesions again were severely impaired, showing no significant capacity for symmetry.

In another study, rats were trained on a series of four odour discrimination problems with shared items such that the odour set could be construed as a hierarchy, and then were tested to determine if they could infer transitive relations according to the hierarchical organization (Dusek & Eichenbaum, 1997). Rats were first trained on a series of two-item odour discriminations called premise pairs that collectively included five different odours (e.g. A+ versus B–, B+ versus C–, C+ versus D–, D+ versus E–, where + or – refers to which item is rewarded). Learning could occur by representing each of the separate discrimination problems individually, or they could instead be represented within an orderly hierarchy that includes all five items. To examine which of the representations was actually employed by the animals, they were given probe tests derived from pairs of non-adjacent elements. When presented with the probe pair B versus D, two non-adjacent and non-end elements, consistently choosing B provides unambiguous evidence for transitive inference. Note that correctly choosing A when presented with the probe pair A versus E could be entirely guided by the independent reinforcement histories of these elements individually, because choices of A during premise training were always rewarded and choices of E were never rewarded. Thus the combination of the probe tests B versus D and A versus E provided a powerful assessment of capacities for making novel judgements guided by inferential expression of the orderly organisation of the distinct experiences or by reward history of the individual elements, respectively.

After achieving solid performance on the premise pairs, probe trials containing the critical B versus D problem and the control A versus E problem were presented intermingled with repetitions of the premise pairs. On these probe trials, animals were rewarded for the "correct" (transitive) selection, in order to avoid dissuading them from making transitive choices and maintain performance on the probe trials. To minimise new learning of the B versus D problem, probes were presented only twice per test session and were widely spaced among repetitions of premise pairs. In addition, to test for possible contamination by new learning of the B versus D problem, all animals were subsequently tested for their ability to learn about new odour cues presented in the probe test format.

The performance of normal rats was compared to that of rats with fornix transections, which disconnects the hippocampus from subcortical areas, or ablation of perirhinal and entorhinal cortices, which disconnects the hippocampus from cortical regions. Both normal rats and rats with either type of hippocampal damage achieved criterion performance on each training phase very rapidly. In addition, all rats readily reached criterion with randomly presented premise pairs in an equivalent number of trials. In probe testing, all rats continued to perform well on the premise pairs during the test sessions. All groups demonstrated a serial position curve, such that performance was best on pairs that included one of the end items. On the critical B versus D probe test, normal subjects demonstrated robust transitive inference. Their performance on B versus D trials significantly exceeded chance level and was not different from their performance on premise pairs that included items B and D (the B versus C and C versus D pairs). In striking contrast, the rats with either type of hippocampal damage performed no better than chance on the BD probe—their performance on the B versus D problem was much lower than that on the premise pairs that included B and D, and much worse than the performance of normal animals on this test of transitivity.

A further analysis of transitivity examined performance on the very first presentation of the B versus D pair, which can be considered a "pure" test of inferential responding uncontaminated by food reinforcements given on repeated probe trials. Of the normal subjects, 88 per cent chose correctly on the first B versus D probe, whereas only 50 per cent of the rats with either type of hippocampal damage were successful on the initial B versus D judgement. Thus, by several measures, the data strongly indicate that rats with hippocampal damage have no capacity for transitive inference, despite their having learned each of the premise problems as well as normal subjects.

Analyses of performance on other types of probe trials demonstrated the selectivity of the deficit in transitive inference in rats with either type of hippocampal damage. All rats performed extremely well on the A versus E trials, which can be solved without a transitive judgement, with no group differences in performance on this problem. Conversely, all groups showed minimal evidence of learning during presentations of the new odour pairs, again with no group differences in performance on these problems. The contrast between robust performance on B versus D problems and poor performance for new odour pairs in normal rats strongly indicates that their judgements on the B versus D pairs reflected inferential capacity. The striking inability of animals with either type of hippocampal damage to show this inferential capacity on the B versus D probe trials, despite normal performance on the premise pairs, suggests that they had learned the premise pairs in a way that did not involve the orderly relations among the odour cues.

Combining the results across these experiments, the findings extend the memory impairment following hippocampal damage to non-spatial, in this case olfactory, learning, and show a similar pattern of spared and impaired learning and memory capacities following damage to the hippocampus itself or to its major connections via the fornix or perirhinal and entorhinal cortex. The results also show that even rather complicated learning can be accomplished in the absence of hippocampal function. In the examples provided here, multiple complex discrimination problems, involving combinations of stimuli each of which have ambiguous reward histories, can be acquired concurrently at a normal rate in animals with different types of hippocampal damage. However, animals with hippocampal damage cannot express their memory for variants of this type of learning when required to make judgements that depend on links between the different problems, indicating an inability in organising the separate representations.

Social transmission of food preferences: Single episode learning with flexible memory expression

My final example involves a form of naturalistic and non-spatial learning in a single episode. In this study, Bunsey and Eichenbaum (1995) assessed the role of the hippocampal region in a type of social olfactory learning and memory, the social transmission of food preferences. Social transmission of food preferences involves alterations in food choice patterns consequent to experience with a conspecific that has recently eaten a particular food. When an "observer" rat encounters another ("demonstrator") rat that has recently eaten a distinctively scented food, the probability that the observer will later select that same food over other foods increases (Galef, 1990; Strupp & Levitsky, 1984). This form of social learning is interpreted within the heuristic that a food recently consumed by a conspecific is safe, and thus transmitting this information is adaptive in rat social groups.

In a series of studies, Galef (1990) had shown that the mechanism underlying this learning involves an association between two odours present in the observer rat's breath, the odour of the recently eaten food and an odorous constituent of rat's breath, carbon disulfide. It is of particular importance that exposing the observer to the distinctive food odour alone, or to carbon disulfide alone, have no effect on later food preference. Thus, the shift in food choice cannot be attributed to mere familiarity with the food odour. By contrast, exposure to the scented food mixed with carbon disulfide, even without the social context in which this association is usually experienced, increased later consumption of food with the same odour. The implication from these studies is that the formation of a specific stimulus–stimulus association, acquired in a single social encounter in the absence of any primary reinforcement, is both necessary and sufficient to support the shift in food selection. Furthermore, memory for the social transmission of food preference involves the formation of a specific stimulus–stimulus association in a single training episode, plus expression of the memory in a situation different from the learning event, both consistent with the critical property of flexible, inferential expression in declarative memory.

Following on a previous observation that this type of learning is dependent on the hippocampal region (Winocur, 1990), the role of the hippocampus itself was investigated in this task, assessing both immediate memory and delayed (1 day) memory for social exposure to the odour of a novel food (Bunsey & Eichenbaum, 1995). Normal rats subsequently showed a strong selection preference for the trained food odour in both tests. By contrast, rats with damage selective to the hippocampus itself showed intact short-term memory, but their performance fell to chance within 24 hours. These findings, similar to the pattern of sparing and impairment in human amnesics, indicate that the hippocampus is not required for perceptual or motivational components of learning or the ability to express the learned choice preferences. But the hippocampus itself is required for long-term memory of the association when it must be expressed outside repetition of the learning context. In addition, Wincur's (1990) study showed hippocampal damage produced within a day of training, but not after 5 days, resulted in a retrograde loss of memory for the odour–odour association. This study provides the clearest example of a deficit in memory for non-spatial materials acquired in a single learning episode, revealed in the distinction between intact short-term memory and impaired delayed memory in a situation that requires expression of memory in a situation quite different from the circumstances of initial learning.

A NEURAL CODING MODEL FOR HIPPOCAMPAL REPRESENTATION OF DECLARATIVE MEMORIES

How are these memory capacities mediated within the circuitry of the hippocampus? Recent observations from extracellular recordings in behaving animals suggest that hippocampal neuronal networks might represent sequences of events and places that compose episodic memories. The content of information encoded by the firing patterns of these neurons includes both specific conjunctions of events and places unique to particular experiences and features that are common to overlapping experiences. Indeed, there is now evidence that the hippocampus creates separate but linked, episodic-like representations even when the overt behaviours and places where they occur are the same but the events are parts of distinct experiences.

Hippocampal principal cells exhibit firing patterns that are readily related to a broad range of events that occur during sequences of behaviour in all tasks examined (Eichenbaum et al., 1999). For example, as rats perform spatial tasks where they are required to shuttle between a common starting location and one or more reward locations, hippocampal "place" cells fire during each moment as the animal traverses its path, with each neuron activated when the animal is in a particular place and moving towards the goal. A largely different set of cells fires similarly in sequence as the rat returns to the starting point, such that each cell can be characterised as an element of a network representing an outbound or inbound part of the episode. One can imagine the network activity as similar to a "video-clip" of each trial episode, with each cell capturing the information about where the rat is and what it is doing in each sequential "frame" of the clip.

Similarly, in both simple and complex learning tasks, hippocampal cells fire at virtually every moment associated with specific relevant events. For example, in an experiment where rats performed an odour discrimination task, hippocampal cells fired during each sequential event, with different neurons firing during the approach to the odour stimuli, sampling of odours, execution of a behavioural response, and reward consumption. Again, it is as if each hippocampal cell encodes one of the sequential trial events with its activity reflecting both aspects of the ongoing behaviour and the place where that behaviour occurred. In all of these situations, some cells fire during common events or places that occur on every trial, whereas other cells fire associated with events that occurred only during a particular type of episode, such as sampling a particular configuration of two odours presented on that trial.

In an extension of these studies, we were recently able to distinguish hippocampal neurons that encoded both specific combinations of events and places that were unique to particular experiences as well as particular features that were common across many related experiences (Wood, Dudchenko, & Eichenbaum, 1999a). In this experiment, rats performed an odour memory task at several locations in an open field. Again, different cells fired during each sequential trial event. Some cells were activated only associated with an almost unique event, for example, when the rat sniffed a particular odour at a particular place and it was a non-match with the odour presented on the previous trial. Other cells fired associated with features of the task that were common across many trials: cells that fired as the rat approached the odour stimulus, or as it sniffed a particular odour, regardless of where the trial was performed, and cells fired as the rat performed the trial at a particular location regardless of what odour was presented.

Finally, there is emerging evidence of coding for information specific to particular types of episodes even in situations where the overt behavioural events and the locations in which they occur are identical between multiple types of experience. For example, as rats performed a spatial memory task, some hippocampal cells were activated when the rat was pressing one of two levers only during the sample or only during the test phase of the task (Hampson, Simeral, & Deadwyler, 1999). These cells can be characterised as elements encoding one temporally, spatially, and behaviourally defined event in the network representation of a particular trial type. The firing of other cells was associated with common events—a particular lever position, regardless of trial phase, or during the sample or test phase regardless of location; these cells could be used to link the separate representations of different trial phases or episodes, and these codings were segregated topographically within the hippocampus. More direct evidence of episodic-like coding was found in a recent study where rats performed a spatial alternation task on a T-maze. Each trial commenced when the rat traversed the stem of the "T" and then selected either the left- or the right-choice arm (Wood et al., 1999b). To alternate successfully the rats were required to distinguish between their left-turn and right-turn experiences and to use their memory for the most recent previous experience to guide the current choice. Different hippocampal cells fired as the rats passed through the sequence of locations within the maze during each trial. Most important, the firing patterns of many of the cells depended on whether the rat was in the midst of a left- or right-turn episode, even when the rat was on the stem of the T and therefore running similarly on both types of trials. Other cells had the same firing pattern when the rat was on the stem on either trial type. Thus, the hippocampus encoded both the left-turn and right-turn experiences using distinct representations, and included elements that could link them by their common features. In each of these experiments, the representations of event sequences, linked by codings of common events and places, could constitute the substrate of a network of episodic memories.

These considerations, based on observations about hippocampal neuronal firing patterns, suggest a scheme that ties together many of the properties of hippocampal dependent memory discussed above. First, the hippocampus is a circuit that is particularly structured to encode regularities in the broadest variety of conjunctions of events, or common features of events. However, it is part of only one of multiple pathways that can represent stimulus features, stimulus significance, or stimulus–response links, and so these simpler aspects of representation and association can be mediated by other brain areas and systems independent of the hippocampus. These other structures and systems are sufficient to support short term and working memory, as well as long-term representations of the significance of individual stimuli and stimulus–response associations and chains (see Eichenbaum & Cohen, 2000, for a comprehensive review). Thus, whereas the hippocampus is well suited to encode stimulus regularities, and indeed likely does so differently than all other brain structures, other brain systems are seen as mediating the eventual permanent storage of detailed declarative memories, as well as non-declarative forms of memory.

In addition, the property by which the expression of remotely acquired memories is independent of the hippocampus is seen as arising from the organisational function of hippocampal circuitry. This organisational cap-acity, as described earlier, involves the ability to rapidly encode a sequence of events that make up an episodic memory, to retrieve that memory by re-experiencing one facet of the event, and to link the ongoing experience to stored episodic representations. It appears that the neuronal elements of the hippocampus contain the fundamental coding properties that can support this kind of organisation. However, it is unlikely that the hippocampus has the storage capacity to contain all of one's episodic memories, and the find-ings on sparing of memories remotely obtained before hippocampal damage indicate that the hippocampus is not the final storage site (Scoville & Milner, 1957). Therefore, it seems likely that the hippocampal neurons are involved in mediating the re-establishment of detailed representations, rather than stor-ing the details themselves, and these detailed representations are probably accomplished in widespread areas of the cerebral cortex that are connected with the hippocampus. Furthermore, one can imagine that repetitive inter-actions between those cortical areas and the hippocampus, and these inter-actions serve to repeatedly coactivate widespread cortical areas so that they eventually develop linkages between detailed memories without hippocampal mediation. In this way, the networking provided by the hippocampus might also underlie its temporary role in the consolidation of cortical memories (Eichenbaum et al., 1999; McClelland, McNaughton, & O'Reilly, 1995; Squire & Alvarez, 1995).

REFERENCES

Bechera, A., Tranel, D., Hanna, D., Adolphs, R., Rockland, C., & Damasio, A.R. (1995). Double dissociation of conditioning and declarative knowledge relative to the amygdala and hippocampus in humans. *Science, 269,* 1115–1118.

Bunsey, M., Eichenbaum, H. (1995). Selective damage to the hippocampal region blocks long term retention of a natural and nonspatial stimulus–stimulus association. *Hippocampus, 5,* 546–556.

Bunsey, M., & Eichenbaum, H. (1996). Conservation of hippocampal memory function in rats and humans. *Nature, 379,* 255–257.

Corkin, S. (1984). Lasting consequences of bilateral medial temporal lobectomy: Clinical course and experimental findings in H.M. *Seminars in Neurology, 4,* 249–259.

Dusek J.A., & Eichenbaum, H. (1997). The hippocampus and memory for orderly stimulus relations. *Proceedings of the National Academy of Sciences USA, 94,* 7109–7114.

Eichenbaum, H. (2000). Cortical–hippocampal system for declarative memory. *Nature Reviews Neuroscience, 1,* 41–50.

Eichenbaum, H., Alvarez, P., & Ramus, S. (2000). Animal models of amnesia. In L. Cermak (Ed.) *Handbook of neuropsychology* (2nd ed., vol. 4, pp. 1–24). New York: Elsevier Sciences.

Eichenbaum, H., & Cohen, N.J. (2000). From conditioning to conscious recollection: Memory systems of the brain. Oxford: Oxford University Press.

Eichenbaum, H., Dudchenko, P., Wood, E., Shapiro, M., & Tanila, H. (1999). The hippocampus, memory, and place cells: Is it spatial memory or memory space? *Neuron, 23,* 1–20.

Eichenbaum, H., Stewart, C., & Morris, R.G.M. (1990). Hippocampal representation in spatial learning. *Journal of Neuroscience, 10,* 331–339.

Galef, B.G. (1990). An adaptionist perspective on social learning, social feeding, and social foraging in Norway rats. In D.A. Dewsbury, (Ed.) *Contemporary issues in comparative psychology* (pp. 55–79). Sunderland, MA: Sinauer.

Hampson, R.E., Simeral, J.D., & Deadwyler, A. (1999). Distribution of spatial and nonspatial information in dorsal hippocampus. *Nature, 402,* 610–614.

Knowlton, B.J., Mangels, J.A., & Squire, L.R. (1996). A neostriatal habit learning system in humans. *Science, 273,* 1399–1401.

McClelland, J.L., McNaughton, B.L., & O'Reilly, R.C. (1995). Why there are complementary learning systems in the hippocampus and neocortex: Insights from the successes and failures of connectionist models of learning and memory. *Psychological Review, 102,* 419–457.

Milner, B., Corkin, S., Teuber, H.L. (1968). Further analysis of the hippocampal amnesic syndrome: 14-year follow-up study of H.M. *Neuropsychologia, 6,* 215–234.

Morris, R.G.M., Garrud, P., Rawlins, J.P., & O'Keefe, J. (1982). Place navigation impaired in rats with hippocampal lesions. *Nature, 297,* 681–683.

Murray, E.A. & Bussey, T.J. (1999). Perceptual–mnemonic functions of the perirhinal cortex. *Trends in Cognitive Sciences, 3,* 142–151.

Murray, E.A., Gaffan, D., Mishkin, M. (1993). Neural substrates of visual stimulus–stimulus association in rhesus monkeys. *Journal of Neuroscience, 13,* 4549–4561.

Rempel-Clower, N.L., Zola, S.M., Squire, L.R., & Amaral, D.G. (1996). Three cases of enduring memory impairment following bilateral damage limited to the hippocampal formation. *Journal of Neuroscience, 16,* 5233–5255.

Saunders, R.C., & Weiskrantz, L. (1989). The effects of fornix transection and combined fornix transection, mamillary body lesions and hippocampal ablations on object pair association memory in the rhesus monkey. *Behavioural Brain Research, 35,* 85–94.

Scoville, W.B. & Milner, B. (1957). Loss of recent memory after bilateral hippocampal lesions. *Journal of Neurology, Neurosurgery, and Psychiatry, 20,* 11–21.

Squire, L. (1992). Memory and the hippocampus: A synthesis from findings with rats, monkeys, and humans. *Psychological Review, 99,* 195–231.

Squire, L.R. & Alvarez, P. (1995). Retrograde amnesia and memory consolidation: A neuro-biological perspective. *Current Opinion in Neurobiology*, *5*, 169–177.

Strupp, B.J., & Levitsky, D.A. (1984). Social transmission of food preferences in adult hooded rats (*Rattus norvegicus*). *Journal of Comparative Psychology*, *98*, 257–266.

Vargha-Khadem F., Gadin, D.G., Watkins, K.E., Connelly, A., Van Paesschen, W., & Mishkin, M. (1997). Differential effects of early hippocampal pathology on episodic and semantic memory. *Science*, *277*, 376–380.

Whishaw, I.Q., & Tomie, J. (1997). Perseveration on place reversals in spatial swimming pool tasks: Further evidence for place learning in hippocampal rats. *Hippocampus*, *7*(3), 361–370.

Whishaw, I.Q., Cassel, J-C., & Jarrard, L.E. (1995). Rats with fimbria–fornix lesions display a place response in a swimming pool: A dissociation between getting there and knowing where. *Journal of Neuroscience*, *15*, 5779–5788.

Winocur, G. (1990). Anterograde and retrograde amnesia in rats with dorsal hippocampal or dorsomedial thalamic lesions. *Behavioral Brain Research*, *38*, 145–154.

Wood, E.R., Dudchenko, P.A., & Eichenbaum, H. (1999a). The global record of memory in hippocampal neuronal activity. *Nature*, *397*, 613–616.

Wood, E.R., Dudchenko, P.A. & Eichenbaum, H. (1999b). Episodic determinants of hippocampal place cell activity during T-maze spatial alternation. *Society for Neuroscience Abstracts*, *25*, 1381.

Zola-Morgan, S.M., Squire, L.R., & Amaral, D.G. (1986). Human amnesia and the medial temporal region: Enduring memory impairment following a bilateral lesion limited to field CA1 of the hippocampus. *Journal of Neuroscience*, *6*, 2950–2967.

CHAPTER TEN

The "what" and "where" of event memory: Independence and interactivity within the medial temporal lobe

Timothy J. Bussey
Department of Experimental Psychology, University of Cambridge, UK

John P. Aggleton
School of Psychology, Cardiff University, UK

INTRODUCTION

Memory has often been described by the use of metaphor, many early examples of which seem amusing to contemporary psychologists. Plato, for example, referred to memory as an aviary, the act of remembering corresponding to the capture of one of the resident birds (and the act of forgetting corresponding to the capture of the wrong bird). Both Plato and Aristotle likened memory to a cube of wax upon which various impressions could be made and stored for posterity. And both William James and Sigmund Freud conceived of memory as a house, with specific memories likened to objects in the house (for discussion of these and other metaphors of memory, see Roediger, 1980). But whatever the metaphor of choice, these early conceptions of memory envisaged an entity or process that is *single, unitary,* and *indivisible*. Arguably the most important single discovery in the modern era of memory research, therefore, was that memory cannot be regarded as a unitary entity or process; rather, there appear to be different kinds of memory, and these different kinds of memory are mediated by anatomically distinct regions of the brain. Much research has been directed at attempting to characterise these different divisions of memory, resulting in a variety of mnemonic taxonomies usually taking the form of a dichotomy, for example, long- versus short-term memory, implicit versus explicit memory, or declarative versus procedural memory.

Particularly influential has been the declarative/procedural distinction, which posits a fractionation of long-term memory into declarative memory for facts and events, and procedural memory for skills and habits (Cohen & Squire, 1980). The difference between these types of memory is illustrated by the famous anecdote concerning the neurologist Claparede, who hid a pin in his hand when shaking hands with one of his amnesic patients. On future encounters the patient recoiled from shaking hands with Claparede, although she could not explain why. Her motor response indicated memory, but she had no declarative knowledge of the learning episode (Claparede, 1911). Further support was presented by Weiskrantz and Warrington (1979), who demonstrated intact classical conditioning in amnesic patients. But the evidence most often cited in favour of such dissociations comes from studies of the neurological patient H.M., first studied by Milner and colleagues (Scoville & Milner, 1957), who, following bilateral damage to the medial temporal lobes, suffered profound impairments in declarative memory, with relatively spared procedural memory. These studies, and subsequent experiments in animals, have provided support for the existence of distinct types of memory, and moreover have focused attention on a region of the brain thought to be particularly important for declarative memory, the medial temporal lobe. Early research focused primarily on the hippocampus, but more recently the closely interlinked perirhinal, entorhinal, and parahippocampal cortices have been included with the hippocampus in a putative "medial temporal lobe (MTL) memory system" thought to underlie declarative memory (Squire & Zola-Morgan, 1991).

Evidence has been presented to suggest that these various subregions of the putative MTL memory system function cooperatively, in an interdependent manner. Perhaps the most influential evidence of this type has come from a study by Zola-Morgan, Squire, and Ramus (1994). This study analysed the effects of experimental damage to various components of the putative MTL memory system in monkeys. It was concluded that, the greater the damage to any part of the MTL memory system, the greater the impairment in declarative memory. This type of evidence has led to the widely accepted view that the various subregions of the putative MTL memory system function in a obligatory, interdependent manner, mediating specifically declarative memory. Attempts to decompose the putative declarative memory system further into, for example, separate episodic versus semantic memory systems (Nadel, 1995; Tulving & Markowitsch, 1998; Vargha-Kadem et al., 1997) have met with critical opposition (e.g., Squire & Zola, 1998; Zola-Morgan, Squire, & Ramus, 1995).

Whereas the concept of a unitary MTL memory system has provided an invaluable heuristic framework, it is clearly an oversimplification. It seems highly unlikely, for example, that the hodologically and cytoarchitectonically distinct regions within the putative MTL memory system are functionally identical. Indeed, despite the findings of Zola-Morgan, Squire, and Ramus

(1994) indicating a seemingly unitary MTL system, these authors themselves speculated that the subregions of the MTL could make distinct contributions to declarative memory. Logically this suggests that declarative memory is further fractionable. For example, perhaps episodic and semantic memory could have distinct neural substrates. Perhaps spatial memory, shown in animal experiments to depend critically upon the integrity of the hippocampal system, could be the particular domain of this subregion of the putative MTL memory system. Perhaps these various types of memory—spatial and object, episodic and semantic—could be brought together in a comprehensive theory of declarative memory in the temporal lobe.

The chapter addresses these issues and speculates as to possible ways toward a resolution. In a nutshell, we will propose that structures in the MTL memory system are functionally distinct, yet work together in the service of certain types of memory. They are independent, yet might also interact. Such interaction, we submit, might underlie complex, everyday "episodic" memories.

PART I: INDEPENDENCE

In a series of recent studies, we have tested the idea that structures of the putative MTL memory system have distinct and dissociable functions. These studies, using rats, have sought to compare the effects of hippocampal dysfunction with dysfunction of the parahippocampal regions perirhinal and postrhinal cortex. These latter regions are thought to correspond to monkey perirhinal and parahippocampal cortex, respectively (Burwell, Witter, & Amaral, 1995). To study hippocampal dysfunction, we have primarily used radiofrequency lesions of the fornix, a fibre bundle that conveys signals to and from the hippocampus. This lesion induces hippocampal dysfunction without any danger of direct damage to parahippocampal regions. That the integrity of parahippocampal structures was preserved was of paramount importance, because our aim was to compare the effects of dysfunction in hippocampal and parahippocampal regions. Furthermore, fornix lesions are well known to produce a pattern of behavioural effects that closely resembles that associated with hippocampal lesions (Aggleton & Brown, 2002; Barnes, 1988), and recent immediate early gene activation studies have shown how fornix damage can suppress activity throughout the hippocampal formation (Vann, Brown, Erichsen, & Aggleton, 2000). To study the effects of parahippocampal region dysfunction, we used excitotoxic lesions of the perirhinal and postrhinal cortices. These were intentionally large lesions that damaged much of the extrahippocampal tissue in the putative MTL memory system. At the same time, these lesions included almost negligible hippocampal damage.

One advantage of using rats is the availability of a well-characterised battery of allocentric spatial tasks that are known to be sensitive to damage to the fornix and hippocampus. Such tasks include the Olton radial arm maze task, the Morris swim task, and spatial T-maze alternation (Aggleton, Hunt, & Rawlins, 1986; Morris, Garrud, Rawlins, & O'Keefe, 1982; Olton, Becker, & Handelmann, 1979; Rasmussen, Barnes, & McNaughton, 1989). Thus we began our behavioural investigations in a straightforward and obvious way. If the various components of the putative MTL memory system function in an interdependent manner, as suggested by the data of Zola-Morgan, Squire and Ramus (1994), then our large peri-postrhinal cortex lesions should impair these tasks. We therefore tested rats with peri-postrhinal cortex lesions on all of these various tasks. These tasks are very well known, and the results are very straightforward. We will therefore discuss them very briefly, taking each task in turn.

Radial arm maze

In the classic Olton radial arm maze task, the rat is allowed to forage in an eight-arm radial maze for eight food rewards, one reward placed in each of the eight arms. Well-trained rats exhibit optimal foraging strategy, visiting and obtaining food from each arm only once. An error is scored every time the rat visits an unbaited arm. Good performance requires that the rat remember which arms it has visited during a trial. Thus this task has been thought to require spatial working memory.

Combined perirhinal and postrhinal cortex lesions had no effect on this hippocampus-dependent task (Bussey, Muir, & Aggleton, 1999). Indeed, lesioned rats significantly outperformed control rats on three of the twelve training trials. Following acquisition, a probe test was conducted to assess the use of possible non-allocentric strategies, and to make the task more difficult in an attempt to bring out any latent deficits. Rats were allowed to forage in four of the eight arms. This was followed by a 30-min delay during which the maze was rotated 45 degrees clockwise or anticlockwise. The four unvisited arms were then baited and the number of errors (entries into unbaited arms) was recorded. Despite the increase in task difficulty, there was no hint of an effect of the lesion. Thus, lesions of structures of the putative MTL memory system that do not damage the hippocampus have no effect on performance in the radial arm maze. This result is replicable, and has been observed in several studies to date (Bussey, et al., 1999, 2001; Ennaceur & Aggleton, 1997) (compare this, however, with the contrary evidence from the work of Bilkey and colleagues, discussed later).

Morris swim task

In the Morris swim task, the rat is placed in a pool of cool water from which it attempts to escape. The rat can escape from the water by climbing onto a slightly submerged and thus invisible platform that is in the same location in the pool every day. The rat, however, is put into the pool in a different location every day. Across days, normal rats learn the location of the platform and become highly proficient at rapidly finding the platform, no matter where in the pool they are placed. This task has been referred to as a test of spatial reference memory.

Combined peri- and postrhinal lesions had no effect on the acquisition of this task (Bussey et al., 1999). As training progressed, control rats learned to find the hidden platform increasingly rapidly. So did rats with peri-postrhinal cortex lesions. There were no significant differences between the groups at any point during acquisition. Swim-path lengths were also examined, and again, according to this measure, lesioned and control animals did not differ. Following acquisition, a probe test was given in which the hidden platform was removed and the rat placed in the pool in the quadrant directly across from the quadrant in which the platform had been previously located. Control rats search predominantly in the quadrant where the platform was previously located. Rats with peri-postrhinal cortex lesions show the same pattern of behaviour. Thus, lesions of structures of the putative MTL memory system that do not damage the hippocampus have no effect on performance in the Morris swim task. This result is replicable, and preserved spatial memory following lesions including perirhinal cortex has been reported in other water maze tasks, including those examining spatial working memory (Glenn & Mumby, 1998; Kolb, Buhrmann, McDonald, & Sutherland, 1994; Mumby & Glenn, 2000).

T-maze

The T-maze alternation task consists of a "sample phase" followed by a "choice phase". At the start of the sample phase the rat is placed in a goal box at the bottom of the stem of a T-shaped maze, and allowed to travel up the stem to the junction of the T, where it makes either a right or left turn (depending on which arm the experimenter leaves unblocked) to enter the arm and obtain a reward pellet. In the choice phase, which occurs after a variable delay, the rat begins in the start box as before, but now is given a choice between the right and left arms. Entering the arm that is different from the sample arm results in food reward.

In a recent experiment we compared the performance of rats with lesions of the fornix or peri-postrhinal cortex on the T-maze alternation task, initially using a 15s delay (Bussey, Duck, Muir, & Aggleton, 2000b). The fornix lesions had a devastating effect on performance in this task. Whereas control rats performed at nearly 90 per cent correct responses, rats with fornix lesions performed near chance levels. In contrast, rats with large peri-postrhinal cortex lesions showed the same high levels of performance as did controls. It was conceivable, however, that the lack of effect of the peri-postrhinal cortex lesions was due to control animals performing at a behavioural ceiling. We therefore increased the delay to 60s delay to bring control performance down from ceiling. Not only did this manipulation not reveal any hidden deficits in the rats with peri-postrhinal cortex lesions, it revealed quite the opposite: under the 60s condition the lesioned animals significantly outperformed controls. Other studies that have reported preserved performance in the T-maze following lesions of MTL structures other than hippocampus include Aggleton, Keen, Warburton, & Bussey (1997) and Ennaceur, Neave, & Aggleton (1996).

Object recognition

It is abundantly clear from the foregoing analysis that rats with lesions of structures thought to comprise the putative MTL memory system can be unimpaired or indeed facilitated in tasks requiring allocentric spatial memory. The performance of these animals does not resemble that of rats with hippocampus or fornix lesions. Such animals are consistently impaired on all of the above classic spatial tasks (Aggleton et al., 1986; Bussey et al., 2000a, 2000b; Bussey, Warburton, Aggleton, & Muir, 1998; Morris et al., 1982; Olton et al., 1979; Rasmussen et al., 1989).

However, with peri-postrhinal cortex lesions to perform a task that requires the use, not of information about spatial locations, but of information about individual objects, the picture became very different. The object task we used was a test of spontaneous object recognition memory, which allows the assessment of the rats' ability to recognise whether an object has been seen previously. Briefly, rats are placed in an open field containing two identical objects, and are allowed to explore these novel objects. Following a delay (of 15min, in our case), rats are placed back into the arena, which now contains a third copy of this now-familiar object, along with a second, novel object. Normal rats explore the novel object in preference to the familiar object, indicating memory for the familiar object.

Unlike the allocentric spatial task described above, rats with peri-postrhinal cortex lesions were significantly impaired on this task (Bussey et al., 1999). Note that these were the very same rats that were unimpaired in the radial maze and Morris swim tasks described above. That lesions including perirhinal cortex can impair object recognition is now well established (e.g. Aggleton et al., 1997; Bussey et al., 1999a, 2000b; Meunier, Bachevalier, Mishkin, & Murray, 1993; Mumby & Pinel, 1994; Suzuki, Zola-Morgan, Squire, & Amaral, 1993). Importantly, it has also been reported, in studies using both rats and monkeys, that lesions of the fornix or hippocampus can spare object recognition, or at the very least lead to mild deficits far smaller in magnitude than those observed following lesions including perirhinal cortex

(Aggleton et al., 1986; Bachevalier, Parkinson, & Mishkin, 1985; Bussey et al., 2000b; Cassaday & Rawlins, 1995, 1997; Duva et al., 1997; Ennaceur et al., 1996; Ennaceur, Neave, & Aggleton, 1997; Mumby et al., 1996; Mumby, Wood, & Pinel, 1992; Murray & Mishkin, 1998; Rothblat & Kromer, 1991; Shaw & Aggleton, 1993; Zola-Morgan, Squire, & Amaral, 1989). Indeed a recent meta-analysis of studies using non-human primates reports a negative correlation between degree of hippocampal damage and the magnitude of recognition memory impairment (Baxter & Murray, 2001). This same study found a positive correlation between the degree of perirhinal cortex and the magnitude of recognition memory impairment. Taken together, these studies indicate a double dissociation between the effects of hippocampus or fornix lesions, and the effects of lesions of extrahippocampal structures within the putative MTL memory system on tests of spatial memory and object recognition. Yet at the same time, other workers have reported object recognition deficits following lesions of the hippocampus that spare parahippocampal cortical regions (Beason-Held, Rosene, Killiany, & Moss, 1999; Clark, Zola, & Squire, 2000; Zola et al., 2000). How can these results be reconciled?

Before turning to this issue, it should be noted that recent data have shown that impairments following lesions of parahippocampal regions are not confined to object recognition tasks, in which rats make a familiarity or novelty judgement, but also certain forced-choice object discrimination tasks involving repeated presentations of familiar objects. For example, perirhinal cortex lesions have been reported to impair concurrent visual discriminations when a large set of stimuli is used (Buckley & Gaffan, 1997), and when the discrimination has "configural" properties (Buckley & Gaffan, 1998a; Bussey, Saksida, & Murray, 2002a; Eacott, Machin, & Gaffan, 2001). This has led some workers to broaden their conception of the proposed functions of perirhinal cortex from "object recognition" to "object identification" (Buckley & Gaffan, 1998b; Murray, Malkova, & Goulet, 1998). More recent work has attempted to define more precisely how the perirhinal cortex operates in the service of object identification, as part of the ventral visual stream or "what" pathway (Bussey & Saksida, 2002; Murray & Bussey, 1999).

The foregoing evidence thus indicates that structures of the putative MTL memory system carry out their own distinct and experimentally dissociable functions. The hippocampus is important for allocentric spatial memory, and the perirhinal cortex is important for object identification. It should be made clear, however, that the focus here is on whether functional dissociations within the putative MTL memory system are possible. A separate (but clearly related) issue is what, exactly, the various components of the system do. We have used allocentric spatial tasks and object recognition tests to provide evidence for functional dissociations within the putative MTL memory system. This does not mean that we advocate, for example, an exclusively spatial view of hippocampal function. Deficits have been reported following hippocampus or fornix lesions on tasks with no obvious spatial component (see Chapter 9; Brasted, Bussey, Murray, & Wise, 2002; Honey, Watt, & Good, 1998; Moyer, Deyo, & Disterhoft, 1990). We have found, for example, that fornix lesions and peri-postrhinal cortex lesions have very different effects on spontaneous locomotor activity, peri-postrhinal lesions having little effect but fornix lesions leading to greatly increased levels of activity (Bussey et al., 2000b). This indicates yet another way in which the effects of hippocampal system dysfunction do not resemble the effects of damage to non-hippocampal regions of the putative MTL memory system. Thus a precise formulation of the distinct functions of the MTL subregions awaits further work, but whatever the details of such formulations, they will need to account for the spatial and object-related functions of the hippocampus and perirhinal cortex, respectively.

A perhaps surprising corollary conclusion that can be drawn from these results is that, to carry out its role in spatial memory, the hippocampus does not seem necessarily to require the use of object information from the ventral visual stream. This is because our peri-postrhinal cortex lesions were intentionally large, encompassing perirhinal cortex, postrhinal cortex, and much of the lateral entorhinal cortex. This lesion virtually disconnects the hippocampus from highly processed object information from the ventral visual stream. It appears, therefore, that such highly processed object information is not necessary for the solution of standard allocentric spatial task based on distal cues. How then does the hippocampal system get its visual information to construct the "spatial map" of landmarks thought to underly performance on such spatial tasks? It is now established that many brain regions other than the hippocampus are involved in the performance of standard allocentric spatial memory tasks, making it possible that visual information to the hippocampus can by-pass the ventral visual stream (Aggleton, Vann, Oswald, & Good, 2000).

Although the foregoing ideas are speculative and require further testing, they can, perhaps, shed some light on an important issue that we have hitherto avoided. This is that although we and others have consistently obtained dissociations between the effects of hippocampal and parahippocampal lesions on object and spatial memory, some researchers have not. For example, in a comprehensive series of experiments, Liu and Bilkey have consistently obtained deficits following lesions including perirhinal cortex on allocentric spatial tasks (Liu & Bilkey, 1998a,b,c, 1999, 2001; Wiig & Bilkey, 1994). Furthermore, as mentioned above, hippocampal dysfunction has been reported to impair object recognition memory (Beason-Held et al., 1999; Clark et al., 2000; Liu & Bilkey, 2001; Zola et al., 2000). What is one to make of these contradictory findings? Our view is that all of these data, taken at face value, are more readily accommodated by the idea that structures in the MTL can function independently, than by the view that these MTL structures form a unitary, functionally homogeneous system. This is because although a unitary system account is by definition able to accommodate the finding of similar effects of damage to different structures, it cannot account for functional dissociations of the kind outlined above. In contrast, the functional heterogeneity view can, by definition, account for such dissociations, and it can also accommodate the finding of similar behavioural effects of damage to different structures. How? By simply entertaining the possibility that certain ostensibly "spatial" tasks could involve an "object" component, and that certain ostensibly "object" tasks could involve a "spatial" component. It has been shown, for example, that perirhinal cortex is important when object discriminations become perceptually difficult (Buckley, Booth, Rolls, & Gaffan, 2001; Bussey, Saksida, & Murray, 2002b)—what if certain spatial tasks recruited the object identification pathway because of the perceptual similarity of object landmarks? In such cases, perirhinal cortex damage might be expected to have a deleterious effect on performance. Or conversely, what if in certain cases object recognition or identification could be facilitated by the use of spatial contextual information? In such cases the hippocampus might become involved in what is ostensibly a purely "object" task. This latter possibility has been suggested previously (Nadel, 1995; Zola et al., 2000; Gaffan, 1994b) and is consistent with the observation that object recognition deficits following hippocampal lesions, when observed, are typically milder than those observed following perirhinal cortex lesions. These predictions remain to be tested experimentally. These speculations notwithstanding, however, it is fairly easy to imagine ways in which large lesions of two anatomically related structures might lead to similar deficits on complex tasks. In contrast, it is very difficult to imagine how double dissociations of the type outlined above could have happened by "accident". Thus we conclude that the extant data, taken at face value and including those that ostensibly provide evidence for a unitary system view, are more consistent with a view of heterogeneity of function within the putative MTL memory system.

PART II: INTERACTION

The foregoing analysis indicates independence of function amongst the structures of the putative MTL memory system. We have already touched on the idea, however, that independence might not be the rule; there could be interaction amongst these functionally distinct regions. Indeed, it would be rather surprising, considering the anatomical connections between these regions, if such interactions never occurred. The foregoing discussion suggests that one circumstance in which such interaction might occur is when a task requires that object and spatial information be integrated. Thus, having determined that hippocampus and peri-postrhinal cortex are functionally distinct, we set about investigating under what circumstances these structures might interact, by examining the effects of lesions on tasks that bring together both object and spatial information. Our hypothesis was that lesions of these two regions of the putative MTL memory system should have similar effects on such tasks.

In our first such experiment we modified the spontaneous object recognition test described above to include a spatial recognition component (Bussey et al., 2000b). In this version of the task four objects were presented, followed by a delay, followed by re-presentation of the same four objects, but with two of the objects' positions switched. Thus, following the delay, two of the four objects remained in the same location but the other two objects appeared in different locations. Normal rats preferentially explore the objects in the new locations. Notice that this behaviour requires the integration of both spatial and object information: none of the objects are novel, and neither are the four possible locations, but two of the object/place combinations are novel.

The effects of the lesions as analysed in the usual manner, i.e. by comparing group means, were variable, making interpretation difficult. But when we simply asked whether these groups of rats were able to discriminate the novel from the familiar object/place combinations at a level significantly greater than chance, a much clearer pattern emerged. According to either difference scores or discrimination ratios, control rats demonstrated the expected preference for novel object/place combinations. Rats with peri-postrhinal cortex lesions, however, failed to discriminate according to either measure. Rats with fornix lesions also failed to discriminate according to the discrimination ratio measure (Bussey et al., 2000b). These results provide some evidence that, as predicted, both fornix and peri-postrhinal cortex lesions can disrupt performance in tasks requiring the integration of information about object and place.

Encouraged by these results, we embarked on a second experiment to investigate this issue further (Bussey et al., 2001). Rather than use a spontaneous exploration paradigm, we opted for a rewarded, forced-choice task that would similarly require the integration of object and space. Briefly, the experiment was carried out in a "double Y-maze" apparatus that allowed the presentation of pairs of objects at either end of a long runway, thus creating two "places" in which the objects could be presented. Only two objects were used, which we can refer to as A and B. On a given trial, the rat would proceed down the runway to the end of the arm, where it would encounter a choice between A and B, one of which was correct, having a reward pellet hidden beneath it, the other being incorrect, hiding no pellet. The critical feature of the task was that in one end of the arm, i.e. in one place, object A was correct and B was incorrect. At the other end of the arm—in the other place—the opposite contingency applied, i.e. B was correct and A was incorrect. Again, correct performance on this task required the integration of information about both object and place.

Previous studies have shown that this type of task depends on the integrity of the hippocampal system. Thus, fornix lesions in monkeys have been shown to impair acquisition of a very similar place–object conditional task (Gaffan & Harrison, 1988, 1989). In our experiment, therefore, we made lesions of perirhinal cortex in rats to see what effect this might have on this hippocampus-dependent task.

As predicted, perirhinal cortex lesions had a highly deleterious effect on the ability of rats to acquire this place–object conditional task. Thus, our work with rats, combined with those from monkeys, has led us to the conclusion that dysfunction of either hippocampus or perirhinal cortex can lead to deficits in tasks in which object and place information must be integrated. Work with monkeys has yielded further compelling evidence for interaction amongst MTL structures. Gaffan and Parker (1996), for example, found that "crossed" unilateral lesions of perirhinal cortex and fornix, which disconnect a putative circuit involving these two structures, led to impairments on a computerised task involving object–place integration. Importantly, work from the same laboratory, and others, using monkeys has also yielded evidence for independence, perirhinal cortex lesions having different effects from fornix lesions on tests of object or spatial ("scene") memory (Gaffan, 1994a). It is only under circumstances in which object and place information are integrated that these investigators find evidence for interactivity.

The results of the experiments outlined above allow us to conclude that a normally functioning hippocampus and perirhinal cortex is necessary for normal performance in tasks in which object and spatial information must be integrated. Furthermore, the foregoing data regarding independence of function within the putative MTL memory system suggest that the hippocampus mediates the "spatial" component of these tasks, while the perirhinal cortex contributes object information. This is consistent with the view that perirhinal cortex comprises part of the ventral visual stream, which contains the representations of visual stimuli including objects (Bussey & Saksida, 2002; Murray & Bussey, 1999). Importantly, however, further tests have indicated that rats and monkeys with perirhinal cortex lesions are able to learn to discriminate between a rewarded and a non-rewarded object in a conventional object discrimination procedure (e.g. Aggleton et al., 1997; Bussey et al., 1999, 2000b, 2001, 2002b). Murray and Bussey (1999) and Bussey and Saksida (2002) have argued that this preserved object discrimination ability following perirhinal cortex lesions might be mediated by other, intact regions of the ventral visual stream. Thus, it could be that perirhinal cortex is anatomically ideally situated to pass object information to the hippocampal system under conditions in which place and object information must be integrated. This idea requires further examination.

The space–object continuum

In this chapter we have outlined evidence for both independence and inter-action among the subregions of the putative MTL memory system. We have also alluded to the possibility that object identification might find its way into ostensibly spatial tasks, and that spatial information could be useful in the solution of certain object-based tasks. Taken together, these considerations suggest that behavioural tasks, and specific memories, are not always easily classified as either purely spatial or purely object. Similarly, the functional relationships amongst the various MTL structures are not always easily classified as purely independent, or interactive. Instead, we submit that independence and interaction, and likewise object and place memory, are best conceived of as lying on a continuum. At the ends are behavioural tasks or memories that are purely spatial or purely object-based. In the middle are tasks or memories that involve both spatial and object information. Of course, the "pure" types of memory lying at the ends of this continuum exist perhaps almost exclusively in the laboratory, and assessing the brain regions critical for these types of memory depends on careful experimentation to avoid confounding different kinds of information. By contrast, real-life epi-sodic memories, which are usually complex and multimodal, are typically of the type lying between the two extremes. It is in this majority of cases that the structures of the putative MTL memory system operate in an interactive manner.

Episodic and semantic memory

We have already touched on the idea that real-life episodic memories are of this complex, multimodal variety; they lie between the extremes of the space–object continuum. Thus the use of tasks requiring object–place integration might be a way towards modelling this aspect of episodic memory in animals (Bussey et al., 2001; Clayton & Dickinson, 1998; Gaffan, 1994b). Usually contrasted with context-dependent episodic memory is context-independent semantic memory. Semantic memory about objects, divorced from the spatial context in which they are presented, might therefore—as we are confining our discussion here to spatial and object information—be considered to be repre-sented in our scheme as lying at the "object" end of the object–space con-tinuum. Thus, the use of tasks requiring object identification and association might be a way towards modelling semantic memory in animals (Murray & Bussey, 1999; Parker & Gaffan, 1998).

But is there any evidence that episodic and semantic memory can be dis-sociated in the human brain? There is, and, moreover, this evidence suggests that episodic and semantic memory might share some of the neural sub-strates we have been discussing. For example, Vargha-Khadem et al. (1997)

have studied children who, at an early age, suffered apparently selective damage to the hippocampus. These children have severely impaired episodic memory, but semantic memory that appears to be intact. Kitchener et al. (1998) have reported a similar result in an adult with selective hippocampal damage, namely impaired episodic memory and intact semantic memory. A converse pattern of mnemonic deficits has been reported in patients with semantic dementia. These patients exhibit impaired semantic memory but relatively intact episodic memory (Hodges, Patterson, Oxbury, & Funnell, 1992). The pathology in these cases is variable but appears to be centred on lateral temporal cortical regions. Although the damage appears not necessarily to include the region along the collateral sulcus considered to be human perirhinal cortex, it might include regions functionally analogous to monkey and rodent perirhinal cortex (for a discussion of this and related issues, see Bussey & Murray, 1999; Simons, Graham, & Hodges, 1999). These considerations notwithstanding, these cases taken together constitute a double dissociation consistent with the ideas outlined above.

CONCLUSION

This chapter began by showing how the structures of the putative MTL memory system can operate independently. The fornix and hippocampus are important for spatial memory, and parahippocampal structures, particularly perirhinal cortex, are important for object identification. Having established that these structures can work independently, we then described cases in which they appear to interact, i.e. cases in which object and spatial information must be integrated. At least a large subset of real-life complex, multimodal memories will be of this type, where visual information is set against a background "scene". In these cases, then, the components of the putative MTL memory system might indeed operate as part of a "system": a system underlying complex, everyday memories.

REFERENCES

Aggleton, J.P., & Brown, M.W. (2002). Integrating systems for event memory: Testing the contribution of the fornix. In L.R. Squire & D. Schacter (Eds.) *Neuropsychology of memory* (pp. 397–394). New York: Guilford Press.

Aggleton, J.P., Hunt, P.R., & Rawlins, J.N.P. (1986). The effects of hippocampal lesions upon spatial and non-spatial tests of working memory. *Behavioural Brain Research, 19*, 133–146.

Aggleton, J.P., Keen, S., Warburton, E.C., & Bussey, T.J. (1997). Extensive cytotoxic lesions involving both the rhinal cortices and area TE impair recognition but spare spatial alternation in the rat. *Brain Research Bulletin, 43*, 279–287.

Aggleton, J.P., Vann, S.D., Oswald, C.J., & Good, M. (2000). Identifying cortical inputs to the rat hippocampus that subserve allocentric spatial processes: A simple problem with a complex answer. *Hippocampus, 10*, 466–474.

Bachevalier, J., Parkinson, J.K., & Mishkin, M. (1985). Visual recognition in monkeys: Effects of separate vs. combined transection of fornix and amygdalofugal pathways. *Experimental Brain Research, 57,* 554–561.

Barnes, C.A. (1988). Spatial learning and memory processes: The search for their neurobiological mechanisms in the rat. *Trends in Neurosciences, 11,* 163–169.

Baxter, M., & Murray, E.A. (2001). Opposite relationship of hippocampal and rhinal cortex damage to delayed nonmatching-to-sample deficits in monkeys. *Hippocampus, 11,* 61–71.

Beason-Held, L.L., Rosene, D.L., Killiany, R.J., & Moss, M.B. (1999). Hippocampal formation lesions produce memory impairment in the rhesus monkey. *Hippocampus, 9,* 562–574.

Brasted, P.J., Bussey, T.J., Murray, E.A., & Wise, S.P. (2002). Fornix transection impairs conditional visuomotor learning in tasks involving nonspatially differentiated responses. *Journal of Neurophysiology*.

Buckley, M.J., Booth, M.C., Rolls, E.T., & Gaffan, D. (2001). Selective perceptual impairments after prirhinal cortex ablation. *Journal of Neuroscience, 21,* 9824–9836.

Buckley, M.J., & Gaffan, D. (1997). Impairment of visual object-discrimination learning after perirhinal cortex ablation. *Behavioral Neuroscience, 111,* 467–475.

Buckley, M.J., & Gaffan, D. (1998a). Perirhinal cortex ablation impairs configural learning and paired-associate learning equally. *Neuropsychologia, 36,* 535–546.

Buckley, M.J., & Gaffan, D. (1998b). Perirhinal cortex ablation impairs visual object identification. *Journal of Neuroscience, 18,* 2268–2275.

Burwell, R.D., Witter, M.P., & Amaral, D.G. (1995). Perirhinal and postrhinal cortices of the rat: A review of the neuroanatomical literature and comparison with findings from the monkey brain. *Hippocampus, 5,* 390–408.

Bussey, T.J., Dias, R., Amin, E., Muir, J.L., & Aggleton, J.P. (2001). Perirhinal cortex and place-object conditional learning in the rat. *Behavioral Neuroscience, 115,* 776–785.

Bussey, T.J., Dias, R., Redhead, E.S., Pearce, J.M., Muir, J.L., & Aggleton, J.P. (2000a). Intact negative patterning in rats with fornix or combined perirhinal and postrhinal cortex lesions. *Experimental Brain Research, 134,* 506–519.

Bussey, T.J., Duck, J., Muir, J.L., & Aggleton, J.P. (2000b). Distinct patterns of behavioural impairments resulting from fornix transection or neurotoxic lesions of the perirhinal and postrhinal cortices in the rat. *Behavioural Brain Research, 111,* 187–202.

Bussey, T.J., Muir, J.L., & Aggleton, J.P. (1999). Functionally dissociating aspects of event memory: The effects of combined perirhinal and postrhinal cortex lesions on object and place memory in the rat. *Journal of Neuroscience, 19,* 495–502.

Bussey, T.J., & Murray, E.A. (1999). What does semantic dementia reveal about the functional role of the perirhinal cortex? (Reply). *Trends in Cognitive Sciences, 3,* 245–250.

Bussey, T.J., & Saksida, L.M. (2002). The organization of visual object representations: A connectionist model of effects of lesions in perirhinal cortex. *European Journal of Neuroscience, 15,* 355–364.

Bussey, T.J., Saksida, L.M., & Murray, E.A. (2002a). Perirhinal cortex resolves feature ambiguity on complex visual discriminations. *European Journal of Neuroscience, 15,* 365–374.

Bussey, T.J., Saksida, L.M., & Murray, E.A. (2002b). The role of perirhinal cortex in memory and perception: Conjunctive representations for object identification. In M.P. Witter & F.G. Wouterlood (Eds.) *The parahippocampal region, organization and role in cognitive functions.* Oxford: Oxford University Press.

Bussey, T.J., Warburton, E.C., Aggleton, J.P., & Muir, J.L. (1998). Fornix lesions can facilitate acquisition of the transverse patterning task: A challenge for "configural" theories of hippocampal function. *Journal of Neuroscience, 18,* 1622–1631.

Cassaday, H.J., & Rawlins, J.N. (1995). Fornix–fimbria section and working memory deficits in rats: Stimulus complexity and stimulus size. *Behavioral Neuroscience, 109,* 594–606.

Cassaday, H.J., & Rawlins, J.N. (1997). The hippocampus, objects, and their contexts. *Behavioral Neuroscience, 111,* 1228–1244.

Claparede, E. (1911). Recognition of moiite. *Archives de Psychologie*, *11*, 75–90.

Clark, R.E., Zola, S.M., & Squire, L.R. (2000). Impaired recognition memory in rats after damage to the hippocampus. *Journal of Neuroscience*, *20*, 8853–8860.

Clayton, N.S., & Dickinson, A. (1998). Episodic-like memory during cache recovery by scrub jays. *Nature*, *395*, 272–274.

Cohen, N.J., & Squire, L.R. (1980). Preserved learning and retention of pattern-analyzing skill in amnesia: dissociation of knowing how and knowing that. *Science*, *210*, 207–210.

Duva, C.A., Floresco, S.B., Wunderlich, G.R., Lao, T.L., Pinel, J.P., & Phillips, A.G. (1997). Disruption of spatial but not object-recognition memory by neurotoxic lesions of the dorsal hippocampus in rats. *Behavioral Neuroscience*, *111*, 1184–1196.

Eacott, M.J., Machin, P.E., & Gaffan, E.A. (2001). Elemental and configural visual discrimination learning following lesions to perirhinal cortex in the rat. *Behavioural Brain Research*, *124*, 55–70.

Ennaceur, A., & Aggleton, J.P. (1997). The effects of neurotoxic lesions of the perirhinal cortex combined to fornix transection on object recognition memory in the rat. *Behavioural Brain Research*, *88*, 181–193.

Ennaceur, A., Neave, N., & Aggleton, J.P. (1996). Neurotoxic lesions of the perirhinal cortex do not mimic the behavioural effects of fornix transection in the rat. *Behavioral Brain Research*, *80*, 9–25.

Ennaceur, A., Neave, N., & Aggleton, J.P. (1997). Spontaneous object recognition and object location memory in rats: The effects of lesions in the cingulate cortices, the medial prefrontal cortex, the cingulum bundle and the fornix. *Experimental Brain Research*, *113*, 509–513.

Gaffan, D. (1994a). Dissociated effects of perirhinal cortex ablation, fornix transection and amygdalectomy: Evidence for multiple memory systems in the primate temporal lobe. *Experimental Brain Research*, *99*, 411–422.

Gaffan, D. (1994b). Scene-specific memory for objects: A model of episodic memory impairment in monkeys with fornix transection. *Journal of Cognitive Neuroscience*, *6*, 305–320.

Gaffan, D., & Harrison, S. (1988). A comparison of the effects of fornix transection and sulcus principalis ablation upon spatial learning by monkeys. *Behavioural Brain Research*, *31*, 207–220.

Gaffan, D., & Harrison, S. (1989). Place memory and scene memory: Effects of fornix transection in the monkey. *Experimental Brain Research*, *74*, 202–212.

Gaffan, D., & Parker, A. (1996). Interaction of perirhinal cortex with the fornix–fimbria: Memory for objects and "object-in-place" memory. *Journal of Neuroscience*, *16*, 5864–5869.

Glenn, M.J., & Mumby, D.G. (1998). Place memory is intact in rats with perirhinal cortex lesions. *Behavioral Neuroscience*, *112*, 1353–1365.

Hodges, J.R., Patterson, K., Oxbury, S., & Funnell, E. (1992). Semantic dementia: Progressive fluent aphasia with temporal lobe atrophy. *Brain*, *115*, 1783–1806.

Honey, R.C., Watt, A., & Good, M. (1998). Hippocampal lesions disrupt an associative mismatch process. *Journal of Neuroscience*, *18*, 2226–2230.

Kitchener, E., Hodges, J., & McCarthy, R. (1998). Acquisition of post-morbid vocabulary and semantic facts in the absence of episodic memory. *Brain*, *121*, 1313–1327.

Kolb, B., Buhrmann, K., McDonald, R., & Sutherland, R.J. (1994). Dissociation of the medial prefrontal, posterior parietal, and posterior temporal cortex for spatial navigation and recognition memory in the rat. *Cerebral Cortex*, *4*, 664–680.

Liu, P., & Bilkey, D.K. (1998a). Excitotoxic lesions centered on perirhinal cortex produce delay-dependent deficits in a test of spatial memory. *Behavioral Neuroscience*, *112*, 512–524.

Liu, P., & Bilkey, D.K. (1998b). Lesions of perirhinal cortex produce spatial memory deficits in the radial maze. *Hippocampus*, *8*, 114–121.

Liu, P., & Bilkey, D.K. (1998c). Perirhinal cortex contributions to performance in the Morris water maze. *Behavioral Neuroscience*, *112*, 304–315.

Liu, P., & Bilkey, D.K. (1999). The effect of excitotoxic lesions centered on the perirhinal cortex in two versions of the radial arm maze task. *Behavioral Neuroscience, 113*, 672–682.

Liu, P., & Bilkey, D.K. (2001). The effect of excitotoxic lesions centered on the hippocampus or perirhinal cortex in object recognition and spatial memory tasks. *Behavioral Neuroscience, 115*, 94–111.

Meunier, M., Bachevalier, J., Mishkin, M., & Murray, E.A. (1993). Effects on visual recognition of combined and separate ablations of the entorhinal and perirhinal cortex in rhesus monkeys. *Journal of Neuroscience, 13*, 5418–5432.

Morris, R.G.M., Garrud, P., Rawlins, J.N.P., & O'Keefe, J. (1982). Place navigation impaired in rats with hippocampal lesions. *Nature, 297*, 681–683.

Moyer, J.R., Deyo, R.A., & Disterhoft, J.F. (1990). Hippocampectomy disrupts trace eye-blink conditioning in rabbits. *Behavioral Neuroscience, 104*, 243–252.

Mumby, D.G., & Glenn, M.J. (2000). Anterograde and retrograde memory for object discriminations and places in rats with perirhinal cortex lesions. *Behavioural Brain Research, 114*, 119–134.

Mumby, D.G., & Pinel, J.P. (1994). Rhinal cortex lesions and object recognition in rats. *Behavioural Neuroscience, 108*, 11–18.

Mumby, D.G., Wood, E.R., Duva, C.A., Kornecook, T.J., Pinel, J.P., & Phillips, A.G. (1996). Ischemia-induced object-recognition deficits in rats are attenuated by hippocampal ablation before or soon after ischemia. *Behavioral Neuroscience, 110*, 266–281.

Mumby, D.G., Wood, E.R., & Pinel, J.P.J. (1992). Object-recognition memory is only mildly impaired in rats with lesions of the hippocampus and amygdala. *Psychobiology, 20*, 18–27.

Murray, E.A., & Bussey, T.J. (1999). Perceptual–mnemonic functions of perirhinal cortex. *Trends in Cognitive Sciences, 3*, 142–151.

Murray, E.A., Malkova, L., & Goulet, S. (1998). Crossmodal associations, intramodal associations, and object identification in macaque monkeys. In A.D. Milner (Ed.) *Comparative neuropsychology* (pp. 51–67). Oxford: Oxford University Press.

Murray, E.A., & Mishkin, M. (1998). Object recognition and location memory in monkeys with excitotoxic lesions of the amygdala and hippocampus. *Journal of Neuroscience, 18*, 6568–6582.

Nadel, L. (1995). The role of the hippocampus in declarative memory: A comment on Zola-Morgan, Squire, and Ramus (1994). *Hippocampus, 5*, 232–239.

Olton, D.S., Becker, J.T., & Handelmann, G.E. (1979). Hippocampus, space, and memory. *Behavioral and Brain Sciences, 2*, 313–365.

Parker, A., & Gaffan, D. (1998). Memory systems in primates: Episodic, semantic, and perceptual learning. In A.D. Milner (Ed.) *Comparative neuropsychology* (pp. 109–126). Oxford: Oxford University Press.

Rasmussen, M., Barnes, C.A., & McNaughton, B.L. (1989). A systematic test of cognitive mapping, working-memory, and temporal discontiguity theories of hippocampal function. *Psychobiology, 17*, 335–348.

Roediger, H.L. (1980). Memory metaphors in cognitive psychology. *Memory and cognition, 8*, 231–246.

Rothblat, L.A., & Kromer, L.F. (1991). Object recognition memory in the rat: The role of the hippocampus. *Behavioural Brain Research, 42*, 25–32.

Scoville, W.B., & Milner, B. (1957). Loss of recent memory after bilateral hippocampal lesions. *Journal of Neurology, Neurosurgery and Psychiatry, 20*, 11–21.

Shaw, C., & Aggleton, J.P. (1993). The effects of fornix and medial prefrontal lesions on delayed non-matching-to-sample by rats. *Behavioural Brain Research, 54*, 91–102.

Simons, J.S., Graham, K.S., & Hodges, J.R. (1999). What does semantic dementia reveal about the functional role of the perirhinal cortex? *Trends in Cognitive Sciences, 3*, 248–249.

Squire, L.R., & Zola, S.M. (1998). Episodic memory, semantic memory, and amnesia. *Hippocampus, 8*, 205–211.

Squire, L.R., & Zola-Morgan, S. (1991). The medial temporal lobe memory system. *Science, 253,* 1380–1386.

Suzuki, W.A., Zola-Morgan, S., Squire, L.R., & Amaral, D.G. (1993). Lesions of the perirhinal and parahippocampal cortices in the monkey produce long-lasting memory impairment in the visual and tactual modalities. *Journal of Neuroscience, 13,* 2430–2451.

Tulving, E., & Markowitsch, H.J. (1998). Episodic and declarative memory: role of the hippocampus. *Hippocampus, 8,* 198–204.

Vann, S.D., Brown, M.W., Erichsen, J.T., & Aggleton, J.P. (2000). Using fos imaging in the rat to reveal the anatomical extent of the disruptive effects of fornix lesions. *Journal of Neuroscience, 20,* 8144–8152.

Vargha-Kadem, F., Gadian, D., Watkins, K., Connely, A., Van Paesschen, W., & Mishkin, M. (1997). Differential effects of early hippocampal pathology on episodic and semantic memory. *Science, 277,* 376–380.

Weiskrantz, L., & Warrington, E.K. (1979). Conditioning in amnesic patients. *Neuropsychologia, 17,* 187–194.

Wiig, K.A., & Bilkey, D.K. (1994). The effects of perirhinal cortical lesions on spatial reference memory in the rat. *Behavioural Brain Research, 63,* 101–109.

Zola, S.M., Squire, L.R., Teng, E., Stefanacci, L., Buffalo, E.A., & Clark, R.E. (2000). Impaired recognition memory in monkeys after damage limited to the hippocampal region. *Journal of Neuroscience, 20,* 451–463.

Zola-Morgan, S., Squire, L.R., & Amaral, D.G. (1989). Lesions of the hippocampal formation but not lesions of the fornix or the mamillary bodies produce long-lasting memory impairment in monkeys. *Journal of Neuroscience, 9,* 898–913.

Zola-Morgan, S., Squire, L., & Ramus, S.J. (1995). The role of the hippocampus in declarative memory: A reply to Nadel. *Hippocampus, 5,* 235–239.

Zola-Morgan, S., Squire, L.R., & Ramus, S.J. (1994). Severity of memory impairment in monkeys as a function of locus and extent of damage within the medial temporal lobe memory system. *Hippocampus, 4,* 483–495.

CHAPTER ELEVEN

Mediating from memory to attention: Necessity of the accumbens connection?

Helen J. Cassaday and Christine Norman
School of Psychology, University of Nottingham, UK

> *There is nothing more frightful than ignorance in action.*
>
> (Goethe, 1774)

INTRODUCTION

In *Remembering: A study in experimental and social psychology* (Bartlett, 1932) Bartlett argued that perception and recognition are dynamically influenced by past experience, so that they are tuned to both the current contingencies and motivational states. Today, with the rapid development of new technologies in the neurosciences, there is an explosion of interest in the biological substrates of the processes that contribute to memory. For example, we are using increasingly selective interventions to produce dissociations in forgetting that tell us how memory is organised in terms of both cognitive processes and brain mechanisms, so as to develop neuropsychological theories. Attention is a much harder nettle to grasp because the term covers wide-ranging aspects of cognition: for example, general level of engagement with the environment or vigilance, span of apprehension or breadth of attention, attentional filtering or selection amongst the sensory impressions, aspects typically, but not necessarily, associated with "consciousness". Behaviourally, attention has been operationalised through the measurement of orienting reactions to events of interest and by the use of selective learning tasks that manipulate the predictive validity of different signals. Here we will consider the "top-down" attentional processes through which past experience normally contributes to the selectivity seen in associative learning, shown as conditioned reactions to environmental stimuli and appropriate instrumental action.

235

Learning is interesting, first, because we show memory with the expression of prior learning, second, because the interrelationship between learning and memory cuts two ways. Thus, forgetting tells us about constraints on encoding as well as retrieval processes, and learning is attentional in the sense that it is normally directed by what is already known. In rats, various two-stage paradigms are used to investigate how previously acquired associations direct current learning. For example, prior experience of a stimulus as irrelevant retards the capacity to learn about it later; similarly, prior experience with a relevant predictor later retards the capacity to learn about an added stimulus that is uninformative in the absence of any change in the outcome. In each case, the associative strength is measured behaviourally by the animal's conditioned reactions (e.g. nosepoking for food or response suppression to a signal for footshock). In single-stage procedures, after many pairings of the same stimulus–outcome relationship, but when the outcome is not presented immediately, the influence of the passage of time can be measured by changes in the level and type of conditioned responses that reflect the animal's anticipation of the food or shock. Differential responding during the delay to be expected on the basis of previous learning trials provides evidence of memory for temporal context. Thus, behavioural measures can tell us how memory affects attention and so learning. The rat provides an attractive model to investigate the neural substrates of this memory mediation because it conditions readily and many of the paradigms in use are readily adapted for parallel investigations in human subjects. Moreover, although the work with rodent models is inevitably behaviourally based, much of what we see points to them having declarative representations (see Bunsey & Eichenbaum, 1996; Dickinson, 1980).

In this chapter, we discuss a variety of selective learning phenomena and how their dysfunction might lend insight into psychiatric disorders that are characterised by attentional problems. Investigation of the neurochemical basis of schizophrenia is steered by the dominant dopamine hypothesis and related amphetamine model (Ellison & Eison, 1983) and, consistent with this hypothesis, a range of selective learning effects (to which memory contributes) have been found to be affected by dopaminergic treatments like amphetamine. Schizophrenia was originally termed *dementia praecox* because it is characterised by an early onset and can progress to a chronic state of cognitive impairment. Dementias in general are characterised by a broader failure of cognitive ability that most obviously includes memory failure. Although the memory loss seen in schizophrenia is more like that seen in classical amnesia than dementia (McKenna et al., 1990; Stip, 1996), and schizophrenia includes additional features such as particularly bizarre thought disorder, there is overlap between the possible psychological and neural substrates of the dementias (Morgan, May, & Finch, 1987; Soares & Gershon, 1997). So far, the role of the dopaminergic system in memory and dementia has received relatively little attention (Wilkerson & Levin, 1999) but this role might have been underestimated because of an initial focus on neurotransmitters found in the hippocampus. Now, given its intimate connections to the nucleus accumbens (a predominantly dopaminergic structure) and the shift from centre, based on (components of) discrete brain structures, to systems-based approaches in specifying functional neuroanatomy in terms of interconnected circuitries, there is increasing interest in how the functional interplay between memory and attention might map onto the hippocampus, nucleus accumbens, and their interconnections.

NORMAL SELECTIVE LEARNING AND ITS DYSFUNCTION

The effect of memory on attentional selectivity is well illustrated by a series of phenomena that show the sensitivity of animals to past contingencies. In latent inhibition (LI), animals show that past irrelevance is a powerful bar to later learning. Knowledge of irrelevance is established in stage 1 of the conditioning procedure, by repeated presentation of a stimulus (e.g. a tone) later to be conditioned but at present without any consequences. In stage 2, the prior stimulus pre-exposure reliably retards any subsequent conditioning to that same tone, even though it now predicts food deliveries. In blocking, animals show that if an event like food delivery is already fully predicted (e.g. by a novel tone stimulus) there will be little further conditioning to any additional stimulus (e.g. a light) that is effectively redundant in the absence of any change in the quantity or quality of food delivered. In trace conditioning, separation in time between conditioned stimulus (CS) and unconditioned stimulus (UCS) weakens the expression of learning on some response measures whereas, over a series of pairings, alternative response measures show anticipation in temporal interval to be expected between CS and UCS.

Investigation of the neural substrates of memory mediation through the use of selective interventions necessarily results in disorder in normal processes, and so also provides us with a model of dysfunction. Disruption in the normal interaction between what we know from past experience and currently apprehend, results in deficits that are more subtle, yet potentially just as devastating, as those seen in classic amnesia. For example, schizophrenia results in behavioural confusion and inappropriate reactions and the effects of drugs and lesions in selective learning tasks reveal similarly confused reactions in animals. This gives an invaluable window on the bases for deterioration from orderly to disorderly behaviour. As is the case for classic amnesia, we need a behavioural approach to the basis of symptoms to allow the development of neuropsychological hypotheses and treatments better targeted to core psychological deficits. This line of approach does not assume that schizophrenia is necessarily a unitary syndrome, and the understanding of dysfunction that arises when normal mediational processes are disordered through the use of drugs or lesions will have a broader relevance to other conditions (like Parkinson's disease and attention deficit disorder) in which selective learning and the dopamine system have been implicated.

Thus, past experience provides one basis for assessing the predictive reliability of a stimulus, and having the wrong memory at the wrong time provides a model for aspects of schizophrenic attention disorder. In the normal animal, stimuli that signal the later arrival of a significant outcome can elicit a series of attentional and anticipatory responses. Disorder in this process could also contribute to the inappropriate responding so characteristic of schizophrenia. The pattern of dissociations across task and lesion will reveal the best neuropsychological account of the processes necessary to, for example, the appropriate control of retrieval, the normal orchestration of anticipatory responses and the liberation of attention by surprise. In support of this kind of model, there is clinical evidence for the focus on the control of retrieval in that schizophrenics get confused about temporal context, i.e. they know that an event has occurred, but not when (Rizzo, Danion, Van der Linden, & Grange, 1996). This deficit could well contribute to other difficulties, such as distinguishing stimuli that are currently relevant from those that would be irrelevant on the basis of past experience in that context. When animals do respond in the here and now without showing any effect of their prior experience of the relationship between the events at issue, we would expect that they should orient to an irrelevant or redundant stimulus just the same as they might to any novel stimulus. Clinically, the phenomenon of *jamais vu* has already been identified as a contributing factor to delusional disorder (Ellis, Luaute, & Retterstol, 1994; Marcel & Schiopu, 1998).

This work has already begun with an extensive series of investigations into latent inhibition and blocking, both of which rely on the appropriate control of retrieval to direct current attentional learning.

NEURAL SUBSTRATES OF LATENT INHIBITION AND BLOCKING

Impairment in filtering on the basis of past experience has been investigated (in rats and schizophrenics) using the latent inhibition and blocking models, in which stimuli are set up as irrelevant or redundant (see Gray et al., 1991; Weiner & Feldon, 1997). The neural substrates for such "attentional learning" are in part dopaminergic, confirming, in line with the dopamine hypothesis of schizophrenia, that this system has a critical role in the selection of stimuli for adaptive responding.

In the rat, latent inhibition is disrupted by acute (Weiner, Lubow, & Feldon, 1988) or chronic (Solomon et al., 1981; Weiner, Lubow, & Feldon, 1984) treatment with the indirect dopamine agonist, amphetamine. Although these studies provide an intriguing link with schizophrenia, supported by some clinical evidence (Baruch, Hemsley, & Gray, 1988a,b) they do not (on their own) allow us to locate the neural substrates of latent inhibition. There have been a number of reports that damage to the septohippocampal system abolishes latent inhibition (Clark, Feldon, & Rawlins, 1992; Han, Gallagher, & Holland, 1995; Kaye & Pearce, 1987; Solomon & Moore, 1975; see Weiner, 1990, for review) and, despite some apparently contradictory reports (Killcross & Robbins, 1993), there is also evidence that microinjections in (Solomon & Staton, 1982) or lesions to (Tai, Cassaday, Feldon, & Rawlins, 1995) nucleus accumbens are sufficient to disrupt latent inhibition. Multilevel theoretical syntheses put these data together to propose a neuropsychology of latent inhibition and, by inference, schizophrenia, with the hypothesis that the normal interaction between hippocampus and nucleus accumbens plays a critical role in attention (Gray et al., 1991; Weiner, 1990). However, it was subsequently found that neurotoxic lesions to hippocampus produced with ibotenic acid, which spares fibres of passage, do not abolish latent inhibition (Honey & Good, 1993). And there is even some evidence that hippocampal lesions, neurotoxic and conventional, and conventional lesions to the nucleus accumbens might actually enhance latent inhibition (Harrington & Purves, 1995; Purves, Bonardi, & Hall, 1995; Reilly, Harley, & Revusky, 1993). In short, although the data are contradictory in terms of the direction of effects, the rat studies suggest that the limbic system is critically involved in the normal development of latent inhibition. More lesion work will be required to establish which pathways are critical for the normal development of latent inhibition and what determines the direction of effects seen. In part, the inconsistencies might arise because of the differing demands of the task variants in use on attention and memory. Already, a neural network model has identified relative novelty (the mismatch between predicted and observed events) as an important determinant of latent inhibition and this model has been shown to accommodate the apparently conflicting effects of a variety of hippocampal lesions (Buhusi, Gray, & Schmajuk, 1998).

Blocking, which demonstrates the normal ability to "tune out" redundant stimuli, can also be impaired by non-specific hippocampal lesions (Solomon, 1977) and in human schizophrenics (Jones, Gray, & Hemsley, 1992). Again, the impairment results in increased conditioning, in this case despite redundancy rather than prior irrelevance. Thus, the critical role of the limbic system across a variety of two-stage procedures (Gray et al., 1991; Weiner, 1990) is consistent with the neuropathology believed to be associated with schizophrenia (Bogerts et al., 1993; Pakkenberg, 1990). Whereas attention is obviously necessary for learning, some instances of learning failure do not necessarily arise from attention deficit. Indeed, an apparent "attentional failure" to a particular stimulus could arise precisely because attention is selective to some alternate predictor. One approach to disentangling the various psychological processes involved is to measure attention and associative learning together in the same rats to determine the relationship between them. Orienting is already established as an appropriate measure and is seen when animals "look over" or rear to events of potential interest (Swan & Pearce, 1988). This approach ties in with the analysis of latent inhibition in terms of habituation and (encouragingly) hippocampal lesions affect both (Kaye & Pearce, 1987). It is also consistent with the role of relative novelty in determining how hippocampal lesions will affect latent inhibition (Buhusi et al., 1998).

Trace conditioning provides a further instance of selectivity in the learning mechanism and could even depend on the same psychological processes as latent inhibition (DeVietti et al., 1987). In any event, the normal animal will show some conditioning to a stimulus that predicts (on the basis of past experience) that the outcome of interest will eventually occur. Although the literature is mixed (see Rawlins & Tanner, 1998) there is some evidence that hippocampal lesions can impair trace conditioning (Solomon et al., 1986) and recent imaging data confirms the involvement of limbic structures (Buchel, Dolan, Armony, & Friston, 1999).

Thus, we can model aspects of attention deficit that might be impaired in schizophrenia. First, we need to determine where such effects would sit with respect to current neuropsychological theories.

ATTENTIONAL THEORIES OF HIPPOCAMPAL FUNCTION

In latent inhibition and blocking, establishing the reliability of a signal on the basis of experience necessarily introduces a memory component, consistent with their dependence on hippocampal structures (see Gray et al., 1991). In trace conditioning, the neuropsychological evidence supports the view that the hippocampus is necessary for processing over time, the temporal discontiguity theory of hippocampal function (Marr, 1971; Rawlins, 1985; Wallenstein, Eichenbaum, & Hasselmo, 1998) and the related notion that it functions as an associator, necessary to show declarative knowledge (e.g. Clark & Squire, 1998; Eichenbaum, 1997).

Attentional theories of hippocampal function have a long history. For example, Vinogradova (1975) suggested that hippocampal circuitry modulated habituation to signals depending on their information value as conditional stimuli. Recent evidence supports this kind of hypothesis, showing that the hippocampus is engaged when the relations between stimuli (as distinct from their physical identities) are varied, consistent with the view that it is necessary to an associative mismatch process (Honey, Watt, & Good, 1998). Whereas the orienting response does not depend on absolute novelty, mismatch renewed orienting in normal, but not in hippocampectomised, rats.

Although based on attentional (unconditioned) reactions such data supports memory mediation theories of hippocampal function (Weiskrantz, 1977, 1982). How far are the connections between the hippocampus and the nucleus accumbens necessary to this function? The reasons for incorporating the nucleus accumbens in any such neuropsychological theory are as follows: (1) there are intimate neuroanatomical connections between the hippocampus and nucleus accumbens (see later); (2) existing evidence already suggests that the hippocampus and nucleus accumbens are involved in some of the same cognitive processes (e.g. latent inhibition); (3) although the hippocampus could modulate dopaminergic activity in connected structures, the lack of dopaminergic innervation to the hippocampus makes it an unlikely substrate of schizophrenic dysfunction; and (4) the nucleus accumbens is part of the mesolimbic dopamine system already found to show signs of pathology in schizophrenia (Pakkenberg, 1990).

ATTENTION TO THE NUCLEUS ACCUMBENS?

The effects of amphetamine and dopaminergic lesions in two-stage procedures, predominantly latent inhibition, have been used to develop theories of nucleus accumbens function (Gray, 1982; Weiner, 1990; Weiner & Feldon, 1997). Although initial explanations of the mechanisms involved in latent inhibition centred on the pre-exposure stage (Lubow, 1989; Mackintosh, 1975; Pearce & Hall, 1980), findings that the disruptive effects of amphetamine occurred at the conditioning and not the pre-exposure stage (Weiner et al., 1984, 1988) changed the focus of interest. This led to the idea that the drugs and lesions might enhance cognitive "switching" from old to new environmental contingencies Weiner (1990). Similarly, neuropsychological disruptions of latent inhibition and blocking have been explained in terms of the lack of effect of "memories of past regularities", a likely model for schizophrenia (Gray et al., 1991; Hemsley, 1993).

Basically, in normal latent inhibition, the reinforcement contingency of the CS changes from pre-exposure (non-reinforced) to conditioning (reinforced), but behaviour continues to be controlled by the past experience of non-reinforcement. The findings that low doses of amphetamine disrupt latent inhibition only at conditioning suggests that it impairs not the ability to learn about the pre-exposed CS, but rather the capacity of that past learning to control behaviour when a change in reinforcement takes place. In other words the hyperdopaminergic animal is controlled by the immediate contingency and not past regularities. This enhancement of "switching" from old to new contingency is not restricted to the latent inhibition paradigm, e.g. amphetamine promotes response shifting between two levers in instrumental conditioning (Robbins & Everitt 1982; Robbins & Sahakian, 1983). Indeed Robbins and Everitt (1982) attributed this result to a general effect of low doses of amphetamine on behavioural switching, which can secondarily result in increased locomotor activity.

Weiner's switching hypothesis (Weiner, 1990; Weiner & Feldon, 1997) extends earlier theories on hippocampal attentional function (Gabriel, Sparenborg, & Stolar, 1986; Gray, 1982; Schmajuk & Moore, 1985, 1988) to include the nucleus accumbens. The mechanism proposed is that upon encountering a stimulus, the hippocampus allocates processing resources by inhibiting (or not) the nucleus accumbens from switching cognitive or behavioural resources towards that stimulus. This is achieved by a comparator function of the hippocampus evaluating the match between past and present predictive values of the stimulus at issue to produce a likely "associative value" that reflects the probability that this stimulus will now control behaviour. Using the example of the mismatch seen between pre-exposure and conditioning in latent inhibition, the comparison of old and new contingencies would result in a low value being attributed to the stimulus presently relevant, as past experience of its irrelevance would normally dominate. Thus, the hippocampus would normally inhibit the nucleus accumbens from switching, and so the past contingency would control behaviour. A signal to switch would only ensue if the CS associability reached a value that required it to receive processing. According to this theory then, latent inhibition is disrupted by amphetamine as a result of increased dopaminergic action in the nucleus accumbens activating the switching mechanism to allocate processing resources to the new CS–UCS contingency, despite the fact that on past experience the hippocampus should consider the case closed on the most likely contingency. However, whereas increased associability can result (for example) from novelty, in the absence of novelty it is not clear what would be a sufficient change to trigger switching.

The proposed route of hippocampal input is primarily via the subicular–accumbens projection. In support of such connections, hippocampal lesions lead to changes in dopaminergic activity in the nucleus accumbens (Springer & Isaacson, 1982). Additionally, an indirect pathway from hippocampus to ventral tegmental area (via the lateral septum) to nucleus accumbens provides an alternative route. This focus on the dopamine system does not preclude a role for other neurotransmitters: for example, Weiner (1990) proposes that accumbens dopaminergic activity is modulated by the serotonergic system originating in the medial raphe, either directly via the ventral tegmental area connection to the nucleus accumbens, or indirectly via the hippocampal connection. This is based on evidence that destruction of the medial raphe enhances ventral tegmental area dopaminergic cells innervating the nucleus accumbens (Deakin, 1983; Herve et al., 1981) and results in depletion of hippocampal serotonin (Dray et al., 1978; Lorens et al., 1976), and that medial raphe lesions enhance the locomotor activity induced by low doses of amphetamine (Geyer et al., 1976).

The switching model fits the latent inhibition data already presented, in that it predicts the disruption of latent inhibition by hippocampal lesions (which would destroy the comparator function and leave only present contingencies as the basis for responding). The further neuropsychological specification is also consistent with the effects of non-dopaminergic treatments on latent inhibition (see Weiner, 1990, for review) and activation of the nucleus accumbens dopaminergic system pharmacologically at conditioning (which would activate the switching mechanism). It also accounts for the evidence that neuroleptics enhance latent inhibition when given only at conditioning (Feldon & Weiner, 1991; Weiner & Feldon, 1997; Peters & Joseph, 1993) and more particularly when injected directly into the nucleus accumbens at conditioning (Gray et al., 1997).

Initially, theories of accumbens function did not take much account of its heterogeneity, in particular the distinction between shell and core subregions. However, it has since been found that destruction of the shell of the accumbens (but not the core) disrupts latent inhibition and as would be expected this disruption is antagonised with haloperidol to restore latent inhibition (Weiner, Rawlins, & Feldon, 1996). These recent findings suggested that the shell lesion resulted in dopamine hyperactivity, possibly due to the destruction of terminals of the hippocampal projection to the shell, which are thought to be inhibitory. If the mechanism for switching resides in the core, this would account for the observation that core lesions leave latent inhibition intact or even enhanced (Weiner et al., 1996, 1999; Weiner & Feldon, 1997). These authors further suggest that release of dopamine in the core activates switching, and that the core is inhibited indirectly by the ventral subiculum and entorhinal cortex afferents to the shell, the evidence to support this being tracing studies demonstrating that the major afferents to the shell are from the ventral subiculum and entorhinal cortex (Groenewegen, Vermeulen-Van der Zee, te Kortschot, & Witter, 1987), and that NMDA lesions of these structures disrupt latent inhibition (Yee, Feldon, & Rawlins, 1995). The pathway proposed from shell to core is GABA-ergic output from shell to A10 of the ventral tegmental area, which inhibits A10 dopaminergic activation of the core of the nucleus accumbens.

Thus, the model is well defined anatomically, but behaviourally less so. Being developed principally to explain latent inhibition, it is not always clear how it could apply more generally in other learning situations. For example, it does not specify the details of how a new CS contingency comes to dominate over the old one, which is necessary before predictions about its application to other learning paradigms can be made. In short, it is currently unclear under what conditions animals would stay or shift to the new contingency, especially when attention is liberated by surprising UCS factors rather than a change in the CS.

A number of recent models of nucleus accumbens function have attempted to unify theories of the role of nucleus accumbens dopamine in reward, aversion, conditioning, and locomotor activity. For example, Ikemoto and Panksepp (1999) propose that nucleus acumbens dopamine has a dual function in first integrating sensorimotor input from salient or novel stimuli to invigorate approach responses towards them (what they term "seeking" or flexible approach responses). This facilitates the second function, which is the allocation of incentive properties to stimuli of biologically significance (UCSs) or those predictive of such biologically significant stimuli (CSs), i.e. conditioning. The approach behaviour directs attentional resources to the stimuli and consequently allows them to acquire (conditioned incentive) properties that reflect their motivational significance.

By this account, interventions decreasing nucleus accumbens activity, e.g. haloperidol, attenuate the arousal to approach stimuli rather than affecting the perceptual and retrieval processes that recognise the salience of the stimuli or decreasing locomotor ability. Thus, they explain the role of nucleus accumbens in at least instrumental conditioned reinforcement, and also Pavlovian conditioning that involves approach behaviour. The theory defines brain reward phenomena, such as nucleus accumbens dopamine release in brain stimulation reward (Liebman & Butcher, 1973; Olds & Milner 1954) and self-administration of dopamine agonists into the nucleus accumbens (Hoebel et al., 1983), not in terms of hedonic properties of the increased dopamine activity but rather in terms of activation of incentive to obtain the reward, i.e. "wanting" as distinct from "liking" (see Berridge & Robinson, 1988). Ikemoto and Panksepp (1999) also include aversive conditioning in the model by characterising responses to aversive stimuli as approach towards safety. However, this theoretical move still does not account for freezing responses that are commonly seen in conditioning paradigms using nucleus accumbens dopamine manipulations, and that have been found to elicit nucleus accumbens dopamine release (Salamone, Cousins, & Snyder, 1997; Young, Joseph, & Gray, 1993).

Gray, Kumari, Lawrence, & Young (1999) propose a model of nucleus accumbens function comparable to that of Ikemoto and Panksepp in terms of the range of phenomena for which it accounts, but that is better specified in terms of functional neuroanatomy. The model similarly ascribes to the nucleus accumbens a role in selection and integration of perceptual information, based on the evidence from latent inhibition and pre-pulse inhibition (in which the startle response to an intense auditory stimulus is reduced by presentation of a less intense stimulus immediately before it). They provide evidence that the nucleus accumbens is activated by the salience of stimuli rather than just their reinforcing properties, for example, nucleus accumbens dopamine release occurs in the presence of stimuli not directly reinforcing or paired with a reinforcer (in a sensory preconditioning paradigm; Young et al., 1998). Gray and co-workers suggest a circuitry (see Gray et al., 1999, for the details) by which the nucleus accumbens receives sensory input so that the degree of stimulus salience can influence motor activity (compare this with Ikemoto & Panksepp's (1999) "seeking" behaviour). The model accounts for the attentional dysfunction seen in hyperdopaminergic animals and schizophrenics in that the increase in nucleus accumbens dopamine activity makes stimuli seem more salient and thereby reinforces the relationships between them, despite no actual contingency in real terms. It accounts for the reward literature in the same way as Ikemoto and Panksepp (1999), i.e. not in terms of dopamine release producing euphoria but rather assigned stimulus salience, and therefore the incentive properties that motivate behaviour.

The behavioural switching theory caters for many of the behavioural effects observed after nucleus accumbens lesions. Is there any evidence in support of the elaboration that the nucleus accumbens is necessary to mediate from memory to attention? Whereas behaviourally switching animals would most probably show orienting responses as they adjust to a new environmental contingency, the switching hypothesis does not formally include orienting. However, there is evidence that the mesolimbic system is necessary to orienting. First, whereas orienting to novel stimuli can be normal without a hippocampus, hippocampectomy does affect the animal's ability to show (through orienting) both decreased attention with repeated stimulus presentation (Kaye & Pearce, 1987) and increased attention given associative mismatches (Honey et al., 1998).

What of the mesolimbic dopamine system? Although comparable lesion data is not yet available for the nucleus accumbens, there is electrophysiological evidence both from recording in the toad (Buxbaum-Conradi & Ewert, 1999) and from stimulating in the cat ventral striatum that supports its involvement in orienting and the switching of attention (Crescimanno, Sorbera, Emmi, & Amato, 1998). Similarly, in the rat, single-unit, microdialysis and voltammetry studies show that, in addition to their role in reward, mesolimbic dopamine neurons respond to novel or intense stimuli (Horvitz, 2000). In human positron emission tomography studies, although no single study is definitive there is convergent evidence that points in the same direction. For example, Koepp et al. (1998) found that endogenous dopamine was released in human striatum in an attentionally demanding task; Berns, Cohen, and Mintun (1997) found that introducing a change in the sequence of events in a simple reaction time task resulted in increased blood flow in the ventral striatum with a time course consistent with its role in dealing with novelty. Detection of, and reaction to, stimuli is inevitably confounded with the use of behavioural measures but this problem can in principle be circumvented by functional measures like electrophysiology, *in vivo* neurochemistry and brain imaging to track the neural substrates of orienting. This evidence is consistent with Gray et al.'s (1999) position that the nucleus accumbens has outputs to (as well as inputs from) perceptual systems.

Finally, no theory of nucleus accumbens function can ignore its connections with the rest of the limbic circuitry. For example, there is good anatomical evidence that nucleus accumbens acts as an important conduit for information from hippocampus and amygdala (Groenewegen et al., 1999a). Whereas the switching hypothesis seems to be about the attraction of the here and now (Weiner, 1990), switching depends on whether the memory comparator in the hippocampus is inhibited or not. It is as if the accumbens is normally subject to discipline from a hippocampus that is wise from experience. When this input becomes inconsistent, disorder results. Variants on the two-stage procedures already described will provide critical tests of exactly how accumbens mediates from memory to attention, e.g. by using the liberation of attention by surprise in unblocking procedures, described later. The amygdala too has been implicated in the regulation of attentional processes (Gallagher & Holland, 1994). However, there is no evidence that amygdala is critical to the two-stage procedures that normally show the influence of past experience and some clear evidence that it is not necessary, e.g. for latent inhibition (Weiner, Tarrasch, & Feldon, 1995).

NEURAL AND COGNITIVE RESOLUTION

Patterns of neuropsychological dissociation will tell us which cognitive processes are functionally related and which depend on different neural substrates. Given the uncertainties that surround the use of diagnostic categories clinically, it is more rational to model psychopathology one symptom at a time using a variety of behavioural diagnostics to develop neuropsychological theories.

To follow up on the theoretical developments arising out of the work on latent inhibition (Gray et al., 1991; Weiner, 1990; Weiner & Feldon, 1997), we need to know how far memory contributes to the (in)ability to take past relevance into account (compare with Bouton, 1993). The latent inhibition literature clearly points to the nucleus accumbens as a substrate for the psychological processes necessary for attentional learning and memory. Although the nucleus accumbens is a heterogenous area, anatomically and neurochemically diverse and likely to contribute to a variety of functions, e.g. in the mediation of motivation to action (Mogenson & Yang, 1991), a combination of restricted lesions and selective behavioural tasks will clarify the role of nucleus accumbens subregions in allowing prior associations to direct current attention. This hypothesis is compatible with its connections to prefrontal cortex and hippocampal formation, and not incompatible with its role in motivation to action given the evidence that different subregions have different input–output characteristics (Groenewegen et al., 1999b). There is already some evidence for functional dissociation in core and shell subregions, for both low level functions like activity (Maldonado-Irizarry &

Kelley, 1995; West, Boss-Williams, & Weiss, 1999) and in the cognitive processes necessary to latent inhibition (Weiner & Feldon, 1997; Weiner et al., 1996, 1999).

Various experiments can be used to bring the interplay between attentional and memory processes into focus, but it is from the animals' actions that we must infer these processes. Given the well-established role of the dopaminergic system in motivation to action (Mogenson & Yang, 1991), it is important also to consider changes in general activity (see e.g. West et al. 1999) and interest in the UCS (see Berridge & Robinson, 1998; Ikemoto & Panksepp, 1999) produced by the various dopamine treatments in use. Trace conditioning procedures not only provide an alternative test of selective attention, that might even rely on the same processes as latent inhibition (De Vietti et al., 1987), they also allow us to compare the effects of treatments that increase learning normally weakened through stimulus pre-exposure (in latent inhibition) with those seen in a procedure that also involves weakened learning (in this case by the introduction of a trace interval between CS and UCS). Comparison between these tasks will allow us to dissociate basic effects on learning. When trace conditioning is abolished we see a reduction in animals' ability to associate events in spite of their temporal separation, i.e. reduced learning, whereas the abolition of latent inhibition is shown as increased learning, in spite of prior irrelevance. In contrast to the pattern of effects that might be expected if trace conditioning and latent inhibition were functionally similar, Parkinson, Robbins and Everitt (1999) found no effect of nucleus accumbens shell lesions in an aversive trace conditioning procedure, whereas lesions to the core impaired conditioning to the CS so that there was no difference between short and long trace conditioned groups (both showed little suppression). However, in similar latent inhibition procedures, the difference between groups that should show normal conditioning and groups for which learning has been reduced by stimulus preexposure is abolished by shell but not core lesions to nucleus accumbens and because of an increase in conditioning in the weak learning group rather than because of a decrease in conditioning in the strong learning group (Weiner et al., 1996, 1999).

However, trace conditioning procedures that rely on a single response measure might underestimate the level of conditioning that has occurred. Put another way, learning can be reflected in the appearance of anticipatory responses other than the designated conditioned responses: for example, foot flexion versus response suppression to tone that signals footshock and rearing versus magazine activity to light that signals food (Holland, 1980). It is as if the rat "licks his lips" in the time period during which food delivery is postponed, performing responses consistent with consummation only when the waiting is over. Whenever alternative attentional and anticipatory responses are reliably observed, focusing on a single conditioned response can obviously lead us to underestimate the effects of our treatments on the normal orchestration of these reactions. For example, in a study of sexual trace conditioning, Aktins and Domjan (1996) found that the requirement to wait for mating access resulted in alternative rather than weaker conditioned responding in their quail subjects. They used a two-compartment conditioning box and in each case the male's anticipation was reflected in their preference for the side on which the female would be delivered, the trace groups responding was different but only in the sense that they showed preference for a wider area in the interval between CS presentation and access to the female. Studies like this raise questions as to how we should measure the "strength" of learning when there are a range of responses that quantify the animals' expectations. In Atkins and Domjan's (1996) study, the trace-conditioned quail just showed decreased spatial specificity of the same loitering response.

These behavioural studies suggest that we need to re-examine the neural substrates of trace conditioning taking the likely orchestration of responses into account. Behavioural disorder will arise not only from a failure of selective learning but also from the disorganisation that will arise when, for example, end-point consummatory activity appears much earlier than is appropriate for the particular environmental schedule of contingencies. However, a model only of disinhibition would be of limited interest. We would predict that the neural substrate necessary to appropriate memory mediation would also, when damaged, result in delayed "early" anticipatory behaviours out of step with the imminence of the UCS. By contrast, whereas the switching model (Weiner, 1990) would presumably predict an increase in behavioural transitions in the trace interval in the dopaminergically disordered animal, it would not seem to predict temporal disorder of otherwise relevant responses. To extend the earlier example, on our account, the behaviourally disordered quail would preen affectedly in some distant corner of the conditioning chamber, and thereby miss his opportunity to copulate. Emitting the appropriate series of responses necessarily requires memory mediation and such an insensitivity to temporal context would be consistent with clinical evidence in schizophrenics (Rizzo et al., 1996).

Variants on the blocking procedure provide a further way to distinguish effects on attention and memory. Basic blocking is seen when, on past experience, the UCS is already fully predicted by some CS, so that there is little advantage in learning about any further potential signal for that outcome (blocking), e.g. if food is already fully predicted by a tone, there will be little later learning about an incidental light that predicts nothing new. In such cases, selective learning is obviously based on past experience introducing a memory component to normal attention (because memory is necessary to decide whether a stimulus is redundant). Like latent inhibition, the blocking paradigm provides a very useful test of attentional memory (Gray et al., 1991). Simple memory loss should reduce blocking as the previous predictor would be forgotten; memory improvement should increase blocking as the memory of the previous predictor would be highly accessible. Any effects attributable to alteration in the subjects' ability to integrate across experimental stages should be demonstrable across a variety of two-stage procedures (e.g. second-order conditioning and associative interference). That is, a general deficit in cognitive mediation will have effects in tasks other than blocking, and irrespective of the motivational significance of the stimuli in use. These kinds of effect are predicted just as well by the switching model of nucleus accumbens function (Weiner, 1990; Weiner & Feldon, 1997) as by our hypothesis that it is critical to direct current attention on the basis of past experience. On either account, the observed effects are difficult to distinguish from those of simple memory failure.

However, a differential prediction arises when we consider unblocking. Blocking is dramatically reduced when things do change so that the outcome is interestingly different, e.g. more or less food is delivered than would be expected on the basis of the established CS (up- or down-shift unblocking; Holland, 1988). In this variant, surprise liberates attention for learning and we can assess the effects of dopamine treatments under conditions that allow us to partial-out any direct effects that reduce the size of the blocking effect. From the point of view of the switching hypothesis, it is already not that easy to tell how one CS contingency comes to dominate over another, so this hypothesis makes no obvious prediction about the liberation of attention for learning produced by increasing or decreasing the size of the UCS.

THEORETICAL TRAJECTORIES

Putting disordered conditioning on the neuroanatomical map allows us to develop functional theories of psychological disorder through the use of animal models. As well as the theoretical impetus provided by existing theories of nucleus accumbens function, continuing developments in associative learning theory inform this process. For example, the variety of responses that can reflect a CS–UCS association has been formally included within a theory that allows for distinct representations of both the emotive and sensory qualities of the UCS ("AESOP"; Wagner & Brandon, 1989), following an earlier distinction in the level of general preparatory versus focused consummatory behaviour supported by the emotive versus sensory qualities of the UCS (Konorski, 1967). There is empirical support for the distinction between the processing of emotive and sensory representations (Brandon & Wagner, 1991; McNish, Betts, Brandon, & Wagner, 1997), which, through a better understanding of its neuropsychological basis could lend insight into associative processes in normal and abnormal states. Disordered classical conditioning will both result in confused cognitive states and secondarily propel animals into inappropriate reactions and misinformed action because instrumental responding is guided by environmental stimuli. We already know that the mesolimbic dopamine system is involved in reward (Berridge & Robinson, 1998). Reinforcement is what enables us to profit from experience and reinforcement is often secondary, guided by classically conditioned stimuli (Gray, 1975; Mowrer, 1960). Yet to be tested, Gray et al.'s (1999) theory that incorporates reward, motor, and sensory processing, could be exactly what we need for a full understanding of nucleus accumbens function. With respect to schizophrenia, although this disorder clearly involves some primary motivational disturbance, e.g. of appetite and sleep patterns, it is clearly more than a motivational disorder: impairment in memory mediation would leave the schizophrenic ignorant of the contingencies relevant to appropriate action.

REFERENCES

Atkins, C.K. & Domjan, M. (1996). The topography of sexually conditioned behaviour: Effects of a trace interval. *Quarterly Journal of Experimental Psychology: Section B*, *49*, 346–356.

Bartlett, F.C. (1932). *Remembering: A study in experimental and social psychology*. Cambridge: Cambridge University Press.

Baruch, I., Hemsley, D.R., & Gray, J.A. (1988a). Differential performance of acute and chronic schizophrenics in a latent inhibition task. *Journal of Nervous and Mental Disease*, *176*, 598–606.

Baruch, I., Hemsley, D.R., & Gray, J.A. (1988b). Latent inhibition and 'psychotic proneness' in normal subjects. *Personality and Individual Differences*, *9*, 777–783.

Berns, G.S., Cohen, J.D., & Mintun, M.A. (1997). Brain regions responsive to novelty in the absence of awareness. *Science*, *276*, 1272–1275.

Berridge, K.C., & Robinson, T.E. (1998). What is the role of dopamine in reward: Hedonic impact, reward learning, or incentive salience? *Brain Research Reviews*, *28*, 309–369.

Bogerts, B., Lieberman, J.A., Ashtari, M., Bilder, R.M., Degreef, G., Lerner, G., Johns, C., & Masiar, S. (1993). Hippocampus–amygdala volumes and psychopathology in chronic schizophrenia. *Biological Psychiatry*, *33*, 236–246.

Bouton, M.E. (1993). Context, time, and memory retrieval in the interference paradigms of Pavlovian learning. *Psychological Bulletin*, *114*, 80–99.

Brandon, S.E., & Wagner, A.R. (1991). Modulation of a discrete Pavlovian conditioned reflex by a putative emotive Pavlovian conditioned-stimulus. *Journal of Experimental Psychology: Animal Behaviour Processes*, *17*, 299–311.

Buchel, C., Dolan, R.J., Armony, J.L., & Friston, K.J. (1999). Amygdala–hippocampal involvement in human aversive trace conditioning revealed through event-related functional magnetic resonance imaging. *Journal of Neuroscience*, *19*, 10869–10876.

Buhusi, C.V., Gray, J.A., & Schmajuk, N.A. (1998). Perplexing effects of hippocampal lesions on latent inhibition: A neural network solution. *Behavioral Neuroscience*, *112*, 316–351.

Bunsey, M., & Eichenbaum, H. (1996). Conservation of hippocampal memory function in rats and humans. *Nature*, *379*, 255–257.

Buxbaum-Conradi, H., & Ewert, J.P. (1999). Responses of single neurons in the toad's caudal ventral striatum to moving visual stimuli and test of their efferent projection by extracellular antidromic stimulation/recording techniques. *Brain Behavior and Evolution*, *54*, 338–354.

Clark, A.J.M., Feldon, J., & Rawlins, J.N.P. (1992). Aspiration lesions of rat ventral hippocampus disinhibit responding in conditioned suppression or extinction, but spare latent inhibition and the partial reinforcement extinction effect. *Neuroscience*, *48*, 821–829.

Clark, R.E., & Squire, L.R. (1998). Classical conditioning and brain systems: The role of awareness. *Science*, *280*, 77–81.

Crescimanno, G., Sorbera, F., Emmi, A., & Amato, G. (1998). Inhibitory effect of A10 dopaminergic neurons of the ventral tegmental area on the orienting response evoked by acoustic stimulation in the cat. *Brain Research Bulletin*, *45*, 61–65.

Deakin, J.F.W. (1983). Roles of serotonergic systems in escape, avoidance and other behaviours. In S.J. Cooper (Ed.) *Theory in pharmacology* (Vol. 2, pp. 144–193). London: Academic Press.

DeVietti, T.L., Bauste, R.L., Nutt, G., Barrett, O.V., Daly, K., & Petree, A.D. (1987). Latent inhibition: A trace conditioning phenomenon? *Learning and Motivation*, *18*, 185–201.

Dickinson, A. (1980). *Contemporary animal learning theory*. Cambridge: Cambridge University Press.

Dray, A., Davies, J., Oakley, N., Tongraoch, P., & Velucci, S. (1978). The dorsal and medial raphe projections to the substantia nigra in the rat: Electrophysiological, biochemical and behavioural observations. *Brain Research*, *151*, 431–442.

Eichenbaum, H. (1997). Declarative memory: Insights from cognitive neurobiology. *Annual Review of Psychology*, *48*, 547–572.

Ellis, H.D., Luaute, J.P., & Retterstol, N. (1994). Delusional misidentification syndromes. *Psychopathology*, *27*, 117–120.

Ellison, G.D., & Eison, M.S. (1983). Continuous amphetamine intoxication: An animal model of the acute psychotic episode. *Psychological Medicine*, *13*, 751–761.

Feldon, J., & Weiner, I. (1991). The latent inhibition model of schizophrenic attention disorder: Haloperidol and sulpiride enhance rats' ability to ignore irrelevant stimuli. *Biological Psychiatry*, *29*, 635–646.

Gabriel, M., Sparenborg, S.P., & Stolar, N. (1986). An executive function of the hippocampus: Pathway selection for thalamic neuronal significance code. In R.L. Isaacson & K.H. Pribram (Eds.) *The hippocampus* (Vol. 4, pp. 1–40). New York: Plenum Press.

Gallagher, M., & Holland, P.C. (1994). The amygdala complex – multiple roles in associative learning and attention. *Proceedings of the National Academy of Sciences USA*, *91*, 11771–11776.

Geyer, M.A., Puerto, A., Menks, D.B., Segal, D.S., & Mandell, A.J. (1976). Behavioral studies following lesions of the mesolimbic and mesostriatal serotonergic pathways. *Brain Research*, *106*, 257–270.

Gray, J.A (1975). *Elements of a two-process theory of learning*. London: Academic Press.

Gray, J.A. (1982). *The neuropsychology of anxiety: An enquiry into the functions of the septo-hippocampal system*. Oxford: Oxford University Press.

Gray, J.A., Feldon, J., Rawlins, J.N.P., Hemsley, D.R., & Smith, A.D. (1991). The neuropsychology of schizophrenia. *Behavioral and Brain Sciences*, *14*, 1–84.

Gray, J.A., Moran, P.M., Grigoryan, G., Peters, S.L., Young, A.M.J., & Joseph, M.H. (1997). Latent inhibition: The nucleus accumbens connection revisited. *Behavioural Brain Research*, *88*, 27–34.

Gray, J.A., Kumari, V., Lawrence, L., & Young, A.M.J. (1999). Functions of the dopaminergic innervation of the nucleus accumbens. *Psychobiology*, *27*, 225–235.

Groenewegen, H.J., Mulder, A.B., Beijer, A.V.J., Wright, C.I., Lopes da Silva, F.H., & Pennartz, C.M.A. (1999a). Hippocampal and amygdaloid interactions in the nucleus accumbens. *Psychobiology*, *27*, 149–164.

Groenewegen, H.J., Vermeulen-Van der Zee, E., te Kortschot, A., & Witter, M.P. (1987). Organisation of the projections from the subiculum to the ventral striatum in the rat. A study using anterograde transport of *Phaseolus vulgaris* leucoagglutinin. *Neuroscience*, *23*, 103–120.

Groenewegen, H.J., Wright, C.I., Beijer, A.V., & Voorn, P. (1999b). Converegence and segregation of ventral striatal inputs and outputs. *Annals of the New York Academy of Sciences*, *877*, 49–63.

Han, J.-S., Gallagher, M., & Holland, P. (1995). Hippocampal lesions disrupt decrements but not increments in conditioned stimulus processing. *Journal of Neuroscience, 15*, 7323–7329.

Harrington, N.R., & Purves, D.G. (1995). Bilateral electrolytic lesions of the nucleus accumbens enhance latent inhibition. *Journal of Psychopharmacology, 9*, A43.

Hemsley, D.R. (1993). A simple (or simplistic) cognitive model for schizophrenia. *Behaviour Research and Therapy, 31*, 633–645.

Herve, D., Simon, H., Blanc, G., Le Moal, M., Glowinski, J., & Tassin, J.P. (1981). Opposite changes in dopamine utilization in the nucleus accumbens and pre-frontal cortex after electrolytic lesions of the medial raphe in the rat. *Brain Research, 216*, 422–428.

Hoebel, B.G., Monaco, A.P., Hernandez, L., Aulisi, E.F., Stanley, B.G., & Lenard, L. (1983). Self infusion of amphetamine directly into the brain. *Psychopharmacology, 81*, 158–163.

Holland, P.C. (1980). CS–US interval as a determinant of the form of Pavlovian appetitive conditioned responses. *Journal of Experimental Psychology: Animal Behavior Processes, 6*, 155–174.

Holland, P.C. (1988). Excitation and inhibition in unblocking. *Journal of Experimental Psychology: Animal Behavior Processes, 14*, 261–279.

Honey, R.C., & Good, M. (1993). Selective hippocampal lesions abolish the contextual specificity of latent inhibition and conditioning. *Behavioral Neuroscience, 107*, 23–33.

Honey, R.C., Watt, A., & Good, M. (1998). Hippocampal lesions disrupt an associative mismatch process. *The Journal of Neuroscience, 18*, 2226–2230.

Horvitz, J.C. (2000). Mesolimbocortical and nigrostriatal dopamine responses to salient non-reward events. *Neuroscience, 96*, 651–656.

Ikemoto, S., & Panksepp, J. (1999). The role of nucleus accumbens dopamine in motivated behavior: A unifying interpretation with special reference to reward-seeking. *Brain Research Reviews, 31*, 6–41.

Jones, S.H., Gray, J.A., & Hemsley, D.R. (1992). Loss of the Kamin blocking effect in acute but not chronic schizophrenics. *Biological Psychiatry, 32*, 739–755.

Kaye, H., & Pearce, J.M. (1987). Hippocampal lesions attenuate latent inhibition and the decline of the orienting response. *Quarterly Journal of Experimental Psychology: Section B, 39*, 107–125.

Killcross, A.S., & Robbins, T.W. (1993). Differential effects of intra-accumbens and systemic amphetamine on latent inhibition using an on-baseline, within-subject conditioned suppression paradigm. *Psychopharmacology, 110*, 479–489.

Koepp, M.J., Gunn, R.N., Lawrence, A.D., Cunningham, V.J., Dagher, A., Jones, T., Brooks, D.J., Bench, C.J., & Grasby, P.M. (1998). Evidence for striatal dopamine release during a video game. *Nature, 393*, 266–268.

Konorski, J. (1967). *Integrative activity of the brain: An interdisciplinary approach.* Chicago: University of Chicago Press.

Liebman, J.M., & Butcher, L.L. (1973). Effects of self stimulation behavior of drugs influencing dopaminergic neurotransmission mechanisms. *Naunyn Schmiedebergs Archives of Pharmacology, 227*, 305–331.

Lorens, S.A., Guldberg, H.C., Hole, K., Kohler, C., & Srebro, B. (1976). Activity, avoidance learning and regional 5-hydroxytryptamine following intra-brain stem 5,7-dihydroxytryptamine and electrolytic midbrain raphe lesions in the rat. *Brain Research, 108*, 97–113.

Lubow, R.E. (1989). *Latent inhibition and conditioned attention theory.* Cambridge: Cambridge University Press.

Mackintosh, N.J. (1975). A theory of attention: Variations in the associability of stimuli with reinforcement. *Psychological Review, 82*, 276–298.

Maldonado-Irizarry, C.S., & Kelley, A.E. (1995). Excitotoxic lesions of core and shell subregions of the nucleus accumbens differentially disrupt body weight regulation and motor activity in rat. *Brain Research Bulletin, 38*, 551–559.

Marcel, E., & Schiopu, B. (1998). Psychic disorders and complex partial epilepsy. *Evolution Psychiatrique, 63*, 395–408.

Marr, D. (1971). Simple memory: A theory for archicortex. *Philosophical Transactions of the Royal Society of London: Series B, 262*, 23–82.

McKenna, P.J., Tamlyn, D., Lund, C.E., Mortimer, A.M., Hammond, S., & Baddeley, A.D. (1990). Amnesic syndrome in schizophrenia. *Psychological Medicine, 20*, 967–972.

McNish, K.A., Betts, S.L., Brandon, S.E., & Wagner A.R. (1997). Divergence of conditioned eyeblink and conditioned fear in backward Pavlovian training. *Animal Learning and Behavior, 25*, 43–52.

Mogenson, G.J., & Yang, C.R. (1991). The contribution of basal forebrain to limbic–motor integration and the mediation of motivation to action. *Advances in Experimental Medicine and Biology, 295*, 267–290.

Morgan, D.G., May, P.C., & Finch, C.E. (1987). Dopamine and serotonin systems in human and rodent brain: Effects of age and neurodegenerative disease. *Journal of the American Geriatrics Society, 35*, 334–345.

Mowrer, O.H. (1960). *Learning theory and behavior*. New York: Wiley.

Olds, J., & Milner, P. (1954). Positive reinforcement produced by electrical stimulation of septal area and other regions of rat brain. *Journal of Comparative Physiology and Psychology, 47*, 419–427.

Pakkenberg, B. (1990). Pronounced reduction of total neuron number in mediodorsal thalamic nucleus and nucleus accumbens in schizophrenics. *Archives of General Psychiatry, 47*, 1023–1028.

Parkinson, J.A., Robbins, T.W., & Everitt, B.J. (1999). Selective excitotoxic lesions of the nucleus accumbens core and shell differentially affect aversive Pavlovian conditioning to discrete and contextual cues. *Psychobiology, 27*, 256–266.

Pearce, J.M., & Hall, G. (1980). A model for Pavlovian learning: Variations in the effectiveness of conditioned but not of unconditioned stimuli. *Psychological Review, 87*, 532–552.

Peters, S.L., & Joseph, M.H. (1993). Haloperidol potentiation of latent inhibition in rats: Evidence for a critical role at conditioning rather than pre-exposure. *Behavioural Pharmacology, 4*, 183–186.

Purves, D., Bonardi, C., & Hall, G. (1995). Enhancement of latent inhibition in rats with electrolytic lesions of the hippocampus. *Behavioral Neuroscience, 109*, 366–370.

Rawlins, J.N.P. (1985). Associations across time: The hippocampus as a temporary memory store. *Behavioral and Brain Sciences, 8*, 479–496.

Rawlins, J.N.P., & Tanner, J. (1998). The effects of hippocampal aspiration lesions on conditioning to the CS and to a background stimulus in trace conditioned suppression. *Behavioural Brain Research, 91*, 61–72.

Reilly, S., Harley, C., & Revusky, S. (1993). Ibotenate lesions of the hippocampus enhance latent inhibition in conditioned taste aversion and increase resistance to extinction in conditioned taste preference. *Behavioral Neuroscience, 107*, 996–1004.

Rizzo, L., Danion, J.-M., Van der Linden, M., & Grange, D. (1996). Patients with schizophrenia remember that an event has occurred, but not when. *British Journal of Psychiatry, 168*, 427–431.

Robbins, T.W., & Everitt, B.J. (1982). Functional studies of the central catecholamines. *International Review of Neurobiology, 23*, 303–365.

Robbins, T.W., & Sahakian, B.J. (1983). Behavioral effects of psycho-motor stimulant drugs: Clinical and neuropsychological implications. In I. Creese (Ed.) *Stimulants: Neurochemical, behavioral and clinical perspectives* (pp. 301–338). New York: Raven Press.

Salamone, J.D., Cousins, M.S., & Snyder, B.J. (1997). Behavioral functions of nucleus accumbens dopamine: Empirical and conceptual problems with anhedonia hypothesis. *Neuroscience & Biobehavioral Reviews, 21*, 341–359.

Schmajuk, N.A., & Moore, J.W. (1985). Real-time attentional models for classical conditioning and the hippocampus. *Physiological Psychology*, *13*, 278–290.

Schmajuk, N.A., & Moore, J.W. (1988). The hippocampus and the classically conditioned nictating membrane response: A real time attentional-associative model. *Psychobiology*, *16*, 20–35.

Soares, J.C., & Gershon, S. (1997). Therapeutic targets in late-life psychoses: Review of concepts and critical issues. *Schizophrenia Research*, *27*, 227–239.

Solomon, P.R. (1977). Role of the hippocampus in blocking and conditioned inhibition of the rabbit's nictating membrane response. *Journal of Comparative and Physiological Psychology*, *91*, 407–417.

Solomon, P.R., Crider, A., Winkelman, J.W., Turi, A., Kamer, R.M., & Kaplan, L.J. (1981). Disrupted latent inhibition in the rat with chronic amphetamine or haloperidol-induced supersensitivity: Relationship to schizophrenic attention disorder. *Biological Psychiatry*, *16*, 519–537.

Solomon, P.R., & Moore, J.W. (1975). Latent inhibition and stimulus generalization of the classically conditioned nictitating membrane response in rabbits (*Oryctolagus cuniculus*) following dorsal hippocampal ablation. *Journal of Comparative and Physiological Psychology*, *89*, 1192–1203.

Solomon, P.R., & Staton, D.M. (1982). Differential effects of microinjections of *d*-amphetamine into the nucleus accumbens or the caudate putamen on the rat's ability to ignore an irrelevant stimulus. *Biological Psychiatry*, *17*, 743–756.

Solomon, P.R., Vander Schaaf, E.R., Thompson, R.F., & Weisz, D.J. (1986). Hippocampus and trace conditioning of the rabbit's classically conditioned nictitating membrane response. *Behavioral Neuroscience*, *100*, 729–744.

Springer, J.E., & Isaacson, R.L. (1982). Catecholamine alterations in basal ganglia after hippocampal lesions. *Brain Research*, *252*, 185–188.

Stip, E. (1996). Memory impairment in schizophrenia: Perspectives from psychopathology and pharmacotherapy. *Canadian Journal of Psychiatry*, *41*, S27–34.

Swan, J.A., & Pearce, J.M. (1988). The orienting response as an index of stimulus associability in rats. *Journal of Experimental Psychology: Animal Behavior Processes*, *14*, 292–301.

Tai, C.-T., Cassaday, H.J., Feldon, J., & Rawlins, J.N.P. (1995). Both electrolytic and excitotoxic lesions of nucleus accumbens disrupt latent inhibition of learning in rats. *Neurobiology of Learning and Memory*, *64*, 36–48.

Vinogradova, O.S. (1975). Functional organization of the limbic system in the process of registration of information: facts and hypotheses. In R.L. Isaacson & K.H. Pribram (Eds.) *The hippocampus* (Vol. 2, pp. 1–70). New York: Plenum Press.

Wagner, A.R., & Brandon, S.E. (1989). Evolution of a structured connectionist model of Pavlovian conditioning. AESOP. In S.B. Klein & R.R. Mowrer (Eds.) *Contemporary learning theories: Pavlovian conditioning and the status of traditional learning theory*. Hillsdale, NJ: Lawrence Erlbaum Associates, Inc.

Wallenstein, G.V., Eichenbaum, H. & Hasselmo, M.E. (1998). The hippocampus as an associator of discontiguous events. *Trends in the Neurosciences, 21*, 317–323.

Weiner, I. (1990). Neural substrates of latent inhibition: The switching model. *Psychological Bulletin, 108*, 442–461.

Weiner, I., & Feldon, J. (1997). The switching model of latent inhibition: An update of neural substrates. *Behavioural Brain Research, 88*, 11–25.

Weiner, I., Gal, G., & Feldon, J. (1999). Disrupted and undisruptable latent inhibition following shell and core lesions. *Annals of the New York Academy of Sciences, 877*, 723–727.

Weiner, I., Gal, G., Rawlins, J.N.P., & Feldon, J. (1996). Differential involvement of the shell and core subterritories of the nucleus in latent inhibition and amphetamine-induced activity. *Behavioural Brain Research, 81*, 123–133.

Weiner, I., Lubow, R.E., & Feldon, J. (1984). Abolition of the expression but not the acquisition of latent inhibition by chronic amphetamine in rats. *Psychopharmacology, 83,* 194–199.

Weiner, I., Lubow, R.E., & Feldon, J. (1988). Disruption of latent inhibition by acute administration of low doses of amphetamine. *Pharmacology, Biochemistry & Behavior, 30,* 871–878.

Weiner, I., Tarrasch, R., & Feldon, J. (1996). Basolateral amygdala lesions do not disrupt latent inhibition. *Behavioural Brain Research, 72,* 73–81.

Weiskrantz, L. (1977). Trying to bridge some neuropsychological gaps between monkey and man. *British Journal of Psychology, 68,* 431–445.

Weiskrantz, L. (1982). Comparative aspects of studies of amnesia. *Philosophical Transactions of the Royal Society of London: Section B, 298,* 97–109.

West, C.H.K., Boss-Williams, K.A., & Weiss, J.M. (1999). Motor activation by amphetamine infusion into nucleus accumbens core and shell subregions of rats differentially sensitive to dopaminergic drugs. *Behavioural Brain Research, 98,* 155–165.

Wilkerson, A., & Levin, E.D. (1999). Ventral hippocampal dopamine D_1 and D_2 systems and spatial working memory in rats. *Neuroscience, 89,* 743–749.

Yee, B.K., Feldon, J., & Rawlins, J.N.P. (1995). Latent inhibition in rats is abolished by NMDA-induced neuronal loss in the retrohippocampal region but this lesion effect can be prevented by systemic haloperidol treatment. *Behavioral Neuroscience, 109,* 227–240.

Young, A.M.J., Joseph, M.H., & Gray, J.A. (1993). Latent inhibition of conditioned dopamine release in the nucleus accumbens. *Neuroscience, 54,* 5–9.

Young, A.M.J., Ahier, R.G., Upton, R.L., Joseph, M.H., & Gray, J.A. (1998). Increased extracellular dopamine in the nucleus accumbens of the rat during associative learning of neural stimuli. *Neuroscience, 83,* 1175–1183.

PART FOUR

Computer models of memory encoding and retrieval

CHAPTER TWELVE

Linking memory and perception: Hebbian models of perceptual learning in animals and humans

Lisa M. Saksida
Department of Experimental Psychology, University of Cambridge, UK

James L. McClelland
Center for the Neural Basis of Cognition and Department of Psychology, Carnegie Mellon University, Pittsburgh, USA

INTRODUCTION

Computational modelling has the potential to be an invaluable tool in under-standing the relationship between brain and behaviour because it addresses not only *what* functions are performed by brain regions, but *how* they are performed (Rolls & Treves, 1997). Although most researchers have a theor-etical framework that informs and motivates their experiments, the particular mechanisms that could yield predicted results are often not made explicit. Computational modelling can be particularly useful in that it brings forward such implicit assumptions. Because of this, models can be important tools for the analysis of data, and can help in the development of clearly motivated experiments with clear predictions. Furthermore, computational models can provide a common language to help with communication across researchers, thereby reducing the perennial problem of ambiguity of terminology.

Just as there are a number of levels in the organisation of the nervous system—from cellular to anatomical systems levels—so there are a number of different levels of computational modelling, each of which is best suited for understanding brain and cognition at a specific resolution. Churchland and Sejnowski (1992) identify seven levels of organisation in the nervous system: molecules, synapses, neurons, networks, maps, systems, and CNS. Each of these levels of organisation has a corresponding level of cognitive neuro-science technique, such as unit recording at the neuronal level, or lesion studies at the systems level. Similarly, each of these levels has a corresponding level of computational modelling technique, for example, Hodgkin and Huxley's (1952) model of the single neuron at the neuronal level or Selverston's model of the stomatogastric ganglion circuit in the lobster at the network level (Selverston, Russell, & Miller, 1976). The goal, with both cognitive neuro-science techniques and with modelling, is not to argue that any one level of study is better than any other. Instead, work should be done by experts at each of the levels, with the idea that research at one level will constrain and motivate research at the surrounding levels.

This chapter focuses on models at the connectionist level. At this level of modelling, information processing is seen as arising from the interactions of large numbers of simple units, and changes in the strength of connections between these units are suggested as the basis for cognitive processes such as learning and memory. Thus, connectionist models are formulated at a rela-tively high level—they attempt to account for psychological data while being inspired by basic facts about the structure of the nervous system. It is import-ant to note that, at this level of modelling, simplification is essential. Includ-ing a great deal of biological detail tends to obscure the essential emergent processes that underlie complex behaviour.

The connectionist approach to learning and memory

The connectionist approach to understanding cognition, and memory in par-ticular, has been around since the early associationists began to consider mechanistic frameworks for studying learning and memory. In 1943, Hull proposed that memory involves the storage of sets of traces. He suggested that short-term memory consists of stimulus traces subject to rapid decay, and that long-term memory consists of associative strengths (or habit strengths) that can persist over longer periods of time. In a connectionist model, Hull's stimulus traces correspond to activity of nodes or units and associative strengths correspond to the strengths of connections between these nodes. Learning, then, consists in the change in these connection strengths over time. These ideas were later expanded and related directly to neurophysiology by Hebb (1949), who was the first to suggest that a stable long-term memory depends on a structural change, and went on to propose a hypothesis for how such a change is achieved: "When the axon of cell A is near enough to excite a cell B and repeatedly or persistently takes part in firing it, some growth process or metabolic change takes place in one or both cells such that A's efficiency, as one of the cells firing B, is increased" (Hebb, 1949, p. 62).

Soon after Hebb's proposal, computational models incorporating prin-ciples of connectionism began to be developed (McCulloch & Pitts, 1943; Rosenblatt, 1962; Selfridge, 1959; Widrow & Hoff, 1960) and applied to understanding the processes underlying perception and discrimination learn-ing. It was at this time that the basic unit for modern connectionist models—a highly abstract neuron—was developed (McCulloch & Pitts, 1943) This model neuron consists of a cell body that has a number of inputs (dendrites) and a single output (axon) (Fig. 12.1). It is usually assumed that the output is either on or off, and that the output depends directly on the inputs—a certain number of inputs must be on at any one time for the neuron to fire. Each input has an associated "weight" (ω), which corresponds to the efficiency of the synapse: more efficient synapses have a higher weight, weaker synapses have a lower weight. The cell body sums together the inputs (Σ), each of which is first multiplied by the weight of its corresponding synapse. This weighted sum is then compared to some internal threshold and if this level is exceeded the output is turned on (i.e. the neuron fires).

These early connectionist models were "single layer" networks, typically consisting of a set of input units and a set of output units[1] (Fig. 12.2). Learning in these networks was achieved through modification of the effi-ciency of the synapses, that is, gradually altering the weight on each input line

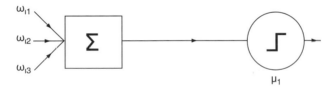

Figure 12.1.   The McCulloch–Pitts neuron (after Hertz, Krogh, & Palmer, 1991, p. 3). ω_{ij} = weight of connection between unit j and unit i; Σ = weighted sum of inputs; μ_i = threshold.

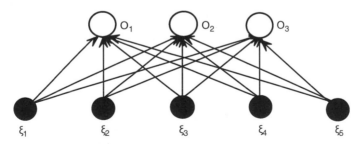

Figure 12.2.   A simple perceptron, which has only one layer (after Hertz, Krogh, & Palmer, 1991, p. 116). ξ = input unit; O = output unit.

---

[1] There are two conventions for counting the number of layers in a network: some authors count the input units as a layer and some do not. The latter convention seems to be more popular, and makes sense for modelling psychological processes because the input layer usually represents a stimulus external to the brain. According to this convention, an N-layer network has N layers of connections and $N-1$ hidden layers.

such that eventually each input led to the desired output. To illustrate, imagine we have a simple network and we want to teach it to differentiate between As and Bs. We want it to output a 1 when an A is presented and a 0 when a B is presented (the network is set-up such that only outputs of 0 or 1 are possible). When the network is first set-up, the weights on the input lines are random. Thus, when an A input is presented and the neuron performs a weighted sum, the chances of it producing a 1 or a 0 are equal. If it randomly outputs a 1, this is the correct response, so there is no need to change any weights. If it outputs a 0, however, this is the incorrect response, so we need to increase the weights on the active input synapses so that next time the A is presented, the sum of weights exceeds the threshold, and the network produces a 1. Likewise for B: if presentation of a B input causes the network initially to produce a 1, we need to decrease the weights on the active input synapses so that next time the weighted sum is beneath the threshold and the unit does not fire. Thus, for the network to learn, we need to increase the weights on the active inputs when we want the output to be active, and decrease them when we want the output to be inactive. In addition, it seems sensible to change the weights by a lot when the weighted sum is a long way from the desired value, but to alter them only slightly when the weighted sum is close to that required to give the correct solution. This modification, the Widrow–Hoff delta rule (Widrow & Hoff, 1960), calculates the difference between the weighted sum and the required output and calls this the error. Weight adjustment is then carried out in proportion to that error. Psychologists will recognise this as identical to the Rescorla–Wagner learning rule (Rescorla & Wagner, 1972).

Single-layer error-correcting networks were seen to be very exciting at first, because they seemed quite powerful for such a simple model. However, in 1969 Minsky and Papert published a report demonstrating that these models were unable to solve many problems, including several that seemed very straightforward. For example, they showed that these networks were unable to solve linearly inseparable problems, such as the exclusive-or logic function.[2] As a result, interest among computational researchers in this type of model decreased drastically, and shifted in favour of serial information processing models of cognition that made little or no connection with brain structure.

In the 1980s, however, there was a resurgence of interest in connectionist models, largely due to the discovery and popularisation of the "back-propagation" algorithm (LeCun, 1985; Parker, 1985; Rumelhart, Hinton, & Williams, 1986) for adjusting connection weights. This algorithm allowed for the development of multiple-layered (with input, output, and "hidden"

---

[2] The exclusive-or function has two inputs and one output. The network has to learn to output a 1 if only one input is on, and otherwise output a 0.

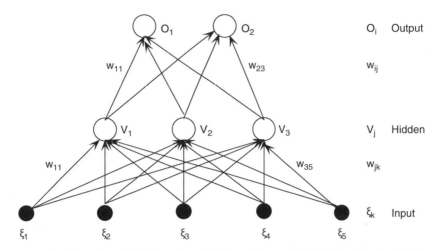

Figure 12.3.   A two-layer feed-forward artificial neural network (after Hertz, Krogh, & Palmer, 1991, p. 116). ξ = input unit; O = output unit; V = hidden unit; ω_{jk} = weight from input unit to hidden unit j; ω_{ij} = weight from hidden unit j to output unit i.

layers) connectionist networks by adjusting weights between all layers based on reinforcement at the output layer (Fig. 12.3). This allowed connectionist networks to solve all manner of problems, thereby rendering irrelevant Minsky and Papert's criticisms.

Backpropagation is a very powerful algorithm and has been used success-fully to model a large number of cognitive processes in humans and animals (Gluck & Myers, 1993; McClelland, McNaughton, & O'Reilly, 1995; Munakata, McClelland, Johnson, & Siegler, 1997; O'Reilly & McClelland, 1994; Schmajuk & DiCarlo, 1991). In fact, it could be argued that, since its discovery, backpropagation has been the standard approach to psychological modelling. Unfortunately, however, it does not seem to neurobiologists to be at all biologically plausible (see Rolls & Treves, 1997). In the backpropagation algorithm, the error for units in the hidden layers is calculated by the back-wards propagation of information based on the errors of all of the output neurons to which a hidden unit is connected. It is thought to be unlikely that the correct information to provide the appropriate error for each hidden unit is sent backwards like this between real neurons. Thus, it is desirable to explore more biologically plausible algorithms that use local learning rules in which connections are strengthened in relation only to correlations in firing between the pre- and the postsynaptic units. One learning rule that has enjoyed considerable support from neurobiological studies is Hebb's (1949) coincidence detection rule, outlined above.

Recently, models based on purely Hebbian principles have been applied to problems in cognitive neuroscience. One area in which significant progress has been made is that of perceptual learning. This is the focus of the present chapter. We first outline the phenomenon of perceptual learning. Next, we provide a basic introduction to a particular type of Hebbian connectionist modelling of learning and memory called competitive learning. Third, we discuss as examples two Hebbian models of different aspects of perceptual learning—a model of perceptual learning, and a model of the *failure* of perceptual learning—and discuss the implications that these models have for the cognitive neuroscience of learning, memory, and perception.

PERCEPTUAL LEARNING

Theoretical models of cognition usually address processes that are said to occur after the perceptual system has completed its work. According to such views, output from a putative perceptual system merely provides the initial information that is fodder for subsequent cognitive operations. This approach is common in the human cognitive psychology literature, in which a set of primitive elements usually forms the building blocks of cognition (Biederman, 1987; Julesz, 1981; Treisman & Gelade, 1980). Many researchers in associative animal learning theory have adopted a similar paradigm by assuming that any event that can be learned about will correspond to a static perceptual representation that is always fully activated in the presence of the stimulus. This division of behaviour into serial stages reflects the sense–think–act paradigm that is also common in the fields of artificial intelligence and robotics. The strength of this approach is that it separates the processes contributing to behaviour, thereby parsing a complex system into a form that may be more easily understood.

The assumptions upon which the above approach is based hold if perceptual representations are static. If perceptual organisation changes as a result of experience, however, this should have a direct impact on cognitive processes. For example, the discriminability of a stimulus could increase or decrease over time, leading to changes in the learning rate as learning proceeds.

An alternative to the sense–think–act approach is to assume that perceptual representations are not fixed or finite but adapt to the requirements of the task for which they are employed. Gibson, an early proponent of this view, suggested that the perceptual interpretation of an event depends on the observer's history, training, and acculturation (Gibson, 1969). No set of primitives exists because the perceptual building blocks themselves are adaptable. Rather than providing an immutable substrate for cognition, representations might instead adapt flexibly to the requirements of cognitive tasks. So, although cognitive processes involved in, for example, learning, might alter perception, the alteration is beneficial because, as a result, perception becomes better tuned to the task at hand.

A large body of data provides evidence for the idea that internal representations of stimuli can change simply as a result of experience (for a review see Hall, 1991). A classic example of this is given by William James (1890). On his or her first taste, a person might barely be able to distinguish a claret from a burgundy. After a few more experiences, the discrimination might still be uncertain, but eventually the person will be able readily to tell the difference between the two. A professional wine taster will be able to make even finer distinctions, and might even be able to identify the vintage or the vineyard. This phenomenon, called perceptual learning (PL), is often studied in the laboratory through a method in which animals are pre-exposed to different stimuli, and are then trained on a discrimination between them. It is often found that, whereas the ease of a discrimination between completely novel stimuli might depend initially only on their similarity, as experience is gained with the stimuli the ease of discrimination, as manifested in the rate of learning of the discrimination, increases.

Gibson and Walk (1956), in the original experimental demonstration of perceptual learning, exposed rats to black metal triangles and circles attached to the walls of their home cages. After some time, control subjects with no exposure and pre-exposed subjects were trained on a food-rewarded discrimination with triangles and circles as the relevant stimuli. The experimental group performed much better than the controls. Subsequent work has confirmed that pre-exposure can facilitate discrimination learning (Bennett & Ellis, 1968; Forgus, 1956; Kawachi, 1965).

A second experimental demonstration of perceptual learning, although not described as such at the time, involves a phenomenon called "transfer along a continuum". Lawrence (1952) found that rats trained from the outset on a discrimination between two stimuli lying close together on a brightness continuum learned this difficult discrimination rather slowly. A second group of rats that were initially trained on an easy task in which the stimuli differed greatly, and then were transferred to the difficult discrimination, learned the difficult discrimination much more quickly than the first group of rats. Lawrence's finding has proven to be robust, with a similar effect having been seen in species ranging from humans (Gonzalez & Ross, 1958; Hogg & Evans, 1975; May & MacPherson, 1971) to honeybees (Walker, Lee, & Bitterman, 1990).

Further evidence for perceptual learning comes from work done since the 1980s by Merzenich and colleagues (for a review see Merzenich, Recanzone, Jenkins, & Grajski, 1990a). In a series of experiments in which monkeys performed tactile discriminations (Allard, Clark, Jenkins, & Merzenich, 1991; Recanzone, Jenkins, Hradek, & Merzenich, 1992a; Recanzone, Merzenich, & Dinse, 1992b; Recanzone, Merzenich, & Jenkins, 1992c; Recanzone, Merzenich, Jenkins, Grajski, & Dinse, 1992d; Recanzone, Merzenich, & Schreiner, 1992e; Xerri, Merzenich, Jenkins, & Santucci, 1999;

Xerri, Merzenich, Peterson, & Jenkins, 1998) they demonstrated training-dependent changes in the discriminability of the stimuli. Furthermore, work from this laboratory has shown that these changes are almost certainly due to changes in the representation of the stimuli in the somatosensory cortex. These authors have defined some critical characteristics of these cortical changes. First, although the improvement in discrimination performance is for the most part specific, some learning apparently transfers to the surrounding skin. Second, there is an enlargement of the territory of representation of skin surfaces in somatosensory cortical areas. Finally, there is a decline in receptive field size that is inversely proportional to the increase in representational territory with training, suggesting that a more refined representation of trained stimuli develops. These changes are dependent on attention, and can return to normal when the behaviour is extinguished.

These authors have also explored the phenomenon of transfer along a continuum, specifically with respect to the development of therapies for children with language-based learning impairments (LLIs) (Tallal et al., 1996). These children present with deficits in recognition of some rapidly successive phonetic elements and non-speech sound stimuli. In a recent experiment, LLI children were engaged in adaptive training exercises designed to drive improvements in temporal processing according to the principle of transfer along a continuum: the interstimulus interval was first lengthened artificially and, as the children became better able to discriminate the phonemes, was then gradually reduced. Within 8 to 16h of training over a 20-day period LLI children improved markedly in their abilities to recognise brief and fast sequences of non-speech and speech stimuli.

We now describe a general connectionist model that provides a mechanism for how such perceptual learning might occur. Next, we describe two specific instantiations of this type of model. The first simulates perceptual learning and transfer along a continuum as observed in laboratory animals. The second simulates how language impairments in adults can develop as a result of failure of perceptual learning, and how these may be ameliorated through a training programme based on transfer along a continuum.

Modelling perceptual learning: Competitive learning and self-organising maps

A basic form of Hebbian neural network learning is called competitive learning (Grossberg, 1976a,b; Kohonen, 1982; Rumelhart & Zipser, 1986). In competitive learning networks, units are not arranged in layers as in the multilayer perceptron; instead all inputs connect to every node in the network (Fig. 12.4). Feedback is restricted to lateral interconnections to immediate neighbouring nodes. Also, there is no separate output layer—each of the units is itself an output node. In competitive learning, only one output unit is

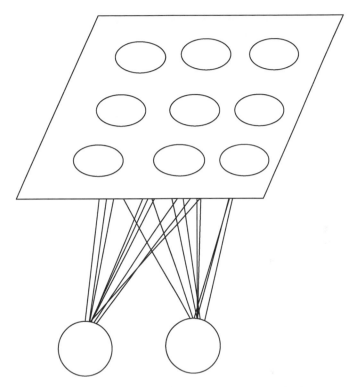

Figure 12.4. A Kohonen network. Note that there is only one layer of units, and that the input nodes are connected to all units.

allowed to fire at a time, thus the output units compete to be the unit that fires.

The objective of competitive learning networks is to categorise the input data. The idea is that similar inputs should be classified as being in the same category and so should fire the same output unit. As no desired output information is provided, the classes must be determined by the network itself from the statistical regularities in the input data.

A biologically motivated variant of the standard competitive learning network is the self-organising map developed by Kohonen (1982). Like a standard competitive learning network, the Kohonen network learns to categorise input pattern vectors, and the categories are formed based on the similarity of input vectors. The topographic map is autonomously organised by an iterative process of comparing input patterns to vectors "stored" at each node. Upon presentation of an input, the network chooses the closest matching stored vector and then increases the similarity of this vector, and those in the neighbouring proximity, to the input. Thus, from a randomly organised set of nodes the grid settles into a topographic map of the features.

A model of perceptual learning and transfer along a continuum

Saksida (1999) has presented a model of perceptual learning based on Kohonen's (1982) topographic mechanism. The model can explain numerous perceptual learning results from the animal learning literature, including the paradoxical result that pre-exposure can sometimes facilitate and can sometimes impair subsequent discrimination learning. In addition, the model can readily account for the phenomenon of transfer along a continuum.

Figure 12.5 illustrates the structure of the network. Inputs to the network consist of points in a two-dimensional stimulus space. Input of a stimulus to the network leads to a "sensation" consisting of the activation of a two-dimensional layer of input units. These input units feed into a

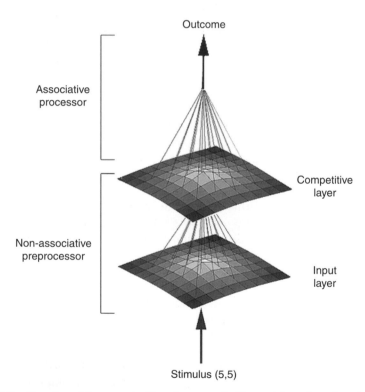

Figure 12.5. Overview of the perceptual learning network. The model consists of two layers of simple units: the input layer and the competitive layer. The input layer is fully connected to the competitive layer via a set of weights that are adjusted by a non-associative (i.e. unsupervised) learning mechanism. The competitive layer is fully connected to a node representing the outcome of the presentation of a stimulus to the network (e.g. response or reinforcer). These weights are adjusted via an associative mechanism.

two-dimensional layer of competitive units, the activation of which comprises a "perception" of the stimulus.

The network can be thought of as consisting of two sections: (1) a non-associative preprocessor comprising the mechanisms that operate on the weights between the input layer and the competitive layer; and (2) an associative processor, comprising the mechanisms that operate on the weights between the competitive layer and the outcome representation. The non-associative preprocessor provides the mechanism for perceptual learning, thus we focus on that part of the model here. The associative processor allows representations to be associated with reinforcement, thereby allowing the network to learn reinforced discriminations.

The non-associative preprocessor consists of two layers of simple units: the input layer and the competitive layer. The input layer is fully connected to the competitive layer via a set of weights that are adjusted by a non-associative learning mechanism. Activation of units in the input layer represents initial processing of an external stimulus and is thus representative of a sensation (e.g. stimulation of the retina). Activation of units in the competitive layer, on the other hand, is reflective of the changeable representation of the stimulus.

A stimulus is represented as a pair of numbers, each of which represents the value of the stimulus on one aspect of a dimension. In this version of the model, stimuli are assumed to be unidimensional. Thus, for a given rectangular stimulus $S = <x,y>$, x might represent the length of the rectangle and y might represent its width. In this case, the dimension represented by the network would be "size". An alternative dimension might be "colour", in which x represents hue and y represents saturation.

On a training trial, the x and y values of a stimulus are fed into the network. This leads to a pattern of activation on the input layer I as follows. The input layer consists of a square set of simple units, with the range of the units being greater than the maximum x or y value of any stimulus that might be presented. Each unit i has a corresponding activation that ranges between 0 and 1. The activation of all units in the input layer is initially zero. When a stimulus $S = <x,y>$ is presented, however, the unit in the input layer whose co-ordinates correspond to the x and y values of S becomes maximally activated (i.e. its activation level is shifted from 0 to 1). This unit affects nearby units such that those that are within a certain radius of the unit will also be activated proportionally to their distance from it. This means that the degree of generalisation between two stimuli can be deduced from either the amount of overlap in their respective input layer activations or by calculating the Euclidean distance between them. For example, two similar stimuli might be represented as $S_1 = <2,2>$ and $S_2 = <3,5>$ whereas two different stimuli would be represented as $S_3 = <2,2>$ and $S_4 = <8,8>$. Note that stimulus representations do not "wrap" around the edges of the grid, meaning that on a 10 by 10 unit grid, <10,10> is the furthest unit from <1,1>.

The weights on the links between the input layer and the competitive layer are at the heart of the Hebbian learning mechanism that contributes to perceptual learning. Each time a stimulus is presented, the weights (w^*) of the winner are adjusted such that they are a bit closer to the pattern of activation on the input layer. Over time, the w^* become closer and closer to the input layer activation pattern a, thus the competitive unit weights of the winner become a better representation of the stimulus.

In addition to the winner, the w_k corresponding to a set of nearby units are also updated in proportion to their proximity to the winner. The result is that after training is complete, nearby competitive units respond to nearby input patterns. The effect of this is to create regions of the competitive layer that code for similar representations, that is, those with common features.

As a result of this competitive mechanism, the discriminability of a stimulus tends to increase with exposure (perceptual learning). To illustrate, consider two similar input stimuli (e.g. S_1 and S_2). Such stimuli are usually captured by topographically close competitive units (e.g. c_1 captures S_1 and c_2 captures S_2), which means that the two winning units will tend to be in each other's neighbourhoods (see Fig. 12.6A). The closer that S_1 and S_2 are, the more activated c_1 will be when S_2 is shown. As a result, when S_1 and S_2 are repeatedly presented, a competition ensues in which each of the competitive units, when its corresponding input stimulus is delivered, moves its weight vector as well as the other winner's weight vector toward the value of the stimulus. That is, when S_1 is presented, c_1 moves both itself and c_2 toward S_1. When S_2 is next presented, c_2 moves itself and c_1 toward S_2. While this is happening, the other competitive units in the winner's neighbourhood are moved as well, proportionally to their distance from the winners. If they fall into both winner's neighbourhoods, then they are moved back and forth between S_1 and S_2 as well. However, a unit c_3 which is in the neighbourhood of c_2 but not in the neighbourhood of c_1 will be affected only when c_2 wins. Over time, because c_2 is pulled toward S_1 but c_3 is not, c_3 develops a better representation of S_2 and wins over c_2 when S_2 is presented (Fig. 12.6B). This means that the new winning units, c_1 and c_3 are more separated on the competitive grid thus there is less overlap in their distributions of activation. Over time, as the above process continues, the two winning units become more and more separated on the competitive grid, thus lessening their effect on each other and facilitating discrimination by lessening generalisation. As this happens, the area around the winning units becomes tuned toward the two input stimuli, that is, the weight vectors of many units are moved in the direction of the stimuli.

In essence, the mechanism outlined above results in an expansion of the area of the competitive layer that is devoted to the stimuli being

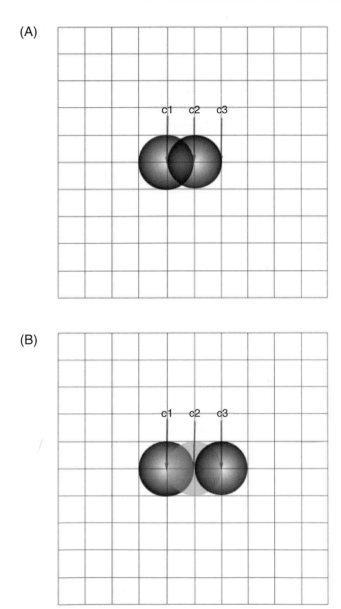

Figure 12.6. (A) Initial activation of the competitive layer after presentation of two similar stimuli, S_1 and S_2. The winning unit for S_1 is c_1 and the winning unit for S_2 is c_2. There is considerable overlap in the areas of activation triggered by each winner. Note that unit c_3 is in the neighbourhood of c_2 but not c_1, and so is affected only by c_2. (B) After continued exposure to the stimuli c_3 becomes the new winner because c_2 is in the neighbourhood of c_1 and therefore its weights are shifted towards c_1 when S_1 is presented. Because c_3 is not affected by the position of S_1 and its weights, it eventually become a more accurate representation of S_2.

discriminated. This corresponds well with electrophysiological work from Merzenich and colleagues, mentioned earlier, that shows that an increase in the amount of cortical space devoted to the discriminanda occurs with discrimination training (Jenkins et al., 1990; Merzenich et al., 1990a).

The above mechanism provides a way in which similar stimuli can eventually be discriminated. If the input stimuli are very different, however, separate competitive units will win from the start, so little perceptual learning will be seen. Indeed, in cases like this, pre-exposure often leads to a decrement in the subsequent rate of discrimination learning. This effect is called "latent inhibition", and it also occurs in the current model following pre-exposure to easily discriminable stimuli (see Saksida, 1999).

Application to transfer along a continuum. The phenomenon of transfer along a continuum, in which training on a simple discrimination facilitates acquisition of a more difficult discrimination, is captured in a straightforward manner by the current model. The topographical organisation of the competitive layer, along with the fact that neighbours of winning units are updated proportionally to their distance from the winner, leads the model to the following prediction: exposure to a pair of similar stimuli will facilitate not only discrimination between the exposed pair, but also discrimination between stimuli that are even more similar. This is because two stimuli that are not easily discriminable will initially be represented as nearby winning units in the competitive layer. As the stimuli are presented to the network, the winning units will be pulled apart and each of the units between them will become tuned toward the stimulus to which it is closest. This tuning of intermediate units suggests that pre-exposure to two stimuli will facilitate discrimination of other stimuli whose representations fall between them on the competitive layer.

In a simulation of this phenomenon, two groups of 25 networks each, group Transfer and group Control, were initialised. Group Control was trained for 10 blocks of 50 trials each on a very difficult discrimination between two stimulus pairs, A = <5,5> versus B = <5,5.25>. Group Transfer was trained on a simpler version of the same problem (X = <5,4.5> versus Y = <5,5.75>) for two blocks of 50 trials and was then shifted to the same problem as group Control (A = <5,5> versus B = <5,5.25>) for 8 blocks of 50 trials each. Thus each group experienced the same total number of training trials.

Figure 12.7 shows learning curves for both group Control and group Transfer, averaged over 25 training runs. Clearly, group Transfer was able to learn the discrimination more quickly than group Control. This confirms that the model predicts an advantage in learning if the networks are initially trained on a simpler version of a discrimination between two very similar patterns.

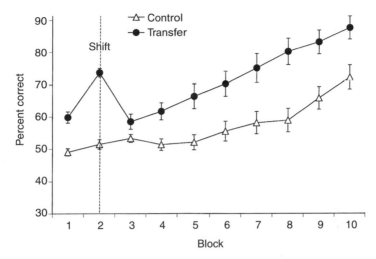

Figure 12.7.   Effect of transfer on a difficult discrimination: learning curves for a discrimination between very similar patterns (A = <5,5> versus B = <5,5.25>). Group Transfer was trained on a simpler version of the discrimination for one block, whereas Group Control was trained on the difficult discrimination from the start. Although the groups were trained for the same total number of trials, Group Transfer acquired the discrimination more quickly.

The reason that the model produces this behaviour is as follows. Group Control was trained on the difficult discrimination from the start. As a result, the patterns were initially categorised as being the same because they activated the same winning competitive unit. Due to the competitive updating, the winning units eventually separated at around Block 5, at which point the discrimination performance reached levels significantly above chance. Around Block 8, the winners separated further, leading to an increase in the rate of learning of the discrimination as a result of reduced overlap between associative links. Group Transfer, on the other hand, was initially trained on a discrimination in which the patterns were further separated than those in the target discrimination. The networks were able immediately to separate on the competitive layer the patterns of the initial discrimination, and thus began learning the discrimination quickly. When they were shifted to the more difficult discrimination, separate units on the competitive layer won for the two stimuli because of changes in the competitive layer that had occurred as a result of the initial discrimination. Thus group Transfer learned the difficult discrimination much more quickly than group Control.

An alternative to the foregoing "non-associative" account is that transfer along a continuum is due merely to associative transfer (see Logan, 1966). In other words, it could be the case that the improvement in the transfer group in Lawrence (1952) was not due to an improvement in perceptual distinction between the stimuli, but to the fact that during the initial, simpler discrimination the animal built up an association between the S+ and reinforcement, and this transferred to the S+ in the more difficult discrimination.

Evidence against such a view, however, has been reported by Mackintosh and Little (Mackintosh & Little, 1970). In this study, pigeons were trained on an easy wavelength discrimination prior to a more difficult one, but the values of the stimuli (positive or negative) were reversed between training phases. That is, if the longer of the two wavelengths was rewarded during the initial training phase, then in the subsequent phase the shorter wavelength was rewarded. The authors demonstrated that subjects given reversed pretraining were initially worse on the difficult discrimination task, but they eventually overtook the group that was trained only on the hard task.

Associative accounts of perceptual learning that rely on transfer of associative strength to explain transfer along a continuum (McLaren, Kaye, & Mackintosh, 1989; McLaren & Suret, 2000) cannot account for these data. The current model, on the other hand, suggests that this result follows directly from an account of perceptual learning in which stimulus representations become more differentiated as a result of pretraining. Specifically, the pretrained group will benefit from the tuning and separation of the competitive units, but at the same time will suffer from generalisation of associative strength between the new and the pretrained winners. These two effects will counteract each other and the behaviour observed will depend on the relative strength of each of them. Thus, as the winning units become more separated, generalisation of associative strength between them will decrease and performance will improve. This property, combined with the advantage of extra separation between the new winners gained during pretraining, is sufficient for the current model to reproduce the pattern of data observed by Mackintosh and Little (1970).

In a simulation of this effect, two groups of 25 networks each, group Reversed Transfer and group Control, were initialised. Group Control was trained for 10 blocks of 50 trials each on a difficult discrimination with <5,5> as the S+ and <5,5.25> as the S–. Group Reversed Transfer was trained on an easier version of the same problem with S+ and S– reversed (<5.75,5> as the S+ and <5,4.5> as the S–) for two blocks of 50 trials. In other words, the stimulus in the easy discrimination that was most similar to the S+ in the difficult discrimination was not reinforced whereas the stimulus in the easy discrimination that was most similar to the S– in the difficult discrimination was reinforced. The Reversed Transfer group was then shifted to the same problem as group Control (S+ = <5,5> versus S– = <5,5.25>) for 8 blocks of 50 trials each. Thus each group experienced the same total number of discrimination learning trials.

Figure 12.8 shows learning curves for both group Control and group Reversed Transfer, averaged over 25 training runs. Group Reversed Transfer

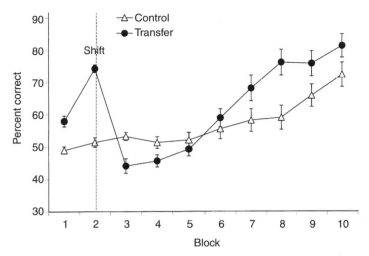

Figure 12.8.   Effect of reversed transfer on a difficult discrimination: learning curves for a discrimination between very similar patterns (A = <5,5> versus B = <5,5.25>). Group Reversed Transfer was trained on a simpler version of the discrimination, with the S+ and S– reversed as compared to the final discrimination, for one block. Group Control was trained on the difficult discrimination for the entire session. Although the groups were trained for the same total number of trials, and associative transfer for group Reversed Transfer impeded learning of the final discrimination for several blocks, overall, Group Reversed Transfer acquired the discrimination more quickly.

demonstrated a severe drop in performance when the final difficult discrimination was introduced at the beginning of Block 3. Because the S+ and S– were reversed in the initial discrimination relative to the S+ and S– in the final discrimination, associative transfer worked against group Reversed Transfer, resulting in worse performance of the transfer group relative to controls during blocks 3 to 5. However, because of the changes made in the competitive layer as a result of training on the initial discrimination, networks in group Reversed Transfer were able to learn the new associations more quickly and so overtook controls and overall were able to learn the discrimination more quickly.

As in the previous simulation of standard transfer along a continuum, group Reversed Transfer was able immediately to separate on the competitive layer the patterns of the initial discrimination, and thus began learning the discrimination quickly. When they were shifted to the more difficult discrimination, separate units on the competitive layer won for the two stimuli as a result of changes in the competitive layer that had occurred during the initial discrimination. Thus, changes in the competitive layer facilitated discrimination of the stimuli. At the same time, however, the S+ had developed negative links with reinforcement whereas the S– had developed positive associative links. This negative associative transfer initially caused the

Reversed Transfer networks to perform worse on the difficult discrimination than controls. However, the advantage gained through further separation on the competitive layer of the stimulus representations outweighed the negative influence of associative transfer, and the Reversed Transfer networks out-performed controls in the long run. This pattern of data, with the reversed transfer group showing an initial decrease in discrimination followed by superior learning performance as compared to controls, mirrors the results found by Mackintosh and Little (1970).

Summary. In this section we described a Hebbian model of perceptual learning. In the model, if two input stimuli are very similar then they will tend to be captured by nearby units on the competitive layer. With more input samples, however, the perceptual learning mechanism causes better separated units eventually to win out over the original winners. This results in the stimulus representations on the competitive layer being pushed apart; as a result pre-exposure will provide an advantage on a subsequent discrimination learning task. The model accounts for several important phenomena reported in the learning literature, and is consistent with cortical neuronal changes thought to underlie perceptual learning (Merzenich, Recanzone, Jenkins, & Grajski, 1990b). In the next section, we describe a similar Hebbian model that provides insights into *failures* of perceptual learning.

A competitive Hebbian model of failure of perceptual learning

When Japanese adults move to an English-speaking country, they often have difficulty discriminating /r/ and /l/. There is evidence that this can improve over time, but this improvement tends to be gradual and difficulties often persist indefinitely. At the same time, it is not difficult for adults to learn new information and skills. So why is it that perceptual discriminations between sounds not differentiated in one's native language are so difficult to acquire?

In this section, we consider a model that explains this difficulty on the basis of the Hebbian learning rule. As mentioned earlier, Hebb (1949) suggested that if one neuron takes part in firing another, the strength of the connection between them will be increased. The logical extension of this principle is that if an input elicits a pattern across many neurons, Hebbian learning will strengthen the tendency to elicit the same pattern of activity on subsequent occasions. Thus, if the mechanism underlying learning is Hebbian, learning will tend to cause the brain to strengthen whatever response it is that the brain makes to specific inputs. Although this mechanism works well for "stamping in" responses in consistent situations, one unfortunate consequence is that if the situation changes it does not distinguish between adaptive responses and responses that have become maladaptive. This leads to the possibility that failures of learning in adulthood might reflect a tendency of Hebbian mechanisms of learning to reinforce formerly appropriate, but now inappropriate, responses.

To explore the failure of Japanese adults to learn to discriminate between /r/ and /l/, McClelland and colleagues (McClelland, Thomas, McCandliss, & Fiez, 1999) constructed a Hebbian model of perceptual learning. The model illustrates how a Hebbian learning mechanism could lead to the failure to learn to discriminate two similar inputs once that ability had been lost because of extensive pretrainng in an environment providing only a single input in that region of perceptual space.

The model is a variant of the standard Kohonen architecture, very similar to that outlined in the previous section. It consists of two layers, each with 49 units arranged in a 7 × 7 array. The first layer is referred to as the "input" layer and the second is called the "representation" layer. Initially, connections between the layers consist of random feed-forward projections that are loosely topographic. When an input is presented, the representation unit receiving the strongest net input is chosen as the winning unit and it and its neighbours are assigned activation values equal to a Gaussian function of the distance from winner. Weights coming into the representation units are then adjusted according to a competitive learning rule.

In a simulation of the failure of perceptual learning, inputs consisted of Gaussian distributions of activity. Two training conditions were used; in both there were four corner inputs occupying the four corners of input space and corresponding to background phonemes.

Training condition 1—English-like. In this condition, two additional overlapping inputs were presented to the network, simulating /r/ and /l/. Given these six inputs, more than 90 per cent of trained networks learned to assign distinct representations to the two overlapping stimuli. This simulation represents the performance of children reared in English speaking countries, who have no previous experience with language, learning to distinguish between /r/ and /l/.

Training condition 2—Japanese-like. In this condition, initially just the four corner inputs and only one other, input (centred between the two overlapping inputs used in condition 1) were presented to the network. Following training, the networks were switched from condition 2 to condition 1 (Japanese-like to English-like). All networks learned to assign a single representation to the Japanese-like centred input, and none subsequently learned to assign different representations to the two overlapping English-like inputs. These networks retained the tendency to treat these inputs the same even though the same mechanisms of plasticity as in the first condition operated without any changes throughout the simulation.

These simulations support the idea that discriminations that can be learned if a distinction is present in a network's original environment might not be learned when distinction is not introduced until after the network's response tendencies are established. This process could account for the loss of plasticity seen in Japanese who learn English as adults.

If these mechanisms do underlie the above example of the failure of perceptual learning, they predict that plasticity could be induced in Japanese adults through the method of transfer along a continuum. Indeed, support for this idea comes from the remediation training studies of Merzenich, Tallal, and colleagues, mentioned earlier (Merzenich et al., 1996; Tallal et al., 1996). To illustrate this idea, McClelland and colleagues added two extra inputs—exaggerated versions of /r/ and /l/—to the English-like environment. Networks that failed to learn to discriminate /r/ and /l/ in the Japanese pretraining condition learned to discriminate these stimuli in only a few epochs after the exaggerated stimuli were included in the training set.

To test the above prediction, McCandliss and colleagues (McCandliss et al., in press) then tested whether this method would ameliorate recognition of /r/ and /l/ in Japanese adults. The authors developed a set of two speech continua, one spanning from the word "rock" to "lock" and a second spanning from "road" to "load". Starting with natural speech tokens generated by native English speakers, 80-item continua were constructed. Each ranged from highly exaggerated tokens of lock or load to highly exaggerated tokens of rock or road. University of Pittsburgh undergraduates categorised the stimuli on each continuum; in each case only 10 steps on the continuum lay in a "grey zone" where they were indistinguishable.

Next, subjects whose initial discrimination ability between /r/ and /l/ was poor were tested in an adaptive (transfer) condition. Each subject was trained on one of the two continua with highly exaggerated tokens near the extreme ends of the continuum. The two selected stimuli were presented in random order and the subject was required to press one button if the stimulus began with /r/ and another if it began with /l/. Whenever a subject made an error, the task was made easier by replacing the stimulus with the next more exaggerated one, until the extremes of the continuum were reached. When a subject was correct on eight trials in a row, the task was made easier. Half of the subjects received feedback after each trial and half did not. All subjects showed substantial improvement within three 20-min sessions, and all showed great improvement in post-training as compared to pretraining performance.

Two further groups of subjects were selected by the same criteria as discussed earlier for participation in the (no transfer) training condition, with or without feedback. The conditions were identical to the adaptive condition, with the exception that these subjects were presented with /r/ and /l/ stimuli just at the edge of the native English speaker grey zone, which was highly confusing to Japanese subjects. The subjects who received these stimuli without feedback failed to show any benefit from the training (compared to a control group that received no training at all). This is consistent with expectations based on Hebbian learning: if the stimuli elicit the same perceptual representation, Hebbian learning might simply reinforce this tendency, resulting in a failure to progress.

The four subjects in the feedback condition, on the other hand, were all able to learn the discrimination. This suggests that there is some sort of interaction between associative (reinforcement-based) and non-associative (Hebbian) learning mechanisms in the brain. A hybrid model that incorporates both types of mechanism, such as the model discussed earlier (Saksida, 1999), could yield insights into how these different mechanisms might work together.

For the most part, it was very easy for the subjects to learn in this experiment: only the subjects receiving highly confusable stimuli without feedback failed to learn. If /r/–/l/ discrimination learning is this easy, why, then, is it so difficult for Japanese adults in real life? A possible explanation is that in the model patterns compete for space, and the outcome of this competition depends on the similarity and frequency of presentation of the stimuli. Under natural conditions, /r/ and /l/ must compete for space with many other inputs. However, if training is focused in isolation on overlapping stimuli, the model will learn to separate them. As a result, subjects who had some ability to discriminate the stimuli from the start capitalised on this and learned rapidly, whereas subjects who were unable to discriminate the stimuli at all did not.

CONCLUSION

We began this chapter by summarising the history of connectionist modelling, arguing that a critical next step will involve an exploration of models that do not rely on non-local learning rules such as backpropagation. We then outlined the process of Hebbian learning, and discussed the instantiation of this rule in the form of self-organising connectionist models. Finally, we provided two examples of Hebbian, competitive models that can account for a large number of behavioural results involving the phenomenon of perceptual learning in animals and humans. These examples show how very simple connectionist models can have powerful explanatory and predictive power. Furthermore, they illustrate how impressive feats of learning and memory can be accomplished without recourse to biologically implausible mechanisms such as backpropagation, instead using local learning rules, which more closely match the properties of real neurons, in real brains.

REFERENCES

Allard, T., Clark, S.A., Jenkins, W.M., & Merzenich, M.M. (1991). Reorganization of somato-sensory area 3b representations in adult owl monkeys after digital syndactyly. *Journal of Neurophysiology, 66*(3), 1048–1058.

Bennett, T.L., & Ellis, H.C. (1968). Tactual-kinesthetic feedback from manipulation of visual forms and nondifferential reinforcement in transfer of perceptual learning. *Journal of Experimental Psychology, 77*, 495–500.

Biederman, I. (1987). Recognition-by-components: A theory of human image understanding. *Psychological Review, 94*, 115–147.

Churchland, P.S., & Sejnowski, T.J. (1992). *The computational brain*. Cambridge, MA: MIT Press.

Forgus, R.H. (1956). Advantage of early over late perceptual experience in improving discrimination. *Canadian Journal of Psychology, 10*, 147–155.

Gibson, E.J. (1969). *Principles of perceptual learning and development*. New York: Appleton-Century Crofts.

Gibson, E.J., & Walk, R.D. (1956). The effect of prolonged exposure to visually presented patterns on learning to discriminate them. *Journal of Comparative and Physiological Psychology, 49*, 239–242.

Gluck, M.A., & Myers, C.E. (1993). Hippocampal mediation of stimulus representation: A computational theory. *Hippocampus, 3*, 491–516.

Gonzalez, R.C., & Ross, S. (1958). The basis of solution by preverbal children of the intermediate-size problem. *American Journal of Psychology, 71*, 742–746.

Grossberg, S. (1976a). Adaptive pattern classification and universal recoding: I. Parallel development and coding of neural feature detectors. *Biological Cybernetics, 23*, 121–134.

Grossberg, S. (1976b). Adaptive pattern classification and universal recoding: II. Feedback, expectation, olfaction, illusions. *Biological Cybernetics, 23*, 187–202.

Hall, G. (1991). *Perceptual and associative learning*. Oxford: Clarendon Press.

Hebb, D.O. (1949). *The organization of behavior*. New York: Wiley.

Hertz, J., Krogh, A., & Palmer, R.G. (1991). *Introduction to the theory of neural computation* (Vol. I). Redwood City, CA: Addison-Wesley.

Hodgkin, A.L., & Huxley, A.F. (1952). A quantitative description of membrane current and its application to conduction and excitation in nerve. *Journal of Physiology (London), 117*, 500–544.

Hogg, J., & Evans, P.L. (1975). Stimulus generalization following extra-dimensional training in educationally subnormal (severely) children. *British Journal of Psychology, 66*(2), 211–224.

Hull, C. (1943). *Principles of behaviour*. New York: Appleton-Century-Crofts.

James, W. (1890). *The principles of psychology*. New York: Holt.

Jenkins, W.M., Merzenich, M.M., Ochs, M., Allard, T., & Guic-Robles, E. (1990). Functional reorganization of primary somatosensory cortex in adult owl monkeys after behaviorally controlled tactile stimulation. *Journal of Neurophysiology, 63*, 82–104.

Julesz, B. (1981). Textons, the elements of texture perception, and their interaction. *Nature, 290*, 91–97.

Kawachi, J. (1965). Effects of previous perceptual experience of specific three-dimensional objects on later visual discrimination behavior in rats. *Japanese Journal of Psychological Research, 7*, 20–27.

Kohonen, T. (1982). *Clustering taxonomy and topological maps of patterns*. Paper presented at the Sixth International Conference on Pattern Recognition, Silver Springs, MD.

Lawrence, D.H. (1952). The transfer of a discrimination along a continuum. *Journal of Comparative and Physiological Psychology, 45*, 511–516.

LeCun, Y. (1985). *Une procedure d'apprentissage pour reseau a seuil assymetruqie.* Paper presented at the Cognitiva 85, Paris.

Logan, F.A. (1966). Transfer of discrimination. *Journal of Experimental Psychology, 71*(4), 616–618.

Mackintosh, N.J., & Little, L. (1970). An analysis of transfer along a continuum. *Canadian Journal of Psychology, 24*(5), 362–369.

May, R.B., & MacPherson, D.F. (1971). Size discrimination in children facilitated by changes in task difficulty. *Journal of Comparative and Physiological Psychology, 75*(3), 453–458.

McCandliss, B.D., Fiez, J.A., Protopapas, A., Conway, M., & McClelland, J.L. (in press). Success and failure in teaching the [r]-[l] contrast to Japanese adults: Predictions of a Hebbian model of plasticity and stabilization in spoken language perception. *Cognitive, Affective, and Behavioral Neuroscience.*

McClelland, J.L., McNaughton, B.L., & O'Reilly, R.C. (1995). Why there are complementary learning systems in the hippocampus and neocortex: Insights from the successes and failures of connectionist models of learning and memory. *Psychological Review, 102,* 419–457.

McClelland, J.L., Thomas, A.G., McCandliss, B.D., & Fiez, J.A. (1999). Understanding failures of learning: Hebbian learning, competition for representational space, and some preliminary experimental data. *Progress in Brain Research, 121,* 75–80.

McCulloch, W.S., & Pitts, W. (1943). A logical calculus of ideas immanent in nervous activity. *Bulletin of Mathematical Biophysics, 5,* 115–133.

McLaren, I.P.L., Kaye, H., & Mackintosh, N.J. (1989). An associative theory of the representation of stimuli: Applications to perceptual learning and latent inhibition. In R.G.M. Morris (Ed.) *Parallel distributed processing: Implications for psychology and neurobiology* (pp. 102–130). Oxford: Clarendon Press.

McLaren, I.P.L., & Suret, M. (2000). Transfer along a continuum: Differentiation or association? In L.R. Gleitman & A.K. Joshi (Eds.) *Proceedings of the Twenty-Second Annual Conference of the Cognitive Science Society* (pp. 994–999). Mahwah, NJ: Lawrence Erlbaum Associates Inc.

Merzenich, M.M., Jenkins, W.M., Johnston, P., Schreiner, C., Miller, S.L., & Tallal, P. (1996). Temporal processing deficits of language-learning impaired children ameliorated by training. *Science, 271*(5245), 77–81.

Merzenich, M.M., Recanzone, G.H., Jenkins, W.M., & Grajski, K.A. (1990a). Adaptive mechanisms in cortical networks underlying cortical contributions to learning and nondeclarative memory. *Cold Spring Harbor Symposia on Quantitative Biology, 55,* 873–886.

Merzenich, M.M., Recanzone, G.H., Jenkins, W.M., & Grajski, K.A. (1990b). Adaptive mechanisms in cortical networks underlying cortical contributions to learning and nondeclarative memory. *Cold Spring Harbor Symposia on Quantative Biology, 55,* 873–887.

Minsky, M.L., & Papert, S. (1969). *Perceptrons: An introduction to computational geometry.* Cambridge, MA: MIT Press.

Munakata, Y., McClelland, J.L., Johnson, M.H., & Siegler, R.S. (1997). Rethinking infant knowledge: Toward an adaptive process account of successes and failures in object permanence tasks. *Psychological Review, 104*(4), 686–713.

O'Reilly, R.C., & McClelland, J.L. (1994). Hippocampal conjunctive encoding, storage, and recall: Avoiding a trade-off. *Hippocampus, 4*(6), 661–682.

Parker, D.B. (1985). *Learning-logic* (TR-47). Cambridge, MA: Massachusetts Institute of Technology.

Recanzone, G.H., Jenkins, W.M., Hradek, G.T., & Merzenich, M.M. (1992a). Progressive improvement in discriminative abilities in adult owl monkeys performing a tactile frequency discrimination task. *Journal of Neurophysiology, 67*(5), 1015–1030.

Recanzone, G.H., Merzenich, M.M., & Dinse, H.R. (1992b). Expansion of the cortical representation of a specific skin field in primary somatosensory cortex by intracortical microstimulation. *Cerebral Cortex*, *2*(3), 181–196.

Recanzone, G.H., Merzenich, M.M., & Jenkins, W.M. (1992c). Frequency discrimination training engaging a restricted skin surface results in an emergence of a cutaneous response zone in cortical area 3a. *Journal of Neurophysiology*, *67*(5), 1057–1070.

Recanzone, G.H., Merzenich, M.M., Jenkins, W.M., Grajski, K.A., & Dinse, H.R. (1992d). Topographic reorganization of the hand representation in cortical area 3b owl monkeys trained in a frequency-discrimination task. *Journal of Neurophysiology*, *67*(5), 1031–1056.

Recanzone, G.H., Merzenich, M.M., & Schreiner, C.E. (1992e). Changes in the distributed temporal response properties of SI cortical neurons reflect improvements in performance on a temporally based tactile discrimination task. *Journal of Neurophysiology*, *67*(5), 1071–1091.

Rescorla, R.A., & Wagner, A.R. (1972). A theory of Pavlovian conditioning: Variations in the effectiveness of reinforcement and nonreinforcement. In A.H. Black & W.F. Prokasy (Eds.) *Classical conditioning II: Current research and theory* (pp. 64–99). New York: Appleton Century Crofts.

Rolls, E., & Treves, A. (1997). *Neural networks and brain function*. Oxford: Oxford University Press.

Rosenblatt, F. (1962). *Principles of neurodynamics*. Washington, DC: Spartan Books.

Rumelhart, D.E., Hinton, G.E., & Williams, R.J. (1986). Learning internal representations by back-propagating errors. In D.E. Rumelhart & J.L. McClelland (Eds.) *Parallel distributed processing* (Vol. 1, pp. 318–362). Cambridge MA: MIT Press.

Rumelhart, D.E., & Zipser, D. (1986). Feature discovery by competitive learning. In D.E. Rumelhart & J.L. McClelland (Eds.) *Parallel distributed processing* (Vol. 1, pp. 151–193). Cambridge, MA: MIT Press.

Saksida, L.M. (1999). Effects of similarity and experience on discrimination learning: A nonassociative connectionist model of perceptual learning. *Journal of Experimental Psychology: Animal Behavior Processes*, *25*, 308–323.

Schmajuk, N.A., & DiCarlo, J.J. (1991). A neural network approach to hippocampal function in classical conditioning. *Behavioral Neuroscience*, *105*, 82–110.

Selfridge, O.G. (1959). *PANDEMONIUM: A paradigm for learning*. Paper presented at the Symposium on the Mechanisation of Thought Processes, National Physics Laboratory, London.

Selverston, A.I., Russell, D.F., & Miller, J.P. (1976). The stomatogastric nervous system: structure and function of a small neural network. *Progress in Neurobiology*, *7*(3), 215–290.

Tallal, P., Miller, S.L., Bedi, G., Byma, G., Wang, X., Nagarajan, S.S., Schreiner, C., Jenkins, W.M., & Merzenich, M.M. (1996). Language comprehension in language-learning impaired children improved with acoustically modified speech. *Science*, *271*(5245), 81–84.

Treisman, A., & Gelade, G. (1980). A feature-integration theory of attention. *Cognitive Psychology*, *12*, 97–136.

Walker, M.M., Lee, Y., & Bitterman, M.E. (1990). Transfer along a continuum in the discriminative learning of honeybees (*Apis mellifera*). *Journal of Comparative Psychology*, *104*(1), 66–70.

Widrow, B., & Hoff, M.E. (1960). *Adaptive switching circuits* (Stanford Electronics Laboratories Technical Report 1553–1). Stanford, CA: Stanford University.

Xerri, C., Merzenich, M.M., Jenkins, W., & Santucci, S. (1999). Representational plasticity in cortical area 3b paralleling tactual motor skill acquisition in adult monkeys. *Cerebral Cortex*, *9*(3), 264–276.

Xerri, C., Merzenich, M.M., Peterson, B.E., & Jenkins, W. (1998). Plasticity of primary somatosensory cortex paralleling sensorimotor skill recovery from stroke in adult monkeys. *Journal of Neurophysiology*, *79*(4), 2119–2148.

CHAPTER THIRTEEN

CHARM²: A multimodular model of human memory

Janet Metcalfe
Columbia University, New York, USA

INTRODUCTION

Results emerging from the cognitive neurosciences are converging on a semi-modular neo-Kantian perspective: different areas of the brain have different functions, and deal with different kinds of information—sometimes exclusively, sometimes only preferentially—and they also transform the information in their care in different manners, so influencing the person's consciousness. The Kantian view—that the mind/brain imposes its own organisation and so alters and limits what the person can perceive and remember—has been multiplied to apply to each separate semimodular sub-system, which emphasises the modalities, features, combinations, and peculiarities for which it has an affinity, and mostly ignores the preferences of the other regions of the brain, except insofar as they alter its input. In contrast to the surely too-simple hope that there would be one universal learning mechanism that would apply throughout the brain and would explain everything, the mind/brain seems to be a Tower of Babel, with some modules speaking Fourier transform, others lateral inhibition, some convolution, or correlation or some other complex learning rule, others spreading activation, still others only summation.

The multimodular view started with research on split-brain patients show-ing that the two hemispheres might disagree with one another (Gazzaniga, 1998; Gazzaniga, Bogen, & Sperry, 1962). In these patients, the right hemi-sphere has what appears to be different thoughts, memories, and reactions from those of the left even in the face of the identical afferent stimuli (Metcalfe, Funnell, & Gazzaniga, 1995; Phelps & Gazzaniga, 1992), and an objectively near-identical past. For example, we (Metcalfe et al., 1995) gave a split-brain patient, J.W. (who has a sizeable vocabulary in both hemispheres) a series of words that were members of a particular category, such as PLUM, BANANA, PEACH, and PEAR, to study freely with both hemispheres. Then we tested the hemispheres separately for what they remembered. Both hemispheres were able to correctly identify the presented items, and to correctly reject unrelated lures. However, when we probed with unpresented category members, such as APPLE, the left hemisphere said "yes" and the right hemisphere said "no". The same finding was observed when we gave categorically related random dot patterns as the to-be-learned stimuli, and tested with unpresented prototypes that were the central tendency of the presented exemplars: the left hemisphere thought that it had seen the prototype; the right hemisphere did not. It seems very clear that the two large and highly complicated systems delineated by the two hemispheres process the same information in a different manner, with cognitive consequences.

The view that there are two minds within one skull has multiplied itself into a *multi*component view. As Kinsbourne (1994) noted, dividing the brain along the corpus callosum is arbitrary (except for the fact that the particular projection is so clear and obvious). The brain could be divided into many different functional areas, with each giving its own view of the events that impinged upon it. Presumably, each of these different semimodules, with its own special processing functions, competes for its voice to be heard. One could ask where this voice—or rather this choir, or symphony, or cacophony—might be heard in the normal person? The probably too-pat answer that will be offered here is that, as long as the connections have not been severed, it appears—superimposed along with all the other voices of the other activated modules—in the person's phenomenological field. The result is an ever-changing phenomenology that differentially emphasises the inputs of the various contributing components, depending on their current activation levels.

I will here review the model of human memory that has evolved out of the CHARM (composite holographic associative recall memory) model (Metcalfe, 1990, 1991, 1993a,b, 1997; Metcalfe Eich, 1982, 1985), in light of this multimodular view of human mind/brain processing. The domain of the model is certainly not the whole of human cognition. No problem solving, or language skills, or motor abilities—to name just a few crucial capabilities—are included. Still, the model begins to give a notion of the functioning and dynamics of a coordinated model that takes seriously the view that the different components first of all *are* different, but that they nevertheless interact, each contributing its own special function. This kind of multimodular model becomes especially interesting when there are conditions under which different modules can be differentially potentiated or inhibited—such as under conditions of stress. Some components become hyperpotentiated whereas others shut down. When this happens, the model begins to take on some of the characteristics of a truly dynamic system, and some of the complexity of online human memory.

In addition to the two basic components of the original CHARM model—a perceptual processor/lexicon, and the distributed holographic episodic encoding and retrieval model proper—two additional components have now been added to the model. (Of course, given that many aspects of human cognitive functioning have been summarily avoided, these two that have been added are not exhaustive of what the model "should" become.) These two new components—a monitoring and control component, and an emotional "hot"-system conditioning component—were made necessary either from consideration of the formal constraints of the model or because of the psychological and neuroscience data themselves. The so-augmented CHARM model, with its four rather than two components, might now more appropriately be called CHARM².

The first component is a perceptual/semantic preprocessor, which leads up to a lexicon. This provides the input to the higher-level episodic memory model and acts as the identification system to interpret the output from memory. The next component, the episodic memory component, is the "core loop" in the original CHARM model. This is a basic hippocampal/episodic memory binding component. It comprises a distributed model of how people associate, store and retrieve items in episodic memory. Its characterisation gives rise to a variety of properties of this particular type of memory, and is distinct from the properties of other components of the CHARM² model. The third component entails monitoring and control. This component was added both because there was an internal problem in the model that required a monitoring/control module, and also because the cognitive neuroscience data suggested that there exists in humans, a separable monitoring function. The fourth component has been added very recently (Metcalfe & Jacobs, 1999), in appreciation of the fact that, in both humans and in animals, there is an interacting but functionally distinct and dissociable system that influences memory proper, which we might dub the "hot" system (Metcalfe & Jacobs, 1998; and see Bechara et al., 1995; Davis, 1992; LeDoux, 1995). This system, which is amygdala-centred rather than hippocampally-centred, selects different elements from the stimulus configuration than the hippocampal system, and it operates on those components in a different manner, supporting conditioning rather than episodic memory. Conditioning is, of course, a form of memory, although it has different characteristics than episodic memory. The hot system interacts with the cool system, and so changes the representations therein. It gives preferential treatment to particular fragmentary features, and it emphasises different parts of the content—those that are survival relevant—to the exclusion of neutral information, which is handled more uniformly by the hippocampal system. These four components, although functionally distinct and mathematically dependent upon different representations and operations, interact with one another and allow transformations to be made from one subsystem to another. Also, and fundamentally, all four components contribute to the individual's phenomenological field. Figure 13.1 provides a diagrammatic overview of the interaction of the four components of memory, and of their interaction with the phenomenological field.

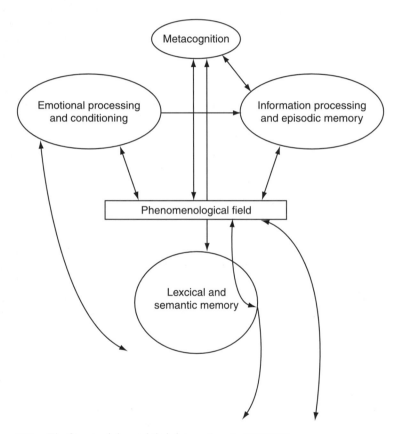

Figure 13.1.   The four modules and their interactions in CHARM[2]

PERCEPTUAL/SEMANTIC PREPROCESSOR
AND LEXICON

The perceptual recognition/semantic lexicon module has some characteristics relevant to memory proper, and so is included as a memory module. It resembles Tulving's (1986) characterisation of semantic memory. Most of the tasks that have been dubbed implicit memory tasks, such as lexical decision, fragment completion, perceptual identification, object identification, and word identification under noisy conditions involve processing by this system. It is not clear, however, whether familiarity-based recognition (e.g. Jacoby et al., 1989; Whittlesea & Leboe, 2000) is done by this system (or by, say, the familiarity monitor—a different module). Relative to the other systems in the CHARM² model, long-lasting learning in this system is very slow at best, although the semantic representations can quickly become activated upon presentation and furthermore other unpresented items can also become activated to the extent to which they have features in common with the presented item.

Why does CHARM need this system?

CHARM uses the semantic lexicon as a preprocessor of outside information. However, the episodic module of the model only requires that its input be in vector form—it does not need these vectors to have any particular characteristic, such as being orthogonal or symbolic or verbal. Therefore, although it is assumed that information is first processed by the semantic lexicon before entering the episodic memory module, in many cases (especially when the to-be-remembered items are not words) this input step is not strictly necessary.

However, the semantic lexicon *is* necessary at the output stage of processing. The model retrieves fuzzy outputs, which can be, for example, superimposed representations of more than a single item (even when the original inputs had been discrete words). But people say discrete, words, when asked. The model, therefore, requires a system that can convert its own output into a discrete wordlike form. For this it uses the lexicon. To give a more concrete example: under some conditions the model will retrieve a superimposed image of, say, a cat and a dog. (If an item A is associated with CAT and then the same items A is associated with a DOG, and then the item A is used as a retrieval cue, the result of retrieval will be both CAT and DOG.) However, given that people know there are no "cdoagts" (or whatever the conjoint image/word might be) a decision needs to be made as to what exactly the retrieved item is, so that the person can speak about it in their recall protocol. The lexicon, then, serves this purpose of allowing discrete output. Note that it can allow both cat and dog to be produced—but separately. Notice, also, that retrieved superimposed items might sometimes match an item that was never presented. Norman Park (1997) gave a lovely example of such an effect in an experiment in which the two input items were "MAN-EATING" and "FISH". People recalled "SHARK" rather than the two separate items. Presumably, the same convergence on a non-presented item may occur in the

Deese, Roediger, and McDermott false memory paradigm (see Dodhia & Metcalfe, 1999).

Although the main reason the model requires the lexicon is to solve this *output* disambiguation problem, there is every reason to suppose that there is also a similar input disambiguation problem, and that the same lexicon is used. As perceptual psychologists have noted, we never see the whole percept, replete, and yet we reliably identify a visual pattern as, say, a dog, despite the limitations of the retinal image. Differences in orientation, and the amount and noisiness of the input are overcome by a perceptual recognition system. CHARM[2] assumes that input and output disambiguation or identification are handled by the same system. This assertion is consistent with a growing body of neuroscience data (Kosslyn, Thompson, & Alpert, 1997; Gabrieli, 2000) showing that the same cortical areas are activated when one perceives an object as when one later remembers it.

What is the form of representation in this system?

One might ask whether this system is a spreading activation net, or a parallel activation system? The functional requirement—that the module be able to disambiguate noisy, fuzzy, and sometimes ambiguous stimuli—provides no basis for ascertaining whether the module uses distributed or localist representations. Indeed, it is imaginable, because the only real requirement is that the pattern that is either input or output needs to map onto or to allow production of an output that will be interpreted as a word, that the representation is not even discrete and finitely differentiable (i.e. symbolic, see Goodman, 1968). Both localist and distributed forms of the lexicon are possible on functional grounds.

Furthermore, it is possible to smoothly translate between them. If one chooses the distributed form of representations, then the lexicon is comprised of multidimensional vectors. The distributed characteristics arise if each element in the vectors is taken as a dimension or a feature or a neuron (or set of neurons), resulting in the characterisation of an item as a pattern of values over a set of such feature dimensions. The values over this ensemble of neurons could be given as their firing rates or potential differences (and so has a certain appeal to neuroscientists).

However, we can think of the same representations as being localist. They could be the endpoints of arrows in multidimensional space, which might vary in magnitude and direction from origin. Thus, as long as the underlying structure of the lexicon is a multidimensional similarity space, the distributed and localist representations amount to the same thing.

The metaphor one uses to think about processing can depend upon one's preference for localist or distributed representations. If one thinks of the representation as feature sets, then one is drawn to a metaphor whereby an externally presented item's features resonate, like a set of tuning forks (Ratcliff, 1979), with the dimensions that are shared in common with it and the items that contain subsets of its features. If one thinks about the representations as localist nodes, then one imagines that a presented item is located in some particular location in the multidimensional space, its activation spreading to nearby neighbours. The consequences for the speed of responding—priming—are more obvious with the localist than the distributed choice of metaphor. Finally, even though one can translate, mathematically, from one to the other, the underlying brain structure might allow us eventually to differentiate the two possibilities.

To take a pragmatic intermediate stance: if it is easier to think about the processing in the lexicon as being spreading activation—a metaphor that psychologists continue to find very compelling—but it turns out that nobody ever finds the grandmother cells, or a brain correlate of the actual multidimensional space, whereas they can and do find sets of features that might correspond to the dimension in the feature-set vector notation, little has been lost. The translation of research findings is straightforward from one form of representation to the other, and so the findings should be equally valid regardless of the metaphor. One need only substitute "as if" for "is" in the theoretical statements.

Data accounted for by this module

Priming.   Many experiments have shown that the presentation of items, even when those items cannot explicitly be recollected, results in later facilitation of processing of those items, in, for example, lexical decision tasks. Repetition and semantic priming, word identification, and disambiguation results are all attributable, without controversy, to this system.

Fluency-based recognition?   Some researchers (Whittlesea & Leboe, 2000; Whittlesea & Williams, 2001a,b) have suggested that inferences about fluency or familiarity might underlie recognition. The question asked here is whether the semantic lexicon could be responsible for familiarity, fluency, or discrepancy-based recognition judgements. The answer that I suggest here is no. However, it does seem likely that people can make recognition judgements based on familiarity of some sort, and there is another module in the model—the familiarity monitoring module—that I prefer as the likely locus of familiarity-based recognition.

The argument that people might be able to use the perceived overactivation of an item in the semantic lexicon to make an inference about whether an item was or was not presented or experienced in the recent past has some implications that make it unlikely. Whereas, people sometimes say they do not think that such and such an item was presented, because they "would have remembered it if it had been", it is not clear that lexical fluency is the basis for these judgements. The difficulty arises when one attempts to ascertain the computational basis—what would the person have to do, and what structures would he or she need to have—to be able to make such a lexical fluency-based recognition judgement? The first question is: How does the person know how active the features (or the node) should have been? Presumably, there must be some record of background or base rate activation. It would appear that an immutable "ghost" lexicon is necessary to provide normative information. Presumably, to say whether an item was retrieved with unusual fluency the person accesses the item in the ghost lexicon, keeping track of the speed or ease of activation in the lexicon that is not subject to change. He or she also accesses the "real" lexicon, which has been modified by recent experience, to see how quickly and easily the item is accessed in that system. Then, the person compares the two activations, concluding that any enhancement in the real lexicon as compared to the ghost lexicon is attributable to, for example, the item having been presented recently. Only then could one make the comparison that gives rise to the inference that "this is out of the ordinary", and the attribution that this unusual fluency must or might be due, for example, to having been presented recently. Other attributions, such as high feeling of knowing judgements, due to the perception of unusual fluency or familiarity, have also been suggested (Koriat, 2000).

I think it extremely unlikely that we have two lexicons that are redundant except insofar as one becomes activated and the other does not. But suppose we do. We need, then, to confront the question of how an immutable lexicon came into being in the first place? Unless one takes an extreme Platonist stance, holding that it is inborn and immutable, this ghost lexicon seems to be an impossibility. I say "seems to" rather than "is" because one might imagine some very complicated scheme wherein this immutable lexicon develops in early life, and then becomes stable. The discovery of such a double lexicon, and its developmental implications, have yet to be spelled out, however. Or one might take the view that once the process one currently needs the ghost lexicon for has been enacted, the old ghost lexicon is updated, so that the new information is now incorporated. The ghost lexicon, in this case, is the $N-1$ back-up, such as people often keep on their computers when writing a manuscript. But, if there is such a back-up system of the lexicon before it was changed by the current experience, why is there only one? Perhaps there are hundreds. If there is only one, and if it is the last back-up that is used to compare to the current system, to allow attritions to be make, then one needs to postulate a machinery for controlling when this back-up lexicon is supposed to be updated, and wipe out the old back-ups. In updating, there would also have to be yet another control processor indicating what information, and how much of the information should be kept. For example, one needs some system to specify whether and to what extent rare items are converted to common items by a given experience. Presumably, rare items are activated relatively more often than common ones by a particular experience. Does that mean that they are now common items, or is the lexicon supposed to modify those activations to take into account that, after all, this item is rare. The postulation of either kind of "ghost" lexicon is, if taken seriously, anything but simple and elegant. How it managed to acquire the normative background fluencies that allow the person to say that something is not normal, is anything but obvious. I think it is extremely unlikely that we have such a ghost lexicon, and, therefore, seek to account for familiarity-based recognition in a different way.

There is another source of familiarity information in CHARM²—the novelty-monitoring component. It can handle familiarity judgements (that do not entail actual retrieval of the content of the items) in a more spare manner. Thus, although I agree with the distinction proposed by Jacoby and others, between familiarity-based and recollectively-based recognition judgements, I do not think—for the reasons outlined earlier—that the familiarity-based judgements are made by comparison of the current fluency or familiarity to the expected fluency or familiarity of the items as given by a ghost lexicon.

The false memory phenomenon?   Roediger, McDermott, and Robinson (1998) have suggested that a spreading activation network is sufficient to account for the false memory effect, in which an unpresented critical item (such as SWEET) is believed to have been present in a list when a number of high associates of that item (such as SUGAR, MAPLE SYRUP, CAKE, HONEY, SOUR) were presented. It is therefore interesting to consider whether this effect might be attributable to the lexical module alone. In attempting to formalise a way in which the lexicon alone could do the job, one must immediately confront the problem, outlined in the preceding section, of how the activation levels in the lexicon are converted into assessments of recognition. Second, one cannot sidestep the problem by allowing a "list item" tag to be attached to each presented items in the semantic network, because then people would not experience a false alarm on the critical items. These considerations are sufficiently problematic that I do not believe the lexicon alone is responsible for the false-memory effect. However, it does have a role to play. The superimposed output from the episodic-memory module, as will be detailed shortly, needs to be identified. The lexicon is responsible for identifying the individual items from this composite and, because of the high degree of feature overlap in the composite output, will readily identify it as the critical item. Dodhia and Metcalfe (1999) have conducted simulations of this process in CHARM and have demonstrated the similarities between this paradigm and the classical categorisation paradigm.

Do we need anything more than this module?

Some theorists have suggested that all of human memory might be based on a spreading activation network, and, indeed, much (priming) data can be explained parsimoniously by this single module. However, there are certain problems that this module either cannot solve, or cannot solve while simultaneously maintaining the capabilities it has that account for similarity priming and inferential generalisation—properties that make this module attractive in the first place. The capabilities of the four different modules are outlined in Table 13.1. The limitations of the semantic lexicon are detailed below.

What about association by contiguity?   A spreading activation network cannot simultaneously handle both association by contiguity and association by similarity. The module can deal elegantly with priming results but it does this by assuming that the proximity structure is based on the similarity of items: "doctor" and "nurse" activate one another because nurse is located close to doctor in multidimensional space, or has much feature overlap. The reason that "truck" is not primed by "doctor" is that it is not close in this pre-existing network.

However, real problems arise if one wishes to associate two unrelated items such as doctor and truck. Even if one were to trace the long pathway between them in the associative network, presumably along the way of getting from doctor to truck in retrieval there are many other nodes that are both closer to the cue, doctor, and likely to be more activated by its occurrence—like nurse, for example. Why do people not give those items as the response? In a network arranged by pre-existing similarity, and capable of giving the elegant priming effects, there is no obvious way to know that truck is the thing one is supposed to produce to the cue doctor.

People, of course, are quite well able to associate unrelated pairs (Tulving & Thompson, 1971), and omit items similar to the cue as the response. There are exceptions: very elderly participants, for instance, will produce the semantic associates rather than the experimentally designated targets. Presumably, though, in these cases, the episodic memory module, which is different from the semantic network and which is responsible for this second kind of memorial performance, is not functioning properly.

Recall of information not present in the cue.   Recall poses a problem for any model or module that relies only on activation of features that are present in the environment. How do we get the features that are in memory but not activated in consciousness? Does DOCTOR somehow "know" that the thing it is supposed to retrieve is TRUCK? The search metaphor (and with it the spreading activation formulation) suffers from the problem that one needs to

TABLE 13.1

Module	Function	Representation	Common tasks	Content	Development	High stress response	Anatomical focus
Semantic lexicon	Identification Knowledge	Nodes spreading activation	Priming Lexical decision identification	Categories	Late infancy	Some impairment	Cortex
Episodic memory	Remembering Associative encoding & retrieval	Distributed vectors composite trace	Recall Recognition	Infomationally neutral, spatial & temporal remembrances	Late infancy	Impairment	Hippocampus/ cortex
Monitoring & control	Habituation modulates learning	Scalar feedback	Novelty & release PI Metacognition Habituation	Unemotional "gut" feeling Judgments	Late childhood	Impairment	Frontal lobes
Hot system	Conditioning Enhance emotional feature weightings	S-R net	Conditioning	Survival specific trigger features, emotion-fear & passion	Prenatal	Enhancement	Amygdala

know what one is looking for to be able to find it. But if one knew what it was one was seeking one would have already recalled the target—the problem of memory retrieval would already have been solved. For these reasons, recall does not seem possible in the lexical module.

Source and contextual memory.   People are often able to provide a great deal of information about the context that co-occurred with a particular event. For example, they can make source judgements (Johnson, Hashtroudi, & Lindsay, 1993). These kinds of contextual associations depend upon the connection of the item with background or with other events. The activation involved in the preprocessor will not support these tasks.

EPISODIC MEMORY

The episodic-memory module is the "core" loop in the original CHARM model. The inputs to this module are multidimensional representations of the patterns of features of the to-be-remembered items. Formally, ordered sets of features are vectors, and in this part of the model they are represented as distributed patterns of features rather than as points in multidimensional space. An item might be associated with another item or with itself by means of the operation of convolution. Convolution—the encoding operation used in holography—effectively smears one representation over the other, such that when one of the items is later presented as a cue, and correlated with the association, the other item is reconstructed. Correlation, following convolution, is a redintegrative process such that if any part of either of the original items is presented, the whole of the other item is reconstructed. This redintegrative property functionally means that every part of an item is bound or glued to every other part, and thus, the whole configuration of the event, as experienced at the time of encoding, is woven together into one unit that is retrieved as a whole. The fact that all of the event is retrieved as a whole is what is meant by episodic binding. Each association is added into a composite trace, which is, therefore comprised of a sum of associations.

In this module, the retrieved item, $\mathbf{R}$, is equal to the correlation between the cue, $\mathbf{Q}$, and the trace, $\mathbf{T}$. the trace consists of: $\mathbf{A}*\mathbf{B}$, $\mathbf{C}*\mathbf{D}$, and so on, where * means association by convolution. The original items, $\mathbf{A}$, $\mathbf{B}$, $\mathbf{C}$, $\mathbf{D}$, etc., can have any similarity with respect to one another. So, $\mathbf{A}$ and $\mathbf{B}$ can be independent of one another, for example, and the similarity, S, between them, would then be 0. They could be identical, in which case the similarity between them would be 1. Or they could be somewhere in between, in which case the extent of the similarity is given by the magnitude of their dot product, which would be somewhere between 0 and 1. The cue, $\mathbf{Q}$, is also a vector, and has a similarity to each of the items. The similarity between the cue and item $\mathbf{A}$ is notated S_{QA}, and is a scalar weighting factor that, as will be illustrated, is applied to the complement item. To further characterise what is retrieved, the similarity between the cue, **Q**, and each of the items is computed and this is the weighting with which the complement item is given in the retrieved item **R**. The result of summing gives the resulting superimposed vector (this vector is then sent to the lexicon for identification). To summarise retrieval, then:

$$\mathbf{R} = \mathbf{Q}\#\mathbf{T}$$

$$= \mathbf{Q} \#\{(\mathbf{A}*\mathbf{B}) + (\mathbf{C}*\mathbf{D}) + (\mathbf{E}*\mathbf{F}) + \ldots\}$$

$$= S_{QA}\,\mathbf{B} + S_{QB}\,\mathbf{A} + S_{QC}\,\mathbf{D} + S_{QD}\,\mathbf{C} + S_{QE}\,\mathbf{F} + S_{QF}\,\mathbf{E} \ldots \tag{1}$$

Notice that the cue retrieves not itself or the items that are similar to it, but rather the items that were convolved with that cue, whether they are similar to it or not. Thus, retrieval here is unlike that in the spreading activation network, where the probe retrieves itself and the things that are like it. In the convolution network the cue retrieves the things that it was associated with—not necessarily itself.

Let us suppose that the cue is **A** and it is unrelated to everything else. Equation 1, then, becomes:

$$\mathbf{R} = 1\,\mathbf{B} + 0 + 0 + 0 + 0 + 0 \ldots$$

$$= \mathbf{B}$$

To give another example, suppose the cue is a category member—say peach—and **A** is also peach, and the other category members are, say pear (**B**), banana (**C**), plum (**D**), orange (**E**), and grape (**F**), etc., and let us assume that, for convenience, they all have a similarity of .5 to one another. The result would be

$$\mathbf{R} = 1\mathbf{B} + .5\mathbf{A} + .5\mathbf{D} + .5\mathbf{C} + .5\,\mathbf{F} + .5\,\mathbf{E} \ldots$$

$$= 1 \text{ pear} + .5 \text{ peach} + .5 \text{ plum} + .5 \text{ banana} + .5 \text{ grape} + .5 \text{ orange}, \ldots$$

which is a superimposed "fruit" that would emphasise the common features among the various retrieved fruits but lean a bit towards pearishness. This kind of output, by the way, gives rise to the false memory effect, because the lexicon might be very likely to identify it as an apple.

Episodic binding

The function that convolution enacts might be called episodic memory binding, insofar as the operation weaves together all of the elements from the two items associated in such a way that if later all or part of one of the items is correlated with the result, the entire other item is reproduced. This module is redintegrative in the true sense: parts of an event that are not present in the cue are reconstituted. This capability of the convolution/correlation operations—to reconstitute the missing parts of the events is what makes it distinctively episodic. An episode is defined in terms of the configuration and peculiarities of that moment—what went together with what at time t. It is this that the convolution/correlation algorithm reconstructs (as opposed to what an item has in common with other items across moments, which is semantic similarity). Two experimental situations might further serve to illustrate this crucial property of the episodic module.

Memory for conjunctions.   Reinitz, Lammers, and Cochran (1992) presented participants with line drawings of faces to remember for a later recognition test. At the time of test, they presented not only old item probes and faces that were made up of entirely new features, but also items consisting entirely of old features, but reconfigured from different old faces. Without knowledge of what was bound to what in a particular episode, there is no way to distinguish between the actual old faces and the conjunction faces, because all of the features in the conjunction faces were old. However, as Reinitz and colleagues showed, normal people can make this discrimination quite well.

When we (Kroll et al., 1996) tested hippocampal patients (many of whom did not seem to be amnesic in their day-to-day lives), they were found to be selectively impaired on just this task. They called the new conjunction faces, conjunction flag patterns, and even, in some cases, conjunction words, old at the same rate at which they called the actual old items old. It was as if features were slipping from event to event, unbound by episodic constraints, as was first observed by Bartlett (1932). The amnesics looked as though they had an impairment in the binding module, whereas the normals were able to bind.

Implicit and explicit repeated fragment completion.   The other finding, in humans, that has been uniquely attributed to binding depends on episodic or explicit-memory instructions, and implicit memory instructions (Hayman & Tulving, 1989). If the convolution algorithm is responsible for episodic memory, then we expect that explicit instructions would give rise to evidence of binding, whereas the implicit instructions might suggest that people need not use the episodic-retrieval module, and could do the task by mere global familiarity matching, which does not involve binding. After presenting participants with a list of items, Hayman and Tulving (1989) gave them a repeated fragment completion task with either given implicit memory instructions (i.e. say the first thing that comes to mind that successfully completes the fragment) or explicit instructions (i.e. think of a word from the list that completes the fragment). Once people had completed the whole list once, they did it a second time, but with the complementary fragments. For SOLILOQUY, people might have been given SO_ _ _OQU_ on the first test, and _ _ LIL _ _ _ Y on the second test. Hayman and Tulving investigated the conditional probability of successfully completing the second fragment given success on the first.

If the word is bound together in memory, such that all of the features form an episode, and both cues retrieve the episode—as the convolution/correlation algorithm of the CHARM model suggests—then if the person was able to retrieve the item from one fragment, he or she should be more able to retrieve it to the other fragment than if it had not been retrieved from the first fragment. A positive dependency should be observed. In contrast, if the features were stored separately, in a non-bound manner, then the probability of activating the target node given one set of non-overlapping features should not necessarily be related to the probability of its retrieval from another set. Independence should be found. Tulving and Hayman found independence when people were given implicit memory instructions but dependence when they were given explicit memory instructions. Our (Metcalfe, Cottrell, & Mencl, 1992; Metcalfe, Mencl & Cottrell, 1994) simulations indicated that this otherwise puzzling finding was that with the implicit instructions people did not have recourse to use the hippocampal system, whereas, when they were asked to retrieve the item from the list to complete the tasks, then they did make use of the binding system.

The relation of animal place cells to episodic memory binding in humans. Since O'Keefe and Nadel's (1978) landmark book, animal researchers have focused on the spatial characteristics of the hippocampus as being a cognitive map, rather than on memory. Recently, work on such phenomena as hippocampal long-term potentiation (Foy, Stanton, Levine, & Thompson, 1987), and fyn mutant mice with a genetically manipulated hippocampal long-term potentiation impairment, who exhibit both spatial and memory impairments (Grant, O'Dell, Karl, Stein, Soriano & Kandel, 1992) has brought some rapprochement with the human memory work. Even so, the finding that hippocampal CA1 cells are place cells, seems unrelated to the mnemonic function in humans. Some intriguing work by Barnes (1988), however, lends credibility to the possibility that place cells serve the binding function.

Barnes (1988) recorded from single cells in rats, freely moving in a environment containing a variety of stimuli. Particular place cells fired at particular locations in the environment, as is usual. Barnes found that the firing of these cells persisted even when many of the objects making up the content of the environment were removed. However, when the locations of the objects were scrambled, the place cells stopped firing. This sensitivity to the co-occurrence of information in the correct configuration led Barnes to conclude that place cells were conjunction cells, their function being binding (see Nadel & Jacobs, 1999). The fact that animal researchers are proposing configural processing or binding as the prime function of the hippocampus suggests a convergence of what had seemed to be unreconcilable research traditions.

Dissociations and overlap

Classic dissociations between priming tasks and episodic memory tasks (Tulving, Hayman, & MacDonald, 1991; Tulving, Schacter, & Stark, 1982; or between implicit and explicit memory tasks, see Schacter, 1987, for a review) have a natural interpretation in the model. The implicit tasks can generally be done by the semantic lexicon (and perhaps the familiarity monitor), whereas the explicit memory tasks, including recall, source and contextual assessments, recognition requiring binding, and recollection are handled by the convolution/correlation module. There are some paradigms that have traditionally been attributed to either explicit or implicit memory that do not require binding—but that, under some circumstances might benefit from it. The model allows us to analyse these multiple determined cases. Performance on those paradigms might be enacted by either module—although with potentially different fine-grained results. Some classification learning experiments could use either (see the above section, and Metcalfe Eich, 1982, for illustrations). Similarly, the false memory paradigm results could be obtained whether binding was used or not (see Dodhia & Metcalfe, 1999, for CHARM simulations of this paradigm).

This redundancy—that different modules can do the same task, using different mechanisms, and with only slightly different results—is the bane of modellers and researchers using dissociation data to separate different brain systems. In the real world, however, this overlap is reassuring. The fact that a task can be accomplished—in a slightly different manner—by different systems in the brain, provides people with a functional redundancy that is very useful in light of our vulnerability of brain injury. Many of the patients with selective damage to the hippocampus, in the study we conducted with Kroll, for example, had no clinically observable amnesia. When they were asked whether they had memory problems, they said no and they performed perfectly well in their daily lives. Furthermore, they performed as well as normals on standard recognition memory tasks. Thus, despite pronounced difficulties when the task was designed to specifically tap into the function that was deficient—in this case memory binding—in most real-world tasks these patients were able to compensate to the point that they often appeared to have no deficit whatever. It is precisely because multiple modules can enact the same task—although in slightly different ways—that we have this buffer that provides us a measure of real-world protection.

MONITORING AND CONTROL

The third module handles monitoring and control. This overseer system is needed for technical reasons in the model, but turns out to have very interesting and adaptive psychological implications. Without a monitor and some means of trace compression, as more and more associative vectors (which are the result of convolution), are added into the composite memory trace, the variability of that trace would increase without limit. Because the variance increases differentially depending on exactly how similar the incoming association is to the trace itself, with associations that are unrelated to the trace augmenting it least, and associations that are highly similar to the trace increasing it most, it is not possible to apply an across-the-board solution (like dividing everything by a constant) to this problem. Instead, the similarity of the incoming item to the cumulative episodic memory trace must be computed and the feedback signal, which adjusts the weightings on the incoming association and the trace, adjusted accordingly. The signal computed by the monitor, thus, is a scalar value that summarises the similarity of the incoming event to a weighted episodic memory trace. This feedback signal is then used to renormalise the trace: those events that are highly similar to the trace receive a low weighting and those that are dissimilar receive a high weighting.

Notice that the value computed by the monitor is a global episodic familiarity value, and could provide the basis for a recognition decision, as discussed by Jacoby, Kelley and Dywan (1989). It is a parsimonious candidate for fast familiarity judgements because: (1) the model requires it anyhow; (2) one does not have to posit a second normative lexicon for purposes of the comparison; (3) the items do not have to be words, for the familiarity to be computed—it could make a familiarity judgement about a pattern that did not have a name, for example, a photographed scene or a face. There is no logical necessity that an item first enter the semantic lexicon in order to be processed by the monitor.

This module contributes a particular form of dynamic to the model. The result of the weighting is that events that are already well known are not given much weight, whereas those that are quite novel, or different from the trace at time t, are given substantial weight. Clearly, habituation effects are the result of this module. Given that this weighting is done on an item-by-item basis, it follows that the order of presentation becomes important (and this module is responsible for effects that depend on order). For example, suppose one were to present a number of category members. When the first one is presented it will be rather different from the trace, and so be given a high weighting. However, when the second one is presented, by virtue of the fact that the first one is now a part of the trace, it will be less different from the trace than was the first, and hence will be accorded a lower weighting. The third will receive a yet lower weighting, because of the presence of the first two. Thus, we expect that the first presented exemplars will tend to pull the category representation towards themselves to a greater extent than will the later presented exemplars, *ceteris paribus*. This priority effect is seen both in the data on classification learning and stereotype formation and in real-life situations.

The effects in the literature that are attributable to this module are: (1) spacing effects; (2) the build-up from proactive inhibition; (3) release from proactive inhibition; (4) the residual primacy effects that are not due to rehearsal; (5) certain metacognitions, particularly either fast feeling of knowing judgements (Reder & Ritter, 1992) or feeling of knowing judgements that are conditional upon the item not having been retrieved (Hart, 1965, 1967; Metcalfe, 2000; Nelson & Narens, 1980); (6) von Restorff effects; (7) cue overload; and (8) familiarity-based recognition judgements. Interestingly, a number of these effects have been dissociated from more basic memory phenomena, that, in the model, would be attributed to the episodic memory component. For example, Janowsky, Shimamura, and Squire (1989) have shown that metacognition can be selectively impaired in frontal patients (and see Shimamura & Squire, 1986, for the problem Korsakoff patients have with metacognition, which differs from the syndrome of hippocampal amnesics). Novelty monitoring, too, seems to be impaired in certain frontal patients (Knight, 1984), and release from proactive inhibition is selectively impaired in Korsakoff but not other amnesics—a finding that suggests that various aspects of this component, as contrasted with the binding component, are jeopardised in that syndrome.

CONDITIONING AND THE HOT SYSTEM

The hot-system module, as well as supporting conditional learning, modulates the episodic-memory module in a quite different manner than does the novelty monitoring/control module. Rather than contributing high level judgements, or altering the weighting as a function of novelty, the hot system has a distinctive emotional input. The functioning of this particular module is especially important in applying the model to memory under traumatic conditions, insofar as the hot-system module becomes dominant under those conditions, whereas the episodic-memory module tends to become disregulated. The hot system is centred on the amygdala, which is selectively responsive to fear-provoking stimuli, and has been shown conclusively, in animals at least, to be the primary locus of fear conditioning (Fanslow, 1994). The addition of the hot-system module to the CHARM model is the most important new addition to the model and is specified in more detail in Metcalfe and Jacobs (1998, 1999).

One of the clearest demonstrations of a distinction between the hot-system and the episodic-memory modules was provided by an experiment conducted by Bechara et al. (1995), who examined the behaviour of patients to a startling event. One of the patients had selective bilateral damage to the amygdala complex as a result of Urbach Weithe syndrome; another patient had hippocampal damage. Subjects were exposed to a series of coloured slides. After presentation of the blue slides, a loud and obnoxious boat horn sounded, resulting in a startle reaction in all patients. Later, the patients were tested in two ways: (1) by asking for their bound memories of the events— what stimulus followed the slides of particular colours; or (2) by measuring their conditioned responses via skin conductance. The hippocampally lesioned patient was unable to say what happened following the blue slide, but did have a conditioned response to it. In contrast, the amygdala patient was perfectly well able to say that the aversive noise followed the blue slide, but had no visceral response to it.

Other studies of this same patient revealed that she appeared to have a scotoma for fear. When she was asked to make ratings of how extreme certain facial expressions were, her range was normal for other emotions such as joy and sadness, but she did not seem to register fear or, to a slightly lesser extent, anger. She was also unable to draw a fearful face, although she did an adequate job of depicting happiness, for example. Profound social dysfunctions have been manifested by non-human primates who have undergone amygdala lesion (Dicks, Myers, & Kling, 1969) and wild amygdalectomy primates have died after amygdelectomy—presumably because of their isolation and inappropriate social behaviour. The effects appear to be much milder in humans but, even so, it appears that knowing what and whom to fear, actually experiencing what can be aversive emotional responses, and acting in the appropriate manner when one does experience them, is highly adaptive.

The amygdala is separated from the hippocampus by only one synapse. And yet the functions of these two modules appear to be quite different. Whereas the hippocampal cells include place cells (which, as we have argued, are configural binding cells) and is informationally neutral, the amygdala is not at all content-neutral in its responses. Single-cell recordings in the amygdala (O'Keefe & Bouma, 1969) indicate that the amygdala responds to features that are highly species survival specific. The specificity could be characterised as a selective responsivity to fragments that either provoke fear or desire. A cat howl or a threatening gesture will excite the amygdala cells in a cat, but a spatial frequency grating, an unemotional context or a simple object will not.

Interaction with other modules

Metcalfe and Jacobs (1998, 1999) proposed that the hot-system representations interact in the phenomenological field, with the more neutral representations from the other three modules. When the hot system is highly activated it will cause an emphasis on those emotional features that are in its domain, resulting in experiences such as weapon focus. In this view, the narrowing of focus (see Easterbrook, 1959) that results with increasing stress is attributable to an increased input from the hot system. The focus should defer to features that are threatening, rather than just those that are conceptually "central".

Two primary variables, other than lesions, result in differential responses of the four modules: developmental level and stress. As can be seen from Table 13.1, the hot system develops early and is functioning at birth, whereas the other systems mature later. Thus, emotional responses, and conditioning, are primitive (see Jacobs & Nadel, 1985; Nadel & Jacobs, 1999, for some consequences of this for phobias).

In addition, the responses of the hot system are potentiated with stress, whereas the reverse is true for the other three modules in the CHARM² model. At low levels of stress (that one might more appropriately call arousal) all systems increase their functioning. However, when the stress levels become very high, the hot-system module is the last to break down. The other three modules become susceptible at lower levels than does the amygdala. The episodic module follows a function much like the Yerkes Dodson law. First its functioning increases with arousal and peaks at some moderate level of stress. With high stress it becomes disregulated (Sapolsky, 1992), and bound episodic memory is impaired. In contrast, the functioning of the hot system increases monotonically with stress, at least up to very high levels (see Metcalfe & Jacobs, 1998). As stress becomes very high, processing in the semantic lexical module functioning becomes fuzzier and fine-grained classifications break down. Finally, although the data are scantier than one would like on this conjecture, it appears likely that the monitoring and judgement module is adversely affected by extremely high stress. Thus, in contrast to the other modules that are impaired, the hot-system module comes into its own when the person faces a threatening and stressful situation.

ACKNOWLEDGEMENTS

This research was supported by National Institute of Mental Health grant MH48066, and by a grant from the James S. McDonnell Foundation. I wish to thank W. J. Jacobs, and Daniel Kimball for their many helpful discussions.

REFERENCES

Adolphs, R., Tranel, D., Damasio, H., & Damasio, A.R. (1995). Fear and the human amygdala. *Journal of Neuroscience, 15*, 5879–5891.

Barnes, C.A. (1988). Spatial learning and memory processes: The search for their neurobiological mechanisms in the rat. *Trends in Neurosciences, 11*, 163–169.

Bartlett, F.C. (1932). *Remembering: A study in experimental and social psychology*. Cambridge: Cambridge University Press.

Bechara, A., Tranel, D., Damasio, H., Adolphs, R., Rockland, C., & Damasio, A.R. (1995). Double dissociation of conditioning and declarative knowledge relative to the amygdala and hippocampus in humans. *Science, 269*, 1115–1118.

Davis, M. (1992). The role of the amygdala in fear and anxiety. *Annual Review of Neuroscience, 15*, 353–375.

Dicks, D., Myers, R.E., & Kling, A. (1969). Uncus and amygdala lesions: Effects on social behavior in the free-ranging monkey. *Science, 165*, 69–71.

Dodhia, R.M., & Metcalfe, J. (1999). False memories and source monitoring. *Cognitive Neuropsychology, 16*, 489–508.

Easterbrook, J.A. (1959). The effect of emotion on cue utilization and the organization of behavior. *Psychological Review, 66*, 183–201.

Fanslow, M.S. (1994). Neural organization of the defensive behavior system responsible for fear. *Psychonomic Bulletin and Review, 1*, 429–438.

Foy, M.R., Stanton, M.E., Levine, S., & Thompson, R.F. (1987). Behavioral stress impairs long-term potentiation in rodent hippocampus. *Behavioral and Neural Biology, 48*, 138–149.

Gabrieli, J. (2000). Invited address to the Memory Disorders Research Society. Toronto, October 2000.

Gazzaniga, M.S. (1998). The split brain revisited. *Scientific American, 279*, 35–39.

Gazzaniga, M.S., Bogen, J.E., & Sperry, R.W. (1962). Some functional effects of sectioning the cerebral commissures in man. *Proceedings of the National Academy of Sciences USA, 48*, 1765–1769.

Goodman, N. (1968). *The languages of art*. Indianapolis: Bobbs-Merrill.

Grant, S.G., O'Dell, T.J., Karl, K.A., Stein, P.L., Soriano, P., & Kandel, E.R. (1992). Impaired long-term potentiation, spatial learning, and hippocampal development in fyn mutant mice. *Science, 258*, 1903–1910.

Hart, J.T. (1965). Memory and the feeling of knowing experience. *Journal of Educational Psychology, 56*, 208–216.

Hart, J.T. (1967). Memory and the memory-monitoring process. *Journal of Verbal Learning and Verbal Behavior, 6*, 685–691.

Hayman, C.A.G., & Tulving, E. (1989). Is priming in fragment completion based on a "Traceless" memory system? *Journal of Experimental Psychology: Learning, Memory, and Cognition, 15*, 941–956.

Jacoby, L.L., Kelley, C.M., & Dywan, J. (1989). Memory attributions. In H.L. Roediger & F.I.M. Craik (Eds.) *Varieties of memory and consciousness: Essays in honor of Endel Tulving* (pp. 391–422). Hillsdale, NJ: Lawrence Erlbaum Associates, Inc.

Jacobs, W.J., & Nadel, L. (1985). Stress induced recovery of fears and phobias. *Psychological Review, 92*, 512–531.

Janowsky, J.S., Shimamura, A.P., & Squire, L.R. (1989). Memory and metamemory: Comparisons between patients with frontal lobe lesions and amnesic patients. *Psychobiology, 17*, 3–11.

Johnson, M.K., Hashtroudi, S., & Lindsay, S.D. (1993). Source monitoring. *Psychological Review, 114*, 3–28.

Kinsbourne, M. (1994). *What kind of modularity?* Invited address to the Memory Disorders Research Society. Boston, October 1994.

Knight, R.T. (1984). Decreased response to novel stimuli after prefrontal lesion in man. *Electroencephalography and Clinical Neurophysiology, 59*, 9–20.

Koriat, A. (2000). The feeling of knowing: Some metatheoretical implications for consciousness and control. *Consiousness and Cognition, 9*, 149–171.

Kosslyn, S., Thompson, W.L., & Alpert, N.M. (1997). Neural systems shared by visual imagery and visual perception: A positron emission tomography study. *Neuro Image, 6*, 320–334.

Kroll, N.E.A., Knight, R., Metcalfe, J., Wolf, E.S., & Tulving, E. (1996). Cohesion failure as a source of memory illusion. *Journal of Memory and Language, 35*, 176–196.

LeDoux, J.E. (1995). Emotion: Clues from the brain. *Annual Review of Psychology, 46*, 209–235.

Metcalfe, J. (1990). A composite holographic associative recall model (CHARM) and blended memories in eyewitness testimony. *Journal of Experimental Psychology: General, 119*, 145–160.

Metcalfe, J. (1991). Recognition failure and the composite memory trace in CHARM. *Psychological Review, 98*, 529–553.

Metcalfe, J. (1993a). Monitoring and gain control in an episodic memory model: Relation to P300 event-related potentials. In A.F. Collins, S.E. Gathercole, M.A. Conway, & P.E. Morris (Eds.) *Theories of memory* (pp. 327–354). Hillsdale, NJ: Lawrence Erlbaum Associates, Inc.

Metcalfe, J. (1993b). Novelty monitoring, metacognition, and control in a composite holographic associative recall model: Implications for Korsakoff amnesia. *Psychological Review, 100*, 3–22.

Metcalfe, J. (1997). Predicting syndromes of amnesia from a composite holographic associative recall/recognition model (CHARM). *Memory, 5*, 2/1.

Metcalfe, J. (2000). Feelings and judgments of knowing: Is there a special noetic state? *Consciousness and cognition, 9*, 178–186.

Metcalfe, J., Funnell, M., & Gazzaniga, M.S. (1995). Right hemisphere memory veridicality: Studies of a split-brain patient. *Psychological Science, 6*, 157–165.

Metcalfe, J., Cottrell, G.W., & Mencl, W.E. (1992). Cognitive binding: A computational-modeling analysis of a distinction between implicit and explicit memory. *Journal of Cognitive Neuroscience, 4*, 289–298.

Metcalfe, J., & Jacobs, W.J. (1998). Emotional memory: The effects of stress on 'Cool' and 'Hot' memory systems. *The Psychology of Learning and Motivation, 38*, 187–221.

Metcalfe, J., & Jacobs, W.J. (1999). 'Hot' emotions in human recollection: Towards a model of traumatic memory. E. Tulving (Ed.) *Memory, consciousness, and the brain: The Tallinn Conference*. Philadelphia: Psychology Press.

Metcalfe, J., Mencl, W.E., & Cottrell, G.W. (1994). Cognitive Binding. In D.L. Schacter & E. Tulving (Eds.) *Memory systems 94*. Cambridge, MA: Bradford Books, MIT Press.

Metcalfe Eich, J. (1985). Levels of processing, encoding specificity, elaboration, and CHARM. *Psychological Review, 91*, 1–38.

Metcalfe Eich, J. (1982). A composite holographic associative recall model. *Psychological Review, 89*, 627–661.

Nadel, L., & Jacobs, W.J. (1999). Traumatic memory is special. *Current Directions in Psychological Science, 7*, 154–157.

Nelson, T.O., & Narens, L. (1980). Norms of 300 general-information questions: Accuracy of recall, latency of recall, and feeling-of-knowing ratings. *Journal of Verbal Learning and Verbal Behavior, 19*, 338–368.

O'Keefe, J., & Bouma, H. (1969). Complex sensory properties of certain amygdala units in the freely moving cat. *Experimental Neurology, 23*, 384–398.

O'Keefe, J., & Nadel, L. (1978). *The hippocampus as a cognitive map*. London: Oxford University Press.

Park, N. (1997). Doctoral dissertation, University of Toronto.

Phelps, E. & Gazzaniga, M.S. (1992). Hemispheric differences in mnemonic processing: The effects of left hemisphere interpretation. *Neuropsychologia, 30*, 293–297.

Ratcliff, R. (1979). Group reaction time distributions and an analysis of distribution statistics. *Psychological Bulletin, 86*, 446–461.

Reder, L.M., & Ritter, F.E. (1992). What determines initial feeling of knowing? Familiarity with question terms, not with the answer. *Journal of Experimental Psychology: Learning, Memory, and Cognition, 18*, 435–452.

Reinitz, M.T., Lammers, W.J., & Cochran, B.P. (1992). Memory-conjunction errors: Miscombination of stored stimulus features can produce illusions of memory. *Memory & Cognition, 20*, 1–11.

Roediger, H.L., III, McDermott, K.B., & Robinson, K.J. (1998). The role of associative processes in creating false memories. In M.A. Conway, S.E. Gathercole, & C. Cornoldi (Eds.) *Theories of memory* (Vol. II, pp. 187–245). Philadelphia: Psychology Press.

Sapolsky, R. (1992). *Stress, the aging brain and the mechanisms of neuron death.* Cambridge, MA: MIT Press.

Schacter, D.L. (1987). Implicit memory: History and current status. *Journal of Experimental Psychology: Learning, Memory, and Cognition, 13*, 501–518.

Shimamura, A.P., & Squire, L.R. (1986). Memory and metamemory: A study of the feeling-of-knowing phenomenon in amnesic patients. *Journal of Experimental Psychology: Learning, Memory, and Cognition, 12*, 452–460.

Tulving, E. (1986). What kind of hypothesis is the distinction between episodic and semantic memory? *Journal of Experimental Psychology: Learning, Memory, and Cognition, 12*, 307–311.

Tulving, E., Hayman, C.A., & MacDonald, C.A. (1991). Long-lasting perceptual priming and semantic learning in amnesia: A case experiment. *Journal of Experimental Psychology: Learning, Memory and Cognition, 17*, 595–617.

Tulving, E., Schacter, D.L., & Stark, H.A. (1982). Priming effects in word fragment completion are independent of recognition memory. *Journal of Experimental Psychology: Learning, Memory, and Cognition, 8*, 336–342.

Tulving, E., & Thomson, D.M. (1971). Retrieval process in recognition memory: Effects of associative context. *Journal of Experimental Psychology, 87*, 116–124.

Whittlesea, B.W.A., & Leboe, J.P. (2000). The heuristic basis of remembering and classification: Fluency, generation, and resemblance. *Journal of Experimental Psychology: General, 129*, 84–106.

Whittlesea, B.W.A., & Williams, L.D. (2001a). The discrepancy–attribution hypothesis: I. The heuristic basis of feelings of familiarity. *Journal of Experimental Psychology: Learning, Memory, and Cognition, 27*, 3–13.

Whittlesea, B.W.A., & Williams, L.D. (2001b). The discrepancy–attribution hypothesis: II. Expectation, uncertainty, surprise and feelings of familiarity. *Journal of Experimental Psychology: Learning, Memory, and Cognition, 27*, 14–33.

CHAPTER FOURTEEN

Building emotional memories: Insights from a computational model of fear conditioning

Jorge L. Armony
Institute of Cognitive Neuroscience, University College London, UK

INTRODUCTION

It is generally accepted that there are different types of memories, involving distinct neural circuits, sometimes working in parallel (Cohen & Eichenbaum, 1993; Gaffan, 1994; Squire & Zola, 1996). For example, explicit declarative memory formation appears to rely chiefly on the hippocampal formation, rhinal cortex, and associated cortical regions (Eichenbaum, 1999; Gaffan, 1994), whereas some forms of implicit procedural memories, such as skill learning, mainly depend on the striatum (Graybiel, 1995). Emotional memories, particularly those associated with painful or otherwise unpleasant experiences are stored in the amygdala and related brain regions (Davis, 1992; Fanselow, 1994; LeDoux, 2000). This system mediates the emotional reactions that are elicited when these stimuli are re-encountered. It can operate at an implicit or unconscious level (LeDoux, 1996; Öhman, Flykt, & Lundqvist, 2000). However, we usually have explicit or conscious memories about emotional situations as well. These, like other explicit memories, are mediated by the medial temporal lobe memory system mentioned above. The implicit memories of emotional events have been called "emotional memories", and the explicit memories have been termed "memories about emotions" (LeDoux, 1996). Implicit emotional memories are elicited automatically in the presence of trigger stimuli and do not require conscious retrieval or recall, whereas explicit memories of emotion are retrieved consciously. In humans, damage to the amygdala interferes with implicit emotional memories but not explicit memories about emotions, whereas damage to the medial temporal lobe memory system interferes with explicit memories about emotions but not with implicit emotional memories (Bechara et al., 1995; LaBar, LeDoux, Spencer, & Phelps, 1995).

The present chapter reviews the neural circuit underlying the formation of emotional memories, specifically fear-related ones, and describes a computational model of this circuit, based on the known anatomy and physiology of the fear neural network.

FEAR CONDITIONING AS A MODEL FOR EMOTIONAL LEARNING

Fear is a normal reaction to danger and is of particular survival value for humans and animals. In humans, disorders of the fear system can give rise to a number of psychiatric disorders, such as phobias, panic attacks, generalised anxiety disorder, and post-traumatic stress syndrome (Charney, Deutch, Southwick, & Krystal, 1995; LeDoux, 1996; Öhman et al., 2000). Furthermore, fear is an emotion that is particularly amenable to laboratory experimentation: it can be elicited readily, and a number of quantitative measures of fear can be used. A commonly used technique for studying fear, both in humans and experimental animals, is classical aversive conditioning, also known as fear conditioning. With this procedure, an innocuous conditioned stimulus (CS), such as a light or a sound, is associated with a biologically aversive unconditioned stimulus (UCS), typically a loud noise or a brief electric shock. As a result of the CS–UCS pairings, the CS will come to elicit a set of innate, species-specific defensive responses that are naturally elicited by a threatening stimulus. In rats, the measured responses include changes in the behaviour (e.g. immobility, or "freezing", and suppression of ongoing behaviour), autonomic (e.g. heart rate and blood pressure) and hormonal systems, as well as potentiation of reflexes (e.g. startle and eyeblink reflexes). In humans, measured conditioned fear responses typically include heart rate changes, skin conductance responses, and pupil dilation. Fear conditioning is a very robust form of learning, requiring few trials (sometimes a single CS–UCS pairing will suffice) and difficult to extinguish. Furthermore, under certain conditions, it can be induced in the absence of conscious awareness (Morris, Öhman, & Dolan, 1998; Öhman et al., 2000).

NEURAL CIRCUITRY OF FEAR CONDITIONING

Research conducted in several laboratories since the 1990s has helped delineate in great detail the neuroanatomy of the fear circuit (for reviews, see Davis, 1992; Fanselow, 1994; Kapp, Whalen, Supple, & Pascoe, 1992; LeDoux, 2000). It is now generally accepted that the amygdala is a critical component of the neural system involved in learning about stimuli that signal threat. Information about the CS and UCS is integrated in the amygdala and its output controls the behavioural, autonomic, and endocrine effector systems located in the brainstem. Most of the research on fear conditioning has been conducted in rodents within the auditory modality, and thus the description that follows focuses mainly on this system (a more detailed description can be found in LeDoux, 1995, 1996, 2000). Nonetheless, most of the results reported here have been also replicated using other sensory modalities, in rodents and other species, including humans (see below).

An auditory CS is transmitted from the ear, through brainstem areas, to the auditory region of the thalamus, the medial geniculate body (MGB). From there, information reaches the amygdala through two parallel pathways. A direct monosynaptic projection originates primarily in the medial division of the MGB (MGm) and the associated posterior intralaminar nucleus (PIN). A second pathway conveys information from all areas of the thalamus, including the tonotopically organised ventral division of the MGB (MGv), to auditory cortex and then, via several corticocortical links, ultimately to the amygdala. Lesion studies have demonstrated that the two pathways are interchangeable if a single, relatively simple auditory stimulus is paired with the UCS during conditioning (Romanski & LeDoux, 1992). That is, either pathway is independently capable of supporting conditioning to a simple pure tone but, although auditory cortex appears not to be necessary for simple frequency discrimination (see later; Armony et al., 1997b), it can become crucial for higher levels of processing involving complex sounds (Whitfield, 1980). This difference between the two pathways is supported by physiological studies showing that neurons in the MGm/PIN projecting directly to the amygdala have broad receptive fields, compared to those in the MGv, which convey information only to primary auditory cortex. Thus, the direct pathway might be limited in its capacity to represent complex auditory stimuli. In contrast, the indirect thalamocortico-amygdala pathway is longer and slower, as it involves several synapses, but it has a much greater capacity to perform a detailed analysis and provide an accurate representation of the conditioned stimulus. The amygdala also receives inputs from higher multimodal association regions, such as perirhinal cortex and hippocampus. These areas provide information about other sensory cues present during conditioning. In particular, the hippocampus appears to be important for learning about the environmental context associated with the fear conditioning experience (Kim & Fanselow, 1992; Phillips & LeDoux, 1992).

Both thalamic and cortical auditory pathways terminate in the lateral nucleus of the amygdala (LA) (Amaral, Price, Pitkänen, & Carmichael, 1992; Bordi & LeDoux, 1992; LeDoux, Farb, & Ruggiero, 1990; Romanski & LeDoux, 1993), often converging onto single neurons (Li, Stutzmann, & LeDoux, 1996), using the excitatory neurotransmitter glutamate. But whereas the cortical pathway acts only via fast AMPA receptors, the thalamic pathway requires the activation of both AMPA and the slower NMDA receptors (Li, Phillips, & LeDoux, 1995; Li et al., 1996). After the stimulus is processed by the cells in LA, it is transmitted to the central nucleus (CE) via several intraamygdala connections (for a review, see Pitkänen, Savander, & LeDoux, 1997). The central nucleus is the main output of the amygdala involved in controlling conditioned responses (Davis, 1992; Kapp et al., 1992). Lesions of the CE interfere with the elicitation of all conditioned fear responses (Davis, 1992; Kapp et al., 1992; LeDoux, 1995), whereas lesions of regions to which the central nucleus projects abolish specific responses. For example, lesions of the central grey disrupt conditioned motor responses, such as "freezing" (Fanselow, 1991; LeDoux, Iwata, Cicchetti, & Reis, 1988; Wilson & Kapp, 1994), lesions of the lateral hypothalamus abolish conditioned sympathetic responses, such as blood pressure elevation (LeDoux et al., 1988; Smith et al., 1980), and lesions of the bed nucleus of the stria terminalis interfere with neuroendocrine changes (Gray et al., 1989, 1993). A schematic of the neural circuit underlying auditory fear conditioning is depicted in Fig. 14.1.

Many cells in the rat LA respond to auditory stimuli, particularly in the high frequency range, above 10kHz (Bordi & LeDoux, 1992). About 90 per cent of auditory-responsive cells in LA also respond to strong somatosensory stimulation (Romanski, Clugnet, Bordi, & LeDoux, 1993). Therefore, LA is a potential site of CS–UCS convergence at the single-cell level. Similar CS–UCS responsive cells are found in the auditory thalamus (Bordi & LeDoux, 1992; Cruikshank, Edeline, & Weinberger, 1992), although the proportion is smaller (less than 40 per cent). Such an intersection of neural pathways transmitting the CS and UCS has long been suggested to be necessary for conditioning (Hebb, 1949; Konorski, 1967; Pavlov, 1927). Consistent with this hypothesis, several studies have demonstrated that neurons in several components of the fear network exhibit changes in their responses to the CS following conditioning. Specifically, cells in MGm, auditory cortex, and amygdala develop conditioning-induced plasticity. In LA, some cells develop short-latency increases to a tone CS after it has been paired with a footshock UCS. The earliest changes occur within 10–20ms after tone onset (Quirk, Repa, & LeDoux, 1995). These changes cannot be accounted for by cortico-amygdala projections, because the earliest plasticity observed in auditory cortex does not occur until 20–40ms after tone onset (Quirk, Armony, & LeDoux, 1997), suggesting that the earliest changes in CS processing in the amygdala are not dependent on cortical inputs. Conversely, lesions of the amygdala do not interfere with short-latency plasticity in auditory cortex (Armony, Quirk, & LeDoux 1998). Thus, it appears that onset plasticity in amygdala and auditory cortex develop independently, and that both are driven by direct inputs from the thalamus (for a discussion, see Quirk et al., 1996).

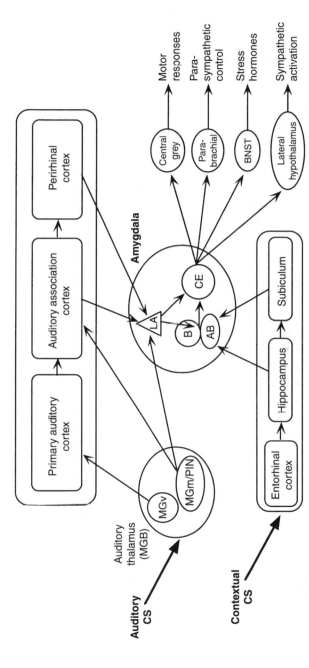

Figure 14.1. The neural circuit underlying fear conditioning to an auditory conditioned stimulus (CS). The lateral nucleus (LA) of the amygdala receives a hierarchical cascade of information from sensory areas in the thalamus and neocortex. Information about the conditioning context reaches the basal (B) and accessory basal (AB) nuclei through the hippocampus and subiculum. The central nucleus (CE) controls the expression of different emotional responses. BNST: bed nucleus of the stria terminalis.

This conditioning-induced plasticity is frequency specific, as evidenced by shifts in the receptive fields of neurons in the lateral amygdala (Bordi, Le Doux, Clugnet, & Pavlides, 1993), as well as in auditory thalamus and auditory cortex, where it was discovered and most extensively studied (for a review, see Weinberger, 1998; Weinberger et al., 1990).

Although most of the findings about the neural basis of fear conditioning have been obtained from studies in experimental animals, particularly rats, recent studies suggest that analogous brain regions and mechanisms are involved in human fear conditioning. For example, patients with temporal lobe lesions that include (LaBar et al., 1995), or are restricted mainly to the amygdala (Bechara et al., 1995) have shown deficits in fear conditioning and in the perception of fear in facial expressions (Adolphs, Tranel, Damasio, & Damasio, 1994) and voices (Scott et al., 1997). In addition, functional neuroimaging studies have now shown activation of the amygdala during fear conditioning (Morris et al., 1998; Büchel et al., 1998, 1999; LaBar et al., 1998; for a review see Büchel and Dolan, 2000) and when processing faces depicting fearful expressions (Morris et al., 1996; Whalen et al., 1998).

A COMPUTATIONAL MODEL OF FEAR CONDITIONING

One of the main goals of cognitive neuroscience is to explain the relation between neural activity and behaviour. In the case of fear conditioning, several hypotheses have been put forward to explain how neural changes occurring in the different components in the circuit lead to the observed behavioural responses (LeDoux, 1996, 2000; Weinberger, 1998). Although useful, these conceptual models are inherently limited in their capacity to provide quantitative tests and predictions of the proposed hypotheses. Computational models, however, are ideally suited for exploring the consistency of, and interactions between, the different assumptions on which the theory is built. Thus, we developed a connectionist model of the fear network to explore the relationship between neurobiological findings and behaviour. That is, our goal was to test whether a set of basic principles could account for a number of neurobiological observations and, at the same time, patterns of behaviour related to the functioning of this neurobiological system.

A diagram of the basic architecture of the model is shown in Figure 14.2. The essential components of the model are the following (more details can be found in Armony et al., 1995, 1997a,b):

(1) *Processing units:* the basic computational elements are non-linear summation units, the output of which can be thought as the time-averaged firing rate of a neuron or a neural assembly that codes redundantly for the same piece of information.

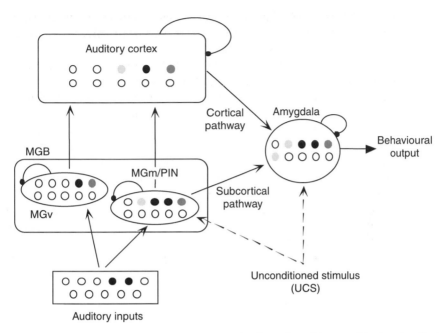

Figure 14.2. Architecture of the network used in the simulation of fear conditioning described in the text. A typical pattern of activation is schematised by representing unit activation with grey shadings (solid circles, maximum activation; open circles, zero activation). Dashed arrows indicate excitatory, non-modifiable connections. Circular arrowheads indicate mutual inhibitory connections between units in each layer. MGv: ventral division of the medial geniculate body (MGB); MGm/PIN: medial division of the MGB and posterior intralaminar nucleus (adapted from Armony et al., 1997b).

(2) *Architecture:* the units are arranged in modules representing the relevant neural structures of the fear circuit: the lemniscal (MGv) and non-lemniscal (MGm/PIN) areas of the auditory thalamus, the auditory cortex, and the amygdala. Connections between units in different modules are feed-forward and excitatory (positive). Units within a module are mutually inhibitory. The strength of this lateral inhibition was used to capture the differences in the response properties (broad versus narrow receptive fields) of the MGm/PIN and amygdala on the one hand, and MGv and auditory cortex on the other hand. Information is processed in two parallel pathways, the direct, or "subcortical", thalamo-amygdala pathway and the indirect, or "cortical", thalamocortico-amygdala stream.

(3) *Sensory inputs:* to train the network, the auditory spectrum was divided into a finite number of pure tones of contiguous frequencies (and equal intensities) in an arbitrary scale. These tones were represented in

the model by overlapping patterns of activation in the input layer. During conditioning, one of these tones was arbitrarily chosen as the CS. The nociceptive input, i.e. the UCS, was represented as an external binary unit projecting to the MGm/PIN and amygdala modules, providing a positive input of equal magnitude to all units in these modules. This design assumption was intended to capture the effect of diffuse somatosensory information associated with a UCS such as footshock. It is based on physiological and anatomical studies showing that cells in these nuclei receive convergent auditory and somatosensory information (as described earlier).

(4) *Behavioural output:* we modelled the behavioural response of the network as the sum of the activation of all the units in the amygdala module. This fairly simplistic assumption was intended to capture the fact that amygdala activation plays a key role in the expression of fear conditioning by controlling the expression of behavioural and autonomic responses, as described earlier.

(5) *Learning:* the strengths of excitatory connections between units were adjusted using a simple modification of the Hebbian learning rule, in which connection strengths are increased between correlated units and decreased for uncorrelated units, by keeping the sum of all incoming weights to a unit constant, through multiplicative normalisation. Together with the lateral inhibitory connections between units within a module, this rule represents a variant of the standard competitive learning rules (Rumelhart & Zipser, 1986), similar to the so-called soft competitive learning (Nowlan, 1990).

Experiments with the model

Conditioning-induced plasticity: From units to behaviour. At the beginning of the simulations, all modifiable weights were set to random values between zero and one and units responded, on average, equally but weakly to all input patterns. Thus, before the conditioning phase, the network was trained in a "development" phase during which all inputs were presented in a random order and the weights adjusted according to the learning rule described above. Following this phase, during which no UCS was presented, units developed receptive fields (RFs): they were activated only by a subset of contiguous tones. The input value eliciting the strongest response is referred to as the unit's best frequency (BF). As described earlier, we adjusted the strength of the lateral inhibitory connections in the different modules to modulate the width of these receptive fields. Accordingly, units in the MGm/PIN and amygdala modules exhibited wide RFs, whereas, by contrast, units in the MGv and auditory cortex modules had narrow receptive fields, responding mainly to their BF and adjacent frequencies. The characteristics of these RFs mimicked those observed in actual cells (Bordi & LeDoux, 1992; Weinberger, 1998; Weinberger et al., 1990).

Following the "development" phase, all inputs patterns were again presented, but this time one of the tones was arbitrarily chosen as the CS, so that its presentation was paired with the delivery of the UCS. As a result of conditioning, some units developed frequency-specific changes in their RFs: units in the MGm/PIN, auditory cortex, and amygdala modules whose RFs prior to conditioning included the CS showed a substantial increase in their response to the CS, in the absence of the UCS, whereas their response to other inputs either remained unchanged or decreased. In many cases, this change resulted in a retuning of the RF, so that the BF shifted towards the CS. Figure 14.3A shows an example of an amygdala unit whose RF showed such a change. Units whose original BFs were relatively distal to the CS and that did not respond to the CS before conditioning did not show a significant change in their receptive fields. Equally, units in the MGv module did not change their response to the CS because they did not receive US input either directly, like the MGm/PIN and amygdala modules, or indirectly, like the auditory cortex module. The unit RF changes observed in the model closely mirrored the changes observed in the exact same areas in animal experiments (see Fig. 14.3B; Bordi & LeDoux, 1993; Weinberger, 1998; Weinberger et al., 1990). This re-representation of the input patterns at the single-unit level in the amygdala was reflected at the behavioural output of the network by an increased response to the CS and neighbouring frequencies, in the form of a stimulus generalisation gradient (SGG), shown in Fig. 14.3C (open symbols). Similar behavioural gradients are observed in animal experiments (Fig. 14.3D, open symbols; see Armony et al., 1997b).

Auditory cortex lesions and stimulus generalisation.   The results described above show that our model of the fear conditioning circuit, although admittedly quite simplistic in many of its features, was able to capture some of the basic physiological and behavioural phenomena observed in fear conditioning experiments. The next step was then to use the model to generate new predictions. In particular, we were interested in the relative contributions of the thalamic (direct) and cortical (indirect) pathways to the amygdala. As described above, the cells of origin of these two inputs differ in their processing capacity; neurons in the MGm/PIN, which provide the direct thalamic projection to the lateral nucleus of the amygdala, have broad receptive fields, whereas cells in auditory cortex are more narrowly tuned. Thus, we hypothesised that lesions of the cortical input to the amygdala would cause an increased generalisation of fear responses to stimuli other than the CS, resulting in a broader stimulus generalisation gradient. We tested this hypothesis in the model by repeating the conditioning simulations described in the preceding section, but setting the connections between the auditory cortex and

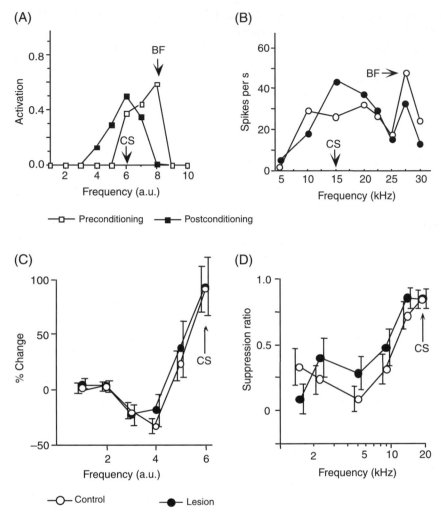

Figure 14.3. Examples of receptive fields (RFs) of amygdala units in the computational model (A) and of amygdala neurons in rats (B), before and after fear conditioning. In both cases, fear conditioning resulted in a shift of RFs, such that the conditioned stimulus (CS) became the new best frequency (BF). This stimulus re-representation, in turn, resulted in increased fear responses to the CS and adjacent frequencies in the model, measured by the output of the amygdala module (C; open symbols) and in rats, measured using suppression of operant responding (D; open symbols), in the form of a stimulus generalisation gradient (SGG). Cortical lesions prior to conditioning did not have a significant effect on the width of the SGG in either case (C, D; filled symbols). a.u., simulated arbitrary frequency units. (A, adapted from Armony et al., 1995; B, based on data from Bordi & LeDoux, 1993; C and D, modified from Armony et al., 1997b).

amygdala units to zero, i.e. "lesioning" the cortico-amygdala pathway. Contrary to our predictions, removal of the cortico-amygdala pathway did not significantly affect the width of the SGG, as shown in Fig. 14.3C. The reason for this lack of effect is intriguing: although units in the MGm/PIN region of the thalamus that provide direct input to the amygdala have broad RFs, the discriminative behaviour mediated by the projection is fairly precise, suggesting that the structure as a whole can be a much better stimulus discriminator, by relying on population coding.

Interestingly, subsequent experiments in rats confirmed the predictions of the model; that is, fairly large lesions of the auditory cortex and associated areas in caudal entorhinal and perirhinal cortices failed to have a significant effect on the conditioned SGG, as shown in Fig. 14.3D. These results, motivated by the predictions of the model, showed that, contrary to what was previously thought (Jarrell et al., 1987; LeDoux, 1995), the direct thalamo-amygdala pathway is capable of supporting some simple forms of stimulus discrimination. Further studies, using both simulations and behavioural experiments, are necessary to elucidate the full capacity, and limitations, of the direct thalamo-amygdala pathway.

Emotional modulation of attention. Top-down selective attention is believed to occur in cortical areas and to result from the competition for allocation of available processing resources, so that task-relevant (i.e. attended) stimuli are focused on at the expense of competing (unattended) ones (Duncan, Humphreys, & Ward, 1997). However, if this mechanism operated unconditionally, adverse consequences could arise in some conditions. For example, if a stimulus signalling the presence of danger appeared in an unattended location of the environment, it would be ignored due to its reduced cortical representation because of attentional filtering. This, however, is not generally the case; we are able to respond to threats arising outside our focus of attention (Öhman et al., 2000). Furthermore, recent neuroimaging studies show that the amygdala responds to fearful faces even when they are presented in unattended locations (Vuilleumier et al., 2001). We have hypothesised (Armony & LeDoux, 2000; Armony et al., 1997a) that the thalamo-amygdala pathway might constitute an attention-independent channel that provides the amygdala with information about threat stimuli that occur outside or inside the focus of attention. We tested this hypothesis by extending our computational model of the fear circuit to include modulation of cortical processing by selective attention (task demand), as proposed by Cohen, Dunbar, and McClelland (1990). The architecture of the network is shown in Fig. 14.4. Two parallel processing streams, representing different aspects of the environment (such as visual or auditory hemifields) or task demands (e.g. colour naming versus word reading in the Stroop task; Stroop, 1935), compete for the limited pool of cortical

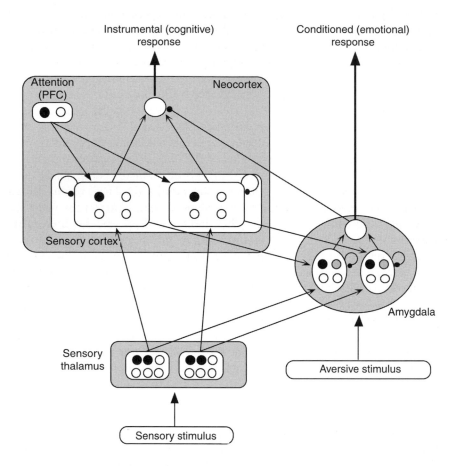

Figure 14.4. Architecture of the network used to model the modulation of attention by fear conditioning. The network represents an integration of the original fear model of Armony et al. (1995, 1997b; see Fig. 14.2) and the model of selective attention of Cohen et al. (1990). Sensory information flows along two parallel processing streams, representing different dimensions of the stimulus space. The two streams compete for cortical resources, which are allocated by externally set attentional input by way of the prefrontal cortex (PFC). Emotional (fear) responses have the capacity to inhibit instrumental responses.

processing resources to determine behavioural responses. Selective attention units, externally set by the task demands and thought to be mediated by projections from prefrontal cortex, bias one cortical representation over the other, depending on the task demand (e.g. attending to the left or naming colours of stimuli), so that the appropriate response is given. This behavioural output resulted from the competition between instrumental (cognitive) responses, determined from the output of the cortical module, and fear-related (emotional) responses, elicited by amygdala activation. This response competition was implemented in a asymmetrical fashion, such that the fear response had the capacity to inhibit instrumental responses. This design was intended to represent, in a simplistic fashion, empirical observations that fear reactions can interfere with, and interrupt, ongoing behaviour in favour of danger-elicited defensive responses (Bouton & Bolles, 1980).

This model predicts that whereas lesions of either pathway will have no effect on fear responses to a conditioned stimulus if it occurs within the focus of attention, lesions of the direct thalamo-amygdala pathway will interfere with fear responses to an unattended CS. Furthermore, results of simulations suggest that significant interference in stimulus processing in cognitive–attentional tasks, such as the Stroop word–colour interference task, can occur when some of the stimuli have acquired strong negative affective value through fear conditioning (Armony et al., 1996, 1997a). Thus, the model shows how emotional processing can operate independently of, and modulate the focus of, attentional mechanisms.

CONCLUSIONS

The neural system involved in learning about dangerous stimuli has evolved very early in the phylogenetic scale and has remained essentially unchanged throughout evolution. The system involves transmission of information, through parallel and complementary channels, to the amygdala. The amygdala has the capacity to integrate and learn this information and, if appropriate, retrieve it and elicit a host of species-typical survival responses.

This chapter described the basic anatomical and physiological features of the neural system underlying fear conditioning, a well-characterised form of emotional learning. Next, a computational model based on this circuit was described. The set of assumptions about connectivity and learning on which the model is based has proven sufficient to account for several of the phenomena observed in animals during fear conditioning, both at the behavioural and single-cell levels. Other models of classical conditioning in the literature can account for several of the findings described here (Grossberg & Gutowski, 1987; Grossberg & Schmajuk, 1987; Myers & Gluck, 1994). However, the approach taken here is different. Previous models have typically attempted to describe a wide range of various complex behaviours, followed by a *post hoc* identification of the underlying neural substrates. In contrast, the modelling work presented here is based on a very specific and well-known system, that of fear conditioning, through which we have tried to establish a link between the circuit level and the physiological and behavioural changes that occur through learning. Further extensions and improvement of this anatomically and physiologically constrained model may continue to help enhance our understanding of the neural mechanisms underlying the formation of emotional memories.

ACKNOWLEDGEMENTS

The work described here was conducted in collaboration with Joseph LeDoux, David Servan-Schreiber and Jonathan Cohen.

REFERENCES

Adolphs, R., Tranel, D., Damasio, H., & Damasio, A.R. (1994). Impaired recognition of emotion in facial expressions following bilateral damage to the human amygdala. *Nature*, *372*, 669–672.

Amaral, D.G., Price, J.L., Pitkänen, A., & Carmichael, S.T. (1992). Anatomical organization of the primate amygdaloid complex. In J.P. Aggleton (Ed.) *The amygdala: Neurobiological aspects of emotion, memory, and mental dysfunction* (pp. 1–66). New York: Wiley-Liss, Inc.

Armony, J.L., & LeDoux, J.E. (2000). How danger is encoded: Towards a systems, cellular, and computational understanding of cognitive–emotional interactions. In M.S. Gazzaniga (Ed.) *The new cognitive neurosciences* (2nd ed.) (pp. 1067–1079). Cambridge, MA: The MIT Press.

Armony, J.L., Quirk, G.J., & LeDoux, J.E. (1998). Differential effects of amygdala lesions on early and late plastic components of auditory cortex spike trains during fear conditioning. *Journal of Neuroscience*, *18*(7), 2592–2601.

Armony, J.L., Servan-Schreiber, D., Cohen, J.D., & LeDoux, J.E. (1995). An anatomically constrained neural network model of fear conditioning. *Behavioral Neuroscience, 109*(2), 246–257.

Armony, J.L., Servan-Schreiber, D., Cohen, J.D., & LeDoux, J.E. (1996). Emotion and cognition interactions in the thalamo-cortico-amygdala network: Theory and model. *Cognitive Neuroscience Society Abstracts*, *3*, 76.

Armony, J.L., Servan-Schreiber, D., Cohen, J.D., & LeDoux, J.E. (1997a). Computational modeling of emotion: Explorations through the anatomy and physiology of fear conditioning. *Trends in Cognitive Sciences*, *1*, 28–34.

Armony, J.L., Servan-Schreiber, D., Romanski, L.M., Cohen, J.D., & LeDoux, J.E. (1997b). Stimulus generalization of fear responses: Effects of auditory cortex lesions in a computational model and in rats. *Cerebral Cortex*, *7*(2), 157–165.

Bechara, A., Tranel, D., Damasio, H., Adolphs, R., Rockland, C., & Damasio, A.R. (1995). Double dissociation of conditioning and declarative knowledge relative to the amygdala and hippocampus in humans. *Science*, *269*(5227), 1115–1118.

Bordi, F., & LeDoux, J.E. (1992). Sensory tuning beyond the sensory system: an initial analysis of auditory properties of neurones in the lateral amygdaloid nucleus and overlying areas of the striatum. *Journal of Neuroscience*, *12*(7), 2493–2503.

Bordi, F., & LeDoux, J.E. (1993). Sensory-specific conditioned plasticity in lateral amygdala neurones. *Society of Neuroscience Abstrract*, *19*, 1227.

Bordi, F., LeDoux, J.E., Clugnet, M.C., & Pavlides, C. (1993). Single unit activity in the lateral nucleus of the amygdala and overlying areas of the striatum in freely-behaving rats: rates, discharge patterns, and responses to acoustic stimuli. *Behavioral Neuroscience, 107,* 757–769.

Bouton, M.E., & Bolles, R.C. (1980). Conditioned fear assessed by freezing and by the suppression of three different baselines. *Animal Learning and Behaviour, 8,* 429–434.

Büchel, C., & Dolan, R.J. (2000). Classical fear conditioning in functional neuroimaging. *Current Opinion in Neurobiology, 10*(2), 219–223.

Büchel, C., Dolan, R.J., Armony, J.L., & Friston, K.J. (1999). Amygdala-hippocampal involvement in human aversive trace conditioning revealed through event-related functional magnetic resonance imaging. *Journal of Neuroscience, 19*(24), 10869–10876.

Büchel, C., Morris, J., Dolan, R.J., & Friston, K.J. (1998). Brain systems mediating aversive conditioning: an event-related fMRI study. *Neuron, 20*(5), 947–957.

Charney, D.S., Deutch, A.Y., Southwick, S.M., & Krystal, J.H. (1995). Neural circuits and mechanisms of post-traumatic stress disorder. In M.J. Friedman, D.S. Charney, & A.Y. Deutch (Eds.), *Neurobiological and clinical consequences of stress: from normal adaptation to PTSD* (pp. 271–287). Philadelphia: Lippincott-Raven.

Cohen, J.D., Dunbar, K., & McClelland, J.L. (1990). On the control of automatic processes: A parallel distributed processing account of the Stroop effect. *Psychological Review, 97,* 332–361.

Cohen, N.J., & Eichenbaum, H. (1993). *Memory, amnesia, and the hippocampal system.* Cambridge, MA: The MIT Press.

Cruikshank, S.J., Edeline, J.-M., & Weinberger, N.M. (1992). Stimulation at a site of auditory–somatosensory convergence in the medial geniculate nucleus is an effective unconditioned stimulus for fear conditioning. *Behavioral Neuroscience, 106,* 471–483.

Davis, M. (1992). The role of the amygdala in conditioned fear. In J.P. Aggleton (Ed.) *The amygdala: Neurobiological aspects of emotion, memory, and mental dysfunction* (pp. 255–306). New York: Wiley-Liss, Inc.

Duncan, J., Humphreys, G., & Ward, R. (1997). Competitive brain activity in visual attention. *Current Opinion in Neurobiology, 7,* 255–261.

Eichenbaum, H. (1999). The hippocampus and mechanisms of declarative memory. *Behavioral Brain Research, 103,* 123–133.

Fanselow, M.S. (1991). Analgesia as a response to aversive pavlovian conditional stimuli: Cognitive and emotional mediators. In M.R. Denny (Ed.) *Fear, avoidance, and phobias: A fundamental analysis* (pp. 61–86). Hillsdale, NJ: Lawrence Erlbaum Associates, Inc.

Fanselow, M.S. (1994). Neural organization of the defensive behaviour system responsible for fear. *Psychonomic Bulletin and Review, 1,* 429–438.

Gaffan, D. (1994). Dissociated effects of perirhinal cortex ablation, fornix transection and amygdalectomy: Evidence for multiple memory systems in the primate temporal lobe. *Experimental Brain Research, 99,* 411–422.

Gray, T.S., Carney, M.E., & Magnuson, D.J. (1989). Direct projections from the central amygdaloid nucleus to the hypothalamic paraventricular nucleus: Possible role in stress-induced adrenocorticotropin release. *Neuroendocrinology, 50,* 433–446.

Gray, T.S., Piechowski, R.A., Yracheta, J.M., Rittenhouse, P.A., Betha, C.L., & van der Kar, L.D. (1993). Ibotenic acid lesions in the bed nucleus of the stria terminalis attenuate conditioned stress induced increases in prolactin, ACTH, and corticosterone. *Neuroendocrinology, 57,* 517–524.

Graybiel, A.M. (1995). Building action repertoires: Memory and learning functions of the basal ganglia. *Current Opinion in Neurobiology, 5,* 733–741.

Grossberg, S., & Gutowski, W.E. (1987). Neural dynamics of decision making under risk: affective balance and cognitive-emotional interactions. *Psychological Review, 94,* 300–318.

Grossberg, S., & Schmajuk, N.A. (1987). Neural dynamics of attentionally modulate Pavlovian conditioning: Conditioned reinforcement, inhibition, and opponent processing. *Psychobiology*, *15*, 195–240.

Hebb, D.O. (1949). *The organization of behaviour*. New York: John Wiley and Sons.

Jarrell, T.W., Gentile, C.G., Romanski, L.M., McCabe, P.M., & Schneiderman, N. (1987). Involvement of cortical and thalamic auditory regions in retention of differential bradycardia conditioning to acoustic conditioned stimuli in rabbits. *Brain Research*, *412*, 285–294.

Kapp, B.S., Whalen, P.J., Supple, W.F., & Pascoe, J.P. (1992). Amygdaloid contributions to conditioned arousal and sensory information processing. In J. P. Aggleton (Ed.) *The amygdala: Neurobiological aspects of emotion, memory, and mental dysfunction*. New York: Wiley-Liss.

Kim, J.J., & Fanselow, M.S. (1992). Modality-specific retrograde amnesia of fear. *Science*, *256*, 675–677.

Konorski, J. (1967). Transient (or dynamic) memory. In J. Konorski (Ed.) *Integrative activity of the brain* (pp. 490–505). Chicago: University of Chicago Press.

LaBar, K.S., LeDoux, J.E., Spencer, D.D., & Phelps, E.A. (1995). Impaired fear conditioning following unilateral temporal lobectomy in humans. *Journal of Neuroscience*, *15*(10), 6846–6855.

LaBar, K.S., Gatenby, J.C., Gore, J.C., LeDoux, J.E., & Phelps, E.A. (1998). Human amygdala activation during conditioned fear acquisition and extinction: A mixed-trial fMRI study. *Neuron*, *20*(5), 937–945.

LeDoux, J. (1996). *The Emotional Brain*. New York: Simon & Schuster.

LeDoux, J.E. (1995). Emotion: Clues from the brain. *Annual Review of Psychology*, *46*, 209–235.

LeDoux, J.E. (2000). Emotion circuits in the brain. *Annual Review of Neuroscience*, *23*, 155–184.

LeDoux, J.E., Farb, C.F., & Ruggiero, D.A. (1990). Topographic organization of neurones in the acoustic thalamus that project to the amygdala. *Journal of Neuroscience*, *10*, 1043–1054.

LeDoux, J.E., Iwata, J., Cicchetti, P., & Reis, D.J. (1988). Different projections of the central amygdaloid nucleus mediate autonomic and behavioural correlates of conditioned fear. *Journal of Neuroscience*, *8*, 2517–2529.

Li, X., Phillips, R.G., & LeDoux, J.E. (1995). NMDA and non-NMDA receptors contribute to synaptic transmission between the medial geniculate body and the lateral nucleus of the amygdala. *Experimental Brain Research*, *105*, 87–100.

Li, X.F., Stutzmann, G.E., & LeDoux, J.E. (1996). Convergent but temporally separated inputs to lateral amygdala neurones from the auditory thalamus and auditory cortex use different postsynaptic receptors: *In vivo* intracellular and extracellular recordings in fear conditioning pathways. *Learning & Memory*, *3*, 229–242.

Morris, J.S., Frith, C.D., Perrett, D.I., Rowland, D., Young, A.W., Calder, A.J., & Dolan, R.J. (1996). A differential neural response in the human amygdala to fearful and happy facial expressions. *Nature*, *383*, 812–815.

Morris, J.S., Öhman, A., & Dolan, R.J. (1998). Conscious and unconscious emotional learning in the human amygdala. *Nature*, *393*(6684), 467–470.

Myers, C.E., & Gluck, M.A. (1994). Context, conditioning, and hippocampal representation in animal learning. *Behavioral Neuroscience*, *108*, 835–847.

Nowlan, S.J. (1990). Maximum likelihood competitive learning. In D.S. Touretsky (Ed.) *Advances in neural information processing systems 2* (pp. 574–582). San Mateo, CA: Morgan Kaufmann Publishers, Inc.

Öhman, A., Flykt, A., & Lundqvist, D. (2000). Unconscious emotion: Evolutionary perspectives, psychophysical data and neuropsychological mechanisms. In R.D. Lane & L. Nadel (Eds.) *Cognitive neuroscience of emotion* (pp. 296–327). New York: Oxford University Press.

Pavlov, I.P. (1927). *Conditioned Reflexes*. New York: Dover.

Phillips, R.G., & LeDoux, J.E. (1992). Differential contribution of amygdala and hippocampus to cued and contextual fear conditioning. *Behavioral Neuroscience*, *106*, 274–285.

Pitkänen, A., Savander, V., & LeDoux, J.E. (1997). Organization of intra-amygdaloid circuitries:

An emerging framework for understanding functions of the amygdala. *Trends in Neuroscience, 20*, 517–523.

Quirk, G.J., Armony, J.L., & LeDoux, J.E. (1997). Fear conditioning enhances different temporal components of tone-evoked spike trains in auditory cortex and lateral amygdala. *Neuron, 19*(3), 613–624.

Quirk, G.J., Armony, J.L., Repa, J.C., Li, X.-F., & LeDoux, J.E. (1996). Emotional memory: A search for sites of plasticity. *Cold Spring Harbor Symposia on Quantitative Biology, 61*, 247–257.

Quirk, G.J., Repa, J.C., & LeDoux, J.E. (1995). Fear conditioning enhances short-latency auditory responses of lateral amygdala neurones: Parallel recordings in the freely behaving rat. *Neuron, 15*, 1029–1039.

Romanski, L.M., Clugnet, M.C., Bordi, F., & LeDoux, J.E. (1993). Somatosensory and auditory convergence in the lateral nucleus of the amygdala. *Behavioral Neuroscience, 107*, 444–450.

Romanski, L.M., & LeDoux, J.E. (1992). Equipotentiality of thalamo-amygdala and thalamo-cortico-amygdala projections as auditory conditioned stimulus pathways. *Journal of Neuroscience, 12*, 4501–4509.

Romanski, L.M., & LeDoux, J.E. (1993). Information cascade from primary auditory cortex to the amygdala: Corticocortical and corticoamygdaloid projections of temporal cortex in the rat. *Cerebral Cortex, 3*, 515–532.

Rumelhart, D.E., & Zipser, D. (1986). Feature discovery by competitive learning. In D.E. Rumelhart & J.L. McClelland (Eds.) *Parallel distributed processing. Volume 1: Foundations.* (pp. 147–193). Boston, MA: MIT Press.

Scott, S.K., Young, A.W., Calder, A.J., Hellawell, D.J., Aggleton, J.P., & Johnson, M. (1997). Impaired auditory recognition of fear and anger following bilateral amygdala lesions. *Nature, 385*, 254–257.

Smith, O.A., Astley, C.A., Devito, J.L., Stein, J.M., & Walsh, R.E. (1980). Functional analysis of hypothalamic control of the cardiovascular responses accompanying emotional behaviour. *Federation Proceedings, 39(8)*, 2487–2494.

Squire, L.R., & Zola, S.M. (1996). Structure and function of declarative and nondeclarative memory systems. *Proceedings of the National Academy of Sciences USA, 93*, 13515–13522.

Stroop, J.R. (1935). Studies of interference in serial verbal reactions. *Journal of Experimental Psychology, 18*, 643–662.

Vuilleumier, P., Armony, J.L., Driver, J., & Dolan, R.J. (2001). Amygdala activation by seen and unseen fearful faces in unilateral spatial neglect: Event-related fMRI. *NeuroImage, 13*, 5482.

Weinberger, N.M. (1998). Physiological memory in primary auditory cortex: Characteristics and mechanisms. *Neurobiology of Learning and Memory, 70*, 226–251.

Weinberger, N.M., Ashe, J., Metherate, R., McKenna, T., Diamond, D., Bakin, J., Lennartz, R., & Cassady, J. (1990). Neural adaptive information processing: A preliminary model of receptive-field plasticity in auditory cortex during Pavlovian conditioning. In M. Gabriel & J. Moore (Eds.) *Learning and computational neuroscience: Foundations of adaptive networks* (pp. 91–138). Cambridge, MA: MIT Press.

Whalen, P.J., Rauch, S.L., Etcoff, N.L., McInerney, S.C., Lee, M.B., & Jenike, M.A. (1998). Masked presentations of emotional facial expressions modulate amygdala activity without explicit knowledge. *Journal of Neuroscience, 18*, 411–418.

Whitfield, I.C. (1980). Auditory cortex and the pitch of complex tones. *Journal of the Acoustic Society of America, 67*, 644–647.

Wilson, A., & Kapp, B.S. (1994). Effect of lesions of the ventrolateral periaqueductal gray on the Pavlovian conditioned heart rate response in the rabbit. *Behavioral and Neural Biology, 62*, 73–76.

CHAPTER FIFTEEN

From spike frequency to free recall: How neural circuits perform encoding and retrieval

Michael Hasselmo, Bradley P. Wyble and Robert C. Cannon
Department of Psychology and Program in Neuroscience,
Boston University, MA, USA

INTRODUCTION

Researchers have described numerous hypotheses of hippocampal function based on lesion data, attempting to present these hypotheses entirely in verbal terms—using terms such as "interference", "response inhibition", "context", "temporal contiguity", "snapshot memory", etc. This method of hypothesis presentation results in an incomplete and distorted perception of the experimental data, as it is filtered through the multiple associations that each individual has with these verbal terms. Even the terms used in the title of this chapter, such as episodic memory and spatial navigation, come laden with semantic associations that can distract from the essential features of hippocampal function.

Theories of hippocampal function will converge on a comprehensive account of a full range of behavioural data only when hypotheses are directly presented in terms of physiological and anatomical data, without any distortion by verbal description. Linking these levels requires computational models that are constructed at a neural level within the constraints of physiological and anatomical data. Ultimately, linking these levels will require not only that the models of information processing proceed on a neural level, but that the input and output of the network should be defined in terms of the actual interactions with the environment. In other words, it will not be enough to build a biological model. We can avoid the distorted perceptions of verbal hypotheses only when biological models interact directly with a virtual animal moving in a virtual environment. Only then can every element of the behavioural data be tested in the context of the biological data.

This chapter presents an overview of existing models of hippocampal function, which constitute only an initial sketch of what must ultimately become a sophisticated computational framework. The first half will focus on some standard models of episodic memory function and important open research questions. The latter half will present models of spatial navigation, including a first attempt at directly guiding navigation behaviour with a neural simulation.

MODELLING HUMAN EPISODIC MEMORY FUNCTION

An extensive literature concerns the mechanisms of human episodic memory (Tulving & Markovitch, 1998). For the purpose of the modelling presented here, episodic memory is defined as the memory of an individual for a set of related events within an episode experienced by the subject within a specific delimited time period at a specific spatial location, and which the subject can access in a flexible and comprehensive manner. This is usually measured with specific laboratory tests using verbal materials. Damage to the hippocampal formation has been demonstrated to impair a number of tasks requiring memory for verbal information in a specific behavioral context. For example, damage to the hippocampus significantly decreases the percentage accuracy of performance on delayed free recall of an encoded list of words, or encoding and retrieval of paired associates (Graf, Squire, & Mandler, 1984; Scoville & Milner, 1957). Selective lesions of hippocampal subregions due to hypoxia cause statistically significant memory impairments in these tasks, although the effects might be somewhat less severe in some cases (Rempel-Clower, Zola, Squire, & Amaral, 1996; Zola-Morgan, Squire, & Amaral, 1986).

Thus, when a subject participates in a specific experiment and learns an arbitrary association between a pair of words (e.g. dishtowel–locomotive), the encoding of that association in the specific experimental context appears to depend upon circuitry within the hippocampal formation. Here we will focus on some features of a model (Hasselmo & Wyble, 1997) that demonstrates how populations of hippocampal neurons might be involved in specific human memory tasks, such as paired associate memory, free recall, and recognition. This model has many features in common with other models of hippocampal memory function (Hasselmo & Wyble, 1997; Levy, 1996; Marr, 1971; McNaughton & Morris, 1987; Treves & Rolls, 1994). The model attributes particular functional roles to individual subregions of the hippocampal formation, as summarised in Fig. 15.1.

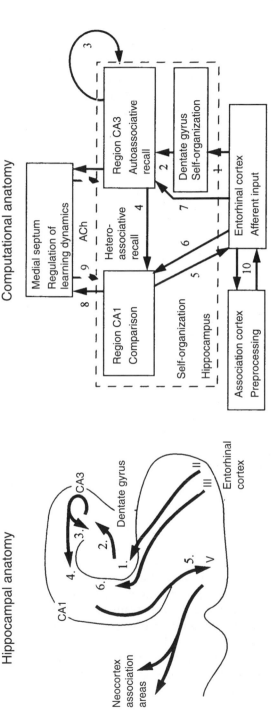

Figure 15.1. Left: overview of the anatomical connectivity of the hippocampal formation. These connections include: 1. perforant path connections from entorhinal cortex layer II to the dentate gyrus; 2. mossy fibres projecting from the dentate gyrus and synapsing on region CA3 pyramidal cells; 3. the longitudinal association fibres providing excitatory recurrent connections between pyramidal cells in region CA3; 4. the Schaffer collaterals connecting pyramidal cells of region CA3 to pyramidal cells of region CA1; 5. excitatory feedback projections from region CA1 and subiculum to deep layers of the entorhinal cortex; 6. direct perforant path projections from entorhinal cortex layer III to region CA1. Most sensory input entering the hippocampus arrives via layers II and III of entorhinal cortex, which receives convergent input from a range of multimodal association cortices. Output to cortical structures projects via deep layers of entorhinal cortex. Right: summary of the basic components of hippocampal memory models. Individual subregions of the hippocampus shown on the left are modelled with populations of processing units with connections summarised on the right. Each rectangle in the figure on the right represents a population of processing units in the model. Arrows represent synaptic connectivity within the models. In addition to the connections summarised in Fig. 3.1, computational models include: 7. direction perforant path projections from entorhinal cortex layer II to region CA3; 8. connections from regions CA1 and CA3 to subcortical circuits influencing the activity of neurons in the medial septum; 9. modulatory cholinergic and GABAergic innervation from the medial septum to the hippocampus; 10. bidirectional connections between entorhinal cortex and higher order association cortices, including perirhinal cortex and parahippocampal gyrus.

Region CA3

In this model, the primary locus for encoding of associations was in region CA3 of the hippocampal formation. Two features of region CA3 make it particularly appealing as the locus for storage of episodic memory: (1) the convergence of multimodal sensory information on this region means that strengthening of synapses here could provide associative links between distinct sensory stimuli without any strong prior associative link, e.g. between the word "dishtowel" and the word "locomotive"; (2) the capacity for rapidly inducing large changes in size of synaptic potentials (long-term potentiation) at the excitatory connections between neurons in this region suggests that this region can more rapidly encode associations than many other pathways. As an initial example, we will consider the role of hippocampal region CA3 in paired associate memory function (Hasselmo & Wyble, 1997), separately considering the dynamics necessary for encoding and retrieval (although, as noted later, these encoding and retrieval dynamics could occur rapidly within short time periods).

Encoding. How might the association between the words "dishtowel" and "locomotive" be stored in neural network models of the hippocampus? First, recognition of the two words activates regions of temporal lobe language cortex. Patterns of activity then spread into populations of neurons in the entorhinal cortex. Physiological and behavioural evidence suggests that the parahippocampal and entorhinal cortices provide the means for holding information about this event for a period of time (Young, Otto, Fox, & Eichenbaum, 1997; Fransen et al., 1999; Hasselmo, Fransen, Dickson, & Alonso, 2000). During this period of entorhinal activity, the activity will also influence the hippocampus. A specific subset of neurons in the dentate gyrus receives input from the entorhinal cortex. These neurons do not represent the use of the words "dishtowel" and "locomotive" in all contexts, but instead represent the specific use of the words in the specific behavioural context. The same neurons will play a role in portions of a wide variety of different memories. These neurons provide the basic code for the episodic memory.

Activity in the dentate gyrus is then passed on to region CA3. In this area, widely distributed connections give the potential for random associations between a number of disparate perceptions. Thus, even if different neurons within the inferotemporal cortex or dentate gyrus become activated the two words, region CA3 has the capability of binding together these disparate items into a unified memory for the event.

This process is summarised in Fig. 15.2. Within region CA3, activity in a subset of neurons representing the word "dishtowel" (item 1) occurs at the same time or as activity in a subset of neurons representing the word "locomotive" (item 2). As this activity repetitively activates the neurons, the

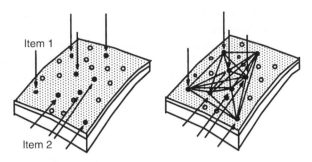

Figure 15.2.   Left: afferent input evokes a pattern of activity in region CA3. Filled circles represent active neurons in the network. Different inputs evoke different patterns of activity in region CA3. For example, presentation of the first word in the context of a specific memory task (item 1) might evoke activity in one set of neurons. Presentation of the second word in that task (item 2) might evoke a second pattern of active neurons. Right: Hebbian synaptic modification strengthens synapses between active neurons.

processes of synaptic modification gradually increases the efficacy of synapses between these two sets of neurons. This forms the basic trace of the event.

Connections within region CA3 might not be the only synapses being modified. Synapses between region CA3 and the entorhinal cortex could also be modified, forming stronger connections between each element of the memory and the patterns of activity occurring in other cortical areas. Whatever the case, this distributed change in the pattern of synaptic connectivity will allow later retrieval of the episodic memory.

Synapses constantly change in synaptic strength, under the influence of a variety of factors. The process of long-term potentiation could result from the same processes altering synaptic strength during learning, and has been studied extensively as an experimental phenomenon (Bliss & Collingridge, 1993; Levy & Steward, 1983). Several different time courses have been described, all of which might map to specific features of the decay of memory. This process of forgetting has been studied extensively on a behavioural level but surprisingly little effort has focused on relating the specific time course of long-term potentiation to the specific time courses of behavioural forgetting.

Retrieval.   What processes allow retrieval of this association? In the paired-associate memory task, the experimenter gives the first word (e.g. "dishtowel") as a cue. First, this information must activate language representations in the auditory cortex. The activity will evoke some activity in the entorhinal cortex, which can activate the episodic representation of that word formed within the dentate gyrus. Activity spreads from the dentate gyrus into region CA3. Within region CA3, the population of neurons associated with the word "dishtowel" becomes active.

As shown in Fig. 15.3, once the population of neurons in region CA3 associated with the word "dishtowel" becomes active, then the activity spreads across the previously modified synapses into a specific separate population of neurons. These are the neurons representing the word "locomotive."

One or more passes of activity through the hippocampus could retrieve other aspects of the episodic event—the expression on the experimenter's face or the layout of furniture in the room. Each of these pieces of information can be extracted from different overlapping sequences, all of which together constitute the episodic memory for that event. The interitem associations necessary to construct this memory depend on the flow of activity across sets of synaptic connections, allowing specific populations of neurons in region CA3 to evoke activity in other specific populations of neurons. Figure 15.4 depicts flexible retrieval within an associative network.

Once the activity has been evoked in region CA3, it will spread along

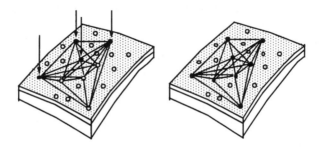

Figure 15.3.   Left: a retrieval cue evokes activity in a subset of neurons in region CA3. Right: activity spreads along excitatory recurrent connections within region CA3 to evoke the full pattern of activity.

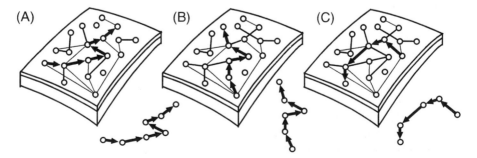

Figure 15.4.   Example of retrieval of distinct relational properties or sequences of events from a network of encoded associations. Responses to different questions about an episodic event can result in different sequences of accessing the necessary information to answer the question.

backprojections into neurons of the entorhinal cortex, and subsequently into neurons of the parahippocampal cortex, temporal cortex, and frontal cortex. An important function for these regions is to receive specific items evoked within sequences in region CA3 and to hold memory for these specific items until the time when the response is necessary. In this way, a full narrative of the event can be generated, or individual specific questions can be answered without requiring repeated access to the original memory.

Free recall and recognition. The same model was used to simulate hippocampal involvement in free recall and recognition (Hasselmo & Wyble, 1997). In free-recall experiments, subjects are presented with a list of words during encoding. In a separate retrieval phase they are asked what words were on the list, and retrieve them in arbitrary order. No specific cue elicits the retrieval of each word, instead, the general experimental context must serve as a cue for retrieval of each word. Thus, in the simulation of free recall (Hasselmo & Wyble, 1997), region CA3 provides a network in which the memory for individual words then takes the form of associations between a single episodic representation of the context and the episodic representation of the individual word items.

In this simulation, activation of the context attractor state causes activity to spread to multiple different item attractors. These item attractors compete, allowing only one item attractor to predominate and be retrieved. After a period of activity, a wave of inhibition shuts off all attractors (possibly analogous to the oscillatory inhibition associated with theta rhythm oscillations). Subsequently, activation of the context attractor state again causes activity to spread to multiple-item attractors, but the previously retrieved item has sufficient residual adaptation that it cannot be retrieved repetitively.

Recognition memory for individual words has been proposed to involve two different processes: (1) explicit remembering of the episode when the word was encoded; and (2) the fluency of activation of single items, regardless of an association to context. The first type of recognition was modelled in conjunction with free recall (Hasselmo & Wyble, 1997), simply using activation of the item as a cue and evaluating whether the context can be activated by spread along strengthened associative synapses. The second type of recognition probably does not involve hippocampal circuits, but might instead be located in the neocortex (O'Reilly, Norman, & McClelland, 1998).

This description focused on simple sequential activation of separate populations of neurons, but the extensive excitatory connections within the network could allow explosive growth of activity. Thus, there must be some mechanism for preventing continuous explosive growth. A simple mechanism for controlling excitatory feedback uses subtractive inhibition (Hasselmo & Wyble, 1997; Hasselmo, Schnell, & Barkai, 1995; Wilson & Cowan, 1972). Other mechanisms for preventing explosive growth of activity include shunting inhibition providing division of activity (Levy, 1996; McNaughton & Morris, 1987; Treves & Rolls, 1994) saturation of excitatory synaptic transmission (Fransen & Lansner, 1998), or imposing a "k-winners-take-all" scheme (O'Reilly et al., 1998), in which only a set number of neurons can be active. Whereas most existing models have focused on obtaining a stable activity level, it might be sufficient to utilise cycles of inhibition on the time course of gamma or theta rhythm oscillations, which will initially allow a spread of activity that is then curtailed (Wallenstein & Hasselmo, 1997).

Problem of differential dynamics during encoding and retrieval

In addition to the potential for causing explosions of activity, excitatory recurrent connections also have the potential to interfere with the encoding of new patterns. This would cause severe proactive interference in episodic memory and would prevent construction of useful associative links for spatial navigation (see Fig. 15.7, below). Because of this, most associative memory models have had separate dynamics during encoding, with clamping of activity to the desired input pattern (Amit, 1988; Kohonen, 1984). In those models, spread of activity along excitatory connections between units within the network is only allowed during retrieval.

What physiological mechanisms could provide these separate dynamics for encoding and retrieval? A number of models have proposed that these separate dynamics can be obtained by selectively regulating the relative strength of three variables: (1) excitatory synaptic transmission within the hippocampus; (2) excitatory input from entorhinal cortex; and (3) long-term potentiation (Hasselmo et al., 1995, 1996, 2002). Modulatory input from the medial septum can potentially cause these changes in network dynamics on different time scales, causing fast changes in dynamics through effects at GABA receptors during theta rhythm (Hasselmo et al., 1996, 2002) and slow changes in dynamics through effects at muscarinic acetylcholine receptors (Hasselmo et al., 1995).

Appropriate encoding dynamics require strong afferent input from entorhinal cortex. At the same time, the internal connections of the hippocampus (including both recurrent connections in region CA3 and the Schaffer collaterals from CA3 to CA1) would undergo strong synaptic modification but weak synaptic transmission. By contrast, retrieval dynamics would have weaker afferent input, with strong internal synaptic transmission but weak synaptic modification. Previous research has not emphasised these requirements but existing physiological data demonstrate these changes during theta rhythm oscillations in the electroencephalogram (EEG). Theta rhythm appears when animals are actively exploring the environment or attending to behaviourally relevant stimuli (Buzsaki, Leung, & Vanderwolf,

1983; Chrobak & Buzsaki, 1994). Physiological data show that theta is associated with sequential phases of strong entorhinal input to region CA1, followed by strong CA3 input to region CA1 (Bragin et al., 1995; Brankack, Stewart, & Fox, 1993; Rudell et al., 1980; Wyble, Linster, & Hasselmo, 2000). The dynamics described above have the paradoxical requirement that long-term potentiation of the connections from region CA3 should be strongest when the synaptic transmission at these connections is weakest. Surprisingly, previous physiological data already support this paradoxical requirement, showing that induction of long-term potentiation (LTP) works best at the peak of local theta—when synaptic transmission is the weakest (Holscher, Anwyl, & Rowan, 1997; Huerta & Lisman, 1993). Thus, theta rhythm dynamics could provide rapid switching between encoding and retrieval dynamics (Hasselmo et al., 2002). The encoding phase would also be enhanced by strong input from the dentate gyrus. Physiological data demonstrates that stimulation of septum enhances dentate gyrus response to entorhinal input, possibly through inhibition of the dentate interneurons (Bilkey & Goddard, 1985; Fantie & Goddard, 1982; Mizumori et al., 1989b) and reversible inactivation of the medial septum reduces spontaneous firing of neurons in dentate gyrus (Mizumori et al., 1989a).

Cholinergic innervation from the medial septum could provide slower changes between encoding and consolidation dynamics. Acetylcholine reduces the strength of synaptic transmission at excitatory recurrent connections in region CA3 (Hasselmo et al., 1995) and from region CA3 to region CA1. Cholinergic modulation also serves to directly enhance modification of synaptic strength, as demonstrated in experiments showing enhancement of long-term potentiation by cholinergic agonists (Huerta & Lisman, 1993). This direct enhancement of changes in synaptic strength ensures that new learning only occurs at the time that the other cholinergic effects are present to set appropriate dynamics for new encoding (Linster & Hasselmo, 2001).

This theoretical role of medial septum in regulating encoding dynamics through cholinergic and GABAergic effects is consistent with data on drug effects, which demonstrate that encoding can be seriously impaired by two types of drugs: (1) drugs that block muscarinic acetylcholine receptors (e.g. scopolamine); and (2) drugs that enhance GABAergic receptor effects (e.g. diazepam or midazolam). Both of these types of drug impair the encoding of words for subsequent free recall but do not impair the free recall of words encoded before administration of the drug (Ghoneim & Mewaldt, 1975).

Sequence storage models

Fixed patterns of activity in networks can be used to model storage of individual items, or simultaneously presented pairs of items, but these fixed patterns do not effectively represent sequential storage of associations between multiple different items, such as the interitem associations that could cause a higher probability of retrieving words that were adjacent on the list.

These interitem and cross-temporal associations can be more effectively represented by storage of multiple patterns in a sequence rather than a single pattern. The storage of a sequence of activity patterns has been proposed as an alternative function of the excitatory recurrent collaterals in region CA3 (Jensen & Lisman, 1996b; Levy, 1996; Marr, 1971; McNaughton & Morris, 1987; Wallenstein & Hasselmo, 1997).

Encoding of multiple overlapping sequences runs into the problem of interference between stored sequences. Theta rhythm oscillations induced by cholinergic and GABAergic input from the medial septum could assist in disambiguating overlapping sequences (Sohal & Hasselmo, 1998a and b). Encoding of sequences provides the flexibility necessary for relational processing in the hippocampus, including both the flexible goal directed retrieval of episodic memories, and the flexible choice of specific pathways during spatial navigation described below.

Relational processing in an associative net

Extensive data suggests that the hippocampus is particularly important for flexible retrieval of relational information about recent events (Cohen & Eichenbaum, 1995). That is, rather than being locked into a particular stereotypical pattern or sequence of patterns, the hippocampus appears to mediate flexible access to causal relationships within a large network of interitem associations.

This framework corresponds to a case of multiple overlapping sequences encoded in region CA3, which can be accessed not only in a rigid manner specific to individual sequences but with flexible transitions across the elements of the network, picking out different components in different sequences.

As an example, imagine an event in which I observe my Siamese cat knock a bowl of cantaloupe off the table. One aspect of episodic memory is the sense of flexible access to multiple different components of the memory, as if a full video of the sequence was available and we could play through segments of it, forwards and backwards with pausing and focused inspection of different elements. This flexible retrieval of different events within an episode, or different relational features, could be obtained if the recurrent connections of region CA3 set up an associative network, within which specific subsequences of activity could be evoked depending on the conditional features of the retrieval cue. This type of flexible access is schematised in Fig. 15.4. If I look at my cat, I might be reminded of the cat knocking the bowl off the table. But if I eat a cantaloupe, I might be reminded of the cantaloupe pieces falling on the carpet after the cat knocked them off the table.

Dentate gyrus

Most theories and models of hippocampal memory function include an important functional role for the dentate gyrus. In these models, the dentate gyrus serves to reduce the overlap between different patterns of activity stored within region CA3 of the hippocampus. The dentate gyrus activity then strongly activates region CA3 pyramidal cells via the mossy fibres.

This problem of reducing overlap relates to the problem of interference between patterns encoded within an associative memory. A simple means of preventing this type of interference between encoded pattern involves pre-processing the patterns to make their representation less overlapping when they activate region CA3. This requires two processes: (1) a mechanism for automatically reducing overlap between multiple sequentially presented patterns; and (2) a mechanism for mapping the altered, less overlapping representations in region CA3 back to the original input patterns in association neocortex. The overlap between stored patterns can be reduced by allowing modification of the perforant path inputs from entorhinal cortex to dentate gyrus. This results in self-organisation of the dentate gyrus representation due to competition between encoded representations.

Many models of episodic memory have proposed self-organisation of input to dentate gyrus, but have utilised interleaved presentation of different patterns (O'Reilly et al., 1998; Rolls, Treves, Foster, & Perez-Vicente, 1997). These networks can obtain competitive self-organisation without modification of inhibition, but the requirement of interleaved learning might be unrealistic for encoding of episodic memories, unless these memories are repeatedly reactivated and utilised to refine the dentate gyrus representation (see discussion of McClelland, McNaughton, & O'Reilly, 1995). By definition, episodic memories are encoded at one point in time. This means that any representation for the initial encoding of this memory must be formed on the basis of that single presentation. The afferent input could persist for a period of time (see discussion of the possible role of entorhinal cortex as a buffer) but it is not intermixed with the reactivation of other encoded memories. Thus, the encoded memories are not interleaved during learning. This presents a special problem for models of the dentate gyrus in episodic memory, as most models of self-organisation and competitive learning utilise interleaved learning of a large set of input patterns.

Sequential self-organisation of representations in the dentate gyrus has been obtained by utilising modification of inhibitory connections (Hasselmo & Wyble, 1997). In the model, individual representations in dentate gyrus are initially activated due to random divergent input. At this point, excitatory feedforward connections undergo Hebbian modification to strengthen the drive on that dentate representation. This would allow smaller entorhinal patterns to activate dentate gyrus, but this excitatory modification is offset by enhancement of inhibitory feedback connections within the dentate gyrus (Hasselmo & Wyble, 1997). These can then prevent any patterns that do not strongly resemble the initial input pattern from activating the same representation.

Region CA1

If the associations encoded in region CA3 require a transformation in the dentate gyrus to make them less overlapping, then there must be some means of reversing the transformation to map the encoded patterns back to the activity patterns associated with sensory processing in association cortex. However, there are no direct connections from region CA3 to neocortical structures such as the entorhinal cortex. How can this mapping back to neocortical sensory activity take place?

Region CA1 appears well suited to this putative mapping function (Hasselmo & Wyble, 1997; Hasselmo et al., 1995; McClelland & Goddard, 1996). However, in addition to simple remapping, region CA1 could play an important role in determining whether the reconstructed pattern in region CA3 satisfies criteria for remapping to neocortical structures, based on a comparison of the region CA3 output with the current sensory input relayed through entorhinal cortex (Eichenbaum & Buckingham, 1989; Gray, 1982; Hasselmo & Wyble, 1997). This process is summarised in Fig. 15.5.

This matching function could be very important for ensuring that incorrect retrieval does not propagate back to entorhinal cortex. For example, if the input pattern has not been previously encoded, the immediate retrieval from region CA3 will not have any useful information. In addition, if there is severe interference of the new pattern with previously stored patterns, the immediate retrieval from region CA3 will contain additional undesired information, which should be restricted from passing back to entorhinal cortex.

Region CA1 has the appropriate anatomical connectivity for this type of comparison function. The output from region CA3 pyramidal cells arrives via the Schaffer collaterals and synapses in stratum radiatum of region CA1. The direct input from the entorhinal cortex arrives via the perforant path and synapses in the stratum lacunosum-moleculare of region CA1. The output of region CA1 pyramidal cells flows back to the entorhinal cortex, either directly or via the subiculum.

Thus, the activity of region CA1 pyramidal cells reflects the convergence of Schaffer collateral input from region CA3 and perforant path input from entorhinal cortex (see Fig. 15.5). If region CA1 pyramidal cells would require inputs from both pathways to fire (or would require the inputs to match if there is perforant path input), then only matching patterns would activate

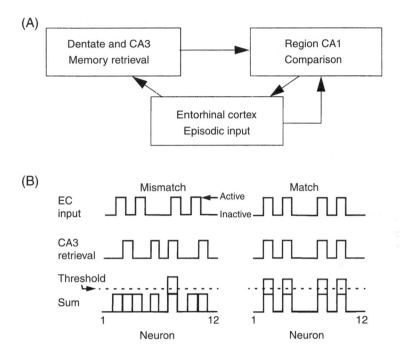

Figure 15.5. Overview of comparison function. (A) Episodic input from entorhinal cortex passes through dentate gyrus and region CA3, where retrieval based on previously encoded representations takes place. This retrieval then passes on via the Schaffer collaterals to region CA1, where there can be a direct comparison with episodic input from entorhinal cortex. If region CA3 and the dentate have not previously encoded the memory, this comparison function might reveal a poor match. (B) Overview of matching function. The top two lines represent activity of synaptic input to specific neurons from different sources (EC input and CA3 retrieval). The bottom line represents the sum of input effects on postsynaptic activity for each neuron relative to threshold. Mismatch: for unfamiliar patterns, the retrieval from region CA3 does not match with EC input, and postsynaptic activity is below threshold for most neurons. Match: for familiar patterns, the retrieval from region CA3 matches EC input and brings neurons in the pattern above threshold.

region CA1 and only matching patterns could spread back to entorhinal cortex.

Region CA3 actually contains direct afferent input from the entorhinal cortex in the stratum lacunosum-moleculare, but the longitudinal association fibres (laf) contact only region CA3 pyramidal cells and interneurons, and the Schaffer collaterals contain only region CA1 pyramidal cells and interneurons. Thus, even if region CA3 performs a comparison function, all output must pass through the potential comparison function of region CA1 as well. Having a separate comparison stage might be important in that it can allow region CA3 to settle into an attractor, without immediately vetoing this attractor or sequence on the basis of input from entorhinal cortex. Thus, region CA3 has the flexibility to generate multiple associations and region CA1 sorts through these to pick out valid retrieval candidates.

The theory of a comparison function in region CA1 has been described verbally in a number of locations (Eichenbaum & Buckingham, 1989; Gray, 1982), but in only a few publications have the actual mechanisms of such a comparison been described in detail and analysed mathematically or simulated (Hasselmo & Schnell, 1994; Hasselmo et al., 1995). In some simulations, the sum of region CA1 activity was utilised to regulate levels of modulatory input from the medial septum (Hasselmo & Schnell, 1994; Hasselmo et al., 1995). Regulation of cholinergic and GABAergic modulatory input from the septum could also determine the capacity for information to flow back to entorhinal cortex.

As shown in Fig. 15.5, retrieval in region CA3 generates predictions that are evaluated by matching in region CA1. This same basic function could be applicable to neocortical function, with supragranular layers II/III playing the same retrieval role as CA3 and holding these predictions in working memory until converging input from layer II/III and other sources (thalamus or lower cortical areas) generates matching activity in infragranular layers (V/VI). This matching criteria would then allow activity to spread to other cortical or subcortical regions. This amounts to a gating process, in which predictions in working memory are matched with current input cues and matching allows progression to a new state. For example, in a simulation of counting, a working memory representation of zero would predict the first presentation of an object. When the object is seen, this match of cue and prediction would cause activation of a gate which would activate the representation of "one". This would then predict the second presentation of input from the exact same object representation. The second presentation of the object would only activate the neuron receiving predictive input from "one", and the activated gate would only activate the new representation for "two". In this manner, matching of prediction and cue could allow gating functions, which could form the basis for rule representations in neocortical circuits.

The general process of comparison between retrieval and input plays an important role in a more abstract class of models described by the term "adaptive resonance theory" (ART). The connectivity of ART networks has not been mapped explicitly to physiological structures but these networks regulate the formation of new representations on the basis of a comparison between the current input and the representations formed in response to previously presented input (Carpenter & Grossberg, 1993).

Entorhinal cortex

In many models of hippocampal memory function, the entorhinal cortex plays a simple role as the source of input and recipient of output from the hippocampus. The entorhinal cortex certainly fits this role with regard to anatomical data. As summarised in Fig. 15.1, input from neocortical association cortices converges on the entorhinal cortex, which provides the primary afferent input to the dentate gyrus as well as providing input to the stratum lacunosum-moleculare of region CA3 and region CA1. On the output side, efferent connections from region CA1 and the subiculum provide a major projection to the deep layers of entorhinal cortex, which send divergent projections to the association neocortex.

The entorhinal cortex can be seen as the gateway to the hippocampus. In this role, it could play an important functional role in regulating whether particular sensory input reaches the hippocampus. The limited capacity of episodic memory storage can be used more efficiently if only important information is relayed. In this context, the modulatory state of entorhinal cortex could be very important. This structure exhibits changes in physiological state associated with different behavioural states, including theta EEG oscillations, which appear to be regulated by the medial septum to provide input to region CA1 that is out of phase with the region CA3 input (Alonso & Garcia-Austt, 1987; Mitchell & Ranck, 1980).

An important means by which entorhinal cortex could regulate input to hippocampus is by acting as a buffer for incoming information, holding behaviourally relevant information for a period of time longer than the presence of the sensory input itself. This potential role is supported by evidence that lesions of the entorhinal cortex and perirhinal cortex impair performance in delayed non-match to sample tasks in non-human primates (Zola-Morgan et al., 1994) and rats (Otto & Eichenbaum, 1992). In these tasks, a stimulus is presented at the start of the trial and, after a delay period, the animals must respond to the object that they did not see at the start of the trial. This lesion effect suggests that entorhinal cortex might retain activity during the delay period.

Electrophysiological recording demonstrates that some neurons in this region do maintain stimulus selective activity during delay periods in a delayed non-matching to sample task (Young et al., 1997). This sustained activity might depend on induction of self-sustained activity on a cellular level as a result of the effects of acetylcholine (Fransen et al., 1999; Hasselmo et al., 2000; Klink & Alonso, 1997). This retention of activity could be very important for providing a sustained source of afferent input for a time period sufficient to induce synaptic modification within the dentate gyrus and hippocampal subregions.

In addition to its potential role in holding input during encoding in the hippocampus, the entorhinal cortex might play an important role in regulating the flow of output from the hippocampus. This could take place both during interaction with the environment and during quiet waking and slow-wave sleep. During interaction with the environment, the validity of retrieved information needs to be compared with sensory input (see the earlier discussion of region CA1). During quiet waking or slow-wave sleep, this output does not play a direct role in guiding behaviour, but could mediate the consolidation of memory function (Hasselmo, 1999).

SPATIAL NAVIGATION MODELS

This section focuses on modelling the mechanisms of spatial navigation—the process of encoding spatial locations and following paths between different locations. Nothing about the mechanisms of cortical or hippocampal function requires that there be a distinction between episodic memory function and spatial navigation. Given that both these functional categories appear to depend upon hippocampus, an effective model of hippocampus should account for both sets of data.

However, at this point in time there is a clear set of empirical data and computational modelling of memory function that focuses specifically on spatial memory function. In particular, many studies of hippocampal function in rats focus on behaviours involving memory for specific locations, and rats provide a greater opportunity for electrophysiological and neurochemical measurements in awake, behaving animals.

Physiological data

Considerable physiological data relevant to rat spatial navigation has been obtained. The responses of many neurons in hippocampus have been defined as "place cells", which respond selectively to a specific location within the environment (O'Keefe & Recce, 1993; Skaggs, McNaughton, Wilson, & Barnes, 1996; Wilson & McNaughton, 1993). This definition of place cell implies a specific role in spatial coding, but these responses could be a specific manifestation of a more general property of encoding events in an episode (Eichenbaum et al., 1999).

In behavioural tasks, hippocampal and entorhinal neurons demonstrate responses to most behaviourally relevant components. For example, in operant conditioning tasks hippocampal neurons respond to task elements including approaching and obtaining water reward (Wiener et al., 1989; Otto & Eichenbaum, 1992; Young et al., 1997), sampling an odour stimulus (Wiener et al., 1989; Otto & Eichenbaum, 1992), sampling local features of the environment such as texture (Shapiro et al., 1997), and making incorrect or correct responses (Wiener et al., 1989; Otto & Eichenbaum, 1992). In addition, during performance of delayed non-match to sample tasks, neurons show specificity for match or non-match trials in hippocampus (Otto et al., 1992) and entorhinal cortex (Young et al., 1997). Neurons show activity during the delay period of the task in entorhinal cortex (Young et al., 1997). In the hippocampus, studies of single neurons do not show distinct delay activity (Otto & Eichenbaum, 1992) whereas the ensemble code appears to maintain information across the delay (Hampson & Deadwyler, 1996). This response to all behaviourally relevant variables suggests that hippocampal neurons are not constrained to any specific sensory dimension but encode a range of events that constitute individual episodes (Eichenbaum et al., 1999).

In recent experiments, it has been explicitly shown that place cells show responses more suggestive of episodic memory function than pure spatial encoding (Frank et al., 2000; Wood et al., 2000). These experiments used tasks in which rats would run along a single central arm of the maze in the same direction, but on different trials they would have to turn either left or right at the end of the central arm. Some neurons recorded in these tasks would show differential responses on "go-left" versus "go-right" trials. Thus, the response depended on the past and future trajectory of the rat, despite the fact that the rat had exactly the same external cues and movements along the central arm.

Computational modelling of spatial navigation

A number of models of spatial navigation have utilised the basic connectivity structure of region CA3. In these models, individual spatial locations are encoded as a pattern of activity across a subpopulation of place cells, and the strengthening of synaptic connections between these place cells allows activity representing one location along a path to evoke the neuronal activity representing the next location along the path. During retrieval, neuronal activity elicited by one location can spread to adjacent locations, depending on the prior strengthening of excitatory recurrent connections during encoding.

These models can be categorised on the basis of differences in the process of encoding the environment. Some models involve encoding of individual paths through the environment, with a global representation built from these pathways, whereas others start with a two-dimensional representation of the full environment which is then modified to encode goal location. Here, these different categories will be termed "path-based" and "grid-based" models.

Path-based models versus grid-based models

The encoding and retrieval of specific pathways through the environment has been modelled in recurrent networks representing region CA3 (Hasselmo et al., 2002; Levy, 1996; Wallenstein & Hasselmo, 1997). In the Levy laboratory, simplified models of region CA3 have been developed with neurons represented by units with binary output states. In these models, the encoding of a path is modelled with sequential activation of different sets of units, for example, pattern A, B, C, D, and E. Application of an asymmetric Hebbian learning rule strengthens connections where the activity of a presynaptic unit precedes the activity of a postsynaptic unit, consistent with neurophysiological data (Levy & Steward, 1983). Retrieval is then obtained by providing input to units in pattern A and allowing the activity to sequentially spread across modified connections to activate units in pattern B, then pattern C, then D, then E.

These models deal with the problem of overlapping components of sequences by allowing strengthening of connections across multiple time steps. For example, synaptic modification can allow units not receiving afferent input to become associated with specific segments of the stored paths; Levy calls these local context units. The local context units enhance the capacity for disambiguating sequences, as well as allowing activity later in the sequence to influence earlier activity.

This type of path-based framework was used in a network of compartmental biophysical simulations of region CA3 pyramidal cells (Wallenstein & Hasselmo, 1997; Wallenstein, Eichenbaum, & Hasselmo, 1998). This network demonstrates many of the pathway-encoding properties of the Levy model, but using a more biologically realistic framework. Theta rhythm oscillations in the model greatly enhanced the encoding of new sequences.

More recent models have focused on the selection of specific pathways dependent upon the current goal location. In these models, activity spreads backwards from the goal location along associative circuits strengthened in the entorhinal cortex. This activity then cues the spread of activity in region CA3, representing the forwards spread from current location. The convergence of the forwards and backwards representations in region CA1 allows selection of the first pathways receiving convergent activation from goal and current location, which usually results in selection of the shortest pathway, as described in the simulation below (Hasselmo et al., in press).

In grid-based models, place cell representations are also assumed to be present when an animal initially encounters a new environment. However, in contrast to the pathway-based models, these representations are assumed to be laid out in a full two-dimensional interconnected grid, presetting the nature of place cell interconnections without any role of context. The grid-based models are proposed to set up a representation that can guide subsequent behaviour. In this framework, the simulated rat performs multiple traversals through the environment, and recently activated connections are modified when the rat reaches the goal location. Eventually, the connections form a two-dimensional gradient of responses which are directed toward the goal location in the network (Blum & Abbott, 1996; Gerstner & Abbott 1997).

The starting conditions of these models are very similar, in that they both assume some initial mapping of sensory features to specific place cell representations. Other models explicitly model the formation of place cell representations through self-organisation of afferent input to the hippocampus (Burgess et al., 1997; Sharp, Blair, & Brown, 1996). The path-based models assume that as an animal passes through different locations along a path, specific place cell representations are activated (implicitly assuming these place cells are initially connected only with the standard default connection strengths). The grid-based models assume a network with homogeneous connectivity, except where the animal has actually traversed the grid and modified connections. Thus, venturing into an area without paths is initially similar to going onto a portion of the grid that has no modified connections. However, if you have a gap and then cross it in one direction, left to right, then later cross it right to left, in the path-based model the initial path would be direction selective, context properties would cause it to have a representation distinct for each direction. These direction-selective responses could then be associated together to provide a non-directional response (Kali & Dayan, 2000). By contrast, in grid-based models the place cell representations are already multidirectional and any directionality would have to involve later modification based on context, i.e. choosing of different grids on the basis of context. Thus, they make different predictions about the initial directionality of place cell representations.

Because grid-based models do not focus on the episodic, context-dependent components of individual pathways, they would be difficult to utilise for showing how separate representations can be set up in the same environment. The use of a single two-dimensional grid results in loss of episodic features that are preserved in a path-based model. Thus, a path-based model would more effectively account for a change in place cell representations when a rat is switched from a broad exploratory task to a specific directional traversal of the same space (Markus et al., 1995), and could account for differential responses in the stem of a T-maze before a rat makes differential responses in a spatial alternation task (Wood et al., 2000).

Guiding a virtual rat with a hippocampal simulation

Many of the hypotheses described above make strong assumptions about the nature of behavioural input during a task and the output required for guidance of movement. These additional assumptions about the input and output can be reduced if the network directly interacts with an agent moving through an environment. This section presents a recent simulation developed in JAVA, in which a hippocampal simulation guides movement of a virtual rat through a virtual environment, and receives its sensory input on the basis of those movements.

This simulation was developed within a general purpose neural simulation package developed by Robert Cannon under the name "catacomb" (Cannon et al., in press; DeSchutter, 2000). This package allows flexible creation of multiple different environments, including arbitrary barrier locations and arbitrary locations for individual objects. A virtual rat can be placed into a given virtual environment, and its movements can be controlled in one of three ways: (1) according to predetermined trajectories; (2) with random choice of direction and speed of movement; and (3) with output from a neural simulation. Numerous parameters of the environment and rat can be adjusted within the simulation.

The hippocampal simulation developed within this package contains the essential features of the simulations described in the preceding sections of this chapter. But the guidance of a rat in an environment required multiple additional functional components of the network. The structure of the network and its interaction with the virtual rat in the virtual environment, is summarised in Fig. 15.6.

Navigation in this model depends upon encoding and retrieval of pathways through the environment, in the form of strengthened excitatory

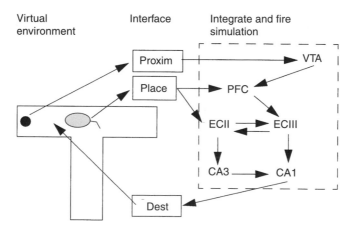

Figure 15.6.   Summary of the essential components of the network simulation. Input from a place representation ("place") depends upon the location of the virtual rat in the virtual environment. This input activates entorhinal cortex layer II, which has intrinsic properties allowing self-sustained activity, and sends excitatory output to entorhinal cortex layer III and region CA3. Region CA3 and entorhinal cortex layer III send converging input to region CA1. The place representation also sends subthreshold input to a prefrontal cortex region. Sensory input for proximity to objects ("proxim") activates a unit representing activation of ventral tegmental area by food reward. The input from ventral tegmental area enters the prefrontal region along with input representing space. The convergence of ventral tegmental and place input to prefrontal cortex causes spiking and activation of intrinsic mechanisms maintaining working memory for reward location. During retrieval phases, the convergence of activity from entorhinal cortex layer III and region CA3 causes spiking in region CA1 indicating the appropriate next location. This spiking output guides the movements of the virtual rat toward the desired goal ("dest").

synapses between individual place cell representations. The network receives direct sensory input representing location within the environment from the "place" node shown in Fig. 15.6. Thus, place cell representations are assumed, *de facto*, similar to other simulations (Blum & Abbott, 1996; Redish & Touretzky, 1998)—the model does not explicitly model processes that could set up place cell representations, such as self-organisation of the excitatory input from entorhinal cortex (Burgess et al., 1997; Sharp et al., 1996), or the self-organisation of excitatory connections arising from region CA3 pyramidal cells (Levy, 1996; Wallenstein & Hasselmo, 1997).

Encoding.   During encoding, the network receives input from precoded trajectories covering the full T-maze. This causes sequential activation of neurons in entorhinal cortex layer II. The activity spreads from entorhinal cortex layer II into region CA3 and entorhinal cortex layer III, and from entorhinal cortex layer III to region CA1. As place cells are activated sequentially, excitatory connections between these place cells are strengthened according to a brief window of Hebbian synaptic modification corresponding to the relative timing of pre- and postsynaptic spiking necessary for induction of long-term potentiation during paired-cell recording (Bi & Poo, 1998; Levy & Steward, 1983). These experiments showed that long-term potentiation would be induced if a presynaptic spike preceded a postsynaptic spike by less than 100ms, and long-term depression would be induced if a presynaptic spike followed a postsynaptic spike by a similar time window. In the simulation, we focus on a single-step function that causes synaptic strengthening for any postsynaptic spike falling within a 70ms period after a presynaptic spike. As can be seen in Fig. 15.7, this results in strengthening of connections in the network between adjacent place cells, but not between non-adjacent place cells.

This aspect of the simulation already raised an important problem not discussed in other simulations. The window of induction for long-term potentiation (Bi & Poo, 1998) is too small relative to the average interval between activation of individual place cells. Rats take seconds or more to cover the distances in the maze, and often pause to investigate individual locations. This slow movement and frequent pausing causes difficulties in forming associations between adjacent locations, unless there is some mechanism for buffering place information to bridge across delays between individual locations. To address this problem, a simplified representation of intrinsic after-depolarisation mechanisms, which have been modelled previously in greater biophysical detail, was incorporated (Fransen et al., 1999; 2002; Hasselmo et al., 2000). In these simplified representations, generation of a single action potential initiates dual exponential time courses to cause a period of after-hyperpolarisation followed by after-depolarisation. This results in repetitive firing of a neuron at about theta frequency for three to

Connectivity pattern

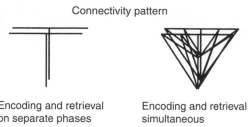

Encoding and retrieval   Encoding and retrieval
on separate phases   simultaneous

Figure 15.7. Pattern of connectivity within region CA3 of the integrate and fire simulation. Lines represent excitatory connections between CA3 pyramidal cells, which have been strengthened during encoding. Connections in opposite directions are offset from one another to illustrate that the strengthened connections are bidirectional in this simulation, although larger scale simulations should be able to function with unidirectional connections. Left: when encoding of sequential input from entorhinal cortex occurs at separate phases from the retrieval activity spreading along recurrent connections in CA3, then the network forms an effective representation of the T-maze, with connections (black lines) only between place cells representing adjacent locations in the maze. Right: when encoding and retrieval are not separated, the spread of activity across the excitatory recurrent connections during encoding causes broadly distributed firing during encoding. This broadly distributed firing causes strengthening of connections between place cells representing locations that are not adjacent, and prevents accurate navigation of the virtual rat within the virtual environment.

four spikes. This repetitive self-sustained intrinsic activity assists in ensuring that activity is sufficient to allow strengthening of all connections between adjacent locations, as shown in Fig. 15.7.

Retrieval. During retrieval dynamics, network activity guided by the location of food reward (goal) and the current location converges within the simulation to activate the appropriate next location for movement toward the chosen goal. The activity within individual regions during this phase is shown in Fig. 15.8, and summarised below.

Entorhinal cortex layer III

This region is activated by the goal location in prefrontal cortex. Each time this goal location is activated, the activity spreads backwards from the goal location across the connections of the network, as shown in the row showing entorhinal cortex in Fig. 15.8. The broad spread of activity within this network results in a much larger place field representation for individual cells in the entorhinal portion of the model, consistent with data from recordings of the entorhinal cortex (Barnes et al., 1990; Frank et al., 2000; Quirk, Muller, Kubie, & Ranck, 1992). The pattern of activity in entorhinal cortex layer III causes subthreshold activation of layer II and region CA1.

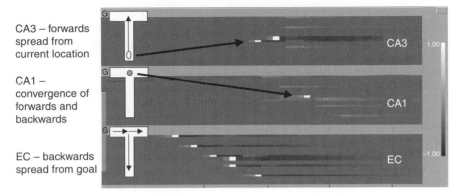

CA3 – forwards
spread from
current location

CA1 –
convergence of
forwards and
backwards

EC – backwards
spread from goal

Figure 15.8. Spread of activity in the network during retrieval. The different rows of this figure show activity in different subregions of the simulation during retrieval (only retrieval dynamics are simulated in this example, to clarify the patterns of activity). Bottom row: entorhinal cortex (EC) – activity spreads backwards from goal location, causing sequential spiking in neurons representing locations throughout the maze. Top row: region CA3 – when the spread in entorhinal cortex reaches the current location, activity spreads forwards in region CA3 from the current location of the rat (at the start of the stem in this example). Middle row: region CA1 – synaptic input from the entorhinal cortex and region CA3 converges in this region, causing spiking of a neuron representing the next desired location (at the T-junction of the maze).

Entorhinal cortex layer II

This region receives subthreshold input from the current location, as well as subthreshold input from entorhinal cortex layer III. When the backwards spread from the goal converges with the input of current location, this causes spiking activity corresponding to current location at the appropriate time. This activity then causes suprathreshold activation of region CA3.

Region CA3

When region CA3 receives suprathreshold input from entorhinal cortex layer II, the spiking activity spreads forward along strengthened excitatory recurrent connections corresponding to previously encoded pathways through the environment, as shown in the row illustrated region CA3 in Fig. 15.8. The spread of activity is terminated by activation of feedback inhibition, which prevents excessive spread of excitation within the region (corresponding to the relatively small size of place fields for neurons recorded in region CA3). Synaptic output from region CA3 causes subthreshold activation of region CA1.

Region CA1

This region receives subthreshold input from both region CA3 and entorhinal cortex layer III. Neurons in this region spike only when they receive simultaneous input from region CA3 and entorhinal cortex layer III, as shown in the row illustrating region CA1 in Fig. 15.8. This input is accurately timed such that it causes spiking only when the forwards spread from current location matches the backwards spread from goal, which activated the current location. Excessive spiking activity is prevented by feed-forward inhibition of region CA1 neurons by the output of region CA3. This activity in region CA1 causes spiking corresponding to the next location a rat needs to enter in order to start moving toward its goal. For each new current location, the cycle repeats to allow updating of the next desired location.

Theta rhythm modulation of network dynamics

In the sections above, encoding and retrieval dynamics are described separately. However, a rat is presumably always able to encode new information, even in the midst of performing a learned navigation task in the maze. Thus, these phases of encoding and retrieval should not persist for long periods.

Theta frequency oscillations provide a mechanism to obtain effective encoding and retrieval in the network during continuous behaviour. These theta rhythm oscillations are large-amplitude 3–10Hz oscillations, which appear in the hippocampal EEG when a rat is actively exploring the environment (Chrobak & Buzsaki, 1994; Buzsaki et al., 1983). In contrast, the EEG shows irregular activity during immobility or consummatory activities such as eating or grooming.

Theta rhythm oscillations in the EEG of region CA1 result from sequential changes in the amplitude of synaptic currents in different layers of region CA1. As proposed in recent publications (Hasselmo et al., 2002), these changes in synaptic current during each cycle of the theta rhythm could correspond to successive phases of encoding and retrieval during each cycle.

During the encoding phase of the theta cycle, afferent input from entorhinal cortex is very strong, whereas the excitatory recurrent connections in region CA3, and the connections from region CA3 to region CA1, are very weak. This allows effective clamping of network activity to the afferent input, which is optimal for strengthening of excitatory recurrent connections to form an accurate representation of environmental features (such as adjacent place cells). Note that this requires that long-term potentiation of the excitatory recurrent connections and Schaffer collaterals should be maximal at the time that synaptic transmission at these connections is the weakest. This is consistent with physiological data showing that long-term potentiation is best induced at the peak of the local EEG, which is the time when synaptic currents are the weakest (Holscher et al., 1997; Huerta & Lisman, 1993).

During the retrieval phase of the theta cycle, afferent input from entorhinal cortex is at its weakest, but the excitatory recurrent collaterals in region CA3 and the Schaffer collaterals from region CA3 to region CA1 are at their strongest. This allows activity to be driven predominantly by spread of activity across previously modified synapses. Note that this retrieval will cause distortion of the pattern of connectivity unless there is no long-term potentiation at these connections during this time (thus, long-term potentiation must be weakest when synaptic transmission is the strongest). If retrieval occurs during encoding, the spread of activity causes spiking to occur in a large number of neurons during the window for induction of long-term potentiation. This retrieval during encoding results in strengthening of connections between distant, non-adjacent locations, causing a severe breakdown in network function, as shown in Fig. 15.7.

Possible mechanisms of selective episodic activity.   This detailed model of the role of the hippocampus in spatial navigation allows generation of multiple potential mechanisms for particular behavioural and electrophysiological phenomena. In particular, the differential firing of neurons in the stem of the T-maze during performance of delayed spatial alternation (Wood et al., 2000) could arise from a number of different network interactions during behaviour, including the following potential mechanisms:

(1) Modification of afferent input from entorhinal cortex could allow gradual separation of firing activity based on slight differences in the context input from neocortical structures. This mechanism would require sufficient differences in neocortical activity, dependent on the next turn, which are amplified by differences in perforant path connectivity to result in distinct cell firing patterns depending on the next turn.

(2) Forwards self-organisation of excitatory connections in region CA3. Prior location of the rat could cause gradual separation of sequence representations in region CA3. In this framework, the network would start out with a single representation of the stem but, as the task becomes more familiar, self-organisation of the excitatory connections within region CA3 could cause distinct activity in different paths, which progressively spreads forward—like the unzipping of a zip.

(3) Backwards self-organisation of region CA3 connections. The future location of the rat could cause activity to spread backwards through the local context units described in previous work (Levy, 1996; Wallenstein & Hasselmo, 1997). This mechanism is unlikely, as activity in region CA3 associated with the end of the pathway is not consistent with the small size of place fields in region CA3.

(4) Backwards spread of activity from the goal could dictate which neurons in region CA1 can fire. In the framework described for spatial navigation above, the backwards spread of activity from a goal location representation in entorhinal cortex can determine which

representation in region CA1 will be activated. In this framework, region CA3 neurons would tend to show non-specific activity in the stem of the maze, but the convergence of this non-specific spread of activity from the current location with the entorhinal input to region CA1 would allow selectivity dependent on the future trajectory.

CONCLUSION

The detailed simulation presented here provides the opportunity to explore these multiple different mechanisms for causing selective firing in the stem of the T-maze, and for determining specific features of spike timing associated with individual hypothetical mechanisms. Thus, the interaction of a detailed spiking model of the hippocampal formation with a virtual rat moving through a virtual environment will provide a means of evaluating detailed quantitative mechanisms directly with regard to both behaviour and physiology, without the mediation of imprecise verbal hypotheses.

REFERENCES

Alonso, A., & Garcia-Austt, E. (1987). Neuronal sources of theta rhythm in the entorhinal cortex of the rat. II. Phase relations between unit discharges and theta field potentials. *Experimental Brain Research, 67*, 502–509.

Amit, D.J. (1988). *Modelling brain function: The world of attractor neural networks*. Cambridge: Cambridge University Press.

Anderson, J.A. (1972). A simple neural network generating an interactive memory. *Mathematical Biosciences, 14*, 197–220.

Barnes, C.A., McNaughton, B.L., Mizumori, S., Leonard, B.W., & Lin, L.H. (1990). Comparison of spatial and temporal characteristics of neuronal activity in sequential stages of hippocampal processing. *Progress in Brain Research, 83*, 287–300.

Bi, G.Q., & Poo, M.M. (1998). Synaptic modifications in cultured hippocampal neurons: Dependence on spike timing, synaptic strength, and postsynaptic cell type. *Journal of Neuroscience, 18*(24), 10464–10472.

Bilkey, D.K., & Goddard, G.V. (1985). Medial septal facilitation of hippocampal granule cell activity is mediated by inhibition of inhibitory interneurones. *Brain Research, 361*(1–2), 99–106.

Bliss, T.V., & Collingridge, G.L. (1993). A synaptic model of memory: Long-term potentiation in the hippocampus. *Nature, 361*, 31–39.

Blum, K.I., & Abbot, L.F. (1996). A model of spatial map formation in the hippocampus of the rat. *Neural Computation, 8*(1), 85–93.

Bragin, A., Jando, G., Nadasdy, Z., Hetke, J., Wise, K., & Buzsaki, G. (1995). Gamma (40–100 Hz) oscillation in the hippocampus of the behaving rat. *Journal of Neuroscience, 15*, 47–60.

Brankack, J., Stewart, M., & Fox, S.E. (1993). Current source density analysis of the hippocampal theta rhythm: Associated sustained potentials and candidate synaptic generators. *Brain Research, 615*(2), 310–327.

Burgess, N., Donnett, J.G., Jeffery, K.J., & O'Keefe, J. (1997). Robotic and neuronal simulation of the hippocampus and rat navigation. *Philosophical Transactions of the Royal Society of London Series B, Biological Sciences, 352*, 1535–1543.

Buzsaki, G., Leung, L.W., & Vanderwolf, C.H. (1983). Cellular bases of hippocampal EEG in the behaving rat. *Brain Research, 287*(2):139–171.

Cannon, R.C., Hasselmo, M.E., & Koene, R.A. (in press). From biophysics to behavior: Catacomb 2 and the design of biologically plausible models for spatial navigation. *Neuroinformatics*.

Carpenter, G.A., & Grossberg, S. (1993). Normal and amnesic learning, recognition and memory by a neural model of cortico-hippocampal interactions. *Trends in Neuroscience, 16*(4), 131–137.

Chrobak, J.J., & Buzsaki, G. (1994) Selective activation of deep layer (V–VI) retrohippocampal cortical neurons during hippocampal sharp waves in the behaving rat. *Journal of Neuroscience, 14*, 6160–6170.

Cohen, N.J., & Eichenbaum, H. (1995). *Memory, amnesia and the hippocampal system.* Cambridge, MA: MIT Press.

DeSchutter, E. (Ed.) (2000). *Computational neuroscience: Realistic modeling for experimentalists.* Boca Raton, FL: CRC Press.

Eichenbaum, H., & Buckingham, J. (1989). Studies on hippocampal processing: Experiment, theory and model. In M. Gabriel & J. Moore (Eds.) *Learning and computational neuroscience: Foundations of adaptive networks* (pp. 171–231). Cambridge, MA: MIT Press.

Eichenbaum, H., Dudchenko, P., Wood, E., Shapiro, M., & Tanila, H. (1999). The hippocampus, memory, and place cells: Is it spatial memory or a memory space? *Neuron, 23*(2), 209–226.

Fantie, B.D., & Goddard, G.V. (1982). Septal modulation of the population spike in the fascia dentata produced by perforant path stimulation in the rat. *Brain Research, 252*(2), 227–237.

Fox, S.E. (1989). Membrane potential and impedance changes in hippocampal pyramidal cells during theta rhythm. *Experimental Brain Research, 77*, 283–294.

Frank, L.M., Brown, E.N., & Wilson, M. (2000). Trajectory encoding in the hippocampus and entorhinal cortex. *Neuron, 27*(1), 169–178.

Fransen, E., Alonso, A.A., & Hasselmo, M.E. (2002). Simulations of the role of the muscarinic-activated, calcium-sensitive, non-specific cation current I (NCM) in entorhinal neuronal activity during delayed matching tasks. *Journal of Neuroscience, 22*, 1018–1097.

Fransen, E., & Lansner, A. (1998). A model of cortical associative memory based on a horizontal network of connected columns. *Network 9*(2), 235–264.

Fransen, E., Wallenstein, G.V., Alonso, A.A., Dickson, C.T., & Hasselmo, M.E. (1999). A biophysical simulation of intrinsic and network properties of entorhinal cortex. *Neurocomputing, 26*, 375–380.

Gerstner, W., & Abbott, L.F. (1997). Learning navigational maps through potentiation and modulation of hippocampal place cells. *Journal of Computing and Neuroscience, 4*, 79–94.

Ghoneim, M.M., & Mewaldt, S.P. (1975). Effects of diazepam and scopolamine on storage, retrieval and organization processes in memory. *Psychopharmacologia, 44*, 257–262.

Graf, P.A., Squire, L.R., & Mandler, G. (1984). The information that amnesic patients do not forget. *Journal of Experimental Psychology: Human Learning and Memory, 10*, 164–178.

Gray, J.A. (1982). *The neuropsychology of anxiety: An enquiry into the functions of the septo-hippocampal system.* New York: Oxford University Press.

Hampson, R.E., & Deadwyler, S.A. (1996). Ensemble codes involving hippocampal neurons are at risk during delayed performance tests. *Proceedings of the National Academy of Sciences USA, 93*(24), 13487–13493.

Hasselmo, M.E. (1999). Neuromodulation: Acetylcholine and memory consolidation. *Trends in Cognitive Science, 3*, 351–359.

Hasselmo, M.E., Bodelón, C., & Wyble, B.P. (2002). A proposed function for hippocampal theta rhythm: Separate phases of encoding and retrieval enhance reversal of prior learning. *Neural Computation, 14*, 793–817.

Hasselmo, M.E., Fransen, E., Dickson, C.T., & Alonso, A.A. (2000). Computational modeling of entorhinal cortex. *Annals of the New York Academy of Science, 911*, 418–446.

Hasselmo, M.E., Hay, J., Ilyn, M., & Gorchetchnikov, A. (in press). Neuromodulation, theta rhythm and rat spatial navigation. *Neural Networks*.

Hasselmo, M.E., & Schnell, E. (1994). Laminar selectivity of the cholinergic suppression of synaptic transmission in rat hippocampal region CA1: Computational modelling and brain slice physiology. *Journal of Neuroscience, 9*, 2737–2763.

Hasselmo, M.E., Schnell, E., & Barkai, E. (1995). Dynamics of learning and recall at excitatory recurrent synapses and cholinergic modulation in hippocampal region CA3. *Journal of Neuroscience, 15*, 5249–5262.

Hasselmo, M.E., & Wyble, B.P. (1997). Simulation of the effects of scopolamine on free recall and recognition in a network model of the hippocampus. *Behavioral Brain Research, 89*, 1–34.

Hasselmo, M.E., Wyble, B.P., & Wallenstein, G.V. (1996). Encoding and retrieval of episodic memories: Role of cholinergic and GABAergic modulation in the hippocampus. *Hippocampus, 6*, 693–708.

Holscher, C., Anwyl, R., & Rowan, M.J. (1997). Stimulation on the positive phase of hippocampal theta rhythm induces long-term potentiation that can be depotentiated by stimulation on the negative phase in area CA1 *in vivo*. *Journal of Neuroscience, 17*(16), 6470–6477.

Huerta, P.T., & Lisman, J.E. (1993). Heightened synaptic plasticity of hippocampal CA1 neurons during a cholinergically induced rhythmic state. *Nature, 364*, 723–725.

Jensen, O., & Lisman, J.E. (1996a). Novel lists of 7 ± 2 known items can be reliably stored in an oscillatory short-term memory network: Interaction with long-term memory. *Learning and Memory, 3*(2–3), 257–263.

Jensen, O., & Lisman, J.E. (1996b). Hippocampal CA3 region predict memory sequences: Accounting for the phase advance of place cells. *Learning and Memory, 3*, 279–287.

Kali, S., & Dayan, P. (2000). The involvement of recurrent connections in area CA3 in establishing the properties of place fields: A model. *Journal of Neuroscience, 20*(19), 7463–7477.

Klink, R., & Alonso, A. (1997). Ionic mechanisms of muscarinic depolarization in entorhinal cortex layer II neurons. *Journal of Neurophysiology, 77*, 1829–1843.

Kohonen, T. (1984). *Self-organization and associative memory*. Berlin: Springer-Verlag.

Levy, W.B. (1996). A sequence predicting CA3 is a flexible associator that learns and uses context to solve hippocampal-like tasks. *Hippocampus, 6*, 579–590.

Levy, W.B., & Steward, O. (1971). Temporal contiguity requirements for long-term associative potentiation/depression in the hippocampus. *Neuroscience, 8*(4), 791–797.

Linster, C., & Hasselmo, M.E. (2001). Neuromodulation and the functional dynamics of piriform cortex. *Chemical Senses, 26*, 585–594.

Markus, E.J., Qin, Y.L., Leonard, B., Skaggs, W.E., McNaughton, B.L., & Barnes, C.A. (1995). Interactions between location and task affect the spatial and directional firing of hippocampal neurons. *Journal of Neuroscience, 15*, 7079–7094.

Marr, D. (1971). Simple memory: a theory for archicortex. *Philosophical Transactions of the Royal Society of London, Series B, Biological Sciences, 262*, 23–81.

McClelland, J.L., & Goddard, N.H. (1996). Considerations arising from a complementary learning systems perspective on hippocampus and neocortex. *Hippocampus, 6*(6), 654–665.

McClelland, J.L., McNaughton, B.L., & O'Reilly, R.C. (1995). Why there are complementary learning systems in the hippocampus and neocortex: Insights from the successes and failures of connectionist models of learning and memory. *Psychological Review, 102*, 419–457.

McNaughton, B.L., & Morris, R.G.M. (1987). Hippocampal synaptic enhancement and information storage within a distributed memory system. *Trends in Neuroscience, 10*, 408–415.

Mitchell, S.J., & Ranck, J.B. (1980). Generation of theta rhythm in medial entorhinal cortex of freely moving rats. *Brain Research, 178*, 49–66.

Mizumori, S.J., Barnes, C.A., & McNaughton, B.L. (1989a). Reversible inactivation of the medial septum: Selective effects on the spontaneous unit activity of different hippocampal cell types. *Brain Research*, *500*(1–2), 99–106.

Mizumori, S.J., McNaughton, B.L., & Barnes, C.A. (1989b). A comparison of supramammillary and medial septal influences on hippocampal field potentials and single-unit activity. *Journal of Neurophysiology*, *61*(1), 15–31.

O'Keefe, J. & Recce, M.L. (1993). Phase relationship between hippocampal place units and the EEG theta rhythm. *Hippocampus*, *3*, 317–330.

O'Reilly, R.C., Norman, K.A., & McClelland, J.L. (1998). A hippocampal model of recognition memory. In M.I. Jordan, M.J. Kearns, & S.A. Solla (Eds.) *Advances in neural information processing systems 10*. Cambridge, MA: MIT Press.

Otto, T., & Eichenbaum, H. (1992). Neuronal activity in the hippocampus during delayed non-match to sample performance in rats: Evidence for hippocampal processing in recognition memory. *Hippocampus*, *2*(3), 323–334.

Quirk, G.J., Muller, R.U., Kubie, J.L., & Ranck, J.B. (1992). The positional firing properties of medial entorhinal neurons: Description and comparison with hippocampal place cells. *Journal of Neuroscience*, *12*(5), 1945–1963.

Redish, A.D., & Touretzky, D.S. (1998). The role of the hippocampus in solving the Morris water maze. *Neural Computation*, *10*, 73–111.

Rempel-Clower, N.L., Zola, S.M., Squire, L.R., & Amaral, D.G. (1996). Three cases of enduring memory impairment after bilateral damage limited to the hippocampal formation. *Journal of Neuroscience*, *16*, 5233–5255.

Rolls, E.T., Treves, A., Foster, D., & Perez-Vicente, C. (1997). Simulation studies of the CA3 hippocampal subfield modelled as an attractor neural network. *Neural Networks*, *10*, 1559–1569.

Rudell, A.P., Fox, S.E., & Ranck, J.B. Jr. (1980). Hippocampal excitability phase-locked to the theta rhythm in walking rats. *Experimental Neurology*, *68*, 87–96.

Scoville, W.B., & Milner, B. (1957). Loss of recent memory after bilateral hippocampal lesions. *Journal of Neurology, Neurosurgery and Psychiatry*, *20*, 11–21.

Shapiro, M.L., Tanila, H., & Eichenbaum, H. (1997). Cues that hippocampal place cells encode: Dynamic and hierarchical representation of local and distal stimuli. *Hippocampus*, *7*(6), 624–642.

Sharp, P.E., Blair, H.T., & Brown, M. (1996). Neural network modeling of the hippocampal formation spatial signals and their possible role in navigation: A modular approach. *Hippocampus*, *6*(6), 720–734.

Skaggs, W.E., McNaughton, B.L., Wilson, M.A., & Barnes, C.A. (1996). Theta phase precession in hippocampal neuronal populations and the compression of temporal sequences. *Hippocampus*, *6*, 149–172.

Sohal, V.S., & Hasselmo, M.E. (1998a). Changes in GABAB modulation during a theta cycle may be analogous to the fall of temperature during annealing. *Neural Computation*, *10*, 889–902.

Sohal, V.S., & Hasselmo, M.E. (1998b). GABAB modulation improves sequence disambiguation in computational models of hippocampal region CA3. *Hippocampus*, *8*(2), 171–193.

Treves, A., & Rolls, E.T. (1994). Computational analysis of the role of the hippocampus in memory. *Hippocampus*, *4*(3), 374–391.

Tulving, E., & Markowitsch, H.J. (1998). Episodic and declarative memory: Role of the hippocampus. *Hippocampus*, *8*, 198–204.

Wallenstein, G.V., Eichenbaum, H.B., & Hasselmo, M.E. (1998). The hippocampus as an associator of discontiguous events. *Trends in Neuroscience*, *21*, 317–323.

Wallenstein, G.V., & Hasselmo, M.E. (1997). GABAergic modulation of hippocampal activity: Sequence learning, place field development, and the phase precession effect. *Journal of Neurophysiology*, *78*(1): 393–408.

Wiener, S.I., Paul, C.A., & Eichenbaum, H. (1989). Spatial and behavioral correlates of hippocampal neuronal activity. *Journal of Neuroscience, 9*(8), 2737–2763.

Wilson, H.R., & Cowan, J.D. (1972). Excitatory and inhibitory interactions in localized populations of model neurons. *Biophysical Journal, 12*, 1–24.

Wilson, M.A., & McNaughton, B.L. (1993). Dynamics of the hippocampal ensemble code for space. *Science, 261*, 1055–1058.

Wood, E.R., Dudchenko, P.A., Robitsek, R.J., & Eichenbaum, H. (2000). Hippocampal neurons encode information about different types of memory episodes occurring in the same location. *Neuron, 27*, 623–633.

Wyble, B.P., Linster, C., & Hasselmo, M.E. (2000). Size of CA1 evoked synaptic potentials is related to theta rhythm phase in rat hippocampus. *Journal of Neurophysiology, 83*, 2138–2144.

Young, B.J., Otto, T., Fox, G., & Eichenbaum, H. (1997). Memory representation within the parahippocampal region. *Journal of Neuroscience, 17*, 5183–5195.

Zola-Morgan, S., Squire, L.R., & Amaral, D.G. (1986). Human amnesia and the medial temporal region: Enduring memory impairment following a bilateral lesion limited to field CA1 of the hippocampus. *Journal of Neuroscience, 6*, 2950–2967.

Zola-Morgan, S., Squire, L.R., & Ramus, S.J. (1994). Severity of memory impairment in monkeys as a function of locus and extent of damage within the medial temporal lobe memory system. *Hippocampus, 4*, 483–495.

CHAPTER SIXTEEN

Conclusion

Edward L. Wilding
School of Psychology, Cardiff University, UK

Amanda Parker
School of Psychology, University of Nottingham, UK

Timothy J. Bussey
Department of Experimental Psychology, University of Cambridge, UK

Cognitive neuroscience is a broad, and still expanding, church. Social cognitive neuroscience (Ochsner & Lieberman, 2001) and cognitive neuropsychiatry (David & Halligan, 1996), for example, are two emerging disciplines that might have a claim to a place in the congregation. The ultimate goal of cognitive neuroscience is no less than a complete understanding of the way that the operations of the brain give rise to the perceptions, thoughts, and actions that comprise our psychological lives. Few would disagree that this goal is a long way off, but set against this there are now certainly more scientists who believe that this is a tractable goal than there were even a decade ago. Furthermore, if the intermediate goal of cognitive neuroscience were couched a little more conservatively—as, perhaps, a discipline that aims simply to provide a more clear understanding of the relationships between neural and mental events than is available currently—there would be few scientists who would dissent with the argument that this goal can be, and indeed is being, accomplished.

The chapters in this volume make it clear that substantial progress has been made not only in studies of memory with humans, but also with monkeys, rats, and increasingly, computational models. Cognitive neuroscience is clearly a multidisciplinary endeavour, involving a variety of species and an even wider variety of methodologies. Indeed, one striking aspect of the chapters in the present volume is the extensive use of new technologies that permit measurement of brain structure and activity, most notably positron emission tomography (PET) and functional magnetic resonance imaging (fMRI).

Rather than supplanting techniques with a somewhat longer heritage, the advent of these new technologies has served to complement more established approaches.

The authors in Part 1 of this volume review data that was gathered primarily using three functional imaging technologies: PET, fMRI, and event-related potentials (ERPs). An important limitation of these techniques, along with similar techniques used in animals (for example, single-cell recording), is that they rely on correlations (for an extended discussion, see Rugg, 1997). That is, the measure of neural activity is the dependent variable and what is manipulated is the cognitive operations that are assumed to be engaged by the task at hand. Consequently, these techniques are restricted to the observation of relationships between a measure of neural activity and a cognitive variable or variables. They cannot, at least when employed in isolation, identify regions that are *necessary* for completion of a particular task.

Other methods, however, are more likely to indicate causal relationships, revealing what brain regions, connections, neurotransmitters, and so on, are necessary for particular cognitive operations. Such methods include lesion studies, drug interventions, and the use of focal magnetic disruption of neural activity (transcranial magnetic stimulation, TMS; see Walsh & Rushworth, 1999). This latter method involves introducing a transient focal magnetic pulse on the outside of the skull that can disrupt neural activity temporarily in a small area of cortex immediately beneath; selective disruption of neural tissue in "deep" brain structures is, however, not possible. This technique is not employed widely at present, but that situation is likely to change in the near future. Furthermore, although these methods can address the question of necessity, they too have their limitations. The most pertinent here is that although they can indicate what brain region, for example, is necessary for a particular function, they can *only indicate* what brain region is necessary: they cannot *identify* brain regions that are typically engaged during a particular task, but which might not be necessary. For this we must turn to the methods that permit *in vivo* monitoring of neural activity generated by the intact brain.

An example of the benefits conferred by studying structure/function relationships using both "causal" and "correlational" approaches comes from studies of prefrontal cortical function during retrieval from episodic memory. Exploration of the likely roles of the left and right prefrontal cortices (PFC) in episodic memory has been pursued rigorously in numerous studies employing PET and fMRI, and emerging empirical regularities have led to detailed proposals about the distinct roles played by separate regions of the prefrontal cortex during episodic retrieval (see Section 1, as well as Fletcher & Henson, 2001). In some cases at least, these results might be considered somewhat counterintuitive, in the sense that prefrontal cortical activation has been observed in tasks on which patients with damage to the prefrontal cortex show little or no impairment. This observation is particularly true of recognition memory tasks, as well as cued-recall procedures (Swick & Knight, 1996).

This example illustrates clearly that a combination of the findings from, say, human lesion and functional imaging studies provides a more complete characterisation of the neural basis of memory processes than would either method when employed in isolation. The distinction between brain regions that are necessary for completion of a given task and those that are employed in the intact brain is one that can be garnered only from the adoption of multiple approaches to understanding relationships between structure and function.

The foregoing example is also useful for another purpose, which is to emphasise that studies of patients with brain damage are often constrained by the fact that damage is seldom restricted to an anatomically defined area of interest, making interpretation of cognitive deficits problematic. Animal models can be used to address this problem. The fact that two sections of this book focus on non-human animals is a reflection of the importance of this work in the field of the cognitive neuroscience, and in particular in the cognitive neuroscience of memory. Issues remain, however, such as those pertaining to selectivity of damage and functional reorganisation. In addition it can be difficult to determine the stage (or stages) of cognitive processing disrupted by a given lesion.

The final section of this volume is concerned with the use of computational modelling in cognitive neuroscience. The use of computational techniques in cognitive neuroscience has been increasing at a striking rate. This is because computational models allow a rigorous way of instantiating and testing theory, one that minimises the "hypothesis drift" of verbal theories. Computational models can make explicit the assumptions and, by running simulations, the predictions of a theory. The four chapters in this final section illustrate the utility of computational modelling in cognitive neuroscience. They provide many examples of the ways in which this powerful technique can be employed to address different kinds of problems in the cognitive neuroscience of memory.

In the following discussion, we first discuss the correspondences and points of contact between the chapters that fall within each section, before taking a broader focus and commenting on the converging (as well as possibly diverging) issues and themes that bridge two or more sections in the volume.

SECTION 1: STUDIES WITH HUMAN PARTICIPANTS

In the first section of this volume, the chapters by Buckner and Logan and Ranganath and Knight share a focus on prefrontal cortical function and functional neuroimaging data. Buckner and Logan recruit evidence from primate lesion studies in support of a model of frontal/temporal interaction whereby specific functionally dissociable regions of frontal cortex interact with distinct structures in medial temporal cortex during memory encoding. They extrapolate this model to support a candidate explanation for some of the memory deficits that accompany old age. Elderly individuals engage regions of prefrontal cortex during episodic encoding that overlap imperfectly with those engaged by young individuals. If one assumes that the neural activity observed in the elderly population reflects inappropriate or perhaps less efficient recruitment of resources mediated by frontal cortex, then this offers one explanation for at least some of the memory deficits that are seen in elderly individuals, and which might also presumably form the basis for a more ambitious cognitive neuroscience explanation of age-related performance changes that occur in tasks that challenge different cognitive domains and which rely on one or more regions of the frontal cortex.

Ranganath and Knight also consider episodic encoding and extend their discussion to include consideration of the roles of the prefrontal cortex in episodic retrieval, as well as in encoding and retrieval operations in semantic memory. They commence with a review of the kinds of performance impairments that accompany damage to the frontal cortex across a variety of tasks. They then employ findings from functional imaging studies of memory encoding and retrieval as converging sources of evidence for functional specialisation at the stage of encoding as well as at the stage of retrieval. The discussion provides an excellent example of the advantages that are conferred by the use of multiple approaches when the goal is a more complete characterisation of the neural basis of long-term encoding and retrieval, as well as the ways in which such accounts could well develop on the basis of findings in tasks that are not primarily mnemonic.

Rugg and Henson focus on studies of episodic retrieval, and contrast the findings obtained in studies using fMRI in event-related designs with those obtained using PET or fMRI in blocked designs. They highlight an important distinction between transient (item-related) and sustained (state-related) neural activity, both of which are engaged during performance of a cognitive task, and which are likely to reflect different classes of cognitive process. Blocked designs implemented in PET or fMRI confound these types of activity because they provide an aggregate measure of neural activity that is summated over several seconds at least. As a consequence, in blocked designs it is difficult to link unambiguously a given change in neural activity with changes in item-related or state-related cognitive processes, respectively. On a related note, it is of course self-evident that neuropsychological studies do not speak to the transient/state-related issue.

Event-related designs, as the descriptor implies, are sensitive only to the transient activity that is evoked by individual stimuli that are presented during a task. As a consequence, the event-related approach allows refinement and/or revision of conclusions that were drawn on the basis of findings in PET and fMRI studies in which blocked designs were employed. In addition to clarifying the likely role(s) of certain brain structures in episodic retrieval, Rugg and Henson also discuss brain regions identified only in event-related designs, which presumably are associated with item-related changes only. Regions active in blocked as well as event-related designs must also reflect item-related activity, but the possibility remains that the region is also associated with state-related activity (Wilding, 2001). The chapter illustrates the advantages that event-related fMRI confers but, at the same time, the authors are at pains to point out that the characterisation of both item-related and state-related processes (and the identification of the brain regions that support them) is an important endeavour, and to this end the emergence of fMRI approaches to conjoint measurement of both classes of process is encouraging.

For electrical measures of neural activity, the ability to monitor state-related as well as item-related neural activity concurrently via scalp electrodes has been available for a considerable period of time. The majority of studies employing electrical measures have, however, focused on one or other class of process, with the vast majority of these concerned with item-related processing only. One reason for this is that item-related studies are often motivated by psychological studies that rely on behavioural measures alone, with which it is difficult to monitor state-related processes directly. Indeed, part of the pressure for the development of event-related fMRI is likely to be due to the appeal of a closer correspondence between the paradigms that could be used in functional imaging studies and those that are employed in mainstream cognitive psychology. A second reason for the focus on item-related processing in electrophysiological studies is that it is more difficult to acquire reliable electrical measures of state-related activity than item-related activity.

The chapter by Donaldson and colleagues reflects this bias, being concerned primarily with event-related potentials (ERPs) that are evoked in response to the presentation of discrete classes of test stimuli. They review studies that have identified electrophysiological indices of successful retrieval and "postretrieval" processing, and explore the degree to which the current electrophysiological literature provides support for the "consensus" view of episodic retrieval. In addition, they focus on "preretrieval" processes in studies of episodic retrieval—a theme also touched on by Rugg and Henson in their contribution. There are at present more ERP studies than there are fMRI studies that have elicited convincing neural correlates of this class of process, and Donaldson and colleagues review some of the empirical regularities that have emerged. They go on to note that it will be important in future studies to separate two putative classes of "preretrieval" process—retrieval orientation and retrieval effort—that may be engaged in pursuit of successful retrieval (Rugg & Wilding, 2000). Disentangling the relative contributions of these two classes of process will require the use of carefully designed paradigms, and identifying the specific structures that support them will necessitate the implementation of these paradigms in conjunction with fMRI recording, which has spatial resolution far superior to that which can be achieved with ERPs alone (for preliminary results, see Ranganath, Johnson, & D'Esposito, 2000).

SECTION 2: PRIMATE STUDIES

In the first chapter of this section, Baxter addresses the question of the forms of memory that are supported by the hippocampus and those that are supported by the perirhinal cortex, albeit at a different level of granularity, and with the principal focus falling on the findings that have been obtained in studies involving selective lesions of structures within the medial temporal lobe. The core of the discussion centres on the distinction between mnemonic and perhaps perceptual operations that are supported either by the rhinal cortex—encompassing the entorhinal and perirhinal cortices—or the hippocampus and the amygdala. The chapter includes a discussion of the rather counterintuitive finding that across three studies the magnitude of damage to the hippocampus correlated negatively with the performance decrement that was observed on the delayed non-matching to sample (DNMS) task. Explanations for this finding are tentative at present, but it is notable that the reverse association—a positive correlation between volume loss and performance decrement—was observed for rhinal cortex. These data are therefore consistent with other evidence that the hippocampus and rhinal cortex play distinct functional roles in support of memory. These findings parallel the data reviewed by Warburton and Brown in the sense that the weight of evidence in both chapters provides little or no support for the claim that medial temporal lobe structures (including the rhinal cortex and hippocampus) are involved jointly in a unitary form of memory processing (Squire & Knowlton, 2000).

Warburton and Brown provide a critical review of single-cell recording and immunohistochemical studies that speak to the question of the neural circuitry that is engaged during recognition memory tasks and variants thereon. Their findings emphasise and extend the claim that two regions of the medial temporal cortex play distinct roles in recognition memory. According to this claim, the perirhinal cortex is relatively more important for familiarity discrimination than is the hippocampus, which itself plays a more central role in recognition memory where spatial or associative information is involved (Aggleton & Brown, 1999). The primary extensions to this model that are made here concern the proposal that whereas entorhinal cortex may be involved with both systems, the temporal association cortices and postrhinal cortex are allied more closely with the perirhinal and hippocampally mediated systems, respectively. Furthermore, Warburton and Brown note that the time course of stimulus processing in prefrontal cortex during recognition memory is consistent with the view that this region is associated with more complex aspects of retrieval than might be necessary to make a simple judgement of prior occurrence. The data critical to this claim is that the time window during which the neuronal responses to novel and familiar stimuli can be distinguished is delayed in prefrontal cortex relative to inferior temporal cortex.

The third chapter in this section is centred on the possibility that the basal forebrain has a crucial role to play in memory encoding. Parker, Easton, and Gaffan first review research into memory encoding in human and non-human primates, which has focused historically on the role of the hippo-campus and anatomically related structures in the medial temporal lobe. This focus came about at least in part because of patients (particularly H.M.; Scoville & Milner, 1957) who had severe anterograde amnesia after large medial temporal lobe lesions. Parker and colleagues, in keeping with the perspective adopted by the previous two contributors in this section, chal-lenge the view that the hippocampus has an important or special role to play in episodic memory, in this case focusing on memory encoding. They outline an alternative possibility, that the basal forebrain, midbrain, and possibly the frontal neocortex (perhaps in a controlling role) are involved with modulating posterior neocortical storage sites in response to different kinds of arousal. They propose that dense anterograde amnesia is produced by interrupting the modulatory effects of basal forebrain neurons upon the object representa-tions that are produced by distributed networks of neurons within the tem-poral lobe. According to this view, surgical approaches to the hippocampus, which transect these modulatory axons, will disrupt memory encoding. The authors discuss data showing that transection of the fornix, amygdala, and anterior temporal stem, thereby disconnecting the temporal cortex from the potentially modulating influence of the basal forebrain and midbrain, caused profound impairments in monkeys on a variety of memory tests including one that involved scene-related object memory (Gaffan, Parker, & Easton, 2001). These results are consistent with the view that the frontal cortex controls the basal forebrain which in turn up-regulates the ability of the inferior temporal cortex to store memories.

The final chapter in this section is in many ways a companion to the third, with the focus switching to retrieval rather than encoding. In this chapter Easton, Parker, and Gaffan discuss the likely anatomical structures and routes that support encoding and retrieval, respectively. They first review candidate routes by which frontal and posterior cortical regions interact with one another to support the completion of memory tasks. The importance of these routes can be tested by transection of the connecting fibre pathways, or by crossed unilateral lesions of the frontal and posterior areas that are hypothesised to interact in the memory task. Results from a series of experiments using these methods are presented, and a model of memory encoding and retrieval in the primate brain is outlined. According to the model, one of the key roles of the frontal cortex in memory retrieval in primates is to signal the relevance of stimuli to the current goals of the animal. This signal is input to the basal forebrain, which modulates object representations in the temporal lobe. During retrieval of established memories, involvement of the basal forebrain is not necessary, and one possible route for the retrieval of established memories is via the interaction of frontal, inferior temporal, and parietal cortical areas. This model provides a template for further empirical and conceptual advance, which will involve careful delineation of the processes supporting retrieval, identification of their neural basis, and specification of the ways in which specialised cortical and subcortical structures interact during memory encoding and retrieval.

SECTION 3: RAT STUDIES

There is a long history of experimentation into the mechanisms of memory using rats. In the first chapter in this section, Eichenbaum reviews the relationship between the characteristics of human amnesia and the types of memory that can be tested in the rat, with particular reference to the specific characteristics of declarative memory and its relationship to the medial temporal lobe. He then considers experiments from his own laboratory that have addressed these issues and outlines a theoretical model of how the hippocampus might encode episodic memories as sequences of events and the places where they occur. The model also accounts for the representation of events and places that are common between related episodes. Eichenbaum proposes that this flexibility might be key to the fundamental properties of declarative memory processing that are supported by the hippocampus.

Bussey and Aggleton review a series of lesion studies in the rat where the principal contrast is between the memory performance deficits that accrue from parahippocampal (perirhinal and postrhinal) lesions and those that accrue from fornix lesions. The latter type lead to selective disruption of the functional integrity of the hippocampus. The authors report a number of functional dissociations, the evidence being consistent with the view that distinct aspects of mnemonic processing are supported by structures within the medial temporal lobe. The authors go on to note, however, that there are good reasons to believe that whereas particular tasks will comprise mnemonic demands that can be met by one or other structure within the medial temporal lobe, other tasks will doubtless require cooperation between specialised structures, in particular tasks that require the utilisation of object as well as spatial information. They report empirical support for this intuition, comprising parallel deficits on conjoint object/spatial tasks following parahippocampal lesions and fornix damage. These findings are important because it is precisely the combination of different elements of an event that is considered to be the hallmark of an "episodic" memory (Tulving, 1983).

The final chapter of this section is concerned with the interaction between learning and memory on the one hand and attention on the other. As Cassaday and Norman point out, this interrelationship cuts both ways, in that the study of forgetting can tell us about the constraints on encoding as well as retrieval processes, and that learning is attentional in that it is normally directed by what the animal already knows about. Several paradigms have been developed to explore the relationship between attention and episodic memory in the rat, and some have been adapted subsequently for use with human participants. Cassaday and Norman explore the use of these paradigms in rat studies where disruptions of attention and memory are seen following manipulation of brain dopamine levels. In human patients, the symptoms of schizophrenia, which include behavioural confusion and inappropriate reactions to stimuli, probably result from disruption of the interface between prior knowledge and appropriately chosen behaviours. The authors present compelling evidence indicating that the hippocampal/nucleus accumbens axis is critical for memory encoding, that attention is a key part of the encoding process, and that dopaminergic modulation is critical in the efficient processing of perceptual inputs and their mapping onto behavioural outputs.

SECTION 4: COMPUTATIONAL MODELS OF MEMORY FORMATION

Connectionist modelling has the potential to be an invaluable tool in the quest to understand the relationship between brain and behaviour. This line of argument is developed by Saksida and McClelland who outline how, unlike many other approaches in cognitive neuroscience, it provides a method of understanding not only *what* functions are performed by brain regions but *how* they are performed. In addition, as Hasselmo and colleagues note, modelling is important because it helps to avoid "distorted perceptions of verbal hypotheses".

Most current connectionist models of learning and memory utilise a learning algorithm called backpropagation. The introduction of this method into computational modelling (Rumelhart & Zipser, 1986) served to increase considerably the power of such models, leading to a resurgence of interest in the field. However, because backpropagation is a non-local learning rule in which error signals are propagated backwards along connections between units, it is usually seen as being biologically implausible. It is therefore desirable to explore more biologically plausible algorithms that use local learning rules. One such rule that has enjoyed considerable support from neurobiological studies is the coincidence detection rule, proposed by Hebb (1949). Models based on purely Hebbian principles have been applied recently to problems in cognitive neuroscience. In their chapter, Saksida and McClelland provide a basic introduction to Hebbian connectionist modelling of learning and memory, and discuss as examples two such models, a model of perceptual learning and a model of the *failure* of perceptual learning. They go on to use these models in a discussion of the broad implications that they have for the cognitive neuroscience of learning, memory, and perception.

In the second chapter in this section, Metcalfe describes in detail the CHARM^2 model of memory encoding and retrieval. This well-known model has been through a number of incarnations. Here, Metcalfe describes four modules that she argues are necessary to model a variety of memory phenomena that have been observed in studies with human as well as with non-human animals. The original CHARM model consisted of two interacting modules. The first was a perceptual and semantic preprocessor, which feeds in to a lexicon. This module interacts at the input and output stages with an episodic memory module, in that it can determine the form of the input to the episodic module as well as interpret and differentiate between competing outputs. The episodic module is hippocampally based and allows for the storage of events and features by superimposition into a composite memory trace. One consequence of the formal structure of this composite trace is that it can become unstable, resulting in dramatically reduced efficiency (Metcalfe & Murdoch, 1981). One way to ameliorate this problem is to introduce a monitoring and control mechanism that operates prior to retrieval and modulates the way in which new traces are integrated with the composite trace on the basis of an initial sampling of the information that is held in the composite trace. This control mechanism is assumed to be supported by frontal cortex, and Metcalfe goes on to describe a number of memory phenomena that might be explained by the addition of this module, one notable example being familiarity as a basis for recognition judgements (Jacoby & Dallas, 1981; Mandler, 1980).

The final module is an emotional "hot" system, which is assumed to be amygdala based. It supports conditioning and is particularly influential during the encoding and retrieval of traumatic memories. Metcalfe argues for the developmental primacy of this module and emphasises that under stressful conditions this system becomes relatively more dominant than the other systems, by virtue of the fact that, as stress levels increase, the "hot" system maintains and might well enhance its functional integrity whereas the integrity of other systems degrades. Data from lesion studies in humans and single-cell recordings in animals are cited in support of the characteristics of this system, and recruited to argue for the necessity of this module in addition to the "core" episodic module. In the discussion of this new module, as well as in the review of the other three components of CHARM^2, Metcalfe provides numerous illustrations of the ways in which a formal consideration of the properties of a computational model can inform theories of human memory at the psychological as well as at the neuro-anatomical level.

Metcalfe's focus on modelling conditioning also complements the contribution that Armony makes to this volume, in which he describes in detail a model of the formation of emotional memories, emphasising the roles played by the amygdala and the thalamus. The chapter reviews what is known about the formation of memories of this type, including an extensive description of the brain regions that support them. Armony goes on to describe a computational model of emotional memory formation, restricting his focus to fear-conditioning for the purposes of this exposition. The model is modular, with the properties of the modules derived closely from what is known about the anatomy and physiology of the brain circuitry that supports emotional memory formation.

One of the key features of the model is that lateral inhibition is used to capture the differences in response properties of the amygdala and thalamus. Training the network is accomplished by pairing "tones" with an arbitrary "negative" input, and learning is Hebbian (see Chapter 12). The litmus test for a computational model of a given system is its ability to mimic the phenomena of interest as well as to generate testable predictions. To this end, Armony provides several examples of the ways in which the properties of the model of fear conditioning have led to testing and confirmation of the roles played by different neural pathways in memory formation. Perhaps the most notable is the predictions that were generated (and confirmed subsequently) in respect of distinct contributions to emotional memory formation by pathways that are distinguished according to whether they provide input to the amygdala directly (via the thalamus) or indirectly (via cortical regions).

In the final chapter in this section, Hasselmo, Wyble, and Cannon provide a critical overview of existing models of hippocampal function and what they can tell us about the ways in which this brain region performs encoding and retrieval operations. The first part of the chapter is a review of models of hippocampal involvement in episodic memory and the second is a review of models of hippocampal involvement in spatial navigation. The authors emphasise that an important issue for future research will be the development of models of hippocampal memory function that can account for the roles that this region plays in both of these types of memory; something that they argue most existing models do not do.

Hasselmo and colleagues' discussion of spatial navigation moves beyond the parameters that are typically incorporated in such models, by modelling the inputs and outputs to and from a simulation of hippocampal function in spatial navigation. They accomplish this by employing a "virtual rat" agent that interacts directly with its environment. The simulation of hippocampal operation controls the interaction of the rat in a virtual environment, and the rat receives "sensory" inputs that depend upon the movements that it makes.

The benefits conferred by this extended approach are primarily that it forces the modeller to delineate the ways in which the core of the model (the simulation of hippocampal control of spatial navigation) interacts with the model's inputs and outputs. By ensuring that these interactions are specified these extended models reduce the number of untestable assumptions that are made in comparison to models in which input and output operations are not incorporated. Hasselmo and colleagues conclude their chapter by providing an example of how their extended "virtual rat" model generates predictions about the differential firing of hippocampal neurons that is observed during delayed spatial alternation tasks.

GENERAL COMMENTARY

Given the wealth of data and the multiple perspectives that have been provided by the contributors to this volume, the challenge for a brief general commentary is not so much to identify points of contact between sections as it is to limit the discussion to only a subset of those points. No reasonably sized volume on the cognitive neuroscience of memory encoding and retrieval can claim to provide coverage of all relevant perspectives and techniques. This volume, none the less, provides numerous insights into the neuroanatomical basis of memory encoding and retrieval, and a variety of perspectives concerning the range of cognitive processes that are or can be engaged during these two fundamental aspects of memory processing.

From a historical perspective, if for no other reason, perhaps a good place to start is in the medial temporal lobe. The question of the memory processes that are supported by the medial temporal lobe is touched on in all four sections in this volume, and plays a central role in the rat and primate sections. In this regard, two important points have been identified by a number of contributors. The first point is that the "medial temporal lobe memory system" can be regarded as being functionally unitary only at a very general level (see in particular Bussey and Aggleton, Chapter 10). The immediate corollary to this, of course, is that there is considerable functional specialisation in both cortical and subcortical medial temporal lobe structures. The second point is that a complete characterisation of the roles of the structures within the medial temporal lobe in memory encoding and retrieval necessitates consideration of the way in which these structures interact, which they undoubtedly do when there is a need to encode or retrieve multiple aspects that in combination comprise an event or "episode".

The contribution of PET and fMRI research to theories of medial temporal lobe function arguably lags some way behind lesion and single-cell recording techniques at present, due in no small part to the fact that the medial temporal lobe is not a region from which it is straightforward to gain high quality images of regional cerebral blood flow. It is to be hoped that approaches to ameliorating this limitation continue to be developed (see Rugg and Henson, Chapter 1, for further comments), to permit theories of medial temporal lobe function that were developed primarily on the basis of studies in primates and rats to be tested in neurologically intact human populations.

A number of contributors to this volume extend the question of functional interactions between brain regions to a consideration of the interplay between frontal cortical regions and medial temporal lobe structures in memory encoding and retrieval. Lesion studies, single-cell recording studies, and functional imaging approaches all point to the importance of the integrity of frontal cortex for at least some kinds of memory encoding and retrieval, but the exact nature of the interaction between this region and the medial temporal lobe is somewhat underspecified. One reason for this is likely to be the fact that frontal cortical function is itself subject to numerous, often disparate, theoretical interpretations. A key challenge for understanding frontal cortical function in the context of memory encoding and retrieval is identifying cognitive processes (and their neural bases) that are domain-specific, and those that also play a role in other processing domains (e.g. working memory).

The emphasis on frontal cortical function is particularly evident in the functional imaging section of this volume, and this can be seen as an indication that these techniques are likely to be at the forefront with regard to developing more specific theories of frontal cortical function. What fMRI and PET do not provide, however, is much information about the time course of neural activity during memory processing, and in this regard the single-cell recording approach, as well as the use of scalp-recorded event-related potentials, have important contributions to make. An important component of any complete characterisation of the interaction between brain regions during, for example, retrieval from episodic memory, is a description of the order in which processing occurs, and the time course of that processing.

Warburton and Brown (Chapter 6) report that neurons in the prefrontal cortex differentiate between novel and familiar stimuli later than neurons in the perirhinal cortex, motivating them to suggest that the prefrontal cortex neurons are involved in either additional retrieval processing, or what can generally be described as "postretrieval" processing. Broadly comparable observations are made by Donaldson and colleagues (Chapter 2), who link neural activity over frontal scalp sites to processes that operate on the products of retrieval. One of the features of this frontal activity is its extended time course relative to other scalp-recorded activity that is also a correlate of successful retrieval but which is mediated by more posterior brain systems. To link these scalp-recorded electrophysiological indices to activity in particular regions of the prefrontal cortex, it will be necessary to refine techniques for determining the likely generator sources of scalp-recorded activity, and several laboratories are engaged in this endeavour. One attractive approach is the conjoint acquisition of ERP and fMRI data and the use of the fMRI data to constrain the identification of the generators responsible for the concurrently acquired scalp-recorded ERPs. This approach offers, at least in principle, to permit a characterisation of the neural circuit that is engaged during performance of a given task, as well as information about the time course of activity within that circuit. This rather simple description does not do justice to the hurdles that need to be overcome in pursuit of this goal (Rugg, 1997; Wilding, 2001), but this observation does not, of course, make the accomplishment of the goal any less desirable.

Finally, the foregoing brief review has focused primarily on the points of contact between the different methodologies and associated theoretical stances that are advocated by the contributors to this volume. The broad picture that emerges is, we believe, one in which the application of a range of methodologies leads to a broader understanding of the probable neural basis of a number of aspects of memory encoding and retrieval, as well as providing significant pointers to the ways in which memory processes should be characterised and fractionated at the cognitive level. Set against this, however, we should consider at least one cautionary note. One linked set of observations is that the application of some techniques is possible in only some species, at least in most circumstances, and more often than not the kinds of tasks that can be and are employed for different species are far from equivalent. When considered alongside the fact that the extent of the cognitive abilities of different species is also variable, these factors emphasise the need for caution, particularly in making general statements about the neural and functional basis of memory retrieval. Although some of these disparities cannot be overcome, they can certainly be minimised, for example by a careful analysis of the processes that are necessary for task performance, and by the use of equivalent or near-equivalent tasks in different participant populations.

This caveat notwithstanding, it is clear that considerable progress towards a clear understanding of the neural and functional basis of memory encoding and retrieval has been made. A particularly encouraging aspect of this is that the rate of progress appears to have increased in the last decade. This can be attributed in part to the development of new techniques for measuring human neural activity *in vivo*, and the corresponding mutually beneficial impact that this has had on research in rats and primates, in computational approaches to memory encoding and retrieval, and in studies of humans with (relatively) circumscribed brain damage. It is to be hoped that one of the purposes that is achieved by volumes such as this is that a balanced account of the contributions that can and have been made by different methodologies will in some small way contribute to the emerging consensus that the way to maximise further progress is a multimodal approach to understanding the neural and functional basis of memory encoding and retrieval.

REFERENCES

Aggleton, J.P., & Brown, M.W. (1999). Episodic memory, amnesia and the hippocampal–anterior thalamic axis. *Behavioural and Brain Sciences, 22*, 425–489.

David, A.S., & Halligan, P.W. (1996). Editorial, *Cognitive Neuropsychiatry, 1*, 1–5.

Fletcher, P.C., & Henson, R.N.A. (2001). Frontal lobes and human memory: Insights from functional neuroimaging. *Brain, 124*, 849–881.

Gaffan, D., Parker, A., & Easton, A. (2001). Dense amnesia in the monkey after transection of fornix, amygdala and anterior temporal stem. *Neuropsychologia, 39*, 51–70.

Hebb, D.O. (1949). *The organization of behavior*. New York: Wiley.

Jacoby, L.L., & Dallas, M. (1981). On the relationship between autobiographical memory and perceptual learning. *Journal of Experimental Psychology: General, 3*, 306–340.

Mandler, G. (1980). Recognising: The judgment of previous occurrence. *Psychological Review, 87*, 252–271.

Metcalfe, J., & Murdoch, B.B. (1981). An encoding and retrieval model of single-trial free recall. *Journal of Verbal Learning and Verbal Behaviour, 20*, 161–189.

Ochsner, K.N., & Lieberman, M.D. (2001). The emergence of social cognitive neuroscience. *American Psychologist, 56*, 717–734.

Ranganath, C., Johnson, M.K., & D'Esposito, M. (2000). Left anterior prefrontal activation increases with demands to recall specific perceptual information. *Journal of Neuroscience (online), 20*, RC108.

Rugg, M.D. (1997). Functional neuroimaging in cognitive neuroscience. In C.M. Brown & P. Hagoort (Eds.) *The neurocognition of language* (pp. 15–36). Oxford: Oxford University Press.

Rugg, M.D., & Wilding, E.L. (2000). Retrieval processing and episodic memory. *Trends in Cognitive Sciences, 4*, 108–115.

Rumelhart, D.E., & Zipser, D. (1986). Feature discovery by competitive learning. In D.E. Rumelhart & J.L. McClelland (Eds.) *Parallel distributed processing* (Vol. 1, pp. 151–193), Cambridge, MA: MIT Press.

Scoville, W.B., & Milner, B. (1957). Loss of recent memory after bilateral hippocampal lesions. *Journal of Neurology, Neurosurgery and Psychiatry, 20*, 11–21.

Squire, L.R., & Knowlton, B.J. (2000). The medial temporal lobe, the hippocampus, and the memory systems of the brain. In M.S. Gazzaniga (Ed.) *The new cognitive neurosciences* (pp. 765–779). Cambridge, MA: MIT Press.

Swick, D., & Knight, R.T. (1996). Is prefrontal cortex involved in cued recall? A neuropsychological test of PET findings. *Neuropsychologia, 34*, 1019–1028.

Tulving, E. (1983). *Elements of episodic memory*. Oxford: Oxford University Press.

Walsh, V., & Rushworth, M. (1999). A primer of magnetic stimulation as a tool for neuropsychology. *Neuropsychologia, 37*, 125–135.

Wilding, E.L. (2001). Event-related functional imaging and episodic memory. *Neuroscience and Biobehavioural Reviews, 25*, 545–554.

Author index

371

Subject index